UNDERSTANDING FORMULAIC LANGUAGE

Understanding Formulaic Language: A Second Language Acquisition Perspective brings together leading scholars to provide a state-of-the-art, interdisciplinary account of the acquisition, processing, and use of formulaic language. Contributors present three distinct but complementary perspectives on the study of formulaic language – cognitive/psycholinguistic, socio-cultural/pragmatic, and pedagogical – to highlight new work as well as directions for future work. This book is an essential resource for established researchers and graduate students in second language acquisition and pedagogy, corpus and cognitive linguistics, psycholinguistics, sociolinguistics, and pragmatics.

Anna Siyanova-Chanturia is Senior Lecturer in Applied Linguistics at Victoria University of Welington, New Zealand.

Ana Pellicer-Sánchez is Senior Lecturer in Applied Linguistics and TESOL at the UCL Institute of Education, UK.

Second Language Acquisition Research Series
Susan M. Gass and Alison Mackey, Series Editors

The *Second Language Acquisition Research* series presents and explores issues bearing directly on theory construction and/or research methods in the study of second language acquisition. Its titles (both authored and edited volumes) provide thorough and timely overviews of high-interest topics, and include key discussions of existing research findings and their implications. A special emphasis of the series is reflected in the volumes dealing with specific data collection methods or instruments. Each of these volumes addresses the kinds of research questions for which the method/instrument is best suited, offers extended description of its use, and outlines the problems associated with its use. The volumes in this series will be invaluable to students and scholars alike, and perfect for use in courses on research methodology and in individual research.

Understanding Formulaic Language
A Second Language Acquisition Perspective
Edited by Anna Siyanova-Chanturia and Ana Pellicer-Sánchez

For more information about this series, please visit:
www.routledge.com/Second-Language-Acquisition-Research-Series/book-series/LEASLARS

Of related interest:

Second Language Acquisition
An Introductory Course, Fourth Edition
Susan M. Gass with Jennifer Behney and Luke Plonsky

Second Language Research
Methodology and Design, Second Edition
Alison Mackey and Susan M. Gass

UNDERSTANDING FORMULAIC LANGUAGE

A Second Language Acquisition Perspective

Edited by
Anna Siyanova-Chanturia
and Ana Pellicer-Sánchez

Routledge
Taylor & Francis Group
NEW YORK AND LONDON

First published 2019
by Routledge
711 Third Avenue, New York, NY 10017

and by Routledge
2 Park Square, Milton Park, Abingdon, Oxon, OX14 4RN

Routledge is an imprint of the Taylor & Francis Group, an informa business

© 2019 Taylor & Francis

The right of Anna Siyanova-Chanturia and Ana Pellicer-Sánchez to be identified as the authors of the editorial material, and of the authors for their individual chapters, has been asserted in accordance with sections 77 and 78 of the Copyright, Designs and Patents Act 1988.

All rights reserved. No part of this book may be reprinted or reproduced or utilised in any form or by any electronic, mechanical, or other means, now known or hereafter invented, including photocopying and recording, or in any information storage or retrieval system, without permission in writing from the publishers.

Trademark notice: Product or corporate names may be trademarks or registered trademarks, and are used only for identification and explanation without intent to infringe.

Library of Congress Cataloging-in-Publication Data
A catalog record for this book has been requested

ISBN: 978-1-138-63496-1 (hbk)
ISBN: 978-1-138-63497-8 (pbk)
ISBN: 978-1-315-20661-5 (ebk)

Typeset in Bembo
by Apex CoVantage, LLC

To our parents – Liubov Siyanova and Yuri Chanturia, Fina Sánchez and Francisco Pellicer – with love and gratitude.

CONTENTS

Notes on Contributors   ix

Formulaic Language: Setting the Scene   1
Anna Siyanova-Chanturia and Ana Pellicer-Sánchez

PART I
Cognitive and Psycholinguistic Perspectives on Formulaic Language   17

1. Acquisition of Formulaic Language from a Usage-Based Perspective   19
  Stefanie Wulff

2. What Online Processing Tells us About Formulaic Language   38
  Anna Siyanova-Chanturia and Diana Van Lancker Sidtis

3. First Language Influence on the Processing of Formulaic Language in a Second Language   62
  Kathy Conklin and Gareth Carrol

4. Formulaic Language and Speech Prosody   78
  Phoebe Lin

PART II
Socio-Cultural and Pragmatic Perspectives on Formulaic Language — 95

5 Formulaic Language in Second Language Pragmatics Research — 97
Kathleen Bardovi-Harlig

6 Humor and Formulaic Language in Second Language Learning — 115
Nancy Bell and Stephen Skalicky

7 Formulaic Language and its Place in Intercultural Pragmatics — 132
Istvan Kecskes

PART III
Pedagogical Perspectives on Formulaic Language — 151

8 Pedagogical Approaches to the Teaching and Learning of Formulaic Language — 153
Ana Pellicer-Sánchez and Frank Boers

9 Testing Formulaic Language — 174
Henrik Gyllstad and Norbert Schmitt

10 From Corpus to CALL: The Use of Technology in Teaching and Learning Formulaic Language — 192
Tom Cobb

11 Formulaic Language in English for Academic Purposes — 211
Phil Durrant

12 Formulaic Sequences in Learner Corpora: Collocations and Lexical Bundles — 228
Sylviane Granger

13 Concluding Question: Why Don't Second Language Learners More Proactively Target Formulaic Sequences? — 248
Alison Wray

Index — 270

NOTES ON CONTRIBUTORS

Kathleen Bardovi-Harlig is Professor of Second Language Studies at Indiana University, where she teaches and conducts research on second language acquisition, L2 pragmatics, and tense-aspect systems. Her work on formulaic language in pragmatics has appeared in *Language Learning*, *Intercultural Pragmatics*, *Language Teaching Research* and *Language Learning & Technology*.

Nancy Bell is Professor at Washington State University. Her research interests centre on the discourse analytic investigation of conversational humor, language play, and linguistic creativity, especially with respect to second language users. Her work has appeared in such journals as *Humor: International Journal of Humor Studies*, *Journal of Pragmatics*, *Language Learning*, *The Modern Language Journal*, and *Intercultural Pragmatics*. She is the author of *We Are Not Amused: Failed Humor in Interaction* (Mouton de Gruyter) and, with Anne Pomerantz, *Humor in the Classroom: A Guide for Language Teachers and Educational Researchers* (Routledge).

Frank Boers is Professor at the University of Western Ontario, Canada. His initial research interests were in the areas of semantics and lexicology, with a special interest in figurative language. His more recent research interests, however, were sparked by his long experience as an EFL teacher and teacher trainer, and he now publishes mostly on issues of second language acquisition and pedagogy, often with a focus on phraseology.

Gareth Carrol is Lecturer in Psycholinguistics at the University of Birmingham. His work focuses on the processing and comprehension of formulaic and figurative language in first and second language speakers.

Tom Cobb is a recently retired Professor of Applied Linguistics. His main career work has been to adapt linguistic and lexicographical computer software to teachers' and learners' purposes and investigate the success of these adaptations in empirical studies. He continues to contribute to the research in this area and develop new software for data-driven learning at his website Lextutor (www.lextutor.ca). He also does curriculum reform work with UNESCO in development settings.

Kathy Conklin is Associate Professor in Psycholinguistics at the University of Nottingham. A major focus of her research is on the application of psycholinguistic methods to the exploration of formulaic language processing in a first and second language.

Phil Durrant is Senior Lecturer in Language Education at the University of Exeter and a former teacher of English for Academic Purposes. His research uses corpus-linguistic methods to study the language of first- and second-language academic writing, both at school and university levels. His most recent work has investigated disciplinary variation in academic vocabulary and phraseology and the development of written language in school children.

Sylviane Granger is Professor Emerita of English Language and Linguistics at the University of Louvain. In 1990 she launched the first large-scale learner corpus project, the *International Corpus of Learner English*, and since then has played a key role in defining the different facets of the field of learner corpus research. Her current research interests focus on the analysis of phraseology in native and learner language and its integration into reference and instructional materials.

Henrik Gyllstad is Associate Professor of English Linguistics at Lund University. His main research interests include second language vocabulary acquisition, phraseology, and testing and assessment. His recent projects have focused on collocational representation and processing, and validation of vocabulary size tests.

Istvan Kecskes is Distinguished Professor of the State University of New York. He teaches graduate courses in pragmatics, second language acquisition, and bilingualism at SUNY, Albany. He is President of the American Pragmatics Association (AMPRA) and the CASLAR (Chinese as a Second Language Research) Association. His latest books are *Intercultural Pragmatics* (OUP, 2013), *Research in Chinese as a Second Language* (DeGruyter, 2013), and an edited volume with Jesus Romero-Trillo, *Research Trends in Intercultural Pragmatics* (DeGruyter, 2013). He is the founding editor of the journal *Intercultural Pragmatics* and the Mouton Series in Pragmatics, as well as the bilingual (Chinese-English) journal *Chinese as a Second Language Research* (CASLAR).

Phoebe Lin is Research Assistant Professor at the Department of English, Hong Kong Polytechnic University. Her research investigates aspects of formulaic language prosody using a range of methods, including controlled experiments, corpus analysis, statistical modelling, and software development. She is the author of the research monograph *The Prosody of Formulaic Sequences: A Corpus and Discourse Approach* published by Continuum/Bloomsbury Academic. She also publishes in the areas of formulaic language, speech prosody, second language acquisition, corpus linguistics, and computer assisted language learning.

Ana Pellicer-Sánchez is Senior Lecturer in Applied Linguistics and TESOL at the UCL Institute of Education. Her research interests centre around the teaching and learning of vocabulary in a second and foreign language, with a particular focus on the use of psycholinguistic techniques to investigate the process of vocabulary learning. Her most recent research examines the incidental acquisition of single words and multiword expressions from reading using the eye-tracking methodology.

Norbert Schmitt is Professor of Applied Linguistics at the University of Nottingham. He is interested in all aspects of second language vocabulary description, acquisition, and use. He has published eight books on lexical and applied linguistics topics, and over 100 articles and book chapters.

Diana Van Lancker Sidtis is Professor of Communicative Sciences and Disorders at New York University, where she served as Chair from 1999–2002; Associate Director of the Brain and Behaviour Laboratory at the Nathan Kline Institute, Orangeburg, NY; and a certified and licensed speech-language pathologist. Her education includes an MA from the University of Chicago, PhD from Brown University, and a National Institute of Health Postdoctoral Fellowship at Northwestern University. Dr. Sidtis currently teaches, mentors students, and performs research in speech science, voice studies, and neurolinguistics. She is author of numerous scientific papers and review chapters, and co-author of *Foundations of Voice Studies* (Wiley-Blackwell).

Anna Siyanova-Chanturia is Senior Lecturer in Applied Linguistics at Victoria University of Wellington. Anna's research interests include formulaic language, frequency effects in language acquisition, processing and use, and quantitative research methods (reaction times, eye movements, learner corpora, EEG/ERPs). Anna has published in applied linguistics and psychology journals, such as *Studies in Second Language Acquisition, Language Learning, Applied Linguistics, Brain and Language, Journal of Experimental Psychology: Learning, Memory, and Cognition,* and others.

Stephen Skalicky received his PhD from the Department of Applied Linguistics at Georgia State University in 2018. His research focuses on variables that affect the comprehension and production of figurative language using psycholinguistic, corpus, and natural language processing methods, with a particular emphasis on examining these phenomena among multilingual language users. His work has appeared in *Language Learning*, *Discourse Processes*, and *Journal of Pragmatics*.

Alison Wray is Research Professor in Language and Communication at Cardiff University, Wales, UK. She has been researching aspects of formulaic language since the mid-1990s and has published over 50 papers, chapters, and books on this topic, across the domains of second language learning, dementia communication, and the evolutionary origins of language. Most notable are her two monographs, *Formulaic Language and the Lexicon* (Cambridge University Press, 2002) and *Formulaic Language: Pushing the Boundaries* (Oxford University Press, 2008).

Stefanie Wulff is Assistant Professor at the University of Florida. Her research interests are in second language acquisition, usage-based linguistics, and corpus linguistics. She is the editor of *Corpus Linguistics and Linguistic Theory* (de Gruyter Mouton).

FORMULAIC LANGUAGE

Setting the Scene

Anna Siyanova-Chanturia and Ana Pellicer-Sánchez

Introduction[1]

Formulaicity and lexical patterning pervade language (e.g., Erman & Warren, 2000; Nattinger & DeCarrico, 1992). Early studies identified a high proportion of formulaic sequences (FSs) in first language (L1) discourse (e.g., Altenberg, 1998; Biber, Johansson, Leech, Conrad, & Finegan et al., 1999; Howarth, 1998; Foster, 2001; Jackendoff, 1995; Pawley & Syder, 1983; Sorhus, 1977), with some estimates suggesting that up to 50% of language may be formulaic in nature (e.g., Erman & Warren, 2000). Such ubiquity warrants two conclusions key to the present volume: (1) native speakers of a language possess extremely large repertoires of FSs that they draw on in both spoken and written discourse; and (2) in order to reach high levels of proficiency, second language (L2) learners must be able to use appropriately the many and varied FSs that exist in language.

Formulaic language (FL), broadly defined, has been of interest to linguists for several decades. Scholars from a variety of linguistic sub-disciplines – theoretical and applied linguistics, educational and corpus linguistics, psycholinguistics and cognitive science, neurolinguistics, and language disorders – have all, at one point or another, turned their attention to the study of FL. The body of research accumulated since the 1980s has contributed to our understanding of what FL is, how it is acquired and used in a variety of contexts, as well as how FL is processed and represented in the brain.

In her seminal monograph on FL, Wray (2002) provided an overview of the research on formulaicity that had been conducted across a variety of disciplines, providing the richest description of FL available at the time. A plethora of empirical studies that have since followed helped us better understand this complex linguistic phenomenon. This research has, to a great extent, motivated the present volume. Multi- and interdisciplinary in nature, the work presented here has brought together leading researchers in the field with the aim of providing a state-of-the-art account of what is known about FL acquisition, processing, and use, focusing in particular on the recent developments and directions for future explorations.

The goal of this introductory chapter is two-fold. First, we introduce and discuss in some detail the notion of FL and the terminology employed, consider the perspectives adopted, and outline the structure of the volume. Second, we introduce each chapter, briefly considering the major concepts and aspects covered, the type/s of FL looked at, and – where relevant – emphasizing some of the prominent gaps pertinent to L2 speakers. Although, as the title suggests, the main focus of the volume is on learners of a second, or additional, language, inevitably, much of the research reviewed concerns both L1 and L2 users. In places, the authors focus on the findings specific to L1 speakers, attesting to the paucity of L2 research and showing where the field may be moving next.

Formulaic Language: Terminology, Characteristics, and Definition

As anyone even vaguely familiar with the study of FL will know, a plethora of terms exist to refer to (apparently) the same phenomenon. Wray (2002) identified over 50 terms used in the literature to describe aspects of formulaicity, including *fixed expressions, formulaic language, conventionalized forms, lexicalized phrases, prefabricated routines*, and many others.

In our quest to choose the most inclusive term – which we deemed important due to a wide range of perspectives, views, and topics covered – we considered *formulaic language/formulaic sequences* versus *multiword expressions*. Although both terms are commonly used in the field of applied linguistics, we felt that *formulaic language* (and by extension, *formulaic sequences*) was broader and hence more inclusive than *multiword expressions*. Interestingly, although the two are often assumed to refer to the same linguistic phenomenon, there are some noteworthy differences. For example, while multiword expressions are, by definition, strings of language above the word level, formulaic language comprises both multiword and single-word items, including expletives and exclamations (*damn, hurrah*), speech formulas (*yeah, bye*), and so on (e.g., Van Lancker-Sidtis & Rallon, 2004; Wray, 2002). This distinction is important in some research contexts, such as, for example, clinical studies involving patients with language disorders (e.g., aphasia), wherein a person's ability to use formulaic speech – broadly defined and necessarily encompassing units of any size, abstractness, and level of complexity – is compared with their ability to use novel speech (e.g., Bridges & Van Lancker Sidtis, 2013; Van Lancker Sidtis, Choi, Alken, & Sidtis, 2015).

Given these considerations, we opted for *formulaic language* as an umbrella term and *formulaic sequences* as one referring to individual instances of FL.[2] We further felt that these terms would bring our terminology in line with Schmitt (2004), Wray (2002, 2008), Wood (2010, 2015), as well as the work of others.

While choosing a term may seem straightforward, defining the underlying phenomenon is far less so. As Wray (2008) explains, the notion of formulaicity, broadly defined, implies that certain words have a strong relationship with each other in creating meaning. Regardless of the term used, formulaicity refers to the phenomenon that makes certain words, in Kecskes' (this volume) terms, "glued together". A number of characteristics affect this relationship and how formulaic language is conceptualized and identified (also see Wray, 2009). Let us consider some of them.

Wray (2002) proposed the use of the term "formulaic sequence" and defined it as

> a sequence, continuous or discontinuous, of words or other elements, which is, or appears to be, prefabricated: that is, stored and retrieved whole from memory at the time of use, rather than being subject to generation or analysis by the language grammar.
>
> (p. 9)

An important assumption of this often cited and adopted definition is that of *holistic storage* for FSs. However, unanswered questions remain as to what holistic storage and processing is and whether or not it actually exists (e.g., Siyanova-Chanturia, 2015; Siyanova-Chanturia & Van Lancker Sidtis, this volume; Wood, 2015). It is important to note that the proposition that FSs are processed as unanalyzed wholes does not feature in all approaches to the study of FL, and, indeed, much of experimental psycholinguistic evidence appears to argue against it (Konopka & Bock, 2009; Peterson, Burgess, Dell, & Eberhard, 2001; Snider & Arnon, 2012; Sprenger, Levelt, & Kempen, 2006). Crucially, Wray's (2002) use of the term *formulaic sequence* and her reference to holistic storage were linked to the purposes of her book and the approach adopted. These considerations have contributed to the recent calls not to use "formulaic language/sequences" as an umbrella term, precisely because it implies – justifiably or not – a holistic storage and processing (Myles & Cordier, 2017). Our stance is that "formulaic language/ sequences" need not be associated with holistic processing *per se*. Regardless of the term adopted, it is crucial to explain how formulaicity is understood for a particular research purpose.

FSs are often defined and identified in relation to their features. For example, FSs can be conceived of in relation to several characteristics that have been found to play a role in their acquisition, processing, and use, such as frequency, familiarity, predictability, fixedness, and pragmatic function, to name a few. *Frequency* is often considered a defining feature of FL. Indeed, many FSs enjoy high frequency of occurrence in language, as attested in large corpora (of note, many FSs, such as idioms, are very infrequent, despite being highly conventional; see following discussion). Frequency plays an important role in how we learn, process, and represent language (both at the word and phrase level); it is also a key factor in the pedagogically oriented decisions as to which FSs are most useful for L2 learners to know. However, at the same time, frequency is not everything. For example, researchers have observed relatively low correlations between corpus frequencies and acquisition of some FSs (Garnier & Schmitt, 2016; González-Fernández & Schmitt, 2015; Macis & Schmitt, 2017). It seems that FL is not learned according to frequency nearly as strongly as individual words are. Interestingly, some FSs, such as idioms, are low-frequency phrases that are, nonetheless, well familiar to L1 speakers (e.g., see Hallin & Van Lancker Sidtis, 2017; Rammell, Pisoni, & Van Lancker Sidtis, in press). Consider, for example, *raining cats and dogs* and *everything but the kitchen sink* – highly conventional sequences with extremely low frequency of occurrence, as attested in the 100 million words of the British National Corpus (two occurrences each; for comparison, *coprolalia* and *dight* also occur twice in the corpus). Not all FL is frequent, but all FL is typically familiar to most members of a speech community. This is why *familiarity*, or conventionality, may be considered a quintessential characteristic of FL. Achieving high levels of proficiency in an L2 may thus entail the need to develop this familiarity, even in the face of very low frequencies of exposure.

Frequency and familiarity are intimately intertwined with another feature of FL – *predictability*. A proficient language user can easily anticipate that *tie the* will most likely be followed by *knot*, that *knife and* will appear next to *fork*, that *extenuating* will inevitably precede *circumstances*. High frequency of occurrence and familiarity of a phrasal configuration are likely to render its final constituents close to redundant, meaning that a reader (uniquely) expects the upcoming word/s and may skip them altogether, or, at the very least, read them faster than the same words in a different (non-formulaic) context. However, the presence of FL in discourse not only makes for more fluent (and hence, more expedient) reading experience, but it also contributes to speakers' greater (perceived) fluency in spoken discourse and, correspondingly, to hearers' easier comprehension (e.g., see Wood, 2002).

Another characteristic that often figures in the literature is the relative fixedness of FL when compared with propositional speech which enjoys full syntactic flexibility. The words in FSs combine together in exclusive combinations. We talk of *silver lining* but not *gold lining* or *yellow lining*. Many instances of FL are fixed or semi-fixed, such that no or few modifications are possible without the phrase losing its meaning. Idioms and proverbs, in particular, are sometimes viewed as rather fixed, word-like expressions. Yet, even in the case of these seemingly rigid phrases, decompositional analyses have been reported, suggesting that during idiom processing, individual words and their literal meanings are activated and accessed separately (e.g., Konopka & Bock, 2009; Peterson et al., 2001; Snider & Arnon, 2012; Sprenger et al., 2006). While some FSs are fixed, others have been shown to allow a certain degree of modifiability. Some sequences can also be used in a truncated form. Take the example of *every cloud has a silver lining*. While words in the complete idiom cannot be easily changed without losing its meaning, the idiom is more typically used in a truncated form, as in *The silver lining of high petrol prices is that pollution goes down as a result of less driving*. The truncated form, however, cannot be understood unless the complete idiom and its meaning are known. FSs can be positioned on a continuum of fixedness, from completely fixed expressions (e.g., *by and large*) to more abstract ones allowing for a great deal of variation (e.g., constructions *it is X, these are Ys*). FSs have also been characterized by their level of transparency or opaqueness (Schmitt & Carter, 2004). Idioms, such as *at the drop of a hat*, are often placed at the opaque end of the continuum, while lexical bundles, such as *I don't know if*, are placed at the transparent end. Fixedness and transparency are crucial in the study of FL in an L2, as these features are likely to affect the learning burden of a FS.

FSs have also been defined according to their pragmatic function. As will be discussed in this volume, FSs are frequently used in speech to perform different actions and realize specific speech acts. Some of these expressions are used to maintain social interaction, express solidarity (e.g., *I see what you mean*), or to organize discourse (e.g., *to sum up, first of all*) (Schmitt & Carter, 2004; Wray, 2002). FSs are therefore key to achieving and maintaining high levels of pragmatic competence, both in an L1 and L2. This characteristic of FL is central to pragmatics research, where FSs are often defined as "conventional expressions representing ways of saying things agreed upon by a speech community" (Bardovi-Harlig, 2012, p. 209).

The many features that characterize FSs are a clear indication of their diversity. Researchers have often drawn on these features in an attempt to categorize FSs. Some instances of FL heavily depend on one (or more) of the features introduced previously. For example, as Wood (2015) explains, the definition of "lexical bundle" relies on the frequency of occurrence. Similarly, certain approaches to the study of FL may rely more strongly on some of these features but not others. For example, a pragmatic approach to the identification of FSs will place emphasis on the functional feature, whereas a psycholinguistic approach may draw more heavily on frequency and predictability of FSs.

In light of this discussion, it is evident that choosing an umbrella term and deciding on a specific definition of formulaicity has not been easy. Given these considerations, the definition of FL adopted in the present volume is deliberately loose, broad, and inclusive, to accommodate any and all instances of formulaicity.

> *FL, as conceived in this book, may comprise strings of letters, words, sounds, or other elements, contiguous or non-contiguous, of any length, size, frequency, degree of compositionality, literality/figurativeness, abstractness and complexity, not necessarily assumed to be stored, retrieved or processed whole, but that necessarily enjoy a degree of conventionality or familiarity among (typical) speakers of a language community or group, and that hold a strong relationship in communicating meaning.*

Although, as noted earlier, FL may comprise elements both at the word and phrase level, the instances of FL explored in the chapters that make up this volume are, by and large, strings above the word level, such as idioms, collocations, lexical bundles, binomials, grammatical constructions, and so on. Drawing on Wray's (this volume, p. 267) definition, we further regard an FS as a string that is "perceived by the agent (i.e. learner, researcher, etc.) to have an identity or usefulness as a single lexical unit". Importantly, depending on the research context, this "identity or usefulness as a single unit", this special relationship, may be construed rather differently. It may entail high frequency of occurrence (since frequently produced strings, other than being useful by virtue of being frequent in language, may also benefit from being treated as a single unit), a teacher's perceived value of a string (no matter how frequent), some sort of holistic storage and processing, a specific pragmatic function, or, indeed, something altogether different.

This broad conceptualization of FL seeks to reflect and embrace the different approaches, topics, and methodologies represented in this volume. However, as some of the authors note, a narrower definition of formulaicity may sometimes be needed. For example, as argued by Gyllstad and Schmitt (this volume) and Bardovi-Harlig (this volume), an all-inclusive definition might not be particularly useful for test design purposes or in the context of sociopragmatic research, respectively. We acknowledge that different purposes and research contexts may require different approaches, although all of the varied target items should be considered under the broad umbrella of formulaic language.

The Structure of the Book

The volume consists of three sections representing three broad perspectives in the study of FL: (1) cognitive and psycholinguistic, (2) socio-cultural and pragmatic, and (3) pedagogical perspectives. Another important category is the description and identification of FL. However, we felt that this was the focus of the earliest studies into FL. Because the field has now (mainly) moved beyond description, we will not focus on this particular aspect in a separate section. In choosing these broad strands of research, we were guided by a number of factors. First, most research into FL can be said to fall under (at least) one of these categories. For example, a wealth of studies has recently focused on the processing of various instances of FL, the role of frequency of exposure, L1, and L2 proficiency, and how usage-based approaches to language learning and use can accommodate the study of FL. Another prominent line of enquiry is how FL is learned and used by L1 and L2 speakers from a socio-cultural standpoint. It has long been argued that the use of FL may signal that an individual, whether an L1 or L2 user, is a member of a given community. Failure to conform to the accepted wording will inevitably suggest that the speaker is an outsider (e.g., Seidlhofer, 2009). Thus, for anyone wishing to be accepted in or associated with a given linguistic community, the importance of acquiring and using a rich repertoire of FSs can hardly be overestimated. This leads us to a third major line of enquiry dealt within the present volume – FL teaching and learning. Given a seemingly infinite number of FSs that an L2 learner needs to master and the often-limited opportunities available, researchers have long sought to find better ways of teaching and learning the many and varied phrasal configurations that exist in a language.

Our choice was further motivated by earlier collections. For example, the seminal issue of *Annual Review of Applied Linguistics* (2012) dedicated to FL focused on the broad cognitive, pragmatic, and pedagogical perspectives. Other edited collections too focused on these strands, albeit more loosely (e.g., Schmitt, 2004). In sum, it is reasonable to conclude that cognitive and psycholinguistic, sociocultural and pragmatic, and pedagogical perspectives cover much, if not all, of the core research into FL specific to the field of applied linguistics.

No doubt, much of research falls under more than one category and, importantly, is bound to have implications for various strands of FL enquiry. For example, the processing research can inform language teaching and learning. Correspondingly, how learners acquire FSs can guide much of the processing research. Critically, any and all strands of FL research – spanning cognition, pragmatics, and pedagogy – can benefit from viewing such sequences of language as a centrepiece in usage-based linguistics.

The volume is organized such that the later chapters within a section build on the earlier contributions that generally have a broader focus and, thus, provide (some) background information for the chapters that follow. Each contribution offers a state-of-the-art review of a topic at hand, focusing, in particular, on recent developments in the field. In addition, the chapters summarize relevant gaps and outline directions for future work, which, we hope, will render the volume particularly valuable for research students and those new to FL research.

The first section in the volume, *Cognitive and psycholinguistic perspectives on formulaic language*, provides an overview of how FL is acquired and processed by L2 learners from a cognitive perspective. This section comprises four chapters. The first chapter, *Acquisition of formulaic language from a usage-based perspective*, by Stefanie Wulff, provides an overview of contemporary usage-based research into the acquisition of FL in L2 speakers. The chapter considers (formulaic) constructions, as defined in usage-based approaches to language learning, which are opposed to rule-based accounts and which share the core assumptions that (1) linguistic input is the primary source for L2 acquisition and (2) the cognitive mechanisms employed by L2 learners are general learning mechanisms, rather than those pertinent solely to language learning. The chapter focuses on the properties that are known to affect the learnability of formulaic constructions, such as frequency, distribution, recency, salience, redundancy, perception of form, functional prototypicality, and contingency of form-function mapping. Although frequency is viewed as a primary factor impacting on FL acquisition, it is also noted that many instances of FSs are low frequency (e.g., idioms and proverbs, see Siyanova-Chanturia & Van Lancker Sidtis, this volume). Finally, addressing important questions, such as: Do L2 learners have constructions? What's the role of formulaic constructions in L2 acquisition?, the chapter argues for a pivotal role of FL in the L2 acquisition process. Wulff notes, however, that FSs are likely to play a lesser role in L2 acquisition when compared to L1 (also see Arnon & Christiansen, 2017; McCauley & Christiansen, 2017; Wray, 2002), and that it is best to view FL as an optional rather than required route for L2 learning.

The second contribution within the cognitive section, *What online processing tells us about formulaic language*, co-authored by Anna Siyanova-Chanturia and Diana Van Lancker Sidtis, reviews a bulk of evidence that comes from psycholinguistic studies employing a range of paradigms, such as behavioural, eye-tracking, and event-related brain potentials (ERPs). The chapter capitalizes on the differences between the processing in an L1 and L2, as well as the differences that may exist between the processing of various kinds of FL – both compositional and non-compositional – such as collocations, binomials, lexical bundles, idioms, and proverbs. Among other things, the chapter examines a variety of (item and learner specific) factors known to play a role in FL processing, such as frequency of occurrence, adjacency, figurativeness/literality, ambiguity, prediction, the relationship between the smaller parts and the larger whole, prosody, L2 proficiency, and age of acquisition of FL. Similar to Wulff (this volume), the authors argue for a key role for frequency in FL processing. They also note, however, that for many instances of FSs, such as idioms and proverbs, familiarity rather than frequency drives their processing advantage. In addition, some of the findings pertinent to the processing of FSs (e.g., idioms and binomials) in L1 and L2 offer support to Wulff's (this volume) proposition that FSs may play a greater role in L1 learning than in L2. Overall, the chapter attests to a huge amount of interest among the research community in the mechanisms engaged in FL processing in L1 and L2; yet, some of the key topics have so far been examined almost entirely in the context of L1 and thus remain ripe for future L2 research (e.g., FL prosody and online production).

First language influence on the processing of formulaic language in a second language, by Kathy Conklin and Gareth Carrol, also centres on the issue of FL processing. However, the chapter's focus is specifically on cross-linguistic influence and the factors associated with it. As the authors argue, one of the challenges that L2 learners face is acquiring a large repertoire of L2 formulaic expressions that overlap, in one way or another, with expressions in the learners' L1. Examining the evidence pertinent to two types of FSs – idioms and collocations – the authors show that an L1 FS is necessarily activated and impacts on the processing of its L2 counterpart. A bulk of evidence is reviewed, attesting to better performance across a range of tasks and paradigms when FSs share form as well as meaning across L1 and L2 (i.e., "congruent" items). On the contrary, when only one aspect is shared between L1 and L2 (e.g., form but not meaning, or meaning but not form, i.e., "incongruent" items), FS processing tends to be more effortful. It is noteworthy that this line of research is still very new, offering a wealth of opportunities for further work. In particular, a range of FSs, and not just collocations and idioms, need to be looked at; an interplay between L2 proficiency, age of acquisition, and cross-linguistic equivalence explored in greater detail; and more powerful models better able to explain the complex relationships between FL in L1 and L2 proposed.

Formulaic language and speech prosody by Phoebe Lin concludes the cognitive and psycholinguistic section. The chapter centres on the role of prosody in language acquisition. It is argued that prosody plays a fundamental role in how FSs are acquired and represented in an L1, and that it can offer reliable cues in the learning of FL in an L2. Drawing on corpus and psycholinguistic evidence from children and adults, L1 and L2 acquisition, Lin explores the question of whether FL may enjoy prosodic characteristics – such as pitch, loudness, timing, and voice quality – which are unique to FL and distinct from those associated with novel, propositional language. One of the key ideas of the chapter is that FSs be reconceptualized and redefined as strings of *sounds* rather than strings of words (a view that we took on board in the definition of FL; see above). Related to this is the author's proposition that L2 learners' difficulty in acquiring a rich repository of FSs may stem from their poor noticing and processing of prosodic cues, which is the result of learners' limited exposure to L2 spoken input. As Lin acknowledges, very little is known about the prosody of FL in L2, which renders this line of research particularly valuable in future investigations.

The second section in the volume, *Socio-cultural and pragmatic perspectives on formulaic language*, provides a review of the acquisition and use of FL by L2 learners from a pragmatic perspective. Three chapters make up this section. *Formulaic language in second language pragmatics research*, by Kathleen Bardovi-Harlig, looks at how conventional expressions are defined, identified, and evaluated in L2 pragmatics research, how the investigation of the acquisition of such expressions contributes to our understanding of L2 pragmatics, and, conversely, how research on L2 pragmatics contributes to our better understanding of the acquisition of L2 FL more broadly. Of note, while much of the early pragmatics research focused primarily on English, more recently researchers have heeded calls for a greater focus on other languages in SLA research (e.g., Ortega, 2009; Siyanova-Chanturia & Spina, 2015) and started to explore the sociopragmatic aspects of FS use in Chinese, French, German, Japanese, and Russian. As Bardovi-Harlig notes, L2 pragmatics research puts an emphasis on those features that can be shown to be readily available in the input but which are absent in learner production. Thus, what is central to this line of research is establishing availability of the target features in learner input, a topic that she reflects on in some methodological detail. The chapter further considers recognition versus production of conventional expressions by L2 learners, the role of environment, transfer, instruction, and other factors known to play a role in the acquisition of FL from a sociopragmatic perspective. Reviewing a wealth of pertinent findings in the sociopragmatic domain, Bardovi-Harlig hints at a need for more "crossover studies" – still very rare – such as that by Edmonds (2014), which explored both pragmatics and online processing of sequences above word level.

In the chapter entitled *Humor and formulaic language in second language learning*, Nancy Bell and Stephen Skalicky present two strands of evidence specific to L1 context, attesting to a complex relation that FL holds with humor and irony. First, drawing on the theories of lexical priming, semantic prosody, and others, the chapter explores humor and irony as non-formulaic constructs, resulting from deviations from typical linguistic patterning. Following this, studies are considered that view humor and irony as highly conventional and formulaic in nature. As the authors acknowledge, due to the scarcity of L2 research into humor, much of the evidence reviewed necessarily pertains to the L1 domain. Thus, the chapter should be viewed as a research agenda, examining how the body of knowledge from L1 studies can inform the development, use, and interpretation of humor and irony in an L2, and outlining possible ways forward for the study of FL and its relation to humor and irony in non-native language use. The section on implications for L2 learners considers some of the challenges non-native speakers face using humor and irony, such as developing sufficiently strong mental representations of frequent patterns and fostering the ability to identify purposeful non-conformities of such patterns (e.g., produced by L1 speakers) to achieve humorous effect. Finally, the authors offer useful suggestions as to how humor and FL can be fruitfully combined and taught together, noting that the former may have a facilitative effect on the recall of L2 vocabulary, and that it may offer learners opportunities for experimenting with new linguistic forms.

The concluding chapter in the sociopragmatic section, *Formulaic language and its place in intercultural pragmatics*, by Istvan Kecskes, discusses the use of L2 FL from the perspective of intercultural pragmatics. It recognizes the importance of FL for both L1 and L2 communication and examines the role of FL when L2 is put to use in intercultural interactions. The chapter first introduces the sociopragmatic approach, which constitutes the theoretical basis of Intercultural Pragmatics and in which both individual prior experience and actual social situational experience are important in meaning construction and comprehension. Kecskes argues for the need to distinguish between frequently occurring word sequences, such as *if they want*, *to do with it*, and those prefabricated expressions that have "psychological saliency" for speakers. According to the sociopragmatic approach, this psychological saliency is achieved not only by frequency of exposure but also by immersion in the culture, acceptance, and willingness to use those FSs. Psychological saliency is also key in explaining the low rate of FL use by L2 speakers. These factors, which are particularly relevant for L2 speakers, might not be present in L1 use to the same extent. It is further argued that L2 speakers in intercultural encounters create new FSs that do not exist in the target language and modify existing sequences to create their own norms of language use (e.g., Kecskes, 2015), which also explains the low rates of FL use in L2 attested in previous studies.

The third and final section of the volume – *Pedagogical perspectives on formulaic language* – adopts a pedagogical approach to the study of FL and provides a comprehensive overview of how knowledge of FSs can be taught and assessed, as well as how they are used and identified in different pedagogical contexts. This section consists of five chapters. The first chapter, *Pedagogical approaches to the teaching and learning of formulaic language*, by Ana Pellicer-Sánchez and Frank Boers, reviews the empirical work conducted in the last two decades examining the effectiveness of the instructional procedures used to teach and learn different types of FSs. The authors classify the existing instructional approaches into two main categories: (1) *incidental learning* conditions, those that increase the chances of incidental learning of FSs from reading and/or listening; and (2) conditions that stimulate the *intentional learning* of FSs, through decontextualized, explicit vocabulary exercises. Because of the overlap between purely incidental and intentional approaches, the authors identify a third category – *semi-incidental conditions* – characterized by steps that direct learners' attention to FSs in a written or spoken text and that lead them to notice those strings in the input. The authors call for caution when comparing learning gains from different empirical studies, as the many methodological differences across studies may affect the validity of the comparisons drawn. The review provided in this chapter shows that, in general, intentional approaches have led to larger gains than purely incidental approaches, although the effectiveness of intentional conditions really depends on the specific type of exercise in question. The empirical evidence available points towards the positive effects of semi-incidental approaches for the learning of FSs and suggests that gains might be similar to those of intentional learning conditions.

Acknowledging that FSs are an important part of language, and that they should therefore be included in pedagogy, implies the need for testing. Thus, developing tests of FL knowledge has become a main concern of language testers and vocabulary researchers. In the second chapter of this section, entitled *Testing formulaic language*, Henrik Gyllstad and Norbert Schmitt review the main tests of FL knowledge that have been used to date, such as the Word Associates Tests (Read, 1998), Collex and Collmatch (Gyllstad, 2009), Disco (Eyckmans, 2009), Contrix, (Revier, 2009), and the Phrase Test (Martinez, 2011), and discuss the main issues to consider in the design of FL tests. These principles for the development of FL tests include: the need to have a clear definition of the construct of formulaicity; the need to develop tests for particular purposes; the identification and selection of target FSs; sampling rate; choice of item format; and how to take advantage of technology to design tests of FL knowledge. The authors argue that, compared to the testing of knowledge of individual words, the testing of FL has proved more difficult due to the diversity of FSs and the complexity in defining the construct. The discussion provided in this chapter informs not only the design of the next generation of FL tests but also the validation of existing tests.

If technological advancement has had a major role in the identification of FSs and in the design of FL tests, it can also play an important role in the teaching of FSs. The third contribution to the pedagogical section, *From corpus to CALL: The use of technology in teaching and learning formulaic language*, by Tom Cobb, explores the use of technology in the teaching and learning of FL. As already noted, technology can be particularly beneficial for the teaching and learning of FSs. This chapter provides a review of the ways in which technology has been used in the teaching of FSs and provides further suggestions for how it can be exploited to the benefit of learners. Cobb argues that technology, in the form of computationally assembled data, can provide the massive exposure to FSs that is necessary for learners to acquire the many and varied FSs, particularly in the context of computer assisted language learning (CALL), where the technology and materials can be exploited, taking into consideration learners' needs, motivation, and curriculum integration. The chapter provides a detailed demonstration of the ways in which teachers and learners can use computing activities to develop an awareness of FL.

Formulaic language in English for academic purposes, by Phil Durrant, highlights the prominent role that the study of FL has played in the English for Academic Purposes (EAP) research. Learners' successful participation in the EAP community is dependent, among other factors, on their knowledge and use of FSs. Given the role of FL knowledge in predicting academic success, the study of FL has become a key concern in EAP research. This chapter first reviews the rationale for including FL in EAP and then provides a critical discussion of the main FL-related issues that have been explored so far in EAP research, including: how analysis of FL can help us understand the nature of academic language; how FL relates to originality and criticality in academic work; how the use of FL influences the grades students receive; and how appropriate formulas for teaching can be identified. On the basis of this discussion, the author identifies key areas for future work, such as the relationship between FL use and perceptions of linguistic proficiency; the relationship between FL use and thought; and the need to explore other means of identifying formulas for teaching.

Finally, *Formulaic sequences in learner corpora*, by Sylviane Granger, reviews the contribution of learner corpus (LC) research to the study of two types of FSs, collocations and lexical bundles. The chapter examines not only how LC research has provided useful insights about learners' use of lexical bundles and collocations but also how the findings of LC studies can be used to inform the design of teaching materials. The author provides a comprehensive review of what LC research has shown about learners' use of collocations and lexical bundles, addressing the following questions: how LC has helped to identify these two types of FSs; how frequent, accurate, and appropriate they are in LC; what LC studies tell us about their development; and what role L1 plays in learners' use of L2 FSs. Granger highlights the difficulty in comparing results across different studies that may define and operationalize collocations and lexical bundles in different ways. Despite this difficulty, some common patterns emerge from this review: (1) learners use a large number of collocations and lexical bundles, but they tend to rely on a small number of highly frequent sequences; (2) L1 transfer plays an important role in L2 FL use; and (3) the quantity and quality of collocations and lexical bundles develop with proficiency. The author calls for more studies using LC to explore individual trajectories, as opposed to group behaviour, and for the need to conduct more mixed-methods and replication studies.

The volume closes with an explorative chapter by Alison Wray, for no edited collection on FL is complete without a contribution by one of the most prominent figures in FL research. In this concluding chapter, Wray seeks to address a novel and, as of yet, unanswered question in the study of FL: *Why don't second language learners more proactively target formulaic sequences?* She looks for answers in the accounts and discussions found in the preceding chapters, to explore all three perspectives represented – cognitive and psycholinguistic, socio-cultural and pragmatic, and pedagogical. There turn out to be a large number of potential explanations for the low level of targeting of FSs by L2 learners, underlining both the complexity of FL as a phenomenon and our still-limited knowledge about how it fits into our L1 and L2 competence. The various responses to this question and the factors considered in the chapter will help researchers and teachers to better understand the complexity and dynamic nature of L2 learning experiences and a key role played by FL.

The different contributions that constitute this volume provide the reader with arguably the richest account available to date of what interdisciplinary and multidisciplinary research has revealed about FL acquisition, processing, and use in an L2. Importantly, the present volume not only provides a comprehensive review of the current state-of-play in FL research, but it also identifies pertinent gaps and outlines directions for future research. We hope this volume will help the reader forge a deeper understanding of the complex cognitive, pragmatic, and pedagogical phenomenon that is FL.

Notes

1 We are grateful to Alison Wray and Norbert Schmitt for their very useful and insightful comments on the earlier draft of this chapter.
2 Due to the specificities of some areas covered in the volume, a number of contributions employ additional (generic) terms – on a par with formulaic language/sequences – that more conveniently describe the target construct, or that are more common in the field under consideration (e.g., Wulff, this volume, uses *formulaic construction*, while Bardovi-Harlig, this volume, uses *conventional expressions*). Of note, specific types of FL are referred to by their names (e.g., collocations, idioms, phrasal verbs, binomials, etc.).

References

Altenberg, B. (1998). On the phraseology of spoken English: The evidence of recurrent word combinations. In A. P. Cowie (Ed.), *Phraseology: Theory, analysis, and application* (pp. 101–122). Oxford: Clarendon Press.

Arnon, I., & Christiansen, M. H. (2017). The role of multiword building blocks in explaining L1-L2 differences, Special issue on multiword units in language. *Topics in Cognitive Science, 9*(3), 621–636.

Bardovi-Harlig, K. (2012). Formulas, routines, and conventional expressions in pragmatics research. *Annual Review of Applied Linguistics, 32*, 206–227.

Biber, D., Johansson, S., Leech, G., Conrad, S., & Finegan, E. (1999). *Longman grammar of spoken and written English*. Harlow: Longman.

Bridges, K. A., & Van Lancker Sidtis, S. (2013). Formulaic language in Alzheimer's disease. *Aphasiology, 27*(7), 799–810.

Edmonds, A. (2014). Conventional expressions. Investigating pragmatics and processing. *Studies in Second Language Acquisition, 36*(1), 69–99.

Erman, B., & Warren, B. (2000). The idiom principle and the open choice principle. *Text, 20*(1), 29–62.

Eyckmans, J. (2009). Toward an assessment of learners' receptive and productive syntagmatic knowledge. In A. Barfield & H. Gyllstad (Eds.), *Researching collocations in another language* (pp. 139–152). New York, NY: Palgrave Macmillan.

Foster, P. (2001). Rules and routines: A consideration of their role in the task-based language production of native and non-native speakers. In M. Bygate, P. Skehan, & M. Swain (Eds.), *Researching pedagogic tasks: Second language learning, teaching, and testing* (pp. 75–94). Harlow: Longman.

Garnier, M., & Schmitt, M. (2016). Picking Up polysemous phrasal verbs: How many do learners know and what facilitates this knowledge? *System, 59*, 29–44.

González-Fernández, B., & Schmitt, N. (2015). How much collocation knowledge do L2 learners have?: The effects of frequency and amount of exposure. *ITL International Journal of Applied Linguistics, 166*, 94–126.

Gyllstad, H. (2009). Designing and evaluating tests of receptive collocation knowledge: COLLEX and COLLMATCH. In A. Barfield & H. Gyllstad (Eds.), *Researching collocations in another language* (pp. 153–170). New York, NY: Palgrave Macmillan.

Hallin, A. E., & Van Lancker Sidtis, D. (2017). A closer look at formulaic language: Prosodic characteristics of Swedish proverbs. *Applied Linguistics, 38*(1), 68–89.

Howarth, P. (1998). The phraseology of learners' academic writing. In A. Cowie (Ed.), *Phraseology: Theory, analysis and applications* (pp. 161–186). Oxford: Oxford University Press.

Jackendoff, R. (1995). The boundaries of the lexicon. In M. Everart, E. van der Linden, A. Schenk, & R. Schreuder (Eds.), *Idioms: Structural and psychological perspectives* (pp. 133–166). Hillsdale, NJ: Lawrence Erlbaum.

Kecskes, I. (2015). Is the idiom principle blocked in bilingual L2 production? In R. Heredia & A. Cieslicka (Eds.), *Bilingual figurative language processing* (pp. 28–53). Cambridge: Cambridge University Press.

Konopka, A., & Bock, K. (2009). Lexical or syntactic control of sentence formulation? Structural generalizations from idiom production. *Cognitive Psychology, 58*(1), 68–101.

Macis, M., & Schmitt, N. (2017). Not just "small potatoes": Knowledge of the idiomatic meanings of collocations. *Language Teaching Research, 21*(3), 321–340.

Martinez, R. (2011). *Putting a test of multiword expressions to a test*. Paper presented at the IATEFL Testing, Evaluation and Assessment SIG. University of Innsbruck: September 16, 2011. Retrieved from https://ufpr.academia.edu/RonMartinez/Talks.

McCauley, S. M., & Christiansen, M. H. (2017). Computational investigations of multiword chunks in language learning. *Topics in Cognitive Science, 9*(3), 637–652.

Myles, F., & Cordier, C. (2017). Formulaic sequence (FS) cannot be an umbrella term in SLA: Focusing on Psycholinguistic FSs and their identification. *Studies in Second Language Acquisition, 39*, 3–28. doi:10.1017/S027226311600036X.

Nattinger, J. R., & DeCarrico, J. S. (1992). *Lexical phrases and language teaching*. Oxford: Oxford University Press.

Ortega, L. (2009). *Understanding second language acquisition*. London: Hodder.

Pawley, A., & Syder, F. H. (1983). Two puzzles for linguistic theory: Nativelike selection and nativelike fluency. In J. C. Richards & R. W. Schmidt (Eds.), *Language and Communication* (pp. 191–226). New York, NY: Longman.

Peterson, R., Burgess, C., Dell, G., & Eberhard, K. (2001). Disassociation between syntactic and semantic processing during idiom comprehension. *Journal of Experimental Psychology: Learning, Memory, and Cognition, 27*(5), 1223–1237.

Rammell, C. S., Pisoni, S., & Van Lancker Sidtis, D. (in press). Perception of formulaic and novel expressions under acoustic degradation: Evidence for a unitary memory trace. *The Mental Lexicon*.

Read, J. (1998). Validating a test to measure depth of vocabulary knowledge. In A. Kunnan (Ed.), *Validation in language assessment* (pp. 41–60). Mahwah, NJ: Lawrence Erlbaum.

Revier, R. L. (2009). Evaluating a new test of whole English collocations. In A. Barfield & H. Gyllstad (Eds.), *Researching collocations in another language: Multiple interpretations* (pp. 125–138). New York, NY: Palgrave Macmillan.

Schmitt, N. (Ed.). (2004). *Formulaic sequences: Acquisition, processing and use*. Amsterdam: John Benjamins.

Schmitt, N., & Carter, R. (2004). Formulaic sequences in action: An introduction. In N. Schmitt (Ed.), *Formulaic sequences: Acquisition, processing, and use* (pp. 1–22). Amsterdam: John Benjamins.

Seidlhofer, B. (2009). Accommodation and the idiom principle in English as a Lingua Franca. *Intercultural Pragmatics, 6*(2), 195–215.

Siyanova-Chanturia, A. (2015). On the "holistic" nature of formulaic language. *Corpus Linguistics and Linguistic Theory, 11*(2), 285–301.

Siyanova-Chanturia, A., & Spina, S. (2015). Investigation of native speaker and second language learner intuition of collocation frequency. *Language Learning, 65*(3), 533–362.

Snider, N., & Arnon, I. (2012). A unified lexicon and grammar? Compositional and non-compositional phrases in the lexicon. In S. Gries & D. Divjak (Eds.), *Frequency effects in language* (pp. 127–164). Berlin: Mouton de Gruyter.

Sorhus, H. (1977). To hear ourselves – Implications for teaching English as a second language. *ELT Journal, 31*, 211–221.

Sprenger, S., Levelt, W., & Kempen, G. (2006). Lexical access during the production of idiomatic phrases. *Journal of Memory and Language, 54*, 161–184.

Van Lancker-Sidtis, D., & Rallon, G. (2004). Tracking the incidence of formulaic expressions in everyday speech: Methods for classification and verification. *Language & Communication, 24*(3), 207–240.

Van Lancker Sidtis, D., Choi, J., Alken, A., & Sidtis, J. J. (2015). Formulaic language in Parkinson's Disease and Alzheimer's Disease: Complementary effects of subcortical and cortical dysfunction. *Journal of Speech, Language, and Hearing Research, 58*(5), 1493–1507.

Wood, D. (2002). Formulaic language acquisition and production: Implications for teaching. *TESL Canada Journal, 20*(1), 1–15.

Wood, D. (2010). *Formulaic language and second language speech fluency: Background, evidence, and classroom applications*. London and New York, NY: Continuum.

Wood, D. (2015). *Fundamentals of formulaic language: An introduction*. London and New York, NY: Bloomsbury.

Wray, A. (2002). *Formulaic language and the lexicon*. Cambridge: Cambridge University Press.

Wray, A. (2008). *Formulaic language: Pushing the boundaries*. Oxford: Oxford University Press.

Wray, A. (2009). Identifying formulaic language: Persistent challenges and new opportunities. In R. L. Corrigan, E. A., Moravcsik, H., Oulali, & K. M. Wheatley (Eds.), *Formulaic language: Volume 1, distribution and historical change*. Typological studies in language (pp. 27–51). Amsterdam: John Benjamins.

PART I
Cognitive and Psycholinguistic Perspectives on Formulaic Language

1
ACQUISITION OF FORMULAIC LANGUAGE FROM A USAGE-BASED PERSPECTIVE

Stefanie Wulff

Introduction

This chapter provides an overview of contemporary research on the second language (L2) acquisition of formulaic language (FL) from a usage-based perspective. Usage-based studies, in particular those based on large-scale and dense corpora of child-directed speech and learners' productions that have become available in the past 20 years, have demonstrated how FL serves as a starting point for inductive construction learning that complements deductive, rule-based learning processes. This process, called bootstrapping, allows learners to move from lexically fully specified exemplars that are assigned a holistic communicative function to low-scope patterns that are only partially lexically fixed to fully schematized constructions (in the Goldbergian sense of the term; see Goldberg, 2006). The following section outlines the understanding of FL as one type of construction in usage-based linguistics. Given that the input learners receive is assigned a central role in the acquisition process, I then discuss the different relevant input characteristics, such as effects based on frequency and distribution, recency, functional prototypicality, and contingency of the form-function mappings in question (Ellis & Wulff, 2015a, b). I then turn to evidence in favour of constructions in the L2 before we look at the contributions of FL to the L2 acquisition process in more detail. The chapter closes with a few suggestions for future research.

This chapter is by far not the first overview of the role of FL in L2 acquisition, and so it draws substantially on previous publications. The interested reader may in particular want to consult Weinert (1995) for a comprehensive review of formulaic sequences (FSs) in non-native language up until the date of publication; Cadierno and Eskildsen (2015) and Eskildsen (2009) for much more in-depth descriptions of usage-based approaches to L2 acquisition in general; and Ellis,

Simpson-Vlach, Römer, Brook O'Donnell, and Wulff (2015) for a recent overview of FL in L2 from a usage-based perspective.

Finally, a quick note regarding what this chapter covers and what it does not. Firstly, so as to avoid overlap with the other chapters in this volume, the reader should consult the respective chapters on processing of FL in the L2, influence of the first language (L1), and FL use in the context of foreign language learning, and specifically from a corpus-linguistics point of view, as this chapter deliberately only alludes to these (crucial) aspects in passing. Secondly, as the title suggests, this chapter only reviews research that falls under the label of usage-based approaches, or is at least compatible with the core assumptions of that set of linguistic frameworks, but in order to obtain a comprehensive understanding of state-of-the-art research on L2 FL use and acquisition, I strongly encourage the reader to look into formalist research such as Bardovi-Harlig and Stringer (2017), Myles (2012), and Myles and Cordier (2017), as this line of research has been advancing our understanding of the topic in important ways.

Formulaic Sequences as Constructions in Usage-Based Linguistics

A variety of linguistic theories fall under the label "usage-based linguistics" (UBL; see Barlow & Kemmer, 2000; Tummers, Heylen, & Geeraerts, 2005); minimally, they all share two working assumptions regarding (both first and) second language (L2) acquisition[1] (Ellis & Wulff, 2015b, p. 75):

(1) The linguistic input learners receive is the primary source for their second language (L2) acquisition.
(2) The cognitive mechanisms that learners employ in language learning are not exclusive to language learning, but are general cognitive mechanisms associated with learning of any kind.

In UBL, language knowledge is defined as a structured inventory of symbolic units or form-meaning pairs (Langacker, 1987, 2000) or constructions (Goldberg, 2006). In crucial opposition to rule-based approaches to language acquisition that define language acquisition as the acquisition of words and rules that specify how to combine them, UBL approaches discard with the traditional dichotomy of syntax and lexicon and instead advocate for a mental lexicon "in which abstract grammatical patterns and the lexical instantiations of those patterns are jointly included, and which may consist of many different levels of schematic abstraction" (Tummers, Heylen, & Geeraerts, 2005, pp. 228–229; see also Bates & Goodman, 1997). In construction grammar, these patterns are referred to as *constructions* (Goldberg, 2006). In keeping with Tummers et al.'s definition, constructions can be morphemes, words, phrases, and syntactic frames (see also Trousdale & Hoffmann, 2013). That is, simple morphemes such as *-licious* (meaning "delightful, attractive") are constructions in the same way as simple words like *raisin* (meaning "partially dried grape"), collocations like *raisin bran*, idiomatic noun phrases like *raisin ranch* (meaning "retirement home"), and abstract syntactic frames like Subject-Verb-Object-Object (meaning that something is being transferred, as realized in sentences as diverse as *Max gave Abigail a raisin*, *Max gave Abigail a hug*, or *Max baked Abigail a cake*, where nuts, hugs, and cakes are being transferred, respectively). As the latter examples illustrate, not all constructions carry meaning in the traditional sense; many constructions rather serve a more functional purpose. The passive construction, for instance, serves the function of shifting the focus of attention in an utterance from the agent of the action to the patient undergoing the action (compare the passive *A cake was baked for Abigail* with its active counterpart *Max baked Abigail a cake*).

Given this definition of constructions, it follows that they have to be simultaneously stored in multiple forms that differ in their level of complexity and abstraction. To give a simple example of different levels of constructional complexity, the words *raisin* and the plural *-s* morpheme are simple constructions; both are stored also as constituent parts of the more complex construction *raisins* ("more than one raisin"). Different levels of constructional abstraction (also referred to as *schematization*) are evident, for example, in the fully lexicalized formula *Thank you* versus the partially schematized slot-and-frame greeting pattern [*Good* + (time of day)], which can be realized as lexicalized phrases like *Good afternoon* and *Good evening;* and the completely schematic [Noun Phrase + Noun Phrase] construction, which could be realized as *raisin bran*, *cake pan*, or *soda can*, to give but three examples. Likewise, sentences are not the product of applying a rule to a number of words to arrange them in a grammatical sequence, but rather a sentence is a specific combination of constructions – some simple, some complex, some lexically specific, some abstract. *What did Max give Abigail*, for instance, is a combination of the following constructions:

- *Max, Abigail, give, what, do* constructions
- VP, NP constructions
- Subject – Verb – Object – Object construction
- Subject – Auxiliary inversion construction

In summary, a speaker's knowledge of their language(s) is a huge warehouse of constructions that vary in complexity and abstraction. More specifically, language knowledge means knowing the properties of constructions that determine what other constructions they can, or have to be, combined with. Typically, these properties are semantic or functional in nature such that any two constructions can only be combined if their meanings/functions are compatible, or if they can at least temporarily attain compatibility in a specific context or discourse situation (Goldberg, 2006).

Given this definition of constructions, UBL sees FL not as fundamentally different from genuinely productive, on-the-fly assemblies; rather, there is a continuum of constructions from simple to complex and from lexically specified to lexically open. In view of the fact that FL constitutes a significant portion of any competent speaker's language knowledge – one estimate for spoken language is 28% (Biber, Johansson, Leech, Conrad, & Finegan, 1999) – placing FL at the centre of language knowledge rather than relegating it to the margins of what speakers do can be seen as a distinct advantage of UBL approaches over formalist theories.

Input Properties Contributing to the Second Language Acquisition of (Formulaic) Constructions

Frequency of Construction in the Input

In usage-based approaches, frequency is a driving force for language acquisition, with type and token frequency playing different roles. Token frequency is the frequency with which a particular construction occurs in the input; type frequency refers to the number of distinct realizations of a given construction. The English past tense morpheme *-ed* has a high token frequency – it occurs frequently – and it has a very high type frequency as it occurs with thousands of different verbs. In contrast, irregular past tense forms as in *blew*, *sang*, or *rode* have low type frequency as they occur with a much smaller number of different verbs. Type frequency drives the productivity of a construction since it gives the hearer varied opportunities to parse the construction in question, which strengthens the schematic representation of the form and makes it more available for re-use and novel uses alike (Bybee & Hopper, 2001). High token frequency likely has the opposite effect since it conserves specific realizations of a construction (see Bybee, 2006 for a detailed discussion of the conserving, form-reducing, and autonomy-stipulating effects of high token frequency).

The more often two constructions co-occur, the more entrenched that particular constructional arrangement becomes (Divjak & Caldwell-Harris, 2015). Ellis (1996, p. 107) refers to "the development of permanent sets of associative connections in long-term memory" as *chunking*, and he points out how chunks form the basis for automaticity and fluency in language use.

At the same time, it is important to point out that not all FL has to be particularly frequent to be acquired – think of rarer formulaic expressions such as *needle in a haystack*, *red herring*, or *bite the dust*. In contrast, the salience and thus learnability of these expressions is based on the salience they obtain by being unusual. Likewise, frequency is not a sufficient condition for status as an FS: n-grams like *and of the* and *but it is* are extremely frequent, yet they are neither psycholinguistically salient nor coherent (Schmitt, 2004). As evidence from psycholinguistic studies and corpus analyses suggests, speakers consider not only a construction's frequency but also a variety of factors, including its sequential dependencies, prototypicality, and reliability of form-function mappings instantiated in the exemplar (see Ellis, 2002 for an overview).

Distribution of Construction in the Input

Acquisition is kick-started by initial exposure to massive, low-variance input that is centered around prototypical realizations (or exemplars) of the target construction (Elio & Anderson, 1981, 1984). Through this focused input, learners can identify the majority of the category members; through continued exposure to the full breadth of exemplar types, learners can later define the category boundaries (Nosofsky, 1988). Accordingly, both children's input and output reflect Zipf's Law (Zipf, 1935): the frequency of a word is inversely proportional to its rank in a frequency table. This means that the most frequent word occurs about twice as often as the second most frequent word, three times as often as the third most frequent word, etc. Goldberg, Casenhiser, and Sethuraman (2004) showed that Zipf's Law holds when counting words in a given sample of authentic speech, and importantly, it also holds for verbs *within* a given construction. According to Goldberg et al., the Zipfian input distribution directs attention to specific typical verbs that are made salient by being extremely frequent in the input, which then can serve as the "path-breaking verbs" for category formation (see also Ninio, 1999, 2006). Ellis and Ferreira-Junior (2009a, 2009b) considered data from naturalistic L2 acquisition and likewise confirmed that the type/token ratio of the verbs in argument structure constructions is Zipfian. Furthermore, they demonstrated that akin to Tomasello's (2003) claims for L1 acquisition, the most frequent and prototypical verbs seem to act as "verb islands" around which verb-argument constructions gradually emerge.

As Gries and Ellis (2015) point out, Zipfian distributions also point to another aspect of how constructions are distributed in the input, namely their dispersion. Constructions can be differently dispersed across the contexts they occur in: one construction may occur with about the same frequency across all its possible contexts (that is, it is evenly dispersed), while another construction clusters more frequently in some contexts than others (that is, it is unevenly dispersed). At least for initial stages of learning, it appears that the dense clusters of occurrences as provided by the most frequent elements in a construction with a Zipfian distribution facilitate their acquisition more than when a construction is more evenly dispersed: when Goldberg, Casenhiser, and Sethuraman (2004) compared two experimental conditions in their learning experiment, namely one in which participants heard five novel verbs 16 times in an evenly dispersed condition (4-4-4-2-2) versus one in which the 16 occurrences were presented less evenly dispersed (8-2-2-2-2), uptake was significantly better in the less evenly dispersed, more Zipfian condition.

Recency of Construction in the Input

Alongside frequency and context, we know from research in cognitive psychology that recency plays a crucial role as well (Anderson, 1989; Anderson & Schooler,

2000). Recency (also called priming or persistence) is an implicit memory effect such that exposure to a stimulus affects a response to a later stimulus. Recency has been shown to impact processing across linguistic levels from phonology to syntax (McDonough, 2006; McDonough & Mackey, 2006; McDonough & Trofimovich, 2008).

Salience, Redundancy, and Perception of Form of the Construction

Salience is the general perceived strength of a stimulus. According to the Rescorla-Wagner (1972) model of associative learning, the amount of learning induced from an experience of a cue-outcome association crucially hinges upon the salience of the cue and the importance of the outcome: low salience cues are less readily learned than high salience cues. Many grammatical structures in English have low salience in the input, for example, inflections like the third person singular *-s* morpheme. Consequently, these grammatical structures pose challenges even for advanced L2 learners.

Many grammatical constructions are not only low in salience but also are redundant in the listener's understanding of an utterance in that they compete with more salient psychophysical forms, which further impedes acquisition. For example, third person singular *-s* encodes present tense, but adverbs like *today* are more salient in the input and effectively overshadow and block acquisition of the morpheme (Ellis, 2006, 2008b; Ellis & Sagarra, 2010b, Goldschneider & DeKeyser, 2001). Accordingly, L2 learners' preference of adverbial over inflectional cues to tense has been well documented in longitudinal studies of naturalistic L2 acquisition (Bardovi-Harlig, 2000; Dietrich, Klein, & Noyau, 1995), training experiments (Ellis & Sagarra, 2010b, 2011), and studies of L2 language processing (Ellis & Sagarra, 2010a; VanPatten, 2006).

Prototypicality of Function

Some members are better exemplars of a category than others. In Prototype Theory (Rosch & Mervis, 1975; Rosch, Mervis, Gray, Johnson, & Boyes-Braem, 1976), the prototype of a category is defined as an idealized mental representation that unites the most representative features of that category. This prototype serves as the gold standard against which other exemplars are judged as more or less central members of the category. To use the now-classic example, sparrows are good examples of the category BIRD because they incorporate various representative attributes (they are average in size, beak size, colour, etc.). Correspondingly, people are fast to confirm that sparrows are birds (even upon first encounter; Posner & Keele, 1970). In comparison, they take considerably longer to confirm that albatrosses are birds, too.

Prototypicality and token frequency can be correlated: exemplars with high token frequencies often form the prototypes of categories. Accordingly, Goldberg et al. (2004) showed that in L1 acquisition, children's first uses of verbs, in particular verb-argument constructions, tend to be highly frequent, semantically typical generic verb types that encapsulate the central meaning of the construction (*go* for verb-locative, *put* for verb-object-locative, and *give* for the ditransitive construction). Similarly, Ellis and Ferreira-Junior (2009a) showed that the verbs first used by L2 learners are highly frequent, prototypical, and generic in function: *go* dominates in the verb-locative construction (*She went home*), *put* in the verb-object-locative construction (*She put the groceries in the bag*), and *give* in the verb-object-object construction (*He gave her a flower*) (see also Divjak & Arppe, 2013).

At the same time, the correlation between prototypicality and frequency is far from deterministic. Taylor (2015) cautions that "an appeal to frequency is no doubt useful as a research heuristic, but as a pointer to prototypicality it needs to be supported by other considerations" (Taylor, 2015, p. 568). For example, studies by Deignan and Potter (2004) and Hilpert (2006) have shown that figurative uses of words for body parts like *eye*, *head*, and *heart* are often at least as frequent as their literal uses, yet this does not license the conclusion that these figurative uses form the prototypes of these categories. Rather, next to frequency, prototypicality arises from a variety of different factors, none of which are sufficient in isolation (Barsalou, 1985).

Contingency of Form-Function Mapping

Next to the form and the function of a given exemplar to be categorized and learned, the contingency of the form-function mapping plays a role as well as it drives associative learning (Shanks, 1995). To return to our bird example, all birds have eyes and wings, and so we encounter these features equally frequently. However, while many other animals have eyes, only birds have wings. That renders wings a much more reliable (or distinctive) cue than eyes for deciding that an animal is a bird. Contingency, and its associated aspects of predictive value, information gain, and statistical association, are at the heart of L2 acquisition theories like MacWhinney's *Competition Model* (MacWhinney, 1987a, 1987b, 1997, 2001).

Ellis and Ferreira-Junior (2009b) inspected the form-function contingencies of verbs in three different argument structure constructions as used by L2 learners captured in the ESF corpus. They determined the association between the verbs and the constructions by calculating DeltaP, a measure that is based on conditional probabilities. Ellis and Ferreira-Junior found that the verbs that are first learned tend to be those that are highly distinctively associated with the three different constructions as expressed in their DeltaP values. Their findings support the idea that the acquisition of lexical and grammatical constructions is intricately intertwined, and they are an illustration of an understanding of prototypicality as not just based on frequency, but also cue validity, measured here as DeltaP.

Formulaic Constructions in the Second Language

Do Second Language Learners Have Constructions?

Several chapters in this volume survey the rich evidence from psycholinguistics and corpus linguistics that language users have rich knowledge of the frequencies of forms and of their sequential dependencies in their native language (see also Ellis, 2002). Language processing has been shown to be sensitive to the sequential probabilities of linguistic elements at all levels (that is, from phonemes to phrases) across comprehension and production (especially when it comes to fluency and idiomaticity in speech production). This sensitivity to sequence information in language processing demonstrates learners' implicit knowledge of memorized sequences of language and forms the basis for linguistic systematicity and creativity (see Ellis, 2012a; Rebuschat & Williams, 2012; Trousdale & Hoffman, 2013).

Given the strong evidence for the psychological reality of constructions in native speakers' language, many research studies in second language acquisition (SLA) have turned to the question if and to what extent constructions also characterize L2 learners' linguistic competence, and whether L2 learners implicitly "tally" and tune their constructional knowledge to construction-specific preferences in terms of the words that preferably occur in those constructions like native speakers do. This section gives a compact review of recent research in favour.

Gries and Wulff (2005) used a sentence completion task to show that advanced German learners of English can be primed for ditransitive (e.g., *The racing driver showed the helpful mechanic...*) and prepositional dative (e.g., *The racing driver showed the torn overall...*) argument structure constructions, and a sorting task to show that learners preferred a construction-based over a verb-based sorting. Gries and Wulff (2009) found similar results for gerundial and infinitival complement constructions, and several other studies have reported similar L2 syntactic priming effects (McDonough, 2006; McDonough & Mackey, 2006; McDonough & Trofimovich, 2008). A replication study of the sorting task by Liang (2002) with three groups of Chinese learners of English at beginning, intermediate, and advanced proficiency levels suggests that the preference to sort by construction rather than by verb gradually develops as language proficiency increases.

Jiang and Nekrasova (2007) investigated how L2 English and native English speakers responded to formulaic and non-formulaic phrases in the representation and processing of FSs using online grammaticality judgement tasks. L2 English and native English speakers were tested with formulaic and non-formulaic phrases matched for word length and frequency (e.g., *to tell the truth* vs. *to tell the price*). Both native and non-native speakers responded to the FSs significantly faster and with fewer errors than they did to non-formulaic sequences. Similarly, Conklin and Schmitt (2008) found that native and non-native speakers read FSs faster than matched non-formulaic phrases.

Ellis and Ferreira-Junior (2009a, 2009b) analyzed data from L2 English learners in the longitudinal *European Science Foundation* corpus (Klein & Perdue, 1992; Perdue, 1993) and found that the verbs naturalistic adult L2 learners use in frequent verb-argument constructions reflect their input experience: the relative ordering of the types in the input predicted uptake with correlations in excess of $r = 0.90$.

In combination, these findings support the usage-based assumption that grammatical and lexical knowledge are not stored or processed in separate mental modules, but form a continuum from heavily entrenched and conventionalized formulaic units (unique patterns of high token frequency) to connected but collaborative elements (patterns of high type frequency) (Bybee, 2010; Ellis, 2008b, c; Ellis & Larsen-Freeman, 2009; Robinson & Ellis, 2008a, b). Wulff and Gries (2011) propose a corresponding definition of L2 accuracy as "the selection of a construction (in the Goldbergian sense of the term) in its preferred context within a particular target variety and genre" (Wulff & Gries, 2011, p. 70).

What is the Role of Formulaic Constructions in Second Language Acquisition?

The previous section summarized the evidence that at least advanced L2 learners do have some mental representation of constructions. This section is devoted to the (far more abundant) literature investigating the specific role of FL in the L2 acquisition process. Space does not permit a detailed discussion of the role of formulaic constructions in L1 acquisition; see Lieven (2014) and Wray (1999) for comprehensive overviews.

The role of FSs for the L2 language development was the focus of quite a number of early studies in the field of SLA. Corder (1973) coined the term *holophrase*, and Brown (1973) defined *prefabricated routines* as unanalyzed multi-word sequences associated with a particular pragmatic function. The main focus of early SLA studies of FL was if and to what extent prefabricated routines challenge the traditional understanding of language learning as exclusively moving from morphemes and words to increasingly complex structures. Could children alternatively and/or additionally first acquire large(r) chunks of language and subsequently decompose them? Initial research was divided on that question (see Krashen and Scarcella, 1978 for a comprehensive overview). For example, Hatch (1972) found evidence for both learning strategies in looking at the English production data of a 4-year-old Chinese boy. Hakuta's (1974, 1976) analysis of data from a 5-year-old Japanese learner of English led him to propose a more fine-grained distinction between prefabricated routines and prefabricated patterns (i.e., low-scope patterns that have at least one variable slot). Wong-Fillmore (1976) devoted her dissertation project to tracking several children over a longer period of time; her data suggested that children do in fact start out with prefabricated patterns, which they gradually break down into their component parts in search for the rules governing their L2 before they ultimately use language creatively.

Studies on adult L2 learners were much scarcer (see Wray, 2002, pp. 172–198 for a detailed overview). The general consensus that emerged was that while adult L2 learners may occasionally employ prefabricated language, grammatical development in particular seemed to be less leaning on prefabricated language than in children's L2 acquisition. Hanania and Gradman's (1977) study of Fatmah, a 19-year-old native speaker of Arabic who had received only little formal education in her native language, for example, revealed that Fatmah used several pragmatic routines in her L2 English, yet was largely unable to analyze these routines into their component parts. Similarly, Schumann (1978) investigated data from several adult L2 learners with different native language backgrounds; neither did he find much evidence in favour of prefabricated language use in the first place, nor any positive effect of prefabricated language knowledge on language development. In contrast, Schmidt (1983) studied Wes, a native speaker of Japanese who immigrated to Hawaii in his early thirties, and Wes seemed to make extensive use of prefabricated routines. Then again, while this significantly boosted Wes's fluency, his grammatical competence remained low. Ellis (1984) investigated the use of prefabricated language in an instructional context and suggested that learners vary considerably in their ability to decompose prefabricated routines in search for the underlying grammatical rules they exemplify. Krashen and Scarcella (1978) even questioned adult learners' ability to merely retain prefabricated routines and advised against directing learners' attention towards them: "The outside world for adults is nowhere near as predictable as the linguistic environment around Fillmore's children was" (Krashen & Scarcella, 1978, p. 298).

Myles (2004; Myles, Mitchell, & Hooper, 1999) presented one of the first larger-scale analyses of secondary school pupils learning French as a foreign language in England. Her corpora captured the oral language of 16 beginning and 60 intermediate learners across various tasks. The data showed that multimorphemic sequences that are well beyond learners' grammatical competence are quite common in early L2 production. While these sequences contained finite verbs, *wh-* questions, and clitics, Myles did not interpret them as evidence for functional projections at initial stages of L2 acquisition because she did not observe these properties outside of FSs. These sometimes syntactically highly complex sequences co-existed alongside very simple (typically verbless) sentences for prolonged periods of time. Likewise, clitics first appeared in FSs containing tensed verbs, which suggested the acquisition of tense is driven by these sequences. Myles characterized these early grammars as consisting of lexical projections and FSs, with no evidence of functional categories: "Chunks do not become discarded; they remain grammatically advanced until the grammar catches up, and it is this process of resolving the tension between these grammatically advanced chunks and the current grammar which drives the learning process forward". (Myles, 2004, p. 152). Her findings furthermore indicated a tight correlation between learners' use of FSs and their overall linguistic development such that learners who failed to retain FSs did not acquire tensed verbs, while learners who did retain FSs moved forward (Myles, 2004, p. 153).

Other studies likewise illustrated that FSs can serve as starting points for further learning. For example, Eskildsen and Cadierno (2007) presented a study on the development of *do*-negation by a Mexican learner of English, who seemed to rely on one specific instantiation of the pattern *I don't know* at initial stages and thereafter gradually expanded it to other verbs and pronouns. Similarly, Mellow (2008) did a longitudinal case study of Ana, a 12-year-old Spanish learner of English, who wrote stories describing 15 different wordless picture books during a 201-day period. Ana initially produced a limited number of complex constructions that were tied to a small set of verbs before gradually deploying an increasing range of constructions.

The conservative behaviour of L2 learners of restricting the use of complex constructions to a subset of verbs in initial stages of acquisition was also observed by Sugaya and Shirai (2009), who followed L1 Russian learner Alla's acquisition of Japanese tense-aspect morphology over 10 months. In that time period, Alla exhibited strong verb-specific preferences such that some verbs (e.g., *siru* "come to know", *tuku* "be attached") were produced exclusively with the imperfective aspect marker *-te i-(ru)* while others (e.g., *iku* "go", *tigau* "differ") were rarely used with *-te i-(ru)*, although Japanese licenses all of these verbs to be used in any of the four basic forms. In a larger cross-sectional follow-up study of 61 intermediate and advanced learners (based on the ACTFL scale), Sugaya and Shirai observed that lower proficiency learners used the individual verbs in verb-specific ways, and this tendency was stronger for the verbs denoting resultative state meaning with *-te i-(ru)* (e.g., achievement verbs) than the verbs denoting progressive meaning with *-te i-(ru)* (e.g., activity, accomplishment, and semelfactive verbs). The authors concluded that at the intermediate level, learning is primarily item-based and gradually proceeds to low-scope patterns and abstract constructions; they also suggested that memory-based and rule-based processes potentially co-exist for particular linguistic forms and that linguistic knowledge should thus be seen as a formulaic-creative continuum (see Bolinger, 1976).

Several studies, however, call the formulaic-creative sequence in L2 acquisition into question. For example, Bardovi-Harlig (2002) examined the emergence of future expression involving *will* and *going to* in a longitudinal study of 16 adult L2 English learners. Her data showed that future *will* is acquired before *going to* and remains by far the more frequent choice across a variety of verbs, so "for most learners, there is either little initial formulaic use of *will* or that it is so brief that it cannot be detected in this corpus" (Bardovi-Harlig, 2002, p. 192). In contrast,

> [f]or 5 of the 16 learners, the use of *I am going to write* stands out. Their production over the months of observation show that the formula breaks down into smaller parts, from the full *I am going to write about* to the core *going to*

> where not only the verb but also person and number vary. This seems to be an example of learner production moving along the formulaic-creative continuum.
>
> *(Bardovi-Harlig, 2002, p. 197)*

For the other learners, however, *going to* was used early on with different verbs (Bardovi-Harlig, 2002, p. 198).

Eskildsen (2009) longitudinally tracked learner Carlo in his use of *can* in classroom interactions. It seemed that the modal was initially tied to the formula *I can write*, yet Eskildsen cautioned that given the context-dependence of formulas, their use is likely transitory in nature and prompted by recurring discourse situations and tasks.

McCauley and Christiansen (2017) turn to computational modelling to investigate the extent to which FL plays a role in L2 acquisition. Their findings based on applying a chunk-based learning model to L1 data from the CHILDES corpus and L2 data from the ESF corpus indeed suggest that FL plays a modest role in L2 learning, as adults appear to learn less useful chunks, are less reliant on them, and arrive at them through different means than do children acquiring their first language (see also Arnon, McCauley & Christiansen, 2017).

Conclusions and Future Directions

In summary, there is evidence that FL plays a significant role for L2 acquisition, with several qualifications in place:

- FL may play a lesser role in L2 acquisition compared to L1 acquisition;
- FSs likely matter more to some learners than others and are therefore best seen as an optional rather than a strictly required route for L2 acquisition;
- FL is tied to specific discourse requirements and tasks, which needs to be borne in mind when we look for evidence of FSs in a given data set.

All this implies that while FL can play a beneficial role in L2 acquisition, it does not follow that all FSs necessarily serve that function (see Wood, 2006 for a comprehensive, usage-based taxonomy of different FSs in learner language). FSs that are frequent and semantically transparent are likely candidates to serve as acquisition kick-starters, but many FSs are quite rare and idiomatic in meaning, making them harder to acquire. Rather than being acquisition kick-starters, one should consider those FSs targets in ultimate attainment stages. In fact, this accounts for ceiling effects in L2 acquisition: even advanced learners mostly do not achieve nativelike idiomaticity (Erman, Forsberg Lundell & Lewis, 2016; Granger, 2001; Pawley & Syder, 1983); see Ellis (2012b) for further discussion of the apparent paradox that while most L2 learners do not achieve nativelike formulaicity and idiomaticity, FSs can provide learners with a databank of complex structures beyond their current grammar, which can drive the learning process forward. Myles and Cordier (2017) provide an appealing solution by distinguishing learner-external and learner-internal FSs, with the former being defined as "multimorphemic clusters which are either semantically or syntactically irregular, or whose frequent co-occurrence gives them a privileged status in a given language as a conventional way of expressing something" (Myles & Cordier, 2017, p. 12), and the latter being defined as "a multiword semantic/functional unit that presents a processing advantage for a given speaker, either because it is stored whole in their lexicon or because it is highly automatized" (Myles & Cordier, 2017, p. 12). Correspondingly, they offer the distinct terms *linguistic cluster* and *processing unit* to refer to the two types of FSs respectively.

As far as future directions of usage-based research into FL and its place in L2 language and the L2 acquisition process is concerned, this review of the research to date suggests several exciting opportunities for research. For one, the vast majority of studies examines L2 English rather than other second languages (but see, for example, Krummes and Ensslin (2017) on FSs in German essays). Likewise, especially in view of the just-mentioned seeming contradiction that FSs kick-start acquisition of certain structures, while other FSs are rarely if ever acquired, underscores the need for longitudinal studies that track learners from the initial state all the way up to their ultimate attainment level in order to improve our understanding of the different kinds of FSs and their role in L2 acquisition and use.

In my opinion, it is by capturing such types of data in corpora, and by applying the latest of corpus linguistic and computational methods available, that we can hope to gain deeper insights into the role of FL in the L2 learning process. (Only) given sufficiently large and dense data sets, we could test, for example, if and to what extent recent advances in statistical learning research apply to FL acquisition (see Baayen, 2011 on naïve discriminant learning), address the question of how L1 and L2 learners rely on formulaic language to different extents and in different stages of their language learning careers (as in McCauley & Christiansen, 2017), or discriminate the various measures of pertinent factors such as contingency in terms of how well they account for FL and its acquisition (see Gries, 2014 for an excellent overview of frequency, probabilities, and association measures in current usage-based linguistics).

Note

1 Throughout this chapter, the terms *acquisition* and *learning* are used interchangeably.

References

Anderson, J. R. (1989). A rational analysis of human memory. In E. Tulving, H. L. Roediger, & F. I. M. Craik (Eds.), *Varieties of memory and consciousness: Essays in honour of Endel Tulving* (pp. 195–210). Hillsdale, NJ: Lawrence Erlbaum.

Anderson, J. R., & Schooler, L. J. (2000). The adaptive nature of memory. In E. Tulving & F. I. M. Craik (Eds.), *The Oxford handbook of memory* (pp. 557–570). London: Oxford University Press.

Arnon, I., McCauley, S. M., & Christiansen, M. H. (2017). Digging up the building blocks of language: Age-of-acquisition effects for multi-word phrases. *Journal of Memory and Language, 92*, 265–280.

Baayen, R. H. (2011). Corpus linguistics and naïve discriminant learning. *Brazilian Journal of Applied Linguistics, 11*(2), 295–328.

Bardovi-Harlig, K. (2000). *Tense and aspect in second language acquisition: Form, meaning, and use*. Oxford: Blackwell.

Bardovi-Harlig, K. (2002). A new starting point? *Studies in Second Language Acquisition, 24*(2), 189–198.

Bardovi-Harlig, K., & Stringer, D. (2017). Unconventional expressions: Productive syntax in the L2 acquisition of formulaic language. *Second Language Research, 33*(1), 61–90.

Barlow, M., & Kemmer, S. (2000). Introduction: A usage-based conception of language. In M. Barlow & S. Kemmer (Eds.), *Usage-based models of language*. Stanford, CA: CSLI.

Barsalou, L. D. (1985). Ideals, central tendency, and frequency instantiation. *Journal of Experimental Psychology: Learning, Memory, and Cognition, 11*(4), 629–654.

Bates, E., & Goodman, J. C. (1997). On the inseparability of grammar and the lexicon: Evidence from acquisition, aphasia and real-time processing. *Language and Cognitive Processes, 12*(5–6), 507–584.

Biber, D., Johansson, S., Leech, G., Conrad, S., & Finegan, E. (1999). *Longman grammar of spoken and written English*. Harlow: Longman.

Bolinger, D. (1976). Memory and meaning. *Forum Linguisticum, 41*(1), 1–14.

Brown, R. (1973). *A first language*. Cambridge, MA: Harvard University Press.

Bybee, J. (2006). *Frequency of use and the organization of language*. Oxford: Oxford University Press.

Bybee, J. (2010). *Language, usage, and cognition*. Cambridge: Cambridge University Press.

Bybee, J., & Hopper, P. (Eds.). (2001). *Frequency and the emergence of linguistic structure*. Amsterdam and Philadelphia: John Benjamins.

Cadierno, T., & Eskildsen, S. W. (Eds.). (2015). *Usage-based perspectives on second language learning*. Berlin and New York, NY: Mouton de Gruyter.

Conklin, K., & Schmitt, N. (2008). Formulaic sequences: Are they processed more quickly than nonformulaic language by native and nonnative speakers? *Applied Linguistics, 29*(1), 1–18.

Corder, S. P. (1973). *Introducing applied linguistics*. New York, NY: Penguin.

Deignan, A. H., & Potter, L. (2004). A corpus study of metaphors and metonyms in English and Italian. *Journal of Pragmatics, 36*(7), 1231–1252.

Dietrich, R., Klein, W., & Noyau, C. (Eds.). (1995). *The acquisition of temporality in a second language*. Amsterdam: John Benjamins.

Divjak, D., & Arppe, A. (2013). Extracting prototypes from exemplars: What can corpus data tell us about concept representation? *Cognitive Linguistics, 24*(2), 221–274.

Divjak, D., & Caldwell-Harris, C. L. (2015). Frequency and entrenchment. In E. Dabrowska & D. Divjak (Eds.), *Handbook of Cognitive Linguistics* (pp. 53–74). Berlin and New York, NY: Mouton de Gruyter.

Elio, R., & Anderson, J. R. (1981). The effects of category generalizations and instance similarity on schema abstraction. *Journal of Experimental Psychology: Human Learning and Memory, 7*(6), 397–417.

Elio, R., & Anderson, J. R. (1984). The effects of information order and learning mode on schema abstraction. *Memory and Cognition, 12*(1), 20–30.

Ellis, N. C. (1996). Sequencing in SLA, phonological memory, chunking, and points of order. *Studies in Second Language Acquisition, 18*(1), 91–126.

Ellis, N. C. (2002). Frequency effects in language processing: A review with implications for theories of implicit and explicit language acquisition. *Studies in Second Language Acquisition*, 24, 143–188.

Ellis, N. C. (2006). Language acquisition as rational contingency learning. *Applied Linguistics*, 27(1), 1–24.

Ellis, N. C. (2008a). Usage-based and form-focused language acquisition: The associative learning of constructions, learned-attention, and the limited L2 endstate. In P. Robinson & N. C. Ellis (Eds.), *Handbook of cognitive linguistics and second language acquisition* (pp. 372–405). London: Routledge.

Ellis, N. C. (2008b). Optimizing the input: Frequency and sampling in usage-based and form-focused learning. In M. H. Long & C. J. Doughty (Eds.), *Handbook of second and foreign language teaching* (pp. 139–158). Oxford: Blackwell.

Ellis, N. C. (2008c). Phraseology: The periphery and the heart of language. In F. Meunier & S. Granger (Eds.), *Phraseology in language learning and teaching* (pp. 1–13). Amsterdam: John Benjamins.

Ellis, N. C. (2012a). Formulaic language and second language acquisition: Zipf and the phrasal teddy bear. *Annual Review of Applied Linguistics*, 32, 17–44.

Ellis, N. C. (2012b). What can we count in language, and what counts in language acquisition, cognition, and use? In St. Th. Gries & D. S. Divjak (Eds.), *Frequency effects in language learning and processing* (pp. 7–34). Berlin: Mouton de Gruyter.

Ellis, N. C., & Larsen-Freeman, D. (2009). Constructing a second language: Analyses and computational simulations of the emergence of linguistic constructions from usage. *Language Learning*, 59(1), 90–125.

Ellis, N. C., & Ferreira-Junior, F. (2009a). Construction learning as a function of frequency, frequency distribution, and function. *Modern Language Journal*, 93(3), 370–386.

Ellis, N. C., & Ferreira-Junior, F. (2009b). Constructions and their acquisition: Islands and the distinctiveness of their occupancy. *Annual Review of Cognitive Linguistics*, 7(1), 188–221.

Ellis, N. C., & Sagarra, N. (2010a). Learned attention effects in L2 temporal reference: The first hour and the next eight semesters. *Language Learning*, 60(s2), 85–108.

Ellis, N. C., & Sagarra, N. (2010b). The bounds of adult language acquisition: Blocking and learned attention. *Studies in Second Language Acquisition*, 32(4), 1–28.

Ellis, N. C., & Sagarra, N. (2011). Learned attention in adult language acquisition: A replication and generalization study and meta-analysis. *Studies in Second Language Acquisition*, 33(4), 589–624.

Ellis, N. C., Simpson-Vlach, R., Römer, U., Brook O'Donnell, M., & Wulff, S. (2015). Learner corpora and formulaic language in second language acquisition research. In S. Granger, G. Gilquin, & F. Meunier (Eds.), *Cambridge handbook of learner corpus research* (pp. 357–378). Cambridge: Cambridge University Press.

Ellis, N. C., & Wulff, S., (2015a). Second language acquisition. In E. Dabrowska & D. Divjak (Eds.), *Handbook of cognitive linguistics* (pp. 409–432). London and New York, NY: Mouton de Gruyter.

Ellis, N. C., & Wulff, S. (2015b). Usage-based approaches in second language acquisition. In B. VanPatten & J. Williams (Eds.), *Theories in second language acquisition: An introduction* (pp. 75–93). London and New York, NY: Routledge.

Ellis, R. (1984). *Classroom second language development*. Oxford: Pergamon.

Erman, B., Forsberg Lundell, F., & Lewis, M. (2016). Formulaic language in advanced second language acquisition and use. In K. Hyltenstam (Ed.), *Advanced proficiency and exceptional ability in second languages* (pp. 111–148). Boston and Berlin: Walter de Gruyter.

Eskildsen, S. W. (2009). Constructing another language – usage-based linguistics in second language acquisition. *Applied Linguistics*, 30(3), 335–357.

Eskildsen, S. W., & Cadierno, T. (2007). Are recurring multi-word expressions really syntactic freezes? Second language acquisition from the perspective of usage-based linguistics. In M. Nenonen, & S. Niemi (Eds.), *Collocations and idioms 1: Papers from the first Nordic conference on syntactic freezes* (pp. 86–99). Joensuu: Joensuu University Press.

Goldberg, A. E. (2006). *Constructions at work: The nature of generalization in language.* Oxford: Oxford University Press.

Goldberg, A. E., Casenhiser, D. M., & Sethuraman, N. (2004). Learning argument structure constructions. *Cognitive Linguistics, 15*(3), 289–316.

Goldschneider, J. M., & DeKeyser, R. (2001). Explaining the "natural order of L2 morpheme acquisition" in English: A meta-analysis of multiple determinants. *Language Learning, 51*(1), 1–50.

Granger, S. (2001). Prefabricated patterns in Advanced EFL writing: Collocations and formulae. In A. P. Cowie (Ed.), *Phraseology: Theory, analysis, and applications* (pp. 145–160). Oxford: Oxford University Press.

Gries, St. Th. (2014). Frequencies, probabilities, and association measures in usage-/exemplar-based linguistics. In N. B. Gisborne & W. Hollman (Eds.), *Theory and data in cognitive linguistics* (pp. 15–48). Amsterdam and Philadelphia: John Benjamins.

Gries, St. Th., & Ellis, N. C. (2015). Statistical measures for usage-based linguistics. *Language Learning, 65*(1), 1–28.

Gries, St. Th., & Wulff, S. (2005). Do foreign language learners also have constructions? Evidence from priming, sorting, and corpora. *Annual Review of Cognitive Linguistics, 3*(1), 182–200.

Gries, St. Th., & Wulff, S. (2009). Psycholinguistic and corpus linguistic evidence for L2 constructions. *Annual Review of Cognitive Linguistics, 7*(1), 163–186.

Hakuta, K. (1974). Prefabricated patterns and the emergence of structure in second language acquisition. *Language Learning, 24*(2), 287–297.

Hakuta, K. (1976). A case study of a Japanese child learning English. *Language Learning, 26*(2), 321–351.

Hanania, E. A. S., & Gradman, H. L. (1977). Acquisition of English structures: A case study of an adult native speaker of Arabic in an English-speaking environment. *Language Learning, 27*(1), 75–91.

Hatch, E. (1972). Some studies in language learning. *UCLA Workpapers in Teaching English as a Second Language, 6*, 29–36.

Hilpert, M. (2006). Keeping an eye on the data: Metonymies and their patterns. In A. Stefanowitsch & Gries, St. Th. (Eds.), *Corpus-based approches to metaphor and metonymy* (pp. 123–152). Berlin and New York: Mouton de Gruyter.

Jiang, N. A. N., & Nekrasova, T. M. (2007). The Processing of formulaic sequences by second language speakers. *The Modern Language Journal, 91*(3), 433–445.

Klein, W., & Perdue, C. (1992). *Utterance structure: Developing grammars again.* Amsterdam: John Benjamins.

Krashen, S., & Scarcella, R. C. (1978). On routines and patterns in language acquisition and performance. *Language Learning, 28*(2), 283–300.

Krummes, C., & Ensslin, A. (2017). Formulaic language and collocations in German essays: From corpus-driven data to corpus-based materials. *The Language Learning Journal, 43*(1), 110–127.

Langacker, R. W. (1987). *Foundations of cognitive grammar: Vol. 1. Theoretical prerequisites.* Stanford, CA: Stanford University Press.

Langacker, R. W. (2000). A dynamic usage-based model. In M. Barlow, & S. Kemmer (Eds.), *Usage-based models of language* (pp. 1–63). Stanford, CA: CSLI Publications.

Liang, J. (2002). *Sentence comprehension by Chinese Learners of English: Verb centered or construction-based* (Unpublished master's thesis). Guangdong University of Foreign Studies.

Lieven, E. (2014). First language development: A usage-based perspective on past and current research. *Journal of Child Language, 41*(s1), 48–63.

MacWhinney, B. (1987a). Applying the competition model to bilingualism. *Applied Psycholinguistics, 8*(4), 315–327.

MacWhinney, B. (1987b). The competition model. In B. MacWhinney (Ed.), *Mechanisms of language acquisition* (pp. 249–308). Hillsdale, NJ: Lawrence Erlbaum.

MacWhinney, B. (1997). Second language acquisition and the Competition Model. In A. M. B. de Groot, & J. F. Kroll (Eds.), *Tutorials in bilingualism: Psycholinguistic perspectives* (pp. 113–142). Mahwah, NJ: Lawrence Erlbaum.

MacWhinney, B. (2001). The competition model: The input, the context, and the brain. In P. Robinson (Ed.), *Cognition and second language instruction* (pp. 69–90). New York, NY: Cambridge University Press.

McCauley, S. M., & Christiansen, M. H. (2017). Computational investigations of multiword chunks in language learning. *Topics in Cognitive Science, 9*(3), 637–652.

McDonough, K. (2006). Interaction and syntactic priming: English L2 speakers' production of dative constructions. *Studies in Second Language Acquisition, 28*(2), 179–207.

McDonough, K., & Mackey, A. (2006). Responses to recasts: Repetitions, primed production and linguistic development. *Language Learning, 56*(4), 693–720.

McDonough, K., & Trofimovich, P. (2008). *Using priming methods in second language research*. London: Routledge.

Mellow, J. D. (2008). The emergence of complex syntax: A longitudinal case study of the ESL development of dependency resolution. *Lingua, 118*(4), 499–521.

Myles, F. (2004). From data to theory: The over-representation of linguistic knowledge in SLA. *Transactions of the Philological Society, 102*(2), 139–168.

Myles, F. (2012). Complexity, accuracy and fluency: The role played by formulaic sequences in early interlanguage development. In A. Housen, F. Kuiken, & I. Vedder (Eds.), *Complexity, accuracy and fluency* (pp. 71–94). Amsterdam and Philadelphia: John Benjamins.

Myles, F., & Cordier, C. (2017). Formulaic sequence (FS) cannot be an umbrella term in SLA: Focusing on psycholinguistic FSs and their identification. *Studies in Second Language Acquisition, 39*(1), 3–28.

Myles, F., Mitchell, R., & Hooper, J. (1999). Interrogative chunks in French L2: A basis for creative construction. *Studies in Second Language Acquisition, 21*(1), 49–80.

Ninio, A. (1999). Pathbreaking verbs in syntactic development and the question of prototypical transitivity. *Journal of Child Language, 26*(3), 619–653.

Ninio, A. (2006). *Language and the learning curve: A new theory of syntactic development*. Oxford: Oxford University Press.

Nosofsky, R. M. (1988). Similarity, frequency, and category representations. *Journal of Experimental Psychology: Learning, Memory, and Cognition, 14*(1), 54–65.

Pawley, A., & Syder, F. H. (1983). Two puzzles for linguistic theory: Native-like selection and native-like fluency. In J. C. Richards & R. W. Schmidt (Eds.), *Language and communication* (pp. 191–226). New York, NY: Longman.

Perdue, C. (Ed.). (1993). *Adult language acquisition: Crosslinguistic perspectives*. Cambridge: Cambridge University Press.

Posner, M. I., & Keele, S. W. (1970). Retention of abstract ideas. *Journal of Experimental Psychology, 83*, 304–308.

Rebuschat, P., & Williams, J. N (Eds.). (2012). *Statistical learning and language acquisition*. Berlin: Mouton de Gruyter.

Rescorla, R. A., & Wagner, A. R. (1972). A theory of Pavlovian conditioning: Variations in the effectiveness of reinforcement and nonreinforcement. In A. H. Black & W. F. Prokasy (Eds.), *Classical conditioning II: Current theory and research* (pp. 64–99). New York, NY: Appleton-Century-Crofts.

Robinson, P., & Ellis, N. C. (2008a). Conclusion: Cognitive linguistics, second language acquisition and L2 instruction – Issues for research. In P. Robinson & N. C. Ellis (Eds.), *Handbook of cognitive linguistics and second language acquisition* (pp. 489–546). London: Routledge.

Robinson, P., & Ellis, N. C. (Eds.). (2008b). *Handbook of cognitive linguistics and second language acquisition*. London: Routledge.

Rosch, E., & Mervis, C. B. (1975). Cognitive representations of semantic categories. *Journal of Experimental Psychology: General, 104*, 192–233.

Rosch, E., Mervis, C. B., Gray, W. D., Johnson, D. M., & Boyes-Braem, P. (1976). Basic objects in natural categories. *Cognitive Psychology, 8*, 382–439.

Schmidt, R. W. (1983). Interaction, acculturation, and the acquisition of communicative competence: A case study of an adult. In N. Wolfson & E. Judd (Eds.), *Sociolinguistics and language acquisition* (pp. 137–174). Rowley, MA: Newbury House.

Schmitt, N. (Ed.). (2004). *Formulaic sequences: Acquisition, processing, and use*. Amsterdam and Philadelphia: Benjamins.

Schumann, J. H. (1978). Second language acquisition: The pidginization hypothesis. In E. M. Hatch (Ed.), *Second language acquisition: A book of readings* (pp. 256–271). Rowley, MA: Newbury House.

Shanks, D. R. (1995). *The psychology of associative learning*. New York, NY: Cambridge University Press.

Sugaya, N., & Shirai, Y. (2009). Can L2 learners productively use Japanese tense-aspect markers? A usage-based approach. In R. Corrigan, E. A. Moravcsik, H. Ouali, & K. M. Wheatley (Eds.), *Formulaic language: Volume 2. Acquisition, loss, psychological reality, functional applications* (pp. 423–444). Amsterdam: John Benjamins.

Taylor, J. R. (2015). Prototype effects in grammar. In: E. Dabrowksa & D. Divjak (Eds.), *Handbook of Cognitive Linguistics* (pp. 562–579). Berlin and Boston: Walter de Gruyter.

Tomasello, M. (2003). *Constructing a language*. Boston: Harvard University Press.

Trousdale, G., & Hoffmann, Th. (Eds.). (2013). *Oxford handbook of construction grammar*. Oxford: Oxford University Press.

Tummers, J., Heylen, K., & Geeraerts, D. (2005). Usage-based approaches in cognitive linguistics: A technical state of the art. *Corpus Linguistics and Linguistic Theory, 1*(2), 225–261.

VanPatten, B. (2006). Input processing in adult SLA. In B. VanPatten & J. Williams (Eds.), *Theories in second language acquisition: An introduction* (pp. 115–135). Mahwah, NJ: Lawrence Erlbaum.

Weinert, R. (1995). The role of formulaic language in second language acquisition: A review. *Applied Linguistics, 16*(2), 180–205.

Wong-Fillmore, L. (1976). *The second time around: Cognitive and social strategies in second language acquisition* (Unpublished doctoral dissertation). Stanford University.

Wood, D. (2006). Uses and functions of formulaic sequences in second language speech: An exploration of the foundations of fluency. *The Canadian Modern Language Review, 63*(1), 13–33.

Wray, A. (1999). Formulaic language in learners and native speakers. *Language Teaching, 32*(4), 213–231.

Wray, A. (2002). *Formulaic language and the lexicon*. Cambridge: Cambridge University Press.

Wulff, S., & Gries, St. Th. (2011). Corpus-driven methods for assessing accuracy in learner production. In P. Robinson (Ed.), *Second language task complexity: Researching the cognition hypothesis of language learning and performance* (pp. 61–88). Amsterdam and Philadelphia: John Benjamins.

Zipf, G. K. (1935). *The psycho-biology of language: An introduction to dynamic philology.* Cambridge, MA: MIT Press.

2
WHAT ONLINE PROCESSING TELLS US ABOUT FORMULAIC LANGUAGE

Anna Siyanova-Chanturia and Diana Van Lancker Sidtis

Introduction

Single-word processing has long been of interest to psycholinguists, neurolinguists, and cognitive scientists, more generally. Numerous studies with first (L1) and second language (L2) speakers have attested to an important role of word frequency, length, polysemy, language proficiency, L1 background, and other factors known to influence lexical processing. In the past decade, however, the research community has witnessed a shift from the study of (single) words to the study of formulaic language, broadly defined (also known as multiword expressions/ items, conventional language, prefabricated language, routines, formulas, etc., see Wray, 2002). The aim of the present chapter is to provide an up-to-date account, grounded in empirical evidence, of what is currently known about the online processing[1] of formulaic language (FL). Although, in line with the general theme of the volume, our primary focus is on FL processing in an L2, the mechanisms associated with FL processing in an L1 also figure prominently in the chapter, so as to gain better understanding of the topic, enable L1/L2 comparisons, and to highlight relevant gaps pertinent to L2 research.

FL comprises a large set of expression-types, which differ from each other in a number of ways, but which have in common the fact that proficient language users know them. Subsets of formulaic sequences (FSs) reviewed in this report include lexical bundles and n-grams (*in the meantime, I don't know*), multiword verbs (*catch up*), collocations (*spread news*), irreversible binomials (*bride and groom*), idioms (*it came straight from the horse's mouth*), and proverbs (*A rolling stone gathers no moss*). FSs are by definition familiar phrases; many – although not all – also enjoy high frequencies of occurrence (as attested in large reference corpora).

As we shall see, frequency and familiarity have far-reaching implications for how FSs are processed.

Although frequency counts may be established for all FSs, an expression may have negligible frequency counts in any given text (e.g., Moon, 1998a, 1998b; Rammell, Van Lancker Sidtis, & Pisoni, 2017) and yet still be highly familiar to language users (e.g., Hallin & Van Lancker Sidtis, 2017). It may be of interest to consider subtypes of FSs in the light of these differences. FSs may differ in the role of text frequency and exposure in their acquisition and use, as well as in other characteristics, such as degree of cohesion, nuanced semantics, and non-literal meaning (see Figure 2.1).

While much of the early research centred almost entirely on how L1 speakers deal with frequent versus novel linguistic information, or with figurative versus literal language, more recently similar questions have been raised with respect to second language (L2) speakers. In particular, the role of exposure and proficiency has been investigated, as well as the nature of the L2 mental lexicon, with parallels between L1 and L2 FL processing being drawn. For example, some studies with L1 and L2 speakers have offered support to the tenet that FSs are processed differently from novel language and that frequency plays a key role in the processing of some kinds of FL. As we shall see, however, L2-specific studies – especially within the production realm – are still a rarity, with some areas having received virtually no attention from L2 researchers.

Online language processing is often conceived of in terms of two distinct modalities: comprehension and production. Consequently, the chapter has two main foci: the online *comprehension* and *production* of familiar phrases, meaning that language processing happens "online", or in "real time", under time pressure with no advance preparation involved. We first cover the studies within the comprehension domain, followed by the research on the production and prosody of FL, focusing on the questions posed, methodologies used, and the findings reported with respect to two broad categories of FL: *literal compositional* and *figurative non-compositional*.

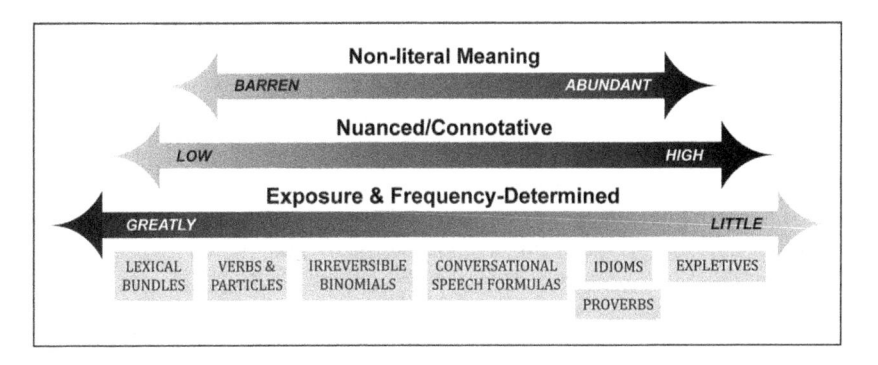

FIGURE 2.1 Visualization of formulaic sequences and possible variations between them.

Comprehension of Formulaic Language

Research into the comprehension of FL has by and large addressed the following questions: First, how do native and non-native speakers process *compositional* sequences? For example, are speakers sensitive to phrase frequency? Does language proficiency play a role in phrasal processing in an L2? Does age of acquisition affect the processing of FSs? Does adjacency play a role in phrasal processing in an L1 and L2? Second, how do native and non-native speakers process *figurative* sequences? For example, how are the two interpretations available in ambiguous idioms processed in L1 and L2 speakers? What is the role of prediction in language comprehension? To what extent can it be said that FSs are characterized by phrasal "cohesion"? To answer these questions, a wealth of methodologies, tasks, and paradigms has been used, and a variety of sequences – literal and figurative – have been explored. In what follows, we review major findings in the field, drawing on evidence from studies employing behavioural methods, eye-tracking, and event-related brain potentials (ERPs).

Comprehension of Compositional Formulaic Language

The earliest (pre-2010) studies looking at the processing of compositional strings of language employed such tasks as a detection task (e.g., Sosa & MacFarlane, 2002; Kapatsinski & Radicke, 2009), timed grammaticality (e.g., Jiang & Nekrasova, 2007), and frequency judgements (e.g., Siyanova & Schmitt, 2008, Study 3). One line of research has focused on the relationship between the constituent parts and the whole. For example, Sosa and MacFarlane (2002) monitored native speaker participants' ability to detect the particle *of* in two-word phrases that varied in frequency (*some of, sense of*), while Kapatsinski and Radicke (2009), in a more carefully controlled study, focused on the particle *up* in verb+up phrases that varied in their phrase frequency (*set up, catch up*). It was hypothesized that there should be a relationship between phrase frequency and accuracy and speed of participants' particle detection. Indeed, both studies attest to the participants' difficulty – in terms of speed and accuracy – in detecting the target particle when it was part of a highly frequent phrase, compared, for example, to a mid-frequency phrase. This led to the conclusion that access to some of the constituents was impeded (Sosa & MacFarlane, 2002), suggesting that frequent encounters with sequences of language make them appear "fused" or, indeed, word-like, supporting a key role of frequency for these kinds of FSs.

Using an online judgement task, Jiang and Nekrasova (2007) and Siyanova and Schmitt (2008, Study 3) not only confirmed the role that phrase frequency plays in L1 processing of some FSs, but also extended these findings to L2 users. In Jiang and Nekrasova (2007), native and non-native participants were both faster and more accurate when performing a grammaticality judgement task on frequent than infrequent phrases of the lexical bundle type (*one of the most* vs. *one of the new*). While the authors' conclusion that the target sequences were processed holistically because they were not subject to the full syntactic analysis cannot be supported by the evidence presented (not least because the issue of syntactic analysis was not investigated directly) and has since been contested (e.g., Edmonds, 2014; Siyanova-Chanturia, 2015), the study is important as it was one of the first to show non-native speaker sensitivity to phrase frequency effects in language processing with respect to these kinds of FSs. Likewise, in Siyanova and Schmitt (2008, Study 3), the authors looked at L1 and L2 users' processing of more versus less frequent phrases. When vastly different, in terms of frequency, sequences were looked at, both L1 and L2 speakers were faster when responding to higher frequency items. However, when the authors compared reaction times to high versus medium frequency items, only L1 speakers maintained the effect, while L2 learners appeared to process the two sets similarly (a finding that was consistent with the results of an offline rating task in Siyanova & Schmitt, 2008, Study 2).

The behavioural research that followed (post-2010) has provided further evidence for L1 (e.g., Arnon & Snider, 2010; Durrant & Doherty, 2010; Kim & Kim, 2012; Millar, 2011; Shantz, 2017; Tremblay, Derwing, Libben, & Westbury, 2011; Tremblay & Baayen, 2010, Experiment 1) and L2 (e.g., Edmonds, 2014; Kim & Kim, 2012; Shantz, 2017; Sonbul, 2015) speakers' sensitivity to phrase frequency and formulaicity in language comprehension. Interestingly, self-paced reading studies (i.e., where a reader sets the pace of his/her own reading by means of a button press to move from one portion of a sentence or phrase to another) have shown a processing advantage for more frequent phrases versus less frequent ones, regardless of the presentation mode, when lexical bundles were examined. For example, in the study by Tremblay et al. (2011) employing lexical bundles (*in the middle of the*) and controls (*in the front of the*), phrase frequency effects were observed irrespective of how the sentences containing the target sequences were presented: word-by-word, phrase-by-phrase, or sentence-by-sentence. More frequent items were also more likely to be remembered and recalled correctly in an offline task, leading the authors to conclude that regular multiword sequences necessarily "leave memory traces in the brain" (p. 595). A similar conclusion was arrived at in a study by Arnon and Snider (2010), who employed a phrasal-decision task to investigate the comprehension of four-word compositional phrases (*I don't know why, I have to say*). Comprehenders were faster to process more frequent phrases relative to less frequent ones, implying that language users store frequency information that is represented in compositional strings of language. In addition, Arnon and Snider (2010) observed that a continuous measure of frequency, rather than a binary one (low vs. high), was a better predictor of response times. On the basis of the results of two experiments, these authors made two methodological recommendations: (1) using continuous measures of frequency, and (2) using regression models for the analysis of continuous predictors – the two now being the norm in FL processing research.

The idea that FSs may be mentally represented as unitary forms by native speakers was tested in a recent perception study by Rammell, Van Lancker Sidtis, and Pisoni (2017). Listeners transcribed spectrally degraded formulaic and novel spoken utterances, matched for grammatical structure and duration, using sinewave vocoded speech. In this treatment, the signal is analyzed and resynthesized, obliterating frequency information and removing temporal fine structure while retaining the original speech envelope. Examples of randomized literal and formulaic sentences, including idioms, n-grams, proverbs, and conversational speech formulas, and a literal counterpart for each are *My record speaks for itself*; *your uncle works with no one*; *When it rains, it pours*; *As I drive, I sing*. Using a spoken corpus, it was seen that formulaic and novel phrases differed in frequency, as might be expected (based on the definition of "novel") but that constituent frequencies were comparable. Listeners correctly transcribed each utterance by typing into a computer what they thought they heard. FSs were correctly transcribed significantly more often than literal utterances. Usage and familiarity ratings correlated positively with transcription accuracy, implying a role of frequency of exposure in the results. However, the utterances with low ratings were also accurately transcribed, reflecting the notion that, under some conditions, FSs may be acquired in other ways (than frequent exposure) into a mental repertory.

More research has focused on the mechanisms involved in the processing of compositional strings of language in an L2 and the role of proficiency and exposure to L2 sequences. Using eye movements, Siyanova-Chanturia, Conklin, and van Heuven (2011) examined the comprehension of English binomials (*time and money*) versus their reversed forms (*money and time*) in native and non-native speakers varying in English language proficiency. As suggested by Arnon and Snider (2010), frequency as a continuous variable was looked at and was found to affect binomial processing in both L1 and higher and lower proficiency L2 speakers. However, L1 and L2 phrasal processing was also found to diverge. While L1 speakers and higher proficiency L2 users were sensitive to the type of phrasal configuration – that is, whether the target phrase was a binomial (conventional) or a reversed form (non-conventional) – lower proficiency L2 speakers' reading patterns were similar for both types of phrases, highlighting the importance of exposure to L2 binomials. Whether or not L2 speakers are attuned to phrase frequency distributions during language comprehension was also studied in Hernández, Costa, and Arnon (2016). Borrowing the items – four-word combinations – and the task – a phrasal-decision task – from Arnon and Snider (2010), these authors focused on L1 and upper intermediate/lower advanced L2 speakers. The role of the type of L2 exposure – immersion-based versus classroom-based – was explored as an additional variable. The study closely replicated the results of the original study, as well as extended the findings to an L2 population: both native and non-native speakers were found to be sensitive to multiword frequency. In fact, the non-natives in both learning settings demonstrated multiword frequency effects on a par with natives, with the learning setting not being a significant predictor. Based on these findings, we can conclude that even when speakers have a relatively limited exposure to a language, they are still remarkably attuned to phrase frequency distributions, at least in language comprehension.

More recently, Arnon and colleagues focused on a question that has received little attention in the literature, but one that is becoming increasingly important – age-of-acquisition (AoA) effects for sequences above word level. Research into lexical (single word) AoA has shown that words that are acquired earlier in life are processed faster than those acquired later in life (e.g., Morrison & Ellis, 1995), even when their adult frequencies, and other factors known to affect the speed of processing, are controlled for. Arnon, McCauley, and Christiansen (2017) have extended the earlier line of AoA research by setting out to investigate whether or not the same holds true for sequences above word level. In a series of phrasal-decision tasks with adult native speakers of English, early-acquired trigrams (*a good girl*) were responded to faster than later-acquired trigrams (*a good dad*), after controlling for such factors as adult frequencies, plausibility ratings, and constituent AoA. Arnon et al. (2017) is the first and only study to date to empirically show that AoA modulates language comprehension at the phrase level just as it does at the word level – another argument in favour of the proposition that the building blocks of language vary in size and complexity and are not limited to single words. This perspective is supported by numerous experts in child language acquisition, who have observed unitary structures alongside grammatically analyzed ones (e.g., Bybee & Torres, 2009; Gleason & Weintraub, 1976; Locke, 1993, 1997; Peters, 1983).

The studies reviewed thus far vary in terms of research questions and methodologies, target items and participants; yet, they all focus on frequent word sequences that are adjacent. However, as Vilkaitė (2016) points out, non-adjacent sequences are just as frequent as, if not more frequent than, adjacent combinations. Despite this, they have received surprisingly little attention in the processing research. To the best of our knowledge, only three published studies to date have looked at the comprehension of non-adjacent sequences. In the first study, using a self-paced reading paradigm, Molinaro, Canal, Vespignani, Pesciarelli, and Cacciari (2013, Experiment 1) were interested in the reading behaviour of L1 speakers of Italian when presented with collocational complex prepositions (*in veste di esperto di*, "in the capacity of an expert") versus their modified versions (*in ufficiale veste di esperto di*, "in the *official* capacity of an expert") embedded in sentence context. These FSs can be said to fall into the category of lexical bundles, for which frequency has been demonstrated to play a large, perhaps exclusive, role. The critical noun (*veste* "capacity") as well as the preposition following it (*di* "of") were both read more slowly in the modified condition compared to the unmodified version. By the second noun in the phrase (*esperto* "expert"), however, the processing difficulty was resolved with the two conditions being read in a similar way. One of the explanations proposed by the authors was that the difference – in reading times – between the two conditions reflected "the processing cost associated with the insertion of an unexpected constituent in a pre-fabricated string" (p. 773).

While Molinaro et al. (2013) focused on whether or not the modification of a conventional phrase resulted in readers slowing down, the other studies by Vilkaitė (2016) and Vilkaitė and Schmitt (2017) employed an eye-tracking paradigm to compare the reading of adjacent (*spread news*) and non-adjacent verb+noun collocations (*spread all the positive news*) versus their controls (*accept news* and *accept all the positive news*) in an L1 and L2, respectively. Consistent with the research reviewed previously, adjacent collocations were read faster than their controls across a range of eye-tracking measures by both L1 and L2 speakers. Non-adjacent items too exhibited a significant processing advantage relative to their controls, but only in the case of L1 speakers (Vilkaitė, 2016). On the contrary, proficient L2 speakers in Vilkaitė and Schmitt (2017) did not show a robust processing advantage. Thus, while modifications of a phrasal configurations may slow down the reader (Molinaro, Canal, Vespignani, Pesciarelli, & Cacciari, 2013), non-adjacent, or modified, frequent sequences still enjoy a processing advantage relative to their controls in the L1 context (Vilkaitė, 2016). This research also suggests that proficiency may play a determinant role in how adjacent and non-adjacent items are processed relative to their controls.

Comprehension of Figurative Formulaic Language

While the studies discussed previously deal with compositional formulaic language, including lexical bundles, verb-particle constructions, and irreversible binomials, idioms have also figured prominently in formulaic language research.[2] Much of relevant research has sought to compare the processing of idioms versus novel controls and the processing of an ambiguous idiom's figurative meaning versus its literal counterpart. Because of the availability of two unrelated interpretations (*kick the bucket* can mean "to pass away" as well as "to kick a pail"), ambiguous idioms have been extensively studied in the linguistic, psycholinguistic, and neurolinguistic literature, and a plethora of theories and hypotheses have been put forward since the 1970s, accounting for the processing of the two meanings in L1 adult speakers (e.g., Bobrow & Bell, 1973; Cacciari & Tabossi, 1988; Gibbs, 1980; Giora, 1997, 2003; Swinney & Cutler, 1979, and others).

More recently, idiom research has examined non-literal language processing in L2 speakers. In a self-paced, line-by-line reading experiment, Conklin and Schmitt (2008) investigated the processing of ambiguous idioms used figuratively (*a breath of fresh air* meaning "a new approach"), same expressions used literally (*a breath of fresh air* meaning "breathing clean air outside"), and control phrases (*a fresh breath of some air*). L1 and L2 speakers read formulaic sequences faster than controls, irrespective of the intended idiom meaning. The authors concluded that both groups of readers enjoyed a comparable processing advantage. The results observed for L2 speakers, however, appear to go against the findings of an earlier study by Cieślicka (2006), who also looked at L2 learners' processing of ambiguous idioms. In this study, participants listened to sentences that contained English idioms (*The young student had cold feet about giving the presentation*) and performed a lexical decision task on one of the four words: a word associated with the idiom's figurative meaning (*nervous*), its control (*leather*), a word associated with the idiom's literal meaning (*toes*), or its control (*toll*). The participants responded more quickly to the words associated with the idiom's literal meaning than to the words associated with the idiom's figurative meaning. Cieślicka (2006) concluded that in L2 idiom comprehension, a literal interpretation of idioms is activated prior to the figurative meaning.

The research into L2 idiom processing that followed has offered support to the proposition that literal meanings of ditropically ambiguous idioms (idioms that have a figurative as well as literal meaning) are easier and faster for L2 speakers to process. In a follow-up to the Conklin and Schmitt (2008) study, Siyanova-Chanturia, Conklin, and Schmitt (2011) employed eye movements to further examine the comprehension of the two meanings available in ambiguous idioms, as well as novel control phrases, in L1 and L2 speakers. The use of eye-tracking allowed for a more in-depth analysis of the data, because a range of measures can be used, both early and late (for an overview of eye-tracking in the context of formulaic language, see Siyanova-Chanturia, 2013). The pattern of results observed offered support to Cieślicka (2006) and was contrary to the findings reported in Conklin and Schmitt (2008). While L1 speakers read idioms faster than control phrases and showed a comparable reading pattern for the figurative and literal interpretation, L2 users did not exhibit differences in the reading of idioms and novel phrases and, in fact, slowed down when reading idioms' figurative uses compared to their literal renderings. It needs to be noted that the idiomatic expressions used in Siyanova-Chanturia, Conklin and Schmitt (2011) were known to the participants (as established in a norming procedure), yet their processing was characterized by a processing cost relative to the literal counterparts. This is in agreement with Cieślicka's (2006) conclusion that literal meaning has a priority over the figurative one in the course of L2 idiom comprehension. In the research that followed, Cieślicka and colleagues found further support for literal facilitation for L2 (ambiguous) idioms, suggesting "the special status that literal meanings of L2 idioms enjoy in the course of their processing by non-native language users" (Cieślicka & Heredia, 2011, p. 146; also see, Cieślicka, 2013; Cieślicka, Heredia, & Olivares, 2014). In sum, it is reasonable to conclude that while L1 speakers read idioms consistently faster than novel controls and do not read figurative and literal meanings differently (e.g., Conklin & Schmitt, 2008; Siyanova-Chanturia, Conklin, & Schmitt, 2011; Underwood, Schmitt, & Galpin, 2004), idiom comprehension appears rather taxing for L2 readers even when the target idioms are known (e.g., Cieślicka, 2006; Cieślicka & Heredia, 2011; Siyanova-Chanturia, Conklin, & Schmitt, 2011.

Research has also looked at how language users deal with unknown (rather than known) figurative language in the L1 context. The possibility of other routes to FL processing (than frequency of exposure, as is the case with compositional FSs) was explored using a naturalistic social setting with children aged 8–14, who were exposed to low-frequency target idioms and matched novel expressions within a conversational context (Reuterskiöld & Van Lancker Sidtis, 2013). The hypothesis was that idioms, due to their unitary, non-literal, nuanced, and linguistic-contextual characteristics, might be acquired from one-time exposure. Following the exposure period, the children recognized having heard significantly more target idioms than novel expressions and scored higher on comprehension of target idioms than on non-target idioms. These results support the notion that idioms, with their load of nuanced meaning, may engage attention and arousal mechanisms to be successfully uploaded into an FL repertory following brief exposure.

Another line of idiom research – idiom priming – has addressed the question of internal structure and how idioms really *are* different from more compositional language. Regular decompositional analyses have been reported in the processing of idiomatic expressions at the level of syntax, phonology, and semantics (e.g., Cutting & Bock, 1997; Konopka & Bock, 2009; Peterson, Burgess, Dell, & Eberhard, 2001; Snider & Arnon, 2012; Sprenger, Levelt, & Kempen, 2006). Much of the research has shown that idioms are amendable to priming just as literal language is, and that they possess "internal structure" (Arnon & Snider, 2012, p. 151). While this evidence may argue against the notion of holistic storage (for a discussion, see Siyanova-Chanturia, 2015), it does not, nevertheless, dispute the fact that idioms are "special" (Arnon & Snider, 2012, p. 149), as clearly they possess highly idiosyncratic semantics that literal, compositional language does not have. While the structure of FSs as unitary in some stage or level of mental representation is plentifully attested (e.g., Conklin & Schmitt, 2008; Horowitz & Manelis, 1973; Osgood & Housain, 1974; Swinney & Cutler, 1979), it is possible that any linguistic structure can be decomposed, especially idioms, given their "surface" structural shape and the available grammatical processes. The hybrid theory of idiomatic processing proposes a reasonable approach. In this proposal, idioms have two kinds of representations, holistic and decomposable according to grammatical rules (e.g., Libben & Titone, 2008; Sprenger et al., 2006).

Idioms are, by definition, highly familiar conventional expressions, and, as a consequence, predictable word strings – the properties that have rendered them particularly interesting for electroencephalography (EEG) researchers. EEG is the recording of electrical activity produced by neurons in the cortex recorded from the scalp. Event-related brain potentials (ERPs) are EEG responses time-locked to a stimulus and averaged over a number of trials (e.g., Luck, 2014). ERPs are represented by positive and negative peaks (e.g., Van Petten & Kutas, 1991) and are associated with different ERP components. An ERP component is "a reflection of the neural mechanisms involved in certain functional (i.e. cognitive or perceptual) processes" (Kaan, 2007, p. 573). Two ERP components in particular have been linked to idiom processing: the N400 and the P300. The N400 is a negative-going deflection between 300 ms and 500 ms post stimulus (e.g., Curran, Tucker, Kutas, & Posner, 1993). The N400 has been found to be affected by word frequency (Van Petten & Kutas, 1990), contextual predictability (e.g., Federmeier & Kutas, 1999), and world knowledge (e.g., Hagoort & Van Berkum, 2007), in that reduced N400 amplitudes are normally observed for more frequent and predictable stimuli versus less frequent and predictable. The P300 is a positive-going deflection between 250 ms and 400 ms post stimulus (e.g., Sutton, Braren, Zubin, & John, 1965). In the context of uniquely predictable linguistic information, Kok (2001) and Roehm, Bornkessel-Schlesewsky, Rösler, and Schlesewsky (2007, Experiment 1) have linked increased P300s to uniquely constraining linguistic scenarios and participants' "awareness that a stimulus belongs or does not belong to the category of a certain memorised target event" (2001, p. 573).

The ERP studies looking at formulaic language have focused mainly on non-literal phrasal processing in an L1 (e.g., Laurent, Denhières, Passerieux, Iakimova, & Hardy-Baylé, 2006; Molinaro & Carreiras, 2010; Rommers, Dijkstra, & Bastiaansen, 2013; Strandburg et al., 1993; Vespignani, Canal, Molinaro, Fonda, & Cacciari, 2010). In one of the earliest such studies by Strandburg et al. (1993), participants were presented with idioms, control phrases, or nonsensical phrases and were required to decide whether the phrase was meaningful or nonsensical. Idiom processing was characterized by reduced N400s relative to the other conditions. Likewise, in Laurent, Denhières, Passerieux, Iakimovac, and Hardy-Baylé (2006), strongly salient idioms (ones that "enjoy a high degree of entrenchment or fixedness", p. 153) elicited reduced N400 amplitudes relative to weakly salient phrases. Both Strandburg et al. (1993) and Laurent et al. (2006) attributed the reduction of the N400 to a processing advantage and easier semantic integration for highly conventional phrases. This conclusion was further confirmed in Vespignani et al. (2010), who observed smaller N400 amplitudes on the idiom's recognition point (point at which an idiom becomes recognizable as a conventional expression) relative to the control condition. However, the word following the recognition point in the idiomatic condition elicited larger P300 amplitudes compared to the control condition. While the N400 effect was taken to reflect easier processing for familiar language, the P300 effect observed post recognition point was interpreted as categorical template matching associated with "the retrieval of prefabricated meaning from the semantic memory" (p. 1696).

Interestingly, a comparable pattern of results was observed in a recent ERP study that looked at L1 readers' comprehension of English compositional phrases, such as binomial expressions (e.g., *knife and fork*) versus associates (e.g., *spoon and fork*) versus semantic violations (e.g., *theme and fork*) (Siyanova-Chanturia, Conklin, Caffarra, Kaan & van Heuven, 2017). The second content word in the binomial condition elicited larger P300s and smaller N400s compared to the other conditions. The findings of these ERP studies suggest that easier processing and semantic integration (indexed by reduced N400 amplitudes) and categorical template matching mechanisms (indexed by larger P300 amplitudes) may be associated with highly conventional language, both literal and figurative (but see

Molinaro & Carreiras, 2010, for some ERP differences observed for literal vs. figurative collocations).

In the context of an L2, the research is relatively scarce. Yet it, too, points to an interplay between familiarity of FL and the reduction of the N400 component. Moreno, Federmeier, and Kutas (2002) focused on English–Spanish bilingual speakers' comprehension of English idiomatic expressions (*Out of sight, out of . . .*) whose completions varied in language and probability: English expected completion (*mind*), its Spanish translation (*mente* "mind"), or English unexpected but plausible completion (*brain*). The expected completion – both English and Spanish – resulted in more positive N400 amplitudes than English unexpected but plausible completion. The finding that high-probability completions are easier to integrate semantically lends support to the research reviewed earlier and, critically, extends it to the L2 domain.

The study by Moreno, Federmeier, and Kutas (2002) looked at idiom processing in highly proficient bilingual individuals. How less proficient L2 speakers process conventional figurative language has been investigated in Paulmann, Ghareeb-Ali, and Felser (2015). These authors looked at late L2 learners' (L1 Arabic) and native English speakers' processing of literal verb+preposition combinations (*run over the old bridge*) versus figurative phrasal verbs (*run over the old farmer*) (see Matlock & Heredia, 2002, for a timed online sentence comprehension experiment employing comparable stimuli with L1 speakers, early and late L2 learners). The analysis of the disambiguating nouns (*bridge* vs. *farmer*) revealed that literal interpretations were associated with larger N400 amplitudes than figurative ones for both L1 and L2 speakers. Thus, late L2 learners "preferred" the figurative meaning, deemed more frequent and, possibly, more anticipated, over the literal one, deemed less frequent and, as a result, less anticipated, just as L1 speakers did.

In sum, at the electrophysiological level, language users benefit from the familiar, prefabricated, and hence highly predictable nature of idiomatic expressions, as suggested by reduced N400s for L1 and L2 speakers, and larger P300s for L1 speakers.

Production of Formulaic Language

In the previous sections, we have reviewed the studies dealing with the online processing of FL from a comprehension perspective. Another line of evidence comes from the studies on the online production (articulation) of FL. These studies have looked at the processing of literal compositional and figurative non-compositional sequences and have primarily sought to address the following questions: How do frequency and predictability effects manifest themselves during the articulation of FL (in naturalistic and elicited speech)? What is the relationship between the smaller parts and the larger whole? Does FL exhibit prosodic characteristics distinct from novel sequences? Does the articulation of figurative FL differ from that of matched literal (novel) sequences? In the following section, we review some of the evidence, focusing first on compositional formulaic sequences and then on figurative language.

Production of Compositional Formulaic Language

Akin to the comprehension studies, production studies have mostly offered support to the tenet that FL is processed differently from matched novel strings of language. Early spoken corpus-based research showed that words are more likely to be phonetically reduced when they are part of frequent and hence predictable phrasal contexts, such as *I don't know* (e.g., Bell, et al., 2003; Bybee & Scheibman, 1999). Using the Switchboard corpus (Godfrey, Holliman, & McDaniel, 1992), Gregory, Raymond, Bell, Fosler-Lussier, and Jurafsky (1999) and Jurafsky, Bell, Gregory, and Raymond (2001) reported that highly probable content and function words were more likely to be reduced in conversational speech. In another perspective, FSs have been described as having phonological coherence, in that the expressions are produced as a single intonation unit (e.g., Lin, 2010).

While early research has looked at spontaneous adult speech from spoken corpora, more recent studies have focused both on naturalistic and elicited speech in adults and children. For example, distinct articulatory patterns for frequent versus infrequent phrases have been observed in children's elicited speech. Using a sentence-repetition task, Bannard and Matthews (2008) showed that children as young as 3 years old are sensitive to phrase frequency distributions: more frequent phrases (*sit in your chair*) were articulated more quickly than their less frequent counterparts (*sit in your truck*). These researchers further showed that children as young as 2 years old were more likely to repeat an utterance correctly if it was frequent rather than infrequent. Thus, phrase frequency affected the speed as well as accuracy with which 2- and 3-year-olds were able to repeat the phrases, suggesting that young children possess "experience-derived knowledge of specific four-word sequences" (p. 246).

A bulk of evidence has come from the studies looking at n-grams varying in size, syntactic structure, and semantics (e.g., Arnon & Cohen Priva, 2013, 2014; Janssen & Barber, 2012; Tremblay & Tucker, 2011). Tremblay and Tucker (2011) investigated the influence of a range of probabilistic measures – unigram, bigram, trigram, and quadgram frequencies, log probability and mutual information (MI) – on the recognition (onset latency) and production (durations) of four-word frequencies, such as *end of the year* and *at the same time*. The amount of experience with an n-gram emerged as the most important predictor in the analysis of articulatory durations. In other words, frequency played a key role in the production of the target four-word sequences. Somewhat unexpectedly, MI (a measure of association strength, or "cohesiveness", p. 321) was not found to be a significant predictor of production times; while log probability contributed minimally to the amount of variance. Interestingly, the analysis of the onset latency (i.e., recognition) data revealed the opposite pattern: log probability surfaced as the most important factor, closely followed by MI, while frequency of occurrence was not found to play a major role. This pattern is reminiscent of the findings in a reading aloud study by Ellis, Simpson-Vlach, and Maynard (2008, Experiment 2), who also found that MI affected voice onset time in native speakers of English, while phrase frequency was not a significant predictor of articulation latency (voice onset time). Interestingly, for the non-native participants in Ellis et al. (2008), the pattern was reversed: frequency but not MI was found to affect articulation latency. Tremblay and Tucker (2011) and Ellis et al.'s (2008) studies are notable in a number of ways, not least because the focus was both on recognition and production, as well as on several families of probabilistic measures.

Siyanova-Chanturia and Janssen (2018) further examined the production of compositional sequences by L1 and L2 users. Borrowing the stimuli from Siyanova-Chanturia, Conklin, and van Heuven (2011), these authors employed a phrase elicitation task in which participants were required to articulate binomial expressions (e.g., *bride and groom*) and their reversed forms (e.g., *groom and bride*). It was found that native speakers' articulatory durations were influenced by phrase frequency (akin to Siyanova-Chanturia, Conklin, & van Heuven, 2011) but not stimulus type – binomial versus reversed (unlike Siyanova-Chanturia, Conklin, & van Heuven, 2011). In contrast, proficient non-native speakers' articulatory durations were not found to be modulated either by phrase frequency or stimulus type. These findings further highlight an important role played by phrase frequency in language production in L1 speakers, suggest possible dissociations between the mechanisms that underpin phrasal comprehension (Siyanova-Chanturia, Conklin, & van Heuven, 2011) and production (Siyanova-Chanturia & Janssen, 2018), as well as point to certain differences between phrasal production in L1 and L2 speakers.

Phrase frequency effects have also been investigated in languages other than English. In Janssen and Barber (2012), native speakers of Spanish (Experiment 1) and French (Experiment 2) produced noun-adjective, noun-noun, and determiner-noun-adjective phrases that were elicited by experimental displays consisting of coloured drawings. In both experiments, production times were influenced by phrase frequency: naming latencies were shorter for higher frequency phrases than for lower frequency sequences. Janssen and Barber (2012) proposed that the language system is sensitive to frequency distributions beyond individual words. Such was also the conclusion of Arnon and Cohen Priva (2013), who investigated the effect of multiword frequency on phonetic duration in excerpts of elicited and spontaneous (corpus-based) speech, as well as the role of syntactic structure in L1 English. Across three experiments, it was shown that phonetic durations were shorter in higher frequency phrases than in lower frequency sequences (*don't have to worry* vs. *don't have to wait*), regardless of the syntactic structure (subject-auxiliary-verb vs. verb-determiner-noun), and that the effects observed were not reducible to the frequency of phrase constituents.

While these studies have focused primarily on how phrase frequency and other probabilistic measures may modulate the production of multiword information,

Arnon and Cohen Priva (2014) explored more directly the relationship between the parts and the whole, and the prominence of smaller constituents within a larger unit, a line of research not unlike that adopted in the earlier detection studies by Sosa and MacFarlane (2002) and Kapatsinski and Radicke (2009). In other words, these authors tested the thesis of FL holistic storage and processing, by investigating the effect of phrasal and single-word frequency on phonetic duration of naturalistically produced speech (using the Buckeye Speech Corpus, Pitt et al., 2007). In particular, Arnon and Cohen Priva (2014) were interested in how the relationship between word and multiword information might change across the frequency continuum. One of the key findings of this study was the observed change in the prominence of single-word versus multiword information with growing phrase frequency. For highly frequent three-word phrases (*all kinds of*, *the fact that*, *little bit more*[3]), the effect of constituent, single-word frequency on phonetic duration decreased but was still significant, while the effect of multiword frequency on phonetic duration increased. Arnon and Cohen Priva (2014) concluded that repeated usage leads to a growing prominence of multiword information, but that repeated usage does *not* eliminate the effect of word information. This is more likely to be the case with FSs that carry little or no figurative meaning, such as lexical bundles and n-grams. That is, no matter how frequent a multiword sequence might be, its constituents remain "present" and impact on the way in which the larger string is processed. The study by Arnon and Cohen Priva (2014) is important in that it provides convincing evidence against holistic storage for frequent lexical bundles (see Siyanova-Chanturia, 2015 for a discussion).

Production and Prosodic Characteristics of Figurative Formulaic Language

The above studies have centred on the phonetic duration of literal, compositional FL in either elicited or spontaneous (spoken corpus) speech. Another line of research comes from the studies on the articulatory durations and prosody[4] of figurative FL – idioms and proverbs – versus novel language, the majority of which have been conducted by Van Lancker Sidtis and colleagues. It needs to be noted, however, that the research into FL prosody described in this section draws on the evidence from production as well as recognition, in the sense that in all but two studies (Hallin & Van Lancker Sidtis, 2017; Siyanova-Chanturia & Lin, 2018), pre-recorded figurative and literal utterances were judged on their prosodic characteristics by a group of listeners.

In the early studies, Van Lancker and Canter (1981) and Van Lancker, Canter, and Terbeek (1981) focused on the prosodic characteristics of ditropically ambiguous idioms' two meanings. In Van Lancker and Canter (1981), it was shown that L1 English listeners were able to successfully identify the intended meaning – figurative or (novel) literal – when speakers purposefully conveyed the distinction between the two. In a follow-up study, Van Lancker et al. (1981) set out to identify the specific cues that helped listeners distinguish plausible figurative versus literal sentences using the stimuli borrowed from Van Lancker and Canter (1981). The follow-up study revealed that literal utterances were characterized by longer durations, increased pausing, and greater numbers of pitch contours compared to figurative utterances. Van Lancker et al. (1981) concluded that distinct physical shape – prosodic cues – marked utterances as either literal or figurative. More recently, again using the recorded materials from Van Lancker and Canter (1981), Van Lancker-Sidtis (2003) further explored auditory recognition of ambiguous idioms by more and less proficient English language users: native American English speakers, native non-American English speakers, highly proficient L2 English speakers, and English as a Second Language (ESL) college students. To the best of our knowledge, this is the only study to date that has investigated the prosody of FL from an L2 perspective. The four groups of participants judged whether the target utterances were intended to be figurative or literal. Native speakers outperformed proficient L2 speakers, while ESL students were not able to reliably distinguish between figurative and literal idiom meanings. Two main conclusions were drawn from this study. First, "quantifiable prosodic cue" (p. 53) helped L1 and, to a lesser extent, proficient L2 speakers successfully differentiate between the idiom meanings, offering support to the thesis that the two are phonetically distinct. Second, the author took the results to suggest that subtle prosodic contrasts, such as those between idiomatic versus literal meanings of otherwise identical utterances (presented in isolation), may be more difficult to acquire in L2 learning than other linguistic elements. The results from the ESL speakers do not support the suggestion by Ashby (2006, see below) that listeners in the earlier study (Van Lancker & Canter, 1981) utilized an acoustic cue strategy (change of sentence focus) to differentiate the utterance types.

It needs to be noted that the speakers who produced the target utterances in the original study by Van Lancker and Canter (1981) were instructed to articulate as distinctly as possible the two contrasting meanings – figurative and literal – implying that the resulting materials (later used in Van Lancker et al, 1981 and Van Lancker Sidtis, 2003) were somewhat unnatural. Indeed, it was argued that the literal as contrasted with the idiomatic exemplars were merely manifesting a different sentence focus (e.g., Ashby, 2006), cueing listeners at the pragmatic level that a different meaning is intended. Nonetheless, the research that followed not only confirmed distinct articulatory features of figurative and literal renderings, but also extended this finding to languages other than English. In particular, Yang, Ahn, and Van Lancker Sidtis (2015) investigated (1) listeners' ability to differentiate between idiomatic and literal renderings of pre-recorded ambiguous idioms in Korean (그 사람이 벌집을 건드렸어. English literal translation "he stirred up a beehive", idiomatic meaning *he caused a big problem*), and (2) specific acoustic cues used by Korean speakers to identify the intended meaning. Although the study was modelled after Van Lancker and Canter (1981), the native speakers of

Korean who were recorded had been instructed to produce the target utterances as naturally as possible, which, arguably, led to more naturalistic data compared to the original study by Van Lancker and Canter (1981). In line with the earlier research, Yang and colleagues (2015) found that native speakers of Korean were able to successfully identify the intended meaning. The acoustic cues investigated were durations (utterance, word, and syllable), pitch contour in final positions, and intensity. Idiomatic sentences were characterized by rising pitch at the end of a sentence, greater intensity, and shorter durations. The authors concluded that distinctive mental representations exist for idiomatic and literal language, and that dissimilar acoustic cues are part of these representations.

Finally, borrowing the stimuli from a reading study by Siyanova-Chanturia, Conklin and Schmitt (2011), Siyanova-Chanturia and Lin (2018) had participants – native speakers of English – read aloud a series of stories that contained ambiguous idioms used either figuratively or literally, as well as control phrases. These authors showed that idioms were articulated faster than controls (in line with Siyanova-Chanturia, Conklin, & Schmitt, 2011), but that figurative meanings were articulated somewhat faster than their literal equivalents (unlike what was shown in Siyanova-Chanturia, Conklin, & Schmitt, 2011). The study is interesting in that direct comparisons can be made between idiom comprehension (Siyanova-Chanturia, Conklin, & Schmitt, 2011) and production (Siyanova-Chanturia & Lin, 2018). However, as the authors note, the reading aloud task involved both the recognition and production stages, pointing to the need for future research to either look at excerpts of spontaneous speech or adopt paradigms that will allow the researcher to tease apart the processes involved in the recognition versus articulation stages.

While most research to date has looked at the prosodic characteristics of idiomatic expressions, Hallin and Van Lancker Sidtis (2017) examined the prosody of another kind of figurative FL – proverbs. Specifically, very low-frequency Swedish proverbs (*borta bra men hemma bäst*, literal English translation "away good but at home best") were looked at versus matched novel sequences (*ute kallt men inne varmt*, literal English translation "outside cold but inside warm"). It needs to be borne in mind that while the proverbs were low frequency (0–0.3 occurrences per million words in a reference corpus), they were, nonetheless, familiar to the participants. A group of native adult and child speakers of Swedish performed an elicitation task in which they were required to read a target sentence silently, and then to articulate it out loud as naturally as possible. The study focused on two aspects: speech rate and tonal patterns. Although there were some differences between the two participant groups, both children and adults produced proverbs faster than novel sentences, akin to the studies with idioms (see earlier discussion). Interestingly, unlike the idiom research, analyses revealed that proverbs exhibited less – rather than more – stressed tonal patterns than matched controls. Based on the pattern of results observed, the authors concluded that a prosodic pattern is stored together with the form of the proverb.

Conclusions and Future Directions

The studies reviewed in the present chapter have been instrumental in our understanding of the role that phrase frequency, predictability, figurativeness, and other factors play in FL processing in an L1 and L2. Despite the heterogeneity of the research reviewed, some common conclusions and venues for future research have emerged.

Arguably, the central finding reported in the studies on the comprehension of compositional FL is a key role of phrase frequency. Not only L1 speakers, but, critically, L2 learners have been shown to be attuned to phrase frequency distributions (e.g., Arnon & Snider, 2010; Hernández et al., 2016; Siyanova-Chanturia, Conklin, & van Heuven, 2011; Tremblay et al., 2011), suggesting that language users of various proficiency levels notice, learn, and store frequency information about sequences above the word level. Interestingly, phrase frequency effects have been observed irrespective of adjacency. Vilkaitė (2016) and Vilkaitė and Schmitt (2017) demonstrated how L1 and L2 readers deal with frequency, adjacency, and the modification of conventional language (often assumed to be fixed, or semi-fixed). Given the scarcity of such research with respect to L2 speakers, future studies should further this line of enquiry by looking at other kinds of non-contiguous FSs in L2 speakers of various proficiencies. Interestingly, despite certain differences having been observed between L1 and L2 processing (e.g., Siyanova & Schmitt, 2008, Study 3; Siyanova-Chanturia, Conklin, & van Heuven, 2011), some researchers have proposed that the similarities between the way in which the language processor deals with multiword information in an L1 and L2 are more apparent than the differences, and that unified, rather than separate, models of L1 and L2 processing are needed (e.g., Hernández et al., 2016). Clearly, this proposition needs further interrogation.

The role of phrase frequency has also been noted in production studies – albeit largely with L1 speakers – with higher frequency and predictability being associated with phonetic reduction and shorter articulatory durations (e.g., Arnon & Cohen Priva, 2013; Bannard & Matthews, 2008; Bell et al., 2003; Bybee & Scheibman, 1999; Janssen & Barber, 2012). With respect to L2 speaker sensitivity to phrase frequency in language production, the jury is still out. It is well established in the second language acquisition literature that receptive vocabulary knowledge precedes productive knowledge (e.g., Nation, 2013), and that receptive learning and use is typically easier than productive learning and use (e.g., Ellis & Beaton, 1993; Nation, 2013). Thus, while the comprehension studies suggest certain parallels between L1 and L2 phrasal processing, production studies may reveal dissimilarities. Language user sensitivity to the distributional properties of FSs has been argued to be problematic for the-words-and-rules view of language. This approach views the lexicon (memorized and stored forms) and grammar (a collection of rules) as distinct entities (e.g., Pinker, 1991, 1999; Pinker & Ullman, 2002). According to this approach, frequency should play a role in the processing of memorized forms, such as morphologically simple forms and idiosyncratic phrases (idioms). Thus, compositional phrases like lexical bundles and binomials are necessarily computed and hence should not be subject to phrase frequency effects. On the contrary, research capitalizing on the role of phrase frequency has offered support to emergentist approaches to language acquisition, processing, and use, such as connectionist models (e.g., Christiansen & Chater, 1999; Elman, 1990; Rumelhart & McClelland, 1986), usage-based theories (e.g., Bybee, 1998; Goldberg, 2006; Langacker, 1987; Tomasello, 2003), and exemplar-based models (e.g., Abbot-Smith & Tomasello, 2006; Bod, 2006; Pierrehumbert, 2001). These approaches argue for an important role of frequency in the processing of all linguistic information, irrespective of size and complexity, at the word, phrase, or sentence level. According to these accounts, the frequency of occurrence is a major factor determining what language learners notice, learn, and represent in the mental lexicon. In sum, phrase frequency effects observed in comprehension (L1 and L2) and production (largely L1) studies have been taken to reflect language users' sensitivity to the distribution of linguistic information at various grain sizes, as well as certain parallels between words and phrases.

Another line of FL research – one investigating the relationship between the parts and the whole – revealed that the access to the constituent parts of an FS can be impeded (e.g., Sosa & MacFarlane, 2002; also see Kapatsinski & Radicke, 2009). While repeated usage clearly leads to a greater prominence of multiword information, the effect of word information is not eliminated, even in the case of highly frequent and "fused" sequences (e.g., Arnon & Cohen Priva, 2014). However, again, these findings pertain mainly to L1 populations. Future research should explore the relationship between smaller parts and the larger whole in L2 speakers. Because L2 users will have had far less exposure to FSs compared to native speakers, the pattern of results may be markedly different.

Several noteworthy conclusions can also be arrived at with respect to figurative FL. Unlike many of the compositional FSs (such as lexical bundles and n-grams), figurative language is far less frequent. Yet, it is highly familiar to proficient language users. At the electrophysiological level, familiar idioms have been shown to be processed qualitatively and quantitatively differently from novel control strings. Reading studies with L1 and, to a lesser extent, proficient L2 speakers have reported electrophysiological markers (e.g., larger P300s, reduced N400s) associated with easier processing and semantic integration, as well as categorical template matching, for conventional language (e.g., Laurent et al., 2006; Moreno et al., 2002; Paulmann et al., 2015; Strandburg et al., 1993; Vespignani et al., 2010).

Another key finding pertains to L2 learners' treatment of figurativeness in those expressions that can be interpreted both literally and figuratively. By and large, evidence suggests that, in L2 idiom comprehension, the literal interpretation of an ambiguous idiom is accessed prior to the figurative meaning, a pattern rather different from that observed for L1 speakers (e.g., Cieślicka, 2006; Siyanova-Chanturia, Conklin, & Schmitt, 2011). It appears that L2 speakers find it easier to process literal meanings of ambiguous idioms than their figurative counterparts.

Finally, the studies on the production of figurative language have shaped our knowledge of prosody of FL. These studies have not only confirmed overall faster articulation for familiar language, but, critically, they have pointed to increased pausing, greater numbers of pitch contours, and (in Korean) lesser intensity in literal versus formulaic utterances, implying that figurative FL is characterized by a quantifiably distinct physical shape stored with the form of the utterance (e.g., Van Lancker-Sidtis, 2003; Van Lancker et al., 1981; Yang et al., 2015). The findings of these studies have been taken to support the tenet that non-literal strings of language and novel sequences may be processed according to different mechanisms. As with other strands of FL processing research, however, this evidence pertains almost exclusively to L1 speakers. How prosodic characteristics of figurative utterances articulated by L2 learners might differ from those produced by L1 speakers remains to be addressed in future research.

In the present review, we sought to cover a large body of evidence attesting to the mechanisms engaged in the processing of the multifarious linguistic, psycholinguistic, and cognitive phenomenon that is formulaic language. In doing so, we hope to have highlighted major findings and set some ground for future research, in particular, with respect to L2 speakers, that will allow us to further advance this ever-growing field of research.

Notes

1 Online processing is one happening in real time or under time pressure. In the present review, we focus on language comprehension (e.g., while reading) and production (e.g., spontaneous and elicited speech) as they unfold in real time. The chapter offers an overview of the studies on the online processing of FL by native and non-native speakers. The chapter, however, does not deal with cross-linguistic influences, i.e., the influence of an L1 on FL processing in an L2 (or vice versa). This issue is explored in Conklin and Carrol (this volume).
2 We define figurative formulaic sequences as non-compositional, non-literal language whose overall meaning is not merely the sum of the literal meanings of their constituents. It is noteworthy that figurative (or non-literal) language encompasses a variety of types, such as idioms, proverbs, metaphors, jokes, and irony. The present review focuses mainly (although not exclusively) on idioms, as this is the only type of non-literal language that has been extensively studied both in the L1 and L2 literature.
3 Examples obtained through personal communication (May 2015).
4 The chapter by Lin (this volume) deals with the issue of prosody of formulaic language from a language acquisition perspective.

References

Abbot-Smith, K., & Tomasello, M. (2006). Exemplar-learning and schematization in a usage-based account of syntactic acquisition. *The Linguistic Review, 23,* 275–290.

Arnon, I., & Cohen Priva, U. (2013). More than words: The effect of multi-word frequency and constituency on phonetic duration. *Language and Speech, 56*(3), 349–371.

Arnon, I., & Cohen Priva, U. (2014). The changing effect of word and multiword frequency on phonetic duration for highly frequent phrases. *The Mental Lexicon, 9*(3), 377–400.

Arnon, I., McCauley, S., & Christiansen, M. H. (2017). Digging up the building blocks of language: Age-of-Acquisition effects for multiword phrases. *Journal of Memory and Language, 92,* 265–280.

Arnon, I., & Snider, N. (2010). More than words: Frequency effects for multi-word phrases. *Journal of Memory and Language, 62,* 67–82.

Ashby, M. (2006). Prosody and idioms in English. *Journal of Pragmatics, 38*(10), 1580–1597.

Bannard, C., & Matthews, D. (2008). Stored word sequences in language learning: The effect of familiarity on children's repetition of four-word combinations. *Psychological Science, 19,* 241–248.

Bell, A., Jurafsky, D., Fosler-Lussier, E., Girand, C., Gregory, M., & Gildea, D. (2003). Effects of disfluencies, predictability, and utterance position on word form variation in English conversation. *The Journal of the Acoustical Society of America, 113,* 1001–1024.

Bobrow, S., & Bell, S. (1973). On catching on to idiomatic expressions. *Memory and Cognition, 1*(3), 343–346.

Bod, R. (2006). Exemplar-based syntax: How to get productivity from exemplars. *The Linguistic Review, 23,* 291–320.

Bybee, J. (1998). The emergent lexicon. *Chicago Linguistic Society, 34,* 421–435.

Bybee, J., & Scheibman, J. (1999). The effect of usage on degree of constituency: The reduction of *don't* in American English. *Linguistics, 37,* 575–596.

Bybee, J., & Torres Cacoullos, R. (2009). The role of prefabs in grammaticization: How the particular and the general interact in language change. In R. L. Corrigan, E. A. Moravcsik, H. Ouali, & M. Wheatley (Eds.), *Formulaic language: Volume 2* (pp. 187–218). Amsterdam: John Benjamins.

Cacciari, C., & Tabossi, P. (1988). The comprehension of idioms. *Journal of Memory and Language, 27,* 668–683.

Christiansen, M., & Chater, N. (1999). Toward a connectionist model of recursion in human linguistic performance. *Cognitive Science, 23,* 157–205.

Cieślicka, A. (2006). Literal salience in on-line processing of idiomatic expressions by second language learners. *Second Language Research, 22,* 115–144.

Cieślicka, A. (2013). Do nonnative language speakers chew the fat and spill the beans with different brain hemispheres? Investigating idiom decomposability with the divided visual field paradigm. *Journal of Psycholinguistic Research, 42*(6), 475–503.

Cieślicka, A., & Heredia, R. (2011). Hemispheric asymmetries in processing L1 and L2 idioms: Effects of salience and context. *Brain & Language, 116,* 136–150.

Cieślicka, A., Heredia, R., & Olivares, M. (2014). It's all in the eyes: How language dominance, salience, and context affect eye movements during idiomatic language processing. In M. Pawlak & L. Aronin (Eds.), *Essential topics in applied linguistics and multilingualism, second language teaching and learning* (pp. 21–42). Switzerland: Springer International Publishing.

Conklin, K., & Schmitt, N. (2008). Formulaic sequences: Are they processed more quickly than nonformulaic language by native and nonnative speakers? *Applied Linguistics, 29*(1), 72–89.

Curran, T., Tucker, D., Kutas, M., & Posner, M. (1993). Topography of the N400: Brain electrical activity reflecting semantic expectancy. *Electroencephalography and Clinical Neurophysiology, 88,* 188–209.

Cutting, J., & Bock, K. (1997). That's the way the cookie bounces: Syntactic and semantic components of experimentally elicited idiom blends. *Memory and Cognition, 25*(1), 57–71.

Durrant, P., & Doherty, A. (2010). Are high-frequency collocations psychologically real? Investigating the thesis of collocational priming. *Corpus Linguistics and Linguistic Theory, 6*(2), 125–155.

Edmonds, A. (2014). Conventional expressions. Investigating pragmatics and processing. *Studies in Second Language Acquisition, 36*(1), 69–99.

Ellis, N. C., & Beaton, A. (1993). Factors affecting foreign language vocabulary: Imagery keyword mediators and phonological short-term memory. *Quarterly Journal of Experimental Psychology, 46A*(3), 533–538.

Ellis, N. C., Simpson-Vlach, R., & Maynard, C. (2008). Formulaic language in native and second-language speakers: Psycholinguistics, corpus linguistics, and TESOL. *TESOL Quarterly, 41*, 375–396.

Elman, J. L. (1990). Finding structure in time. *Cognitive Science, 14*, 179–211.

Federmeier, K., & Kutas, M. (1999). A rose by any other name: Long term memory structure and sentence processing. *Journal of Memory and Language, 41*, 469–495.

Gibbs, R. (1980). Spilling the beans on understanding and memory for idioms in conversation. *Memory and Cognition, 8*, 449–456.

Giora, R. (1997). Understanding figurative and literal language: The graded salience hypothesis. *Cognitive Linguistics, 7*, 183–206.

Giora, R. (2003). *On our mind: Salience, context, and figurative language.* Oxford: Oxford University Press.

Gleason, J. B., & Weintraub, S. (1976). The acquisition of routines in child language. *Language in Society, 5*, 129–136.

Godfrey, J., Holliman, E., & McDaniel, J. (1992). SWITCHBOARD: Telephone speech corpus for research and development. *Proceedings of ICASSP, 92*, 517–520.

Goldberg, A. (2006). *Constructions at work: The nature of generalization in language.* Oxford: Oxford University Press.

Gregory, M., Raymond, W., Bell, A., Fosler-Lussier, E., & Jurafsky, D. (1999). The effects of collocational strength and contextual predictability in lexical production. *Chicago Linguistic Society, 35*, 151–166.

Hagoort, P., & van Berkum, J. (2007). Beyond the sentence given. *Philosophical Transactions of the Royal Society B: Biological Sciences, 362*(1481), 801–811.

Hallin, A. E., & Van Lancker Sidtis, D. (2017). A closer look at formulaic language: Prosodic characteristics of Swedish proverbs. *Applied Linguistics, 38*(1), 68–89.

Hernández, M., Costa, A., & Arnon, I. (2016). More than words: Multiword frequency effects in non-native speakers. *Language, Cognition and Neuroscience, 31*(6), 785–800.

Horowitz, L. M., & Manelis, L. (1973). Recognition and cued recall of idioms and phrases. *Journal of Experimental Psychology, 100*, 291–296.

Janssen, N., & Barber, H. A. (2012). Phrase frequency effects in language production. *PLoS ONE, 7*(3), e33202. doi:10.1371/journal.pone.0033202.

Jiang, N., & Nekrasova, T., M. (2007). The processing of formulaic sequences by second language speakers. *The Modern Language Journal, 91*(3), 433–445.

Jurafsky, D., Bell, A., Gregory, M. L., & Raymond, W. D. (2001). Probabilistic relations between words: Evidence from reduction in lexical production. In J. L. Bybee, & P. Hopper (Eds.), *Frequency and the emergence of linguistic structure* (pp. 229–254). Amsterdam: John Benjamins.

Kaan, E. (2007). Event-related potentials and language processing: A brief overview. *Language and Linguistics Compass, 1*(6), 571–591.

Kapatsinski, V., & Radicke, J. (2009). Frequency and the emergence of prefabs: Evidence from monitoring. In R. Corrigan, E. Moravcsik, H. Ouali, & K. Wheatley (Eds.), *Formulaic language* (pp. 499–522). Amsterdam: John Benjamins.

Kim, S. H., & Kim, J. H. (2012). Frequency effects in L2 multi-word unit processing: Evidence from self-paced reading. *TESOL Quarterly, 46*(4), 831–841.

Kok, A. (2001). On the utility of P300 amplitude as a measure of processing capacity. *Psychophysiology, 38*, 557–577.

Konopka, A., & Bock, K. (2009). Lexical or syntactic control of sentence formulation? Structural generalizations from idiom production. *Cognitive Psychology, 58*(1), 68–101.

Langacker, R. (1987). *Foundations of cognitive grammar* (Vol. 1). Stanford, CA: Stanford University Press.

Laurent, J., Denhières, G., Passerieux, C., Iakimovac, G., & Hardy-Baylé, M. (2006). On understanding idiomatic language. *Brain Research, 1068*, 151–160.

Libben, M. R., & Titone, D. (2008). The multidetermined nature of idiom processing. *Memory and Cognition, 36*, 1103–1121.

Lin, P. M. S. (2010). The phonology of formulaic sequences: A review. In D. Wood (Ed.), *Perspectives on formulaic language: Acquisition and communication* (pp. 174–193). London: Continuum.

Locke, J. L. (1993). *The child's path to spoken language*. Cambridge, MA: Harvard University Press.

Locke, J. L. (1997). A theory of neurolinguistic development. *Brain and Language, 58*, 265–326.

Luck, S. J. (2014). *An introduction to the event-related potential technique*. Cambridge, MA: MIT press.

Matlock, T., & Heredia, R. (2002). Understanding phrasal verbs in monolinguals and bilinguals. In R. Heredia, & J. Altarriba (Eds.), *Advances in psychology: Vol. 134. Bilingual sentence processing* (pp. 251–274). Amsterdam: Elsevier Press.

Millar, N. (2011). The processing of malformed formulaic language. *Applied Linguistics, 32*(2), 129–148.

Molinaro, N., & Carreiras, M. (2010). Electrophysiological evidence of interaction between contextual expectation and semantic integration during the processing of collocations. *Biological Psychology, 83*(3), 176–190.

Molinaro, N., Canal, P., Vespignani, F., Pesciarelli, F., & Cacciari, C. (2013). Are complex function words processed as semantically empty strings? A reading time and ERP study of collocational complex Prepositions. *Language and Cognitive Processes, 28*(6), 762–788.

Moon, R. E. (1998a). *Fixed expressions and text: A study of the distribution and textual behaviour of fixed expressions in English* (Oxford Studies in Lexicography and Lexicology). Oxford: Clarendon Press.

Moon, R. E. (1998b). Frequencies and forms of phrasal lexemes in English. In A. P. Cowie (Ed.), *Phraseology: Theory, analysis, and applications* (Oxford Studies in Lexicography and Lexicology) (pp. 79–100). Oxford: Oxford University Press.

Moreno, E., Federmeier, K., & Kutas, M. (2002). Switching languages, switching *palabras* (words): An electrophysiological study of code switching. *Brain and Language, 80*, 188–207.

Morrison, C. M., & Ellis, A. W. (1995). Roles of word frequency and age of acquisition in word naming and lexical decision. *Journal of Experimental Psychology: Learning, Memory, and Cognition, 21*(1), 116–133.

Nation, I. S. P. (2013). *Learning vocabulary in another language* (2nd Ed.). Cambridge: Cambridge University Press.

Osgood, C. E., & Housain, R. (1974). Salience of the word as a unit in the perception of language. *Perception and Psychophysics, 15*, 168–192.

Paulmann, S., Ghareeb-Ali, Z., & Felser, C. (2015). Neurophysiological markers of phrasal verb processing: Evidence from L1 and L2 speakers. In R. R. Heredia & A. B. Cieślicka (Eds.), *Bilingual figurative language processing* (pp. 245–267). Cambridge: Cambridge University Press.

Peters, A. (1983). *The units of language*. Cambridge: Cambridge University Press.

Peterson, R., Burgess, C., Dell, G., & Eberhard, K. 2001. Disassociation between syntactic and semantic processing during idiom comprehension. *Journal of Experimental Psychology: Learning, Memory, and Cognition, 27*(5), 1223–1237.

Pierrehumbert, J. (2001). Exemplar dynamics: Word frequency, lenition and contrast. In J. Bybee & P. Hopper (Eds.), *Frequency and the emergence of linguistic structure* (pp. 137–157). Amsterdam: John Benjamins.

Pinker, S. (1991). Rules of language. *Science, 253*, 530–535.

Pinker, S. (1999). *Words and rules: The ingredients of language*. New York, NY: Harper Collins.

Pinker, S., & Ullman, M. (2002). The past and future of the past tense. *Trends in Cognitive Sciences, 6*, 456–463.

Pitt, M., Dilley, L., Johnson, K., Kiesling, S., Raymond, W., Hume, E., & Fosler-Lussier, E. (2007). *Buckeye corpus of conversational speech* (2nd release). Columbus, OH: Department of Psychology, Ohio State University. Retrieved from www.buckeyecorpus.osu.edu

Rammell, C. S., Van Lancker Sidtis, D., and Pisoni (2017). Perception of formulaic and novel expressions under acoustic degradation. *The Mental Lexicon, 12*(2), 234–262. http://www.jbe-platform.com/content/journals/10.1075/ml.16019.ram

Reuterskiöld, C., & Van Lancker Sidtis, D. (2013). Retention of idioms following one-time exposure. *Child Language Teaching and Therapy, 29*(2), 219–231.

Rommers, J., Dijkstra, T., & Bastiaansen, M. (2013). Context-dependent semantic processing in the human brain: Evidence from idiom comprehension. *Journal of Cognitive Neuroscience, 25*(5), 762–776.

Roehm, D., Bornkessel-Schlesewsky, I., Rösler, F., & Schlesewsky, M. (2007). To predict or not to predict: Influences of task and strategy on the processing of semantic relations. *Journal of Cognitive Neuroscience, 19*, 1259–1274.

Rumelhart, D., & McClelland, J. (1986). On learning the past tenses of English verbs. In D. Rumelhart & J. McClelland (Eds.), *Parallel distributed processing: Explorations in the microstructure of cognition* (pp. 216–271). Cambridge, MA: MIT Press.

Shantz, K. (2017). Phrase frequency, proficiency and grammaticality interact in non-native processing: Implications for theories of SLA. *Second Language Research, 33*(1), 91–118.

Siyanova, A., & Schmitt, N. (2008). L2 learner production and processing of collocation: A multi-study perspective. *Canadian Modern Language Review, 64*(3), 429–458.

Siyanova-Chanturia, A. (2013). Eye-tracking and ERPs in multi-word expression research: A state-of-the-art review of the method and findings. *The Mental Lexicon, 8*(2), 245–268.

Siyanova-Chanturia, A. (2015). On the "holistic" nature of formulaic language. *Corpus Linguistics and Linguistic Theory, 11*(2), 285–301.

Siyanova-Chanturia, A., Conklin, K., Caffarra, S., Kaan, E., & van Heuven, W. J. B. (2017). Representation and processing of multi-word expressions in the brain. *Brain and Language, 175*, 111–122.

Siyanova-Chanturia, A., Conklin, K., & Schmitt, N. (2011). Adding more fuel to the fire: An eye-tracking study of idiom processing by native and nonnative speakers. *Second Language Research, 27*, 251–272.

Siyanova-Chanturia, A., Conklin, K., & van Heuven, W. J. B. (2011). Seeing a phrase "time and again" matters: The role of phrasal frequency in the processing of multi-word sequences. *Journal of Experimental Psychology: Language, Memory and Cognition, 37*, 776–784.

Siyanova-Chanturia, A., & Janssen, N. (2018). Production of familiar phrases: Frequency effects in native speakers and second language learners. *Journal of Experimental Psychology: Learning, Memory, and Cognition*.

Siyanova-Chanturia, A., & Lin, P. M. S. (2018). Production of ambiguous idioms: A reading aloud study. *International Journal of Applied Linguistics, 28*, 58–70.

Snider, N., & Arnon, I. (2012). A unified lexicon and grammar? Compositional and non-compositional phrases in the lexicon. In S. Gries & D. Divjak (Eds.), *Frequency effects in language* (pp. 127–164). Berlin: Mouton de Gruyter.

Sonbul, S. (2015). Fatal mistake, awful mistake, or extreme mistake? Frequency effects on off-line/on-line collocational processing. *Bilingualism: Language and Cognition, 18*, 419–437.

Sosa, A., & MacFarlane, J. (2002). Evidence for frequency-based constituents in the mental lexicon: Collocations involving the word *of*. *Brain and Language, 83*, 227–236.

Sprenger, S., Levelt, W., & Kempen, G. (2006). Lexical access during the production of idiomatic phrases. *Journal of Memory and Language, 54*, 161–184.

Strandburg, R., Marsh, J., Brown, W., Asarnow, R., Guthrie, D., & Higa, J. (1993). Event-related potentials in high-functioning adult autistics. *Neuropsychologia, 31*, 413–434.

Sutton, S., Braren, M., Zubin, J., & John, E. (1965). Evoked potentials correlates of stimulus uncertainty. *Science, 150*, 1187–1188.

Swinney, D., & Cutler, A. (1979). The access and processing of idiomatic expressions. *Journal of Verbal Learning and Verbal Behaviour, 18*, 523–534.

Tomasello, M. (2003). *Constructing a language: A usage-based theory of language acquisition.* Cambridge, MA and London: Harvard University Press.

Tremblay, A., & Baayen, R. H. (2010). Holistic processing of regular four-word sequences: A behavioral and ERP study of the effects of structure, frequency, and probability on immediate free recall. In D. Wood (Ed.), *Perspectives on formulaic language: Acquisition and communication* (pp. 151–173). London: The Continuum International Publishing Group.

Tremblay, A., Derwing, B., Libben, G., & Westbury, C. (2011). Processing advantages of lexical bundles: Evidence from self-paced reading and sentence recall tasks. *Language Learning, 61*(2), 569–613.

Tremblay, A., & Tucker, B. V. (2011). The effects of N-gram probabilistic measures on the recognition and production of four-word sequences. *The Mental Lexicon, 6*(2), 302–324.

Underwood, G., Schmitt, N., & Galpin, A. (2004). The eyes have it: An eye-movement study into the processing of formulaic sequences. In N. Schmitt (Ed.), *Formulaic sequences* (pp. 153–172). Amsterdam: John Benjamins.

Van Lancker, D., & Canter, G. J. (1981). Idiomatic versus literal interpretations of ditropically ambiguous sentences. *Journal of Speech and Hearing Research, 24*, 64–69.

Van Lancker, D., Canter, G., & Terbeek, D. (1981). Disambiguation of ditropic sentences: Acoustic and phonetic cues. *Journal of Speech and Hearing Research, 24*, 330–335.

Van Lancker-Sidtis, D. (2003). Auditory recognition of idioms by first and second speakers of English. *Applied Psycholinguistics, 24*, 45–57.

Van Petten, C., & Kutas, M. (1990). Interactions between sentence context and word frequency in event-related brain potentials. *Memory and Cognition, 18*, 380–393.

Van Petten, C., & Kutas, M. (1991). Influences of semantic and syntactic context in open- and closed-class words. *Memory and Cognition, 19*, 95–112.

Vespignani, F., Canal, P., Molinaro, N., Fonda, S., & Cacciari, C. (2010). Predictive mechanisms in idiom comprehension. *Journal of Cognitive Neuroscience, 22*(8), 1682–1700.

Vilkaitė, L. (2016). Are nonadjacent collocations processed faster? *Journal of Experimental Psychology: Learning, Memory, and Cognition, 42*(10), 1632–1642.

Vilkaitė, L., & Schmitt, N. (2017). Reading collocations in an L2: Do collocation processing benefits extend to non-adjacent collocations? *Applied Linguistics*.

Yang, S., Ahn, J. S., & Van Lancker Sidtis, D. (2015). The perceptual and acoustic characteristics of Korean idiomatic and literal sentences. *Speech, Language and Hearing, 18*(3), 166–178.

3

FIRST LANGUAGE INFLUENCE ON THE PROCESSING OF FORMULAIC LANGUAGE IN A SECOND LANGUAGE

Kathy Conklin and Gareth Carrol

Introduction

To comprehend and produce formulaic sequences (FSs), language users need to know the complex details of their form, meaning, and use (Van Lancker Sidtis, 2015), which can be illustrated in terms of the examples in (1–2). In (1), because adult native speakers of English know the form of the idiom, they will know that "the straw that broke" is followed by "the camel's back" and not "the horse's cart", or any number of other plausible alternatives. They will know that this idiom means something along the lines of "reaching a final limit after a set of other events", and that it denotes a limit in negative contexts. In the case of non-native speakers, they may not have encountered this expression, or have encountered it infrequently, and therefore will not know it – or may only know some elements of its form, meaning, and use. We can imagine this situation by considering the example in (2). When readers come to the FSs *making the head*, they encounter a form that they have not come across before (unless they speak French and recognize the translated idiom *faire la tête*) and cannot easily interpret it or know the situations and contexts that are appropriate for its use. The context in (2) indicates Mike has not received what he wanted for his birthday, and based on real-world knowledge readers might predict that he is likely to be disappointed and may be sulking or pouting and guess that the idiom has a meaning along these lines. And indeed, it does mean "sulk" or "pout" in French. This French idiom does not have an obvious idiomatic translation in English. In order to "learn" and eventually "know" this idiom, language users will need to encounter it a sufficient number of times for its form, meaning, and use to become entrenched in memory.

(1) Maria's boyfriend left her and then her dog got sick. When her car broke down on the way to the vet, it was the straw that broke . . .
(2) Mike wanted a pony for his fifth birthday, but didn't get one. Now he is making the head.

For non-native speakers, "learning" and "knowing" formulaic language (FL) is complicated by the fact that they have an existing repertoire of formulaic expressions in their first language (L1), which may or may not overlap with the second (L2) in various ways. This situation is illustrated by some examples of idioms from English and French in (3–6). In (3), the English and French idioms largely overlap in meaning and form. Thus, knowing the idiom in one language might facilitate learning it in the other language. However, this potential source of help from the L1 is mediated by the fact that learners will be aware that idioms differ across languages and are often language specific. Kellerman (1979) suggested that learners are generally less willing to translate more idiomatic uses of words for this reason. Therefore, an English speaker learning French cannot simply assume that *throw money out the window* is the same in French. This caution on the part of the learner is justified by the examples in (4–6), which show how phrases can differ in their degree of L1-L2 overlap. In (4), the English and French idioms overlap in meaning but have subtly different forms; in English expensive things cost *an arm and a leg* and in French *the eyes in our head*. The example in (5) demonstrates that English and French can have entirely different phrases to express the same meaning, in this case being sad or depressed. Finally, (6) illustrates the case where one language has an idiom to express a particular meaning, while the other language does not.

(3) "to waste money" in English is *to throw money out the window* and in French *jeter l'argent par les fenêtres*, which literally translates as "to throw money through the windows"
(4) "to be expensive" in English is *to cost an arm and a leg* and in French *coûter les yeux de la tête*, which literally translates as "to costs the eyes in your head"
(5) "to feel sad/depressed" in English is *to feel blue* and in French *avoir le cafard*, which literally translates as "to have the cockroach"
(6) "to have a hangover" has no English idiom but in French is *avoir la gueule de bois*, which literally translates as "to have the wooden face"

The examples in (3–6) demonstrate a few of the complex set of relationships that can exist between an L1 and L2 for idioms. A crucial question is how these relationships influence processing in the L2, and how other types of FS, such as collocations, behave. Exploring the influence of the L1 on L2 FL processing is the focus of this chapter, with a particular emphasis on the effect of cross-language overlap.

Influence of Cross-Language Overlap on Formulaic Processing

The previous section demonstrated that while FL can be the same across languages, it can also differ in various ways. A reasonable assumption might be that when it is the same in two languages, it might help the learner. Conversely, when it differs it might cause difficulty. A related issue is the relationship between learners' conscious awareness of these similarities and differences and how this knowledge is deployed automatically during online processing. For example, German speakers learning English will know that the formulaic expression in German is *mach ein foto* or "make a photo". At the same time, they may know – and even be able to articulate – that in English the correct formulation is *take a picture/photo*. Thus, while they may be consciously aware of this, it is not inconceivable that they would have difficulty deploying this knowledge quickly and automatically, particularly when they have to "override" the German formulation. Under the pressures of real-time communication, some learners might very well say *make a picture/photo* in English.

A number of studies in recent years have investigated how L1-L2 correspondence contributes to online processing. In general, what we see is that when FL shares form *and* meaning across languages (what we will refer to as "congruent"), learners perform better on comprehension and production tasks. In contrast, when there is shared form but not meaning or shared meaning but different formulations (what we will call "incongruent"), processing tends to be slower or disrupted.[1] The vast majority of research in this area has been done on idioms and collocations, and this will be the focus of the discussion in this chapter. It is important to note – as has already been discussed in this book – that the broad category of FL can be defined in a variety of ways. This often makes it difficult to draw clear distinctions between different types of formulaic expressions. Pertinent to this chapter, what one researcher may refer to as collocations could easily be seen as at least partially figurative or idiomatic (e.g., *thick skin* is a collocation meaning "ability to ignore verbal attacks and criticism"). While both collocations and idioms represent specific word combinations, the semantic properties of idioms are often much more complex than non-figurative, literal collocations. Thus, formulaic subtypes exist on a spectrum, rather than being completely separate phenomena. With that important caveat in mind, we look at the influence of the L1 on the L2 for collocations (frequently co-occurring, broadly compositional word combinations) and idioms (lexically fixed or semi-fixed, non-compositional phrases).

Evidence from Collocations and Idioms

Yamashita and Jiang (2010) presented Japanese learners of English with verb-noun and adjective-noun collocations that were either congruent (same/similar form and meaning in both languages) or incongruent (English form does not have a direct translation equivalent in Japanese). Native speakers of English, Japanese ESL speakers, and Japanese EFL learners were asked to judge each phrase on whether it was an acceptable phrase in English.[2] Native speakers showed no difference for the two groups of items. For non-native participants, error rates were higher on the incongruent items for both Japanese ESL speakers and Japanese EFL learners. The EFL learners (but not the ESL learners) also had slower reaction times for the incongruent items. First, these results suggest that both L1 knowledge and L2 exposure contribute to the processing of collocations in the L2. This means that combinations that exist in the L1 are processed more easily in the L2, suggesting that less cognitive effort is required. Second, incongruent collocations remain difficult for learners, even at high levels of proficiency. Acquiring new forms in the L2 is an effortful process that requires high levels of exposure, not simply to instantiate new patterns, but in some cases to reconfigure the way the same ideas are expressed. Third, the difference in error rates but not reaction times for the ESL group suggests that once collocations have become represented in the lexicon, L2 collocations are processed independently of the L1.

Wolter and Gyllstad (2011, 2013) found similar results for the processing of congruent and incongruent collocations by Swedish learners of English. In the first of these studies they used a primed lexical decision task with verb-noun combinations. Learners were shown the first word of each phrase and asked to make a judgement about whether the second word was a real word in English. There was a consistent advantage for items that were collocations in both English and Swedish compared to ones in English only, in both online measures (reaction times to the lexical decision task) and an offline task measuring receptive collocation knowledge. In their second study, they used adjective-noun pairs and asked participants to judge whether each item was a common English phrase. Again, online performance showed an advantage for congruent over incongruent collocations. Notably, despite the clear influence of L1 knowledge (congruent performance better than incongruent), the relative frequency of the congruent collocations in Swedish had little effect on reaction times, whereas L2 frequency (how often the phrase occurs in English) did have a facilitative effect.

Taken together, the results of these studies indicate that knowledge of collocations in the L1 influences the processing of collocations in the L2. More precisely, congruent collocations are recognized and processed more accurately and more quickly than collocations that do not have cross-language equivalence. However, once a collocation has been encountered and registered in the L2 lexicon – regardless of its congruency – its relative frequency in L2 (rather than L1) influences its processing. It is important to note that many of the items that the researchers in these studies refer to as collocations could equally be considered idioms. This is further problematized by the fact that the literal/figurative distinction is confounded with the congruent/incongruent classification. In Yamashita and Jiang (2010), many of the items in the incongruent category could be considered idiomatic (e.g., *kill time, broken heart*). In contrast, most of the items in the congruent category (e.g., *drink soup, famous battle*) are literal, such that the meaning of the whole phrase is more or less a direct combination of the component words. Wolter and Gyllstad likewise include items that could be considered at least partially idiomatic: *break the law, bite the bullet, foot the bill* (2011) and *sweet revenge, straight face, sore losers* (2013). This points to the fact that incongruent items are often at least partially figurative, otherwise a literal translation should be possible (and would therefore be congruent by default).

The discussion thus far demonstrates that collocations, in particular incongruent ones, may cross over into the domain of idioms. In what follows, we will look more specifically at the influence of cross-linguistic overlap on L2 idiom processing, keeping in mind that in some cases idioms may also be collocations.

Titone, Columbus, Whitford, Mercier, and Libben (2015) investigated the influence of cross-language idiom overlap in English and French. Idioms were all of the form pronoun-verb-x-noun (e.g., *she kicked the bucket*) and varied in terms of their cross-language overlap, from no overlap (i.e., the idiom did not exist in French) to word-for-word transliteration, with gradations in between when elements of the form or meaning were shared. English-French bilinguals were presented with sentences word-by-word (at 200-ms intervals) with a meaningfulness judgement at the end of each. Sentences contained an idiom or a matched literal control phrase (e.g., *live/tell a lie*) and were either entirely in English or the final word was code-switched (e.g., *he played with fire/feu*). Titone et al. found that responses to idiom sentences were slower and less accurate than to literal sentences. This contrasts with the widespread finding that idioms are processed more quickly than control phrases (e.g., Swinney & Cutler, 1979; Carrol & Conklin, 2014, 2017). However, it is in line with Gyllstad and Wolter (2016), who asked English native speakers and non-native speakers (Swedish L1) to judge the meaningfulness of English phrases. They found that for both groups there was a "cost" for less transparent items, although L1-L2 overlap was not a consideration in this study. An important parallel between Gyllstad and Wolter and Titone et al. is the use of a meaningfulness judgement task. It may be that while recognition of idioms is in general faster than it is for literal phrases, when participants are required to make explicit semantic judgements, their semi-transparent nature means that idioms require greater consideration.

Importantly, code-switching had the predicted effect, whereby switching languages caused a greater level of disruption for idioms than for literal sentences (in response times but not response accuracy). For phrases where there was a greater degree of cross-language overlap, responses were faster and more accurate. In other words, as the degree of cross-language overlap increased, the disruption caused by the code-switch was reduced. The authors concluded that there is a "substantial direct retrieval component during the comprehension of language-intact idioms in bilinguals" (Titone et al., 2015, p. 190). They suggested that when idioms are familiar in L1 or L2, this familiarity will determine the ease with which that idiom can be accessed.

Pritchett, Vaid, and Tosun (2016) investigated how the existence of an idiom in both the L1 and L2 affected an incidental cued recall task. They asked Russian-English bilingual participants to rate the "pleasantness" of a series of adjective-noun combinations that were either idiomatic in English only (e.g., *blue moon*), idiomatic in Russian only (e.g., *blue distances*), idiomatic in both English and Russian (e.g., *blue blood*), or not idiomatic in either language (e.g., *blue smell*). Participants were then asked to recall as many items as possible. Results showed a clear advantage for word combinations that were idiomatic in both languages (although overall recall rates were fairly low at around 30%). Further, phrases with a figurative meaning in only one language were recalled significantly better than "nonsense" phrases.

Taken together, Titone et al. (2015) and Pritchett et al. (2016) provide an indication that when idioms exist in two languages, this has a facilitative effect on how they are processed or recalled. As it relates to the activation of the idiomatic meaning, the picture is a little less clear. Beck and Weber (2016) set out to investigate how this is affected by congruency with the L1. They presented German-English bilinguals and native English speakers with English idioms that either had word-for-word translations in German or had matching idiomatic concepts but no word-for-word translation. Idioms had the structure verb-x-noun and were presented auditorily in sentences (e.g., *John likes to pull my leg*), which were followed by visually presented target words for a lexical decision task. Targets were related to the idiomatic meaning, the literal meaning, or were a matched control word (literal target = *walk* vs. control = *milk*; figurative target = *joke* vs. control = *ship*). Their overall pattern of results was the same for the native and non-native speakers, such that L1 and L2 listeners had faster response times for targets related to the idiomatic and literal meanings of the phrases compared to their controls. Interestingly, figurative targets were no faster than literal targets for either group. On the crucial question of L1 influence, for the L2 participants, there was no effect of translatability; that is, congruent idioms were not processed any differently to non-congruent ones. Beck and Weber concluded that both L1 *and* L2 participants showed activation for figurative and literal meanings of idioms, hence processing in both languages seemed to follow similar patterns, regardless of whether idioms were shared.

What this research on collocations and idioms seems to point to is a clear cross-language effect, such that L1-L2 overlap aids online processing – or at least some aspects of it. Titone et al. (2015) highlight the importance of distinguishing between formal, semantic or conceptual, and pragmatic levels, which can be equated to our levels of form, meaning, and use. Hence some studies see an advantage in recall and recognition for congruent idioms, whereas others see no effects on the activation of figurative versus literal meaning. Beck and Weber (2016) point out that their online results are not consistent with studies that have shown clear effects of language overlap in offline comprehension and production tasks (e.g., Irujo, 1986), nor with results showing an advantage for the literal meaning of idioms in L2 (e.g., Cieślicka, 2006).

Finally, questions remain about how cross-linguistic overlap interacts with factors such as proficiency and age of acquisition, and aspects like frequency (in L1 and L2). Paquot (2015) found an effect of L1 frequency in a study on how learners used three-word lexical bundles. In a corpus analysis of a set of learner essays, the use of lexical bundles had a strong correlation with the frequency of the translation equivalent forms in the learners' L1 (French or Spanish). Although this is not a processing effect, it does imply that learners utilize the resources from their L1, including knowledge of how words go together. While neither Yamashita and Jiang (2010) nor Wolter and Gyllstad (2011) included L1 or L2 frequency in their analyses, Wolter and Gyllstad (2013) found a significant effect of L2 frequency for both congruent and incongruent collocations. Importantly, no significant effect of L1 frequency for the congruent items was found. Hence beyond the broad general effect of L1 knowledge (congruent collocations are processed faster than L2-only ones), there was a specific effect of how frequent the collocations were in English (and therefore how likely it was that learners would have encountered them) but not how frequent they were in the L1. Although not specifically exploring L1-L2 overlap, Gyllstad and Wolter (2016) also found a significant effect of L2 frequency, whereby more frequent free combinations and collocations were responded to more quickly but not more accurately. They did not report whether L1 frequency values were also included in the analysis.

Evidence from Translated Formulaic Language

Another way to explore the influence of L1 and L2 – and particularly to disentangle any L1 from L2 frequency effects – is to present participants with FL that only exists in the L1, but which is translated into the L2. Although this is a deliberately artificial scenario, it provides a way to eliminate effects of prior knowledge in the L2. In other words, formulaic expressions are "incongruent" in the sense that they are known phrases in the L1, but they have no equivalent form in the L2. It is therefore impossible (or at least extremely unlikely) that any L2 frequency effects will exist to confound the processing of the translated forms. Examples of this come from two studies by Carrol and Conklin (2014, 2017), who investigated the transfer of L1 knowledge to the L2, using Chinese idioms translated into English. Mandarin Chinese has a large set of homogenous idioms or *chengyu*, with the vast majority (around 97%) conforming to a fixed four-character sequence (Zhou, Zhou, & Chen, 2004). Hence the idiom 畫蛇添足 literally translates into English as *draw a snake and add feet*, meaning "to ruin with unnecessary detail". Since this is not a phrase that English native speakers would know, or that language learners would ever be likely to encounter in English, such items can be used to investigate

L1 effects on processing in the L2 relatively independent of any developing L2 knowledge.

Carrol and Conklin (2014) presented English native speakers and Chinese learners of English with English idioms and translated *chengyu*, which had no equivalent in English and which ended in a Chinese character that had a single-word translation equivalent in English. Participants were presented with the initial part of an idiom and then its final word or a matched control word for a lexical decision task (e.g., Chinese = *draw a snake and add feet/hair*; English = *on the edge of your seat/plate*). The results showed a clear dissociation for the two sets of participants. English native speakers had shorter response times to words that completed English idioms (*on the edge of your ... seat*) than equally plausible words that did not (*plate*), and no difference for the Chinese idioms. Chinese native speakers showed the opposite pattern. They demonstrated no difference at all between English idioms and English control phrases, but there were significantly shorter response times for words that completed the Chinese idioms compared to controls. Since the translated *chengyu* were entirely novel in English, only their status as "known" phrases in Chinese could have led to this facilitation. However, as with some of the other studies discussed so far, the nature of the task restricts the claims that can be made. The participants could view the prime for as long as they wanted, giving them ample time to read and possibly translate the phrase into their L1, as well as anticipate what the next word might be. While this does not invalidate the finding of an effect of L1 knowledge, it does make it difficult to determine whether the results reflect online processing. It is also impossible to say anything about whether the participants activated the idiomatic meaning of the translated phrases, rather than just recognizing the form.

Carrol and Conklin (2017) addressed these concerns using a similar set of items and a comparable set of participants. This time the idioms and the controls (e.g., *draw a snake and add feet/hair*) were embedded in short two- to three-sentence contexts that supported the idiomatic meaning, hence the idioms would *only* make sense in the context if they were "known" (for both English and Chinese items). If they were unknown, neither the idiom nor the control would make sense. Using eye-tracking, Carrol and Conklin measured reading patterns for the whole phrase and for the final word. In line with the previous study, for the final word English native speakers read English idiomatic completions faster than controls, but there was no difference for the translated Chinese idioms; Chinese speakers showed this advantage on the final word for the translated idioms but not the English ones. This suggests that known idioms were highly predictable, even in their translated forms. For the whole phrase, English native speakers spent less time reading the idioms than the controls. In contrast, the Chinese native speakers showed no difference between idioms and controls on any of the phrase-level reading times for either Chinese or English idioms. In a second study comparing figurative and literal uses of each phrase, English native speakers showed no difference for English idioms, but literal uses of Chinese idioms were read more quickly overall than figurative ones. Chinese native speakers showed the same pattern for both sets of items (English and translated *chengyu*): literal uses were read consistently more quickly than figurative uses. Taken together, the results of the two studies suggest that although there is some level of activation for the form of idioms that are known in the L2, activation of figurative meaning is more complex, and may interact with a range of other factors such as proficiency, context, plausibility, etc.

Three other studies have investigated cross-linguistic influence in a similar fashion – translating L1 FL into the L2. All three consider what their authors call collocations, although many of their stimuli could be considered to be at least partially idiomatic. Ueno (2009) used word pairs that form common collocations in Japanese but not English (e.g., *forgive marriage* meaning "to consent to marriage"). In a primed lexical decision task (first word of the collocation was presented as a prime and the second required a lexical decision), Ueno presented low-, intermediate-, and high-proficiency Japanese learners of English with English collocations with no Japanese equivalent and Japanese collocations with no English equivalent, as well as unrelated control word pairs. The results showed an advantage for English collocations compared to unrelated word pairs for all three proficiency levels; however, only the highest proficiency participants demonstrated an advantage for the Japanese translations (compared to unrelated controls).

Wolter and Yamashita (2015) studied a similar distribution of items (English collocations with no Japanese equivalent; Japanese translations that are not collocations in English), using verb-noun (e.g., *forgive marriage*) and adjective-noun (e.g., *shallow injury*) combinations. They presented items in a double lexical decision task, whereby both words were presented on-screen (with the first word directly above the second), and participants were asked to make a lexical decision for both words. They compared English native speakers and higher and lower proficiency Japanese learners of English. They found no evidence of an advantage for Japanese translations, either for response times or error rates. They speculated that their results might be partly attributable to the task, which did not require participants to necessarily access collocational knowledge. They addressed this in a follow-up study (Wolter & Yamashita, 2017) using a phrasal acceptability task (which should encourage participants to process the phrases for meaning) on English only, Japanese only, and congruent collocations, all presented in English. Although they found a clear effect of congruency (non-native speakers judged congruent collocations significantly faster than English-only ones), there was again no evidence that the Japanese-only collocations were processed faster than baseline items, by either lower or higher proficiency L2 participants. Wolter and Yamashita suggested that rather than L1 knowledge *per se* contributing to faster processing in congruent phrases, age and order of acquisition effects might instead explain previously seen results.

Carrol, Conklin, and Gyllstad (2016) investigated the effect of the L1 on processing in the L2 using translations of idioms – this time including an additional category of congruent phrases. This allowed them to compare the L1 influence when there was and when there was not an equivalent in the L2. Idioms and translations of Swedish idioms were mostly of the form verb-x-noun and were compared to matched control phrases (e.g., *break/crack the ice*). The stimuli were embedded in single sentences, designed so that the portion preceding the phrase gave no clues as to the intended meaning, but all sentences were completed in such a way that they made sense (e.g., *It was hard to break the ice at the party* vs. *It was hard to crack the ice when the windows froze*). The authors presented the sentences to English native speakers and Swedish advanced learners of English. They compared eye-movement patterns for the final word of each phrase (to establish whether idioms were advantaged compared to controls) and for the phrase as a whole (to consider how the meaning was accessed and integrated into the sentence). English native speakers showed a consistent advantage for any idioms that existed in English (English only and congruent idioms), both in terms of the final word and the phrase as a whole. In contrast, translated Swedish items were read much more slowly, indicating that encountering unknown idioms caused serious disruption for readers. Swedish native speakers showed no real difference in reading times for English-only idioms and their control phrases. Crucially, there was no disruption (like there was with the English native speakers reading translated idioms, and as was seen for non-native speakers in Siyanova-Chanturia, Conklin, & Schmitt, 2011 and Carrol & Conklin, 2017, Experiment 2, both of whom found an advantage for the literal meaning of idioms in L2; see also Cieślicka, 2006). That is, encountering an L2 idiom was no different (or at least not more disruptive) than encountering a comparable literal phrase. For the Swedish-only and congruent idioms, there was a clear advantage for idioms over controls. This was true for the final word, suggesting that a "known" word combination was being activated, and for the phrase overall, suggesting that the figurative meaning was also being triggered more quickly than the literal. Just as interesting was the lack of difference between the two item types, meaning that there was no "added" advantage for congruent idioms that are assumed to be represented in both languages.

These results seem to provide the clearest indication yet that L1 knowledge is activated and utilized during processing in the L2. There was a clear advantage for any items that exist in the L1, compared to control items, regardless of whether they had L2 equivalents. An additional finding from the study was the effect of the relative familiarity of the idioms. All participants were asked to indicate their familiarity with the experimental items after the study. For English native speakers, greater familiarity led to faster reading for all English idioms. For Swedish native speakers, two sets of familiarity ratings were obtained: familiarity with the Swedish forms where these existed, and familiarity with the English forms where these existed. For the English-only items, higher L2 familiarity led to shorter reading times for better-known idioms. For any idioms that existed in Swedish, it was the relative familiarity with the *L1* form that was important; hence, more familiar items in the L1 led to faster processing in the L2. For idioms existing in both languages, specific familiarity with the L2 form had *no* effect. For other studies considered in this section, the results regarding familiarity are mixed. They either show no effect of relative familiarity (e.g., Carrol & Conklin, 2014, 2017) or do not report that it was investigated (Ueno, 2009; Wolter & Yamashita, 2015). As stated at the end of the previous section, Wolter and Gyllstad (2013) found that for both congruent and incongruent collocations, the frequency of the phrases in the L2 (not the L1 for congruent phrases) mattered. Since the participants were comparable in each study (L1 Swedes with advanced proficiency in English), we can speculate that two differences might be important here: the use of idioms as opposed to collocations, and the use of a subjective familiarity rating rather than an objective frequency rating. In particular, differences between idioms and collocations might be very important in explaining discrepancies between the results reported in Carrol et al. (2016) and Wolter and Yamashita (2015, 2017).

As a final word in this section, it is important to mention that not all studies have found that congruence between L1 and L2 leads to facilitation. Cieślicka and Heredia (2013) used eye-tracking to compare Spanish-English bilinguals' reading of congruent idioms (same form and meaning in English and Spanish; e.g., *point of view* and *punto de vista*) and phrases which express the same concept but in a completely different form (e.g., *hit the sack* and *plachar oreja*, literally "iron your ear", both meaning "to go to bed"). Similar idioms took longer to read and had more fixations than different idioms, which they took as evidence that encountering a word-for-word translation of an idiom causes its L1 equivalent to be activated, which in turn leads to competition and requires the L1 lexical entries to be suppressed, slowing down processing. Reconciling this with the other results discussed here (e.g., Titone et al., 2015; Carrol & Conklin, 2014, 2017; Carrol et al., 2016) is tricky, but important differences in the tasks being used, the designations of congruent/incongruent and similar/different idioms, and the nature of the participants (bilinguals vs. second language learners) might all be relevant. Cieślicka and Heredia (2013) point out that multiple factors combined to affect their results, including whether idioms were opaque or transparent, and whether their participants were dominant in English or Spanish. Clearly, further work is required to identify why these studies should lead to conflicting results and to disentangle the many factors at play.

Conclusions and Future Directions

Disentangling effects of L1 knowledge from the increasing experience of FL in the L2 is not straightforward. With the limited research in this area, developing models that explain the L1's influence on FL processing and that account for the role of a wide range of factors known to affect processing more generally (proficiency, frequency, age of acquisition, experience with the L2, task demands, etc.) is challenging. Given the current state of knowledge, such an endeavour is bound to provide an oversimplification of what is assuredly a very complex picture. While keeping this in mind, the following will attempt to summarize what we know and point to some important questions to address in future research.

Overall, the existing evidence tells us that L1 FL exerts an influence on the processing of L2 formulaic expressions. Thus far, we have only alluded to an explanation for this. We believe that this may be in part (or even wholly) due to the fast, automatic activation of L1 translation equivalents while processing in the L2 (e.g., Zhang, van Heuven, & Conklin, 2011). More precisely, reading words in the L2 quickly activates their L1 counterparts. We can consider how this might work using Figure 3.1 and the examples (3–6) from earlier in this chapter.

If we start by considering the situation depicted in A, when an English-French bilingual reads *jeter l'argent par les fenêtres*, the L1 English words "throw", "the", "money", "by", "the" and "window" are automatically activated, which activates the English idiom *throw money out the window* and its associated meaning/concept "waste money". Thus, activation of the individual L1 words activates the L1 formulaic representation – be that a "superlemma" (Sprenger, Levelt, & Kempen, 2006), a duplicate lexical entry encompassing a larger unit (Wray, 2002), or an inter-connected network of words and conceptual representations.[3] Because the L1 representation is activated, properties such as its L1 frequency may influence processing. The example in B illustrates a contrasting case where the translation does not lead to activation of an L1 representation. For example, *avoir la gueule de bois* activates "have", "the", "wooden", and "face", which does not correspond to an idiom in English. Thus, only L2 specific properties, like frequency, influence processing. Crucially, the fact that L2 information influences processing indicates that L2 FL *is* represented, and will become more strongly encoded as a speaker encounters the phrase more often in the L2. At least at lower levels of proficiency, it is likely that this L2 representation will be weaker or less entrenched in memory, which is demonstrated by the smaller representations and weaker connections.

The examples in A and B can be seen as the extremes, where there is complete overlap in form and meaning and when there is no overlap at all. However, there will be many intermediate cases. Take, for example, the situation in C, which is analogous to the example *avoir le cafard* that literally translates as "to have the cockroach", meaning "to feel sad/depressed". This can be expressed idiomatically in L1 English as *to feel blue*. Similar to the situation in B, activation of the corresponding English formulation cannot occur via lexical translation. In contrast, it could occur via conceptual connections. Depending on the strength and/or speed of these connections, an effect of the L1 formulation may (or may not) be evident. Thus, contrary to *avoir la gueule de bois* (which does not have an L1 formulaic equivalent to compete with), *avoir le cafard* may compete with *to feel blue*, thereby resulting in an L1 influence on the L2. More research is needed to explore the situation depicted in C. Another case to consider comes from the example *coûter les yeux de la tête*, which will activate the English words "cost", "the", "eyes", "in", "your", "head". Is this enough to activate the English idiom *cost an arm and a leg*? Likely the amount of conceptual overlap will contribute to L1 activation, as will

A. Congruent L1 and L2 formulaic language: *throw money out of the window / jeter l'argent par les fenêtres*

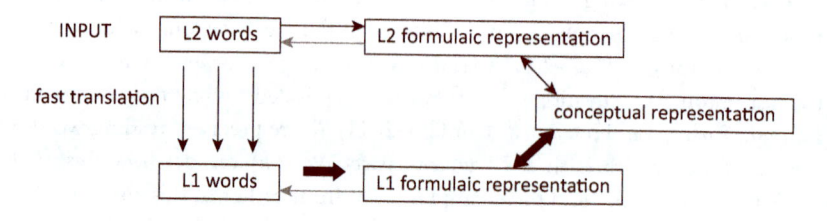

[Diagram: INPUT → L2 words → L2 formulaic representation; fast translation; L1 words → L1 formulaic representation; both formulaic representations connect to conceptual representation]

B. L1 does not have a formulaic expression corresponding to the L2 one: *have a hangover / avoir la gueule de bois*

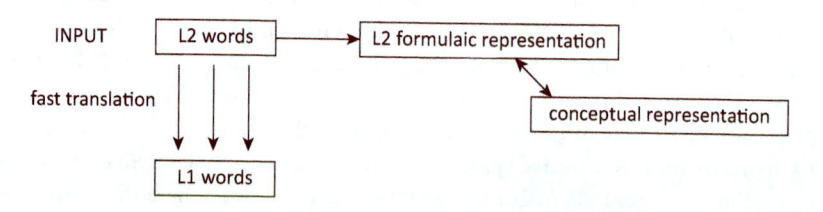

[Diagram: INPUT → L2 words → L2 formulaic representation → conceptual representation; fast translation → L1 words]

C. L1 and L2 have different formulaic expressions meaning similar things: *cost an arm and a leg / couter les yeûx de la tête*

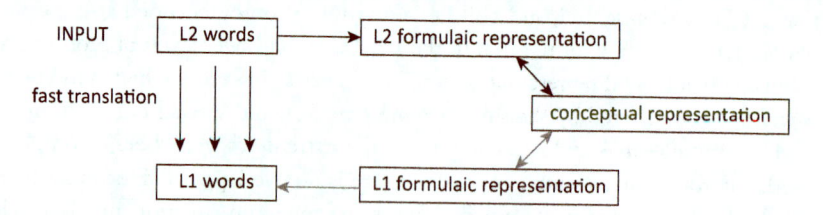

[Diagram: INPUT → L2 words → L2 formulaic representation; fast translation → L1 words → L1 formulaic representation; both formulaic representations connect to conceptual representation]

FIGURE 3.1 Illustration of connections and flow of activation for different relationships between L1 and L2 FL. The size of the L1/L2 lexical and formulaic representations demonstrates the relative strengths of representation, as do the weight and colour of the connecting arrows, with smaller size and gray indicating weaker connections.

the informativeness of the context, proficiency, how often this idiom has been encountered in the L2, etc.

An alternative explanation to the one offered in Figure 3.1 is based on the lemma mediation model (Jiang, 2000). In this approach, the learning of L2 vocabulary involves creating an L2 lexeme/form that is linked to an L1 concept/lemma, which consequently has the properties of the L1 entry in terms of meaning, associations, frequency, etc. Yamashita and Jiang (2010), amongst others, extend this model to encompass collocational knowledge. Learning L2 formulaic expressions is made easier when these cohere with the L1. However, learning new expressions in the L2 is thought to be effortful, and they may remain parasitic on the L1 for a long time.

We should note here that the model outlined in Figure 3.1 accounts well for the data on idiom processing but does not explain the lack of L1 effects reported in Wolter and Yamashita (2015, 2017) for collocations. As we have alluded to throughout this chapter, a wide range of factors influence the processing of FL. In the case of idioms and collocations, fundamental differences between the two types of phrase might be important. For idioms, transparency and decomposability are often factors that are thought to influence processing (for a review, see Cacciari, 2014). For collocations, the degree of transparency often seems linked to whether or not they are congruent, and transparency tends to speed processing (Gyllstad & Wolter, 2016). Idioms, especially longer ones, may be more restricted than collocations in terms of what the final word can be, although the items used in Carrol et al. (2016) were short and non-restrictive and still showed an effect of the L1. In addition, many theories about how idioms are represented and processed posit a dedicated lexico-semantic entry for them; however, the same may not be true for collocations. Theories such as the Constraint-based model suggest that idioms are processed using any and all information available at the time (Libben & Titone, 2008), meaning that a range of variables will affect the different stages or levels. Titone et al. (2015) posit that a Constraint-based model can be applied to L2 idiom processing, and further propose that idioms are prototypical examples of FL, meaning that this type of model can be applied to formulaic expressions *in toto*. Because the findings for idioms and collocations differ somewhat, future research would need to identify and prioritize the constraints that are important for the processing of each.

There are also a whole host of participant variables that might come into play – proficiency, age of acquisition, and type of exposure, to name a few. For example, López and Vaid (2017) explored idiom processing by "language brokers", which refers to "informal translators" like children for their parents in immigrant communities. They found that brokers showed greater activation of idioms in both the L1 and L2, compared to non-brokers. While this study did not specifically explore cross-linguistic overlap, it highlights the range of non-native speaker communities that have been understudied in the literature. Broad group differences and individual speaker variation must be seen as potentially important variables that remain to be explored in detail.

On the whole, the literature shows that when L1 formulaic expressions exist, information about them is activated and influences processing in the L2. This is true whether or not the combination also exists in the L2, at least for idioms, as shown by the research reviewed here. Differences between the results of some studies suggest that much remains to be explored with regards to different types of FL, as well as a wide range of contextual and participant variables.

Notes

1 Some studies consider different degrees of overlap/congruency, but here we consider only items where there is 100% overlap between form and meaning to be "congruent".
2 ESL = English as a second language; EFL = English as a foreign language. In second language acquisition, ESL learners are likely to be acquiring the language in an immersion context, whereas EFL learners are more likely to be taught the second language in an L1 environment.
3 Figure 3.1 depicts "formulaic representations" in boxes simply for convenience, and should not be taken as an indication that these representations are of "holistic" forms. Representation of formulaic language remains an open question, and the model is *not* making claims about the representations themselves *nor* that they are the same for all types of formulaic language.

References

Beck, S., & Weber, A. (2016). Bilingual and monolingual idiom processing is cut from the same cloth: The role of the L1 in literal and figurative meaning activation. *Frontiers in Psychology*, 7, 1350.
Cacciari, C. (2014). Processing multiword idiomatic strings. Many words in one? *The Mental Lexicon*, 9(2), 267–293.
Carrol, G., & Conklin, K. (2014). Getting your wires crossed: Evidence for fast processing of L1 idioms in an L2. *Bilingualism: Language and Cognition*, 17(4), 784–797.
Carrol, G., & Conklin, K. (2017). Cross language priming extends to formulaic units: Evidence from eye-tracking suggests that this idea "has legs". *Bilingualism: Language and Cognition*, 20(2), 299–317.
Carrol, G., Conklin, K., & Gyllstad, H. (2016). Found in translation: The influence of L1 on the processing of idioms in L2. *Studies in Second Language Acquisition*, 38(3), 403–443.
Cieślicka, A. (2006). Literal salience in on-line processing of idiomatic expressions by second language learners. *Second Language Research*, 22(2), 115–144.
Cieślicka, A., & Heredia, R. (2013). *The multiple determinants of eye-movement patterns in bilingual figurative processing*. 25th APS Annual Convention, Washington, DC.
Gyllstad, H., & Wolter, B. (2016). Collocational processing in the light of a phraseological continuum model: Does semantic transparency matter? *Language Learning*, 66(2), 296–323.
Irujo, S. (1986). Don't put your leg in your mouth: Transfer in the acquisition of idioms in a second language. *TESOL Quarterly*, 20(2), 287–304.
Jiang, N. (2000). Lexical representation and development in a second language. *Applied Linguistics*, 21(1), 47–77.
Kellerman, E. (1979). Transfer and non-transfer: Where we are now. *Studies in Second Language Acquisition*, 2(1), 37–57.
Libben, M., & Titone, D. (2008). The multidetermined nature of idiom processing. *Memory and Cognition*, 36(6), 1103–1121.
López, B., & Vaid, J. (2017). Fácil or a piece of cake: Does variability in bilingual language brokering experience affect idiom comprehension? *Bilingualism: Language and Cognition*, 21(2), 340–354.
Paquot, M. (2015). L1 frequency in foreign language acquisition: Recurrent word combinations in French and Spanish EFL learner writing. *Second Language Research*, 33(1), 13–32.

Pritchett, L., Vaid, J., & Tosun, S. (2016). Of black sheep and white crows: Extending the bilingual dual coding theory to memory for idioms. *Cogent Psychology, 3*(1), 1–18.

Siyanova-Chanturia, A., Conklin, K., & Schmitt, N. (2011). Adding more fuel to the fire: An eye-tracking study of idiom processing by native and non-native speakers. *Second Language Research, 27*(2), 251–272.

Sprenger, S., Levelt, W., & Kempen, G. (2006). Lexical access during the production of idiomatic phrases. *Journal of Memory and Language, 54*(2), 161–184.

Swinney, D., & Cutler, A. (1979). The access and processing of idiomatic expressions. *Journal of Verbal Learning and Verbal Behaviour, 18*(5), 523–534.

Titone, D., Columbus, G., Whitford, V., Mercier, J., & Libben, M. (2015). Contrasting bilingual and monolingual idiom processing. In R. Heredia & A. Cieślicka (Eds.), *Bilingual figurative language processing* (pp. 171–207). Cambridge: Cambridge University Press.

Ueno, T. (2009). *An investigation of the relationship between the development of bilingual semantic organisation and interactive connectivity across languages* (Unpublished doctoral dissertation). Trinity College, Dublin.

Van Lancker Sidtis, D. (2015). Formulaic language in an emergentist framework. In B. MacWhinney & W. O'Grady (Eds.), *Handbook of language emergence* (pp. 578–599). Chichester, UK: Wiley-Blackwell.

Wolter, B., & Gyllstad, H. (2011). Collocational Links in the L2 mental lexicon and the influence of L1 intralexical knowledge. *Applied Linguistics, 32*(4), 430–449.

Wolter, B., & Gyllstad, H. (2013). Frequency of input and L2 collocational processing: A comparison of congruent and incongruent collocations. *Studies in Second Language Acquisition, 35*(3), 451–482.

Wolter, B., & Yamashita, J. (2015). Processing collocations in a second language: A case of first language activation? *Applied Psycholinguistics, 36*(5), 1193–1221.

Wolter, B., & Yamashita, J. (2017). Word frequency, collocational frequency, L1 congruency, and proficiency in L2 collocational processing: What accounts for performance? *Studies in Second Language Acquisition*. Advance online publication. doi:10.1017/S0272263117000237.

Wray, A. (2002). *Formulaic Language and the Lexicon*. Cambridge: Cambridge University Press.

Yamashita, J., & Jiang, N. (2010). L1 influence on the acquisition of L2 collocations: Japanese ESL users and EFL learners acquiring English collocations. *TESOL Quarterly, 44*(4), 647–668.

Zhang, T., van Heuven, W., & Conklin, K. (2011). Fast automatic translation and morphological decomposition in Chinese-English bilinguals. *Psychological Science, 22*(10), 1237–1242.

Zhou, S., Zhou, W., & Chen, X. (2004). Spatiotemporal analysis of ERP during Chinese idiom comprehension. *Brain Topography, 17*, 27–37.

4

FORMULAIC LANGUAGE AND SPEECH PROSODY

Phoebe Lin

Introduction

> The trouble is, organic produce is not cheap.
> (British National Corpus, ARJ 325)

The phrases *the thing is* and *the trouble is* are curious cases. They are so familiar and frequent in our everyday speech that they require little effort to produce or comprehend. Parts of these phrases can be skipped in fast speech (i.e., saying *trouble is* and *thing is* instead) and yet hearers will have no problem with comprehension. These characteristics explain why the phrases are considered examples of *formulaic sequences* (FSs). However, the peculiarities in the way that these phrases are articulated are frequently overlooked. They are often articulated in one intonation unit and/or are followed by a pause. This is probably the reason why writers regularly insert a comma after *the thing is* and *the trouble is*. This is intriguing because intonation unit boundaries and pauses often coincide with phrase or clause boundaries, which means that a prosodic break should be inserted between the subject (i.e., *the trouble*) and the predicate (i.e., *is organic produce is not cheap*). The result of this, however, sounds unnatural (i.e., **The trouble, is organic produce is not cheap*). A second peculiarity about this example concerns its accentuation pattern. If a speaker wants to emphasize the meaning of the phrases, the function word will be accented (i.e., *the trouble IS*) even though the tendency in English is for accent to be assigned to the lexical word (i.e., *the TROUble is*). These peculiarities have led to the question of whether FSs might be subject to some special prosodic rules.

Is there a Prosody Special to Formulaic Language?

Beyond the anecdotal observations presented earlier, psycholinguistic evidence seems to point towards the existence of prosodic patterns that may be special to

FSs. In their seminal papers, van Lancker and Canter (1981) and van Lancker, Canter, and Terbeek (1981) investigated whether and how prosody might differ when a class of idioms, which they called ditropic sentences, were articulated with either the intended idiomatic or literal meanings. An example of a ditropic sentence is "she was to keep a stiff upper lip", which can mean, idiomatically, that she is brave or, literally, that she contracts her lip muscles. In their first study, van Lancker and Canter (1981) asked five male speakers to read aloud 15 pairs of ditropic sentences embedded in disambiguating paragraphs. Recordings of the ditropic sentences were then excised from context and played to native English-speaking listeners. However, the listeners were unable to identify whether the stimuli carried the intended idiomatic or literal meanings with above chance accuracy. In their second study, two male speakers read aloud the same 15 pairs of ditropic sentences without context and were instructed to convey the pairs' contrasting meanings as distinctly as possible. This time, the listeners were able to judge, with above chance accuracy, the intended meaning of the stimuli. In the follow-up acoustic analyses, van Lancker et al. (1981) found that these (American English) ditropic sentences could be disambiguated because, compared with their counterparts, the readings with intended literal meanings had longer sentence duration, more internal pauses, more juncture, more pitch contours, and were systematically marked by Accent A as defined by Bolinger (1965). This investigation of the acoustic differences between the idiomatic and literal interpretations of ditropic sentences was later extended to French (Abdelli-Baruh, Yang, Ahn, & van Lancker, 2007) and Korean (Yang, Ahn, & van Lancker, 2010). More recently, Siyanova-Chanturia and Lin (2017) have delved deeper into the question by including matched novel control phrases in the acoustic comparisons. In this experiment, 66 native speakers of British English read aloud three types of stimuli (i.e., idioms used figuratively, idioms used literally, and matched novel control phrases) embedded in disambiguating paragraphs. The acoustic analysis revealed that the idioms had shorter durations than the controls. Furthermore, the idioms also had shorter durations when used figuratively than when used literally.

The prosodic patterns of FSs are also a major area of interest in spoken corpus research. Researchers are particularly keen on detecting patterns in the prosodic features of FSs because such findings will not only shed light on the processing of FSs from a usage-based perspective, but also have substantial practical implications for language teaching and Natural Language Processing (see Lin, 2015, 2018, for further discussion). So far, the list of prosodic features found to be closely associated with FSs includes alignment with intonation unit boundaries (Lin, 2010b; Lin & Adolphs, 2009) and pauses (Wray, 2004), faster rhythm (Lin, 2010b), which may or may not be accompanied by phonological reduction (Bybee & Scheibman, 1999), resistance to internal pauses or hesitations (Wray, 2004), and restricted accentuation patterns (Aijmer, 1996; Lin, 2013). These prosodic patterns, which are opaque for language learners and computers, are vital to the accurate communication of meaning of FSs. To illustrate the point, consider the accentuation pattern of the idiom *my ears are burning* (Ashby, 2006). The accurate use of the idiom necessitates the assignment of accent to the word *burning* (i.e., *my ears are BURNing*). Alternative accentuation patterns (e.g., *my EARS are burning*) are unacceptable. Similarly, for FSs which contain flexible slots (e.g., *as far as ___ is concerned*, *from the ___ point of view*), the default pattern is to accent the word in the flexible slot (Lin, 2013). Deviation from this pattern, though possible, is rare.

Rationale and Aims of the Chapter

This chapter builds upon the aforementioned work describing the prosody of FSs in psycholinguistics and corpus linguistics, and explores the wider cognitive picture within which FSs and speech prosody are situated. This desire to search for a wider cognitive perspective on the relationship between FSs and speech prosody emerged 10 years ago (i.e., Lin & Adolphs, 2009) when we became aware of the fundamental importance of prosody to the contextual meaning of spoken FSs. At that time, corpus linguists tended to apply the same approaches to analyzing FS use in spoken and written corpora. This practice of overlooking prosodic information is questionable because the pragmatic meaning and function of spoken FSs are encoded in and vary with their prosody (see Lin, 2010b for further discussion). On delving deeper into the nature of spoken FSs, the fundamental importance of spoken FSs in everyday communication became even more apparent. As Carter (personal communication, 2012) suggests, the proportion of spoken to written communication in an ordinary person's daily linguistic encounter is believed to be 9:1. If first language (L1) speakers are nine times more likely to acquire and use FSs in speech than in written communication, then the phonological representation of formulaic language (FL) should be far more frequently activated than, say, its orthographic representation. This overwhelming frequency with which L1 speakers activate the phonological representation of FSs justifies why the phonological form of FSs deserves significant research attention. In fact, given that L1 FSs are acquired and accessed through the auditory channel during extensive exposure to spoken communication, a new perspective on FSs may be necessary in which FSs are reconceptualized (and redefined) as strings of sounds, rather than strings of words.

Although the earliest research into the prosody of FSs dates back to the 1970s (e.g., Bloom, 1973; Peters, 1977), and important breakthroughs were made in the 1980s (e.g., Peters, 1983; van Lancker & Canter, 1981; van Lancker et al., 1981), very few empirical studies on this topic have been conducted since then. Recently, however, there has been a renewed interest in the topic within the field of corpus linguistics (e.g., Lin, 2010a, 2010b, 2013, 2018; Lin & Adolphs, 2009) because of the practical applications that the findings will have for both English language teaching and Natural Language Processing. These corpus studies, however, have stopped at the point of capturing the prosodic patterns of automatically identified word sequences. They did not delve further into the cognitive bases underlying the systematicity observed in the prosodic patterns.

This chapter will fill this knowledge gap and explore the uncharted waters of FL and speech prosody from a cognitive perspective. For this exploration, an FS is broadly defined as "a sequence, continuous or discontinuous, of words or other elements, which is, or appears to be, prefabricated: that is, stored and retrieved whole from memory at the time of use, rather than being subject to generation or analysis by the language grammar" (Wray, 2002, p. 9). As an umbrella term, FL subsumes many types of lexicalized word combinations ranging from idioms to proverbs, clichés, conversational routines, collocations, and so on (see Wray, 2002, for a comprehensive review). This chapter examines the idea of speech prosody as a perceptual category that is the result of interactions between four acoustic components, namely pitch, loudness, timing, and voice quality. In the phonological literature, pitch is considered the main contributor to the perception of tones; loudness is considered the main contributor to the perception of stress; and timing is the main contributor to the perception of pauses and rhythm (see Cruttenden, 1997, for further discussion).

The challenge of offering a critical review of FL and speech prosody from a cognitive perspective is substantial, not least because very few empirical studies have directly addressed this topic. Furthermore, the notions of FL and speech prosody are both very broad and complex; therefore, controversies still surround what each entails and how they can be quantified. It is with this background in mind that this chapter provides a critical review of the relevant research findings. Although this chapter attempts to bring together research evidence from across several disciplines, such as phonology, child language research, corpus linguistics, psychology, and biology, the discussion may still appear limited because there are, truly, many research gaps on this topic waiting to be addressed. This review aims to highlight the need for more empirical research on the cognitive aspects of FL and speech prosody and, at the same time, identify possible directions for future empirical studies.

The Emergence of Formulaic Sequences in Child First Language Acquisition

Since the input that children receive is 100% spoken, the phonological representation of FSs is bound to play a prominent role in the mental lexicon of the child. Consequently, child L1 acquisition probably offers the best example to support the conceptualization of FSs as strings of sounds, rather than strings of words.

When comparing the two levels of phonological representation (i.e., prosody and phonemics), prosody appears to play the more fundamental role in L1 acquisition. In one of the earliest FL studies, Peters (1977) examined the productions of an 11-month-old L1 learner, Minh. In Minh's speech, Peters noticed stretches of vocalizations that displayed a distinctive and adult speech-like melody. Despite the lack of phonemic articulatory precision, these vocalizations could be recognized in their immediate speech context as the child's attempts at producing context-bound utterances such as *look at that!* and *what's that?*. That the child was able to produce these utterances was unexpected because he had clearly not yet mastered the grammar, vocabulary, or the phonemes to realize those utterances. Peters (1974) describes this phenomenon as children "learning of a tune before the words". In fact, children's ability to memorize tunes and melodies holistically is remarkable, as people who have spent time with toddlers may observe. Wray (2002) also discussed the case of a 21-month-old child, Ellen, who had managed to memorize and sing the tune *Away in a Manger* perfectly, even though she understood neither the words nor the meaning of the carol. The original lyrics "Away in a manger, no crib for a bed. The little Lord Jesus lay down his sweet head" came out in Ellen's singing as "Away in a manger, no crisp for a bear. The little Lord Jesus lay down on his hair" (see Wray, 2002, p. 109, for further information). While these mis-sung lyrics may bring a light-hearted smile, they nonetheless also provide evidence for the pre-eminence of prosody in child L1 acquisition. When children are exposed to L1 spoken input, the melody (or, indeed, prosody) is very important because it guides their attention to and segmentation of the spoken input. Utterances which form prosodically holistic units such as *look at that!* and *what's that?* are acquired and produced holistically. The length of these prosodically holistic units can extend to the whole tune, as we can see in the case of the carol *Away in a Manger*, but they can also be a shorter phrase, as in the case of *Look at that!*. In both cases, prosody is clearly prioritized; the fact that the child does not understand the meaning or the pronunciation of the words constituting the prosodically holistic units does not appear to hinder the child's acquisition or production of the units. Likewise, the lack of phonemic articulatory precision does not prevent child language researchers from recognizing the presence of holistically learned chunks in the child L1 learner's speech.

That child L1 learners prioritize learning the tune before the words should not be surprising. Recent research has indicated that foetuses and infants are biologically predisposed to rely on prosodic cues to acquire their L1. Due to the abdominal barrier, speech from the outside world is filtered before it reaches the foetus's ears. The vowels and consonants are mumbled, leaving only prosodic cues as the remains of the speech signal (imagine hearing speech under water). For this reason, human foetuses have learned to tune in to the prosodic patterns in the speech signal. Empirical evidence to support the theory that human foetuses tune in and react to the prosodic patterns of their L1 comes from many sources, including a number of studies in biology which recorded and analyzed the cries of newborn babies (e.g., Mampe, Friederici, Christophe, & Wermke, 2009; Wermke & Mende, 2009). In Mampe et al.'s (2009) study, the researchers analyzed the cries of 30 French and 30 German newborn babies and found that the melody of the cries mimicked the prosody of the babies' mother tongues. Since these were newborn babies, it was clear that their acquisition of the melody of their mother tongues had taken place in the womb. This finding has been triangulated by other studies, which have adopted alternative methods to trace the beginning of foetal sensitivity to and memory of linguistic prosody (e.g., DeCasper & Spence, 1986; Ferrari et al., 2016). In DeCasper and Spence's (1986) classic study, pregnant women were asked to read to their foetuses each day during the last 6 weeks of pregnancy. Based on the newborns' response to the sounds of these read passages, the researchers concluded that sensitivity to and memory of linguistic prosody can be traced back to the last trimester of pregnancy. More recently, Ferrari et al. (2016) used two-dimensional ultrasound to directly measure foetal mouth movements in response to their mothers' speech. The study found that, even at 25 weeks of gestation (i.e., the start of the third trimester), foetuses seem to already be responsive to maternal stimuli. These studies involving prenatal and newborn subjects point clearly towards the fact that human foetuses are biologically predisposed to rely on prosodic cues for L1 acquisition, a reliance which seems to extend to infancy (as we see in the cases discussed in Peters, 1977; Bloom, 1973) and toddlerhood (Bannard & Matthews, 2008; Wray, 2002).

Prosody, Grammar, and Formulaic Sequence Acquisition

Prosody plays a vital role in many aspects of L1 acquisition. In the literature, researchers have long been interested in the ways that prosody facilitates L1 grammar acquisition. For example, several studies have investigated whether prosody can offer reliable cues to syntactic and phase structure (e.g., Jusczyk et al., 1992; Kemler Nelson, Hirsh-Pasek, Jusczyk, & Wright Cassidy, 1989). In the prosody literature, prosodic breaks have been classified based on their perceived level of discontinuity. Based on Knowles's (1991) classification, pauses accompanied by audible breathing represent the strongest type of prosodic break (level 5), followed by pause (level 4), pitch discontinuity (level 3), segmental separation features (level 2), segmental run-on cancelled (level 1), and nothing measurable (level 0). What the empirical evidence has shown is that the strength of prosodic breaks may offer child L1 learners cues concerning the hierarchical organization of phrases and syntactic units. For instance, studies by Goldman-Eisler (1972) and Scott (1982) found that pauses (levels 4 and 5 prosodic breaks) were more likely to occur at major syntactic boundaries than arbitrarily within phrases. Pause length also appears to reflect the hierarchical organization of phrases (e.g., Cooper & Paccia-Cooper, 1980; Gee & Grosjean, 1983). Before major syntactic boundaries, the final syllables of the syntactic units tend to be lengthened as well as showing a global decline in pitch (e.g., Cruttenden, 1997; Wichmann, 2000).

Other, corpus-based, studies have examined this question concerning prosodic cues to syntactic and phrase structure from a quantitative angle by asking what kind of syntactic unit do intonation units (IUs) most commonly correspond to between different languages (e.g., Iwasaki & Tao, 1993; Schuetze-Coburn, 1994). These studies have consistently found clauses to be the prototypical correlates of intonation units. In Iwasaki and Tao's (1993) study, 53.6%, 45.4%, and 39.8% of the intonation units in their corpora of English, Japanese, and Mandarin Chinese, respectively, were clauses. These figures are interesting because, contrary to popular belief, the correspondence between intonation units and clauses is far lower than 100%. If prosody guides the segmentation of the input speech signal and influences the unit of lexical storage in the mental lexicon, then the unit of lexical storage could differ according to the child's L1. It seems logical to think that the prosody of L1 Mandarin Chinese (which showed 39.8% of IU-clause correspondence) would be more likely to store alternative types of units (other than clauses) in the mental lexicon when compared with the prosody of L1 English (which showed 53.6% of IU-clause correspondence). Previous research (e.g., Schuetze-Coburn, 1994) has provided the example of sentence fragments as possible alternative types of units with which intonation units may correspond. However, Lin's corpus studies (reviewed later) indicate that intonation units may also correspond to FSs. In other words, following the same logic as L1 grammar acquisition studies (e.g., Jusczyk et al., 1992; Kemler Nelson et al., 1989), it seems that, statistically speaking, prosody is also likely to facilitate the acquisition of L1 FSs.

The fact that adjacent words that form grammatical units appear to be readily chunked by prosodic cues in spoken input (see Iwasaki & Tao's (1993) figures cited earlier) has convinced researchers that prosody serves a bootstrapping function in language acquisition (e.g., Jusczyk et al., 1992; Kemler Nelson et al., 1989). What this means, as Fisher and Tokura (1996) put it, is that prosodic information could provide learners with a linguistically useful, bottom-up means of segmenting speech. Such prosodic evidence, when combined with distributional analyses, may help learners to "rule out conjectures about grammatical structure inconsistent with the audible structure of input sentences" (p. 344).

Since research into the prosodic features of FSs is still in its infancy, there has been extremely little empirical research on the role of prosody in the L1 FS acquisition mechanism. Nevertheless, taking into consideration Lin and her colleagues' corpus research (Lin, 2010b, 2013; Lin & Adolphs, 2009), which found that FSs aligned with pitch discontinuity (level 3 prosodic breaks in Knowles' 1991 classification) approximately 50% of the time, it seems logical to assume that prosody can offer reliable cues which facilitate the acquisition of L1 FSs. In other words, prosody may also serve a bootstrapping function in L1 FS acquisition as well as L1 grammar acquisition.

In psychology and child language acquisition, the closest, indirect evidence for prosody's bootstrapping function in L1 FS acquisition so far comes from Peters (1977, 1983), whose findings seem to illustrate the fact that FSs and prosody are inseparable in the case of child L1 acquisition. The reason for suggesting that Peters' (1977, 1983) studies provide indirect evidence is that these studies' original aim was to draw attention to the fact that language development in children does not appear to proceed in a linear fashion. One-word utterances are not necessarily mastered before two-word utterances or two-word utterances before three-word utterances. Instead, it is also possible for children to memorize and produce larger chunks such as *What's that?* and *Look at that!* even before they master the words or the grammatical structures that constitute those chunks. These studies advocate a careful distinction between utterances which the child has acquired and produced holistically, such as *What's that?* and *Look at that!*, and utterances which are generated by articulating single words in succession. This is because such a distinction will enable child language researchers to reach a more accurate diagnosis of a child's stage of linguistic development (Branigan, 1979; Peters, 1983). The key to distinguishing between these two types of utterances lies, above all, in examining their prosody. As mentioned previously, utterances learned holistically appear to be characterized by their distinctive adult speech-like melody. The words constituting the utterances may be pronounced unclearly and imprecisely, but the delivery, nevertheless, appears to be distinctively fluent. Utterances formed by articulating single words in succession, on the other hand, have an "unmistakable" prosodic pattern whereby "[e]ach word occurred with terminal falling pitch contour, and relative equal stress, and there was a variable but distinct pause between them so that utterance boundaries were clearly marked" (Bloom, 1973, p. 41). Given these findings, there seems to be a clear circularity between FSs and prosody in the case of child L1 acquisition (see also Lin, 2010a). On the one hand, it has been suggested that prosody facilitates child L1 acquisition; but, on the other hand, holistically acquired and memorized chunks (i.e., FSs) in child language are identified based on their prosody. This is why FSs and prosody seem inseparable in the case of child L1 acquisition.

As the child L1 learner's linguistic competence develops, these holistically acquired and memorized chunks eventually undergo one of two processes. They may be "unpacked" as their internal structure is analyzed to different extents as part of the L1 grammar acquisition process, or they may remain as holistic units in the mental lexicon (see Wray, 2002, for further discussion). In the absence of direct empirical research, our knowledge of the ways in which the unpacking process may affect the mental prosodic representation as well as the prosodic realization of the analyzed chunks remains limited. That said, with the advent of dense corpora of child-directed speech (e.g., Bannard & Matthews, 2008), necessary data already exist to assist in answering these important questions.

The Challenges of Formulaic Sequence Acquisition in a Second Language

Knowledge of FSs is considered key to the achievement of nativelike speech fluency (Pawley & Syder, 1983; Wood, 2012). In the literature, many anecdotes have been presented concerning adult second language (L2) learners who seem to be able to speak with distinctive fluency as soon as they start speaking formulaically (see, e.g., Dechert, 1983; Raupach, 1984). In one case (Wray, 2004), a beginner learner was able to give cooking demonstrations on television in Welsh after spending just five days learning context-specific FSs. The fact that FSs seem to offer a "shortcut" to speech fluency has intrigued ELT (English Language

Teaching) professionals. It is believed that L2 learners' speech fluency problems may be partially tackled by facilitating their acquisition of L2 FSs (Meunier & Granger, 2008; Wood, 2012).

Despite the perceived importance of FSs to nativelike fluency, the acquisition of FSs in the L2 does not appear to be straightforward. Studies have reported many challenges confronting L2 FS acquisition. The problems include L2 learners' lack of breadth of FS knowledge, difficulty with memorizing FSs without introducing formal deviations, overuse of familiar FSs and so on (see Bishop, 2004; Meunier & Granger, 2008; Wray & Fitzpatrick, 2008). In the literature, FSs have been described as "the last and most challenging hurdle in attaining near nativelike fluency" (Spöttl & McCarthy, 2004, p. 191) because they are difficult even for advanced-level learners of English. For example, there is no grammatical explanation as to why "nice and easy" is idiomatic while "easy and nice" is not. The preference for the former is only a matter of an L1 speaker's habitual usage.

All over the world, researchers have been exploring ways of facilitating L2 learners' noticing of FSs. For example, Bishop (2004) and Szudarski and Carter (2016) have developed new ways of glossing FSs in written texts, and Granger (2011) has examined how classroom-based FS instruction may be improved (see also Meunier & Granger, 2008).

More recently, Lin (2012, 2016a, 2016b) proposes the need to maximize L2 learners' exposure to L2 spoken input as a way of facilitating their mastery of L2 FSs. It is argued that spoken input will be more conducive to FS acquisition than written input because FSs are prosodically salient. On paper, words are equally delineated by white spaces (Carter, 1987). There are no typographic cues to prompt learners to see that some words constitute relatively fixed chunks and, therefore, ought to be treated holistically (Bishop, 2004). However, the case is different when FSs are acquired through the auditory channel. Words that constitute relatively fixed chunks will tend to be articulated in an intonation unit (see Lin, 2010a, 2010b, 2013; Lin & Adolphs, 2009). This may prompt L2 learners to process and store these chunks holistically. Unfortunately, English as a Foreign Language (EFL) syllabi from many parts of the world tend to emphasize written input over spoken input (Lin, 2012). As a consequence, the imbalance between spoken and written input is severe. As Lin and Siyanova-Chanturia (2014) estimate, the proportion of spoken to written input in some EFL syllabi could be 1:9. On this basis, Lin (2014) advocates greater exposure to internet television outside the curriculum as a fundamental means of addressing this imbalance and maximizing EFL learners' exposure to spoken input in the L2. A new intelligent software package (Lin, 2016a, 2016b) has been developed to facilitate L2 FS acquisition through watching YouTube videos. The tool is designed to highlight pedagogically interesting FSs in L2 learners' self-chosen YouTube videos. It tracks each individual learner's YouTube media history and then automatically generates vocabulary exercises based on users' performance statistics.

Despite the ongoing efforts to increase learners' exposure to spoken input in their L2 (Lin, 2016a, 2016b), whether this will be effective in promoting noticing and gains in knowledge of L2 FSs remains an open question. Although the aforementioned review demonstrates that prosody plays a vital role in many aspects of L1 acquisition, there is still some uncertainty about whether prosody is as significant for L2 acquisition. It is possible that the phonological representation of FSs is less prominent in the L2 than in the L1 mental lexicon. Even if prosody is as important to L2 acquisition as it is to L1, it cannot be assumed that an L2 learner's prosodic processing ability in the L2 will be as efficient as his/her prosodic processing ability in the L1. Therefore, he/she may not be able to fully exploit the prosodic cues in L2 spoken input and acquire L2 FSs in the same way that an L1 learner can. In fact, there is a body of literature which has revealed that learners' prosodic processing ability in their L2 typically fails to match the equivalent ability in their L1 (see the following section). If or when this is the case, the strategy of maximizing L2 learners' exposure to L2 spoken input in the hope that FSs will be noticed and acquired more readily through auditory input may only be effective if other measures are in place to enhance learners' L2 prosodic processing ability.

Learners' Weakness in Noticing and Processing Prosodic Cues in Second Language Input

In the literature on *native listening* (Cutler, 2012), a strand of research has investigated learners' L2 prosodic processing ability. These studies (Akker & Cutler, 2003; Broselow, Hurtig, & Ringen, 1987; Dupoux, Pallier, Sebastian, & Mehler, 1997; Pennington & Ellis, 2000) have shed light on the differences in the ways that native and non-native speakers handle prosodic cues in auditory input. It is now clear that non-native speakers are unable to match native speakers' efficiency in processing prosodic information, and their ability to handle L2 prosodic cues also tends to vary widely depending on their L1 background. In Akker and Cutler's (2003) study, for instance, Dutch learners and native speakers of English completed a phoneme-detection task designed to investigate the strategies they used for processing semantic focus and prosodic accent in the input. The results showed that Dutch learners of English were capable of exploiting the prosodic structure of the L2 spoken input and directing attention to accented words. However, the speed with which they were able to exploit prosodic cues and integrate them with other types of cues in the L2 input, such as semantic focus, was slower than their ability in their L1.

In studies involving learners whose L1 and L2 do not demonstrate similar prosodic structures, however, the conclusion is different. Pennington and Ellis (2000) tested the L2 prosodic processing of Cantonese learners of English using memory recognition tasks. In their experiments, subjects needed to decide whether they had heard identical sentences in a preceding exposure phase. The stimuli included foil items which differed from the originals in terms of either prosody or lexis. The results showed that, while these Cantonese learners of English had no problem with recognizing foil items that differed lexically from the originals, in the absence of explicit instruction, they were unable to recognize those that differed prosodically in terms of semantic focus (e.g., *is HE driving the bus?* vs. *is he driving the bus*), pragmatic interpretation (e.g., *He's a good boy, isn't he?* delivered in a falling vs. a rising tone), phrasing (e.g., *The fight is over Fred* vs. *The fight is over, Fred*), or internal structure (e.g., *She's a lighthouse keeper* vs. *She's a light housekeeper*). These learners' weakness in noticing and processing prosodic cues in the L2 input is thought to have arisen from the fact that their L1 and L2 (i.e., Cantonese and English) have fundamentally different prosodic structures. As Pennington and Ellis (2000) suggest, it is possible that details of the L2 prosodic system are not acquired until an advanced stage of language acquisition. In the case of L2 learners who have not achieved full competence in their L2 by adulthood, they transfer knowledge of their L1 prosodic patterns when processing L2 auditory input. The phenomenon of L1 transfer in prosodic processing is well-evidenced by studies involving speakers of tonal languages who are learning stress languages (Dupoux et al., 1997), as well as those involving speakers of stress languages learning tonal languages (Broselow et al., 1987). The extent to which this L1 transfer in prosodic processing affects the acquisition of L2 FSs from spoken input deserves further, empirical investigation.

Van Lancker (2003) conducted one of the first studies to compare native and non-native speakers' prosodic processing competence in relation to FSs. In the study, non-native speakers from mixed L1 backgrounds (e.g., Hebrew, Arabic, Spanish, Chinese, Korean, German, French, and Hungarian; 23 L1s in total) and native speakers of English listened to a number of prototypical English idioms embedded in sentences (e.g., *She missed the boat; it broke the ice*). These sentences appear semantically ambiguous on paper because they can be interpreted idiomatically or literally. However, the subjects were told that each sentence could be disambiguated prosodically. Their task was to make a forced-choice concerning whether each sentence had been read with an intended idiomatic or an intended literal meaning. Again, the results indicated that the prosodic processing competence of L2 learners was significantly worse than that of native speakers. Even highly fluent L2 learners had difficulties with perceiving the prosodic contrasts between the idiomatic and literal readings of the sentences.

With this in mind, there seems to be considerable empirical evidence for the wide gap between learners' L1 and L2 prosodic processing abilities. While prosodic processing ability probably begins prenatally for native speakers (see the biology studies cited earlier), for non-native speakers the extent of this ability depends on whether their L1 and L2 share similar prosodic structures. Where the prosodic structures of the L1 and L2 are similar, as in the case of the Dutch learners of English, L2 prosodic processing is possible, albeit with reduced efficiency. However, when the L1 and L2 prosodic structures differ considerably, as in the case of the Cantonese learners of English, even highly fluent L2 learners seem to struggle with extracting information about the semantic focus, the pragmatic interpretation, the phrasing and sentence structure from the prosodic cues.

Studies on the Effect of Spoken Input on Formulaic Sequence Acquisition in a Second Language

A decade ago, Fitzpatrick and Wray (2006) and Wray and Fitzpatrick (2008) conducted a series of interesting longitudinal studies to investigate how well L2 learners acquire FSs from spoken input. In these studies, intermediate to advanced-level Chinese and Japanese learners of English (whose L1s have prosodic structures different from that of English as the L2) were given the opportunity to identify practical, daily scenarios that were personally relevant. Authentic and formulaic dialogs appropriate to these scenarios were then prepared and audio-recorded onto CDs. The learners' task was to rote learn the formulaic responses to give in these dialogs in order to perform them in a role-play assessment. Despite having received spoken input, exposure to prosodic cues to formulaicity and repeated practice with the researchers, the learners were still unable to develop accurate memories of the formulaic responses and perform them as they appeared on the audio CDs. Instead, they introduced modifications of various sorts in their production (see Wray and Fitzpatrick, 2008, for details). The fact that these learners were unable to reproduce the formulaic responses intact means that they took an analytical (instead of the holistic, gestalt) approach when processing the spoken input. That the analytical mode was engaged is probably indicative of their lack of attention to prosodic cues which, as discussed earlier, should have facilitated the holistic processing of FSs. Since the learners' L2 prosodic processing ability was neither measured nor controlled, it was impossible to judge whether poor L2 prosodic processing ability had contributed to the poor learning outcome.

Whether poor L2 prosodic processing was the cause of the poor learning of FSs in these studies, other research does exist which suggests that learners' L2 prosodic processing can improve given instruction. While Pennington and Ellis's (2000) first experiment showed that, unaided, even highly fluent Cantonese learners of English struggled with the extraction of information about semantic focus, pragmatic interpretation, phrasing, and sentence structure from prosodic cues, their second experiment showed that statistically significant improvements in L2 prosodic processing could occur if instruction was provided. In the phonological literature, there is a wealth of discussion about speech prosody instruction (Romero-Trillo, 2012; Trouvain & Gut, 2007), although most, if not all, of it has focused on improving the prosody of L2 learners' production, as opposed to ways of enhancing learners' processing of prosody during L2 perception. Considering both the evidence for non-native speakers' weaknesses in L2 prosody processing and its possible link with L2 FS acquisition, the demand for research of the latter type is substantial.

To shed light on the question of whether the imbalance between spoken and written input could be a reason for the lack in breadth of knowledge of L2 FSs that L2 learners seem to demonstrate, Lin (in preparation) is conducting an experiment to investigate: (1) whether spoken input is more conducive to L2 FS acquisition than written input and (2) whether spoken input with natural prosodic cues will be more conducive to L2 FS acquisition than spoken input with word-by-word prosody. At the same time, the study measures and controls for the effect of the subject's L2 processing ability, vocabulary size, and phonological short-term memory capacity. In the study, subjects were exposed to stimuli presented in one of three conditions: written input, spoken input with natural prosody, or spoken input with word-by-word prosody. To address the two research questions, the subjects' gains in knowledge of the FSs will be compared after controlling for the effect of L2 processing ability, vocabulary size, and phonological short-term memory capacity. The findings should provide an answer to key questions highlighted previously, including whether increasing L2 learners' exposure to spoken input is likely to facilitate L2 FS acquisition and whether prosody plays an important role in L2 FS acquisition.

Conclusions and Future Directions

To conclude, this chapter has offered a critical review of the role of prosody in the acquisition of L1 and L2 FSs. Considering the fact that 90% of an ordinary person's daily linguistic encounter in his/her L1 is spoken (Carter, personal communication, 2012) and that L1 FSs are acquired and accessed through the auditory channel during extensive exposure to spoken communication, this chapter proposes that FSs be reconceptualized (and redefined) as strings of sounds rather than strings of words. If this reconceptualization is to take place, it is important that a deeper understanding is gained of the phonological representation of FSs in the mental lexicon.

In fact, empirical evidence from biology and child language research already points to the fundamental role of prosody in FS acquisition in the case of child L1 learners. Foetuses are biologically predisposed to rely on prosodic cues to acquire their L1. Natural speech also contains prosodic patterns that guide the segmentation of the input and influence the unit of lexical storage in the brain. Thus, from a purely statistical point of view, these prosodic patterns could prompt the acquisition of L1 FSs in the same way that they prompt the acquisition of L1 grammar.

Compared with L1 FS acquisition, L2 FS acquisition appears to be much more complex. Studies have investigated why the acquisition of FSs seems surprisingly difficult for L2 learners. One of the proposals traces the cause of the problem to L2 learners' lack of exposure to L2 spoken input and suggests that increased exposure to prosodic cues should prompt learners to notice and acquire FSs. This proposal also predicts that maximizing L2 learners' exposure to L2 spoken input outside the curriculum may help to facilitate L2 FS acquisition.

In this chapter, the proposal was critically examined in the light of recent findings from studies on L2 FS acquisition and native listening, concluding that perhaps maximizing L2 spoken input will facilitate L2 FS acquisition only on the condition that L2 learners have already achieved a certain level of L2 prosodic processing competence. This suggestion is currently being tested in a control experiment.

In terms of future directions, it is noteworthy that previous studies have often considered FSs from a lexical perspective only and overlooked the fact that prosody is vital to the acquisition, processing, and use of spoken FSs. While corpus linguists continue to examine the prosodic patterns of FSs and how they affect contextual meanings, the role of prosody in L1 and L2 FS acquisition remains an uncharted territory. Many fundamental questions are still awaiting empirical testing. For example, while it is clear that spoken input dominates in L1 acquisition and written input dominates in L2 acquisition, it is unclear whether this difference in the dominant mode of input shapes the ways that L1 and L2 FSs are represented in the mental lexicon. If the mode of input does appear to be a significant factor of success in L2 FS acquisition, then it would be useful to note the extent to which that success is moderated by the learner's auditory processing ability. In relation to this, there is the question of whether learners with better L2 prosodic processing ability will master FSs faster than learners with poor L2 prosodic processing ability. The effect of speech prosody instruction on learners' success in L2 FSs acquisition is also an important area for study. If these questions can be answered in the future, we will be one step closer to tackling L2 learners' problems with acquiring L2 FSs.

Acknowledgement

The preparation for this paper was supported by a grant from the Research Grants Council of the Hong Kong Special Administrative Region, China (Project number: PolyU 25612116) and a grant from the Hong Kong Polytechnic University (Project number: 1-ZVET).

References

Abdelli-Baruh, N., Yang, S.-y., Ahn, J. S., & van Lancker, D. (2007). *Acoustic cues differentiating idiomatic from literal expressions across languages*. Paper presented at the American Speech and Hearing Association Convention, Boston, November 15–17, 2007.
Aijmer, K. (1996). *Conversational routines in English*. London: Longman.
Akker, E., & Cutler, A. (2003). Prosodic cues to semantic structure in native and nonnative listening. *Bilingualism: Language and Cognition, 6*(2), 81–96.
Ashby, M. (2006). Prosody and idioms in English. *Journal of Pragmatics, 38*(10), 1580–1597.
Bannard, C., & Matthews, D. (2008). Stored word sequences in language learning: The effect of familiarity on children's repetition of four-word combinations. *Psychological Science, 19*(3), 241–248.

Bishop, H. (2004). The effect of typographic salience on the look up and comprehension of unknown formulaic sequences. In N. Schmitt (Ed.), *Formulaic sequences* (pp. 227–248). Amsterdam: John Benjamins.

Bloom, L. (1973). *One word at a time: The use of single word utterances before syntax*. The Hague: Mouton.

Bolinger, D. (1965). On certain functions of accents A and B. In I. Abe & T. Kanekiyo (Eds.), *Forms of English* (pp. 57–66). Cambridge, MA: Harvard University Press.

Branigan, G. (1979). Some reasons why successive single word utterances are not. *Journal of Child Language, 6*, 411–421.

Broselow, E., Hurtig, R. R., & Ringen, C. (1987). The perception of second language prosody. In G. Ioup & S. Weinberger (Eds.), *Interlanguage phonology* (pp. 350–361). Cambridge, MA: Newbury House.

Bybee, J., & Scheibman, J. (1999). The effect of usage on degrees of constituency: The reduction of don't in American English. *Linguistics, 37*, 575–596.

Carter, R. (1987). *Vocabulary: Applied linguistic perspectives*. London: Allen and Unwin.

Cooper, W. E., & Paccia-Cooper, J. (1980). *Syntax and speech*. Cambridge, MA: Harvard University Press.

Cruttenden, A. (1997). *Intonation* (2nd ed.). Cambridge: Cambridge University Press.

Cutler, A. (2012). *Native listening language experience and the recognition of spoken words*. Cambridge, MA: MIT Press.

DeCasper, A. J., & Spence, M. J. (1986). Prenatal maternal speech influences newborns' perception of speech sounds. *Infant Behavior and Development, 9*(2), 133–150.

Dechert, H. W. (1983). How a story is done in a second language. In C. Faerch & G. Kasper (Eds.), *Strategies in interlanguage communication* (pp. 175–195). London: Longman.

Dupoux, E., Pallier, C., Sebastian, N., & Mehler, J. (1997). A Destressing "Deafness" in French? *Journal of Memory and Language, 36*(3), 406–421.

Ferrari, G. A., Nicolini, Y., Demuru, E., Tosato, C., Hussain, M., Scesa, E., . . . Ferrari, P. F. (2016). Ultrasonographic investigation of human fetus responses to maternal communicative and non-communicative stimuli. *Frontiers in Psychology, 7*, 354–363.

Fisher, C., & Tokura, H. (1996). Prosody in speech to infants: Direct and indirect acoustic cues to syntactic structure. In J. L. Morgan & K. Demuth (Eds.), *Signal to syntax: Bootstrapping from speech to grammar in early acquisition* (pp. 343–363). Hillsdale, NJ and England: Lawrence Erlbaum.

Fitzpatrick, T., & Wray, A. (2006). Breaking up is not so hard to do: Individual differences in L2 memorization. *The Canadian Modern Language Review, 63*(1), 35–57.

Gee, J. P., & Grosjean, F. (1983). Performance structures: A psycholinguistic and linguistic appraisal. *Cognitive Psychology, 15*(4), 411–458.

Goldman-Eisler, F. (1972). Pauses, clauses, sentences. *Language and speech, 15*(2), 103–113.

Granger, S. (2011). From phraseology to pedagogy: Challenges and prospects. In T. Herbst, S. Faulhaber, & P. Uhrig (Eds.), *The phraseological view of language* (pp. 123–146). Berlin: Mouton de Gruyter.

Iwasaki, S., & Tao, H. (1993). *A comparative study of the structure of the intonation unit in English, Japanese, and Mandarin Chinese*. Paper presented at The 67th Annual Meeting of the Linguistic Society of America, Los Angeles, California, January 7–10, 1993.

Jusczyk, P. W., Hirsh-Pasek, K., Kemler Nelson, D. G., Kennedy, L. J., Woodward, A., & Piwoz, J. (1992). Perception of acoustic correlates of major phrasal units by young infants. *Cognitive Psychology, 24*, 252–293.

Kemler Nelson, D. G., Hirsh-Pasek, K., Jusczyk, P. W., & Wright Cassidy, K. (1989). How the prosodic cues in motherese might assist language learning. *Journal of Child Language, 16*, 55–68.

Knowles, G. (1991). Prosodic labelling: The problem of tone group boundaries. In S. Johansson & A.-B. Stenström (Eds.), *English computer corpora* (pp. 149–163). Berlin: Mouton de Gruyter.

Lin, P. (2010a). The phonology of formulaic sequences: A review. In D. Wood (Ed.), *Perspectives on formulaic language* (pp. 174–193). London: Continuum.

Lin, P. (2010b). *The prosody of formulaic language* (Unpublished doctoral dissertation). University of Nottingham, Nottingham, UK.

Lin, P. (2012). Sound evidence: The missing piece of the jigsaw in formulaic language research. *Applied Linguistics, 33*(3), 342–347.

Lin, P. (2013). The prosody of idiomatic expressions in the IBM/Lancaster Spoken English Corpus. *International Journal of Corpus Linguistics, 18*(4), 561–588.

Lin, P. (2014). Investigating the validity of internet television as a resource for acquiring L2 formulaic sequences. *System, 42*(1), 164–176.

Lin, P. (2015). *It's not what you say; It is the way that you say it: The need to specify the intonation of idioms and phraseology in learner dictionaries*. Paper presented at The Asian Association for Lexicography (ASIALEX) conference, The Hong Kong Polytechnic University, Hong Kong, June 25–27, 2015.

Lin, P. (2016a). *How many exposures do learners need to learn a new English phrase*. Paper presented at the Doing Linguistics with Big Data: The 20th Workshop on Linguistics and Language Processing, Kyung Hee University, Seoul, May 29, 2016.

Lin, P. (2016b). *Second language vocabulary acquisition in the age of Internet Television and Social Media*. Paper presented at the Department of English Seminar, The Hong Kong Polytechnic University, November 7, 2016.

Lin, P. (2018). *The prosody of formulaic language: A corpus approach*. London: Continuum.

Lin, P. (in preparation). *Investigating the optimal mode of input for the acquisition of second language formulaic sequences*.

Lin, P., & Adolphs, S. (2009). Sound evidence: Phraseological units in spoken corpora. In A. Barfield & H. Gyllstad (Eds.), *Researching collocations in another language* (pp. 34–48). Basingstoke: Palgrave Macmillan.

Lin, P., & Siyanova-Chanturia, A. (2014). Internet television for L2 vocabulary learning. In D. Nunan & J. C. Richards (Eds.), *Language learning beyond the classroom* (pp. 149–158). London: Routledge.

Mampe, B., Friederici, A. D., Christophe, A., & Wermke, K. (2009). Newborns' cry melody is shaped by their native language. *Current Biology, 19*, 1–4.

Meunier, F., & Granger, S. (Eds.). (2008). *Phraseology in foreign language learning and teaching*. Amsterdam: John Benjamins.

Pawley, A., & Syder, F. H. (1983). Two puzzles for linguistic theory: Nativelike selection and nativelike fluency. In J. C. Richards & R. W. Schmidt (Eds.), *Language and communication* (pp. 191–226). London: Longman.

Pennington, M. C., & Ellis, N. C. (2000). Cantonese speakers' memory for English sentences with prosodic cues. *The Modern Language Journal, 84*(3), 372–389.

Peters, A. M. (1974). *The beginnings of speech*. Papers and Reports on Child Language Development, Stanford University, 8, pp. 26–32.

Peters, A. M. (1977). Language learning strategies: Does the whole equal the sum of the parts? *Language, 53*(3), 560–573.

Peters, A. M. (1983). *The units of language acquisition*. Cambridge: Cambridge University Press.

Raupach, M. (1984). Formulae in second language speech production. In H. W. Dechert, D. Möhle, & M. Raupach (Eds.), *Second language productions* (pp. 114–137). Tubingen: Gunter Narr.

Romero-Trillo, J. (Ed.) (2012). *Pragmatics and prosody in English language teaching*. Dordrecht: Springer.

Schuetze-Coburn, S. (1994). Prosody, syntax, and discourse pragmatics: Assessing information flow in German conversation (Unpublished doctoral dissertation). University of California, Los Angeles.

Scott, D. R. (1982). Duration as a cue to the perception of a phrase boundary. *The Journal of the Acoustical Society of America, 71*(4), 996–1007.

Siyanova-Chanturia, A., & Lin, P. (2017). Production of ambiguous idioms in English: A reading aloud study. *International Journal of Applied Linguistics*, Early View Article, 1–13.

Spöttl, C., & McCarthy, M. (2004). Comparing knowledge of formulaic sequences across L1, L2, L3, and L4. In N. Schmitt (Ed.), *Formulaic sequences* (pp. 191–226). Amsterdam and Philadelphia: John Benjamins.

Szudarski, P., & Carter, R. (2016). The role of input flood and input enhancement in EFL learners' acquisition of collocations. *International Journal of Applied Linguistics, 26*(2), 245–265.

Trouvain, J., & Gut, U. (Eds.). (2007). *Non-native prosody: Phonetic description and teaching practice*. Berlin: Mouton de Gruyter.

van Lancker, D. (2003). Auditory recognition of idioms by native and nonnative speakers of English: It takes one to know one. *Applied Psycholinguistics, 24*(1), 45–57.

van Lancker, D., & Canter, G. J. (1981). Idiomatic versus literal interpretations of ditropically ambiguous sentences. *Journal of Speech and Hearing Research, 46*(1), 64–69.

van Lancker, D., Canter, G. J., & Terbeek, D. (1981). Disambiguation of ditropic sentences acoustic and phonetic cues. *Journal of Speech and Hearing Research, 24*(3), 330–335.

Wermke, K., & Mende, W. (2009). Musical elements in human infants' cries: In the beginning is the melody. In O. Vitouch & O. Ladinig (Eds.), *Musicae scientiae, special issue on music and evolution* (pp. 151–173). Brussels: Presses Universitaires de Bruxelles.

Wichmann, A. (2000). *Intonation in text and discourse*. Harlow: Longman.

Wood, D. (2012). *Formulaic language and second language speech fluency*. London: Continuum.

Wray, A. (2002). *Formulaic language and the lexicon*. Cambridge: Cambridge University Press.

Wray, A. (2004). "Here's one I prepared earlier": Formulaic language learning on television. In N. Schmitt (Ed.), *Formulaic sequences* (pp. 249–268). Amsterdam and Philadelphia: John Benjamins.

Wray, A., & Fitzpatrick, T. (2008). Why can't you just leave it alone? Deviations from memorized language as a gauge of nativelike competence. In F. Meunier & S. Granger (Eds.), *Phraseology in foreign language learning and teaching* (pp. 123–147). Amsterdam: John Benjamins.

Yang, S.-y., Ahn, J. S., & Van Lancker, D. (2010). The perception and acoustic features of Korean ditropic sentences. *Journal of the Acoustical Society of America, 127*(3), 1955–1955.

PART II
Socio-Cultural and Pragmatic Perspectives on Formulaic Language

5
FORMULAIC LANGUAGE IN SECOND LANGUAGE PRAGMATICS RESEARCH

Kathleen Bardovi-Harlig

Introduction

This chapter explores research in the acquisition of second language pragmatics and the acquisition and use of formulaic language (FL).[1] FL, generally referred to as *formulas, routines, conventional expressions,* and *pragmatic routines* in pragmatic research, is one type of pragmalinguistic resource for the realization of sociopragmatics. Pragmatics research has primarily considered the social function of formulaic sequences (FSs); use of specific FSs characterize language use within speech communities, and may mark speakers' membership within those communities. Such conventional expressions can be quite local, with one community favouring an expression such as *I don't mind* and the immediately geographically contiguous community using *I don't care to* for the same situations, meaning, and illocutionary force (namely, willingness to undertake a specified action). Although FL does not characterize the totality of pragmatics, nor even the realization of the majority of speech acts, it is nevertheless a salient feature as FL often indicates the illocutionary force of an utterance when it occurs.[2]

Many claims have been made regarding the utility of acquiring formulas for negotiating second language pragmatics on the part of second language learners, but substantially less empirical research has been conducted concerning their acquisition and use. Early studies examined both the production of formulas (Scarcella, 1979) and the effects of instruction (House, 1996). Increased interest in the use of formulas in the acquisition of second language pragmatics has mirrored the interest in FL in other areas of applied linguistics and has included investigations of use, meaning, recognition in context, and learner attitude toward the targets.

What distinguishes the investigation of FL in pragmatics from other areas of research on FL is the examination of social and pragmatic contexts and use. The majority of the published studies that have investigated FL in the acquisition of second language pragmatics have investigated production (Bardovi-Harlig, 2012a, 2016). Unlike other areas of research into FL, processing is rarely studied as pragmatics inquiry and research design has little to say in that area (but see Edmonds, 2014, for an exception). In second language pragmatics, researchers have been particularly attuned to identifying native speaker use of conventional expressions in specific situations in order to be able to identify clear targets for acquisition by second language learners. Without clear usage patterns of conventional expressions for native speakers, the acquisition research would be necessarily vague.

One other factor in the acquisition of second language pragmatics that distinguishes it from other areas of research is that learners have to use their developing sociopragmatic knowledge to establish or recognize contexts for the use of formulas. If the target community views a particular situation as calling for an expression of gratitude, but the learner views it as a situation that is best served by the use of an apology, the learner will not use any thanking expression that is in play in the speech community. For example, some learners used an apology to close office hours rather than expressing gratitude (Bardovi-Harlig, 2009). Thus sociopragmatics, and not the learner's knowledge of conventional expressions, eliminates the environment for the realization of thanking, and thus any expression of gratitude. Only when speakers recognize the situation as calling for the same speech act, the pragmatic strategy, and the content can the form align in the realization of a conventional expression.

Although research into FL in pragmatics is relatively active, and growing, the focus on the acquisition of specific, empirically identified, conventional expressions in second language acquisition of pragmatics is relatively more limited, but gaining in interest. Research in this area has moved from being focused largely on English to include conventional expressions in Chinese (Bardovi-Harlig & Su, submitted; Taguchi, Li, & Xiao, 2013; Yang, 2016), French (Edmonds, 2014), German (Barron, 2003), Japanese (Tateyama, 2001), and Russian (Furniss, 2016).

In this chapter I will consider how FSs are defined in pragmatics, how they are identified for research, how conventionality is established, how learner knowledge is evaluated, and finally, how the investigation of the acquisition of FSs contributes to our understanding of second language pragmatics and how research on second language pragmatics contributes to a broader understanding of the second language acquisition of FL more generally.

How are Formulaic Sequences Defined in Second Language Pragmatics?

As anyone reading this volume will know, there are many terms for FSs. In pragmatics, four are more commonly used than others, namely *formulas*, *routines*, *conventional expressions*, and *pragmatic routines*. Formulas in pragmatics are (a) multi-word expressions; (b) related to context; (c) characteristic of a speech community; and (d) illocutionarily transparent (Blum-Kulka, 1989; Reiter, Rainey, & Fulcher, 2005). Coulmas's (1981) definition of *routine formula* emphasizes the social aspect of pragmatic formulas, describing them as "tacit agreements, which the members of a community presume to be shared by every reasonable co-member. In embodying societal knowledge they are essential in the handling of day-to-day situations" (p. 4). Terkourafi (2002) focuses on the pragmatic function of formulas as "ready-made solutions to the complex and pertinent problem of constituting one's own and one's addressee's face while simultaneously ensuring that one's immediate goals in interaction are achieved" (p. 196) and argues that formulas may be a significant feature of polite discourse more generally. Because pragmatics research focuses on the social and situational use of multiword units to the relative exclusion of psycholinguistic concerns of processing and storage, Bardovi-Harlig (2009) adopted the term *conventional expressions* to distinguish the pragmatic construct from the psycholinguistic term *formula*, which intrinsically makes claims about storage and retrieval (see also Forsberg, 2010). This chapter adopts *conventional expression* when talking specifically about pragmatics, and *FL* when discussing multiword expressions more generally.

Following the distinction established by Leech (1983) and Thomas (1983), pragmatics research distinguishes between sociopragmatics and pragmalinguistics. Sociopragmatics was defined by Leech as "specific 'local' conditions on language use" (1983, p. 10) and elaborated by Félix-Brasdefer and Hasler-Barker (2015) as "knowledge about and performance consistent with the social norms in specific situations in a given society, as well as familiarity with variables of social power and social distance" (p. 76). Pragmalinguistics is knowledge of the linguistic repertoire needed to carry out the sociopragmatics of the language and culture. Knowledge of conventional expressions is part of pragmalinguistic competence, and knowledge of their use and the contexts in which they occur is part of sociopragmatic competence.

Learner familiarity with conventional expressions relates directly to what Pawley and Syder (1983) have called *the puzzle of nativelike selection*, which describes the problem of how native speakers select conventional expressions from among a "range of grammatically correct paraphrases, many of which are non-nativelike or highly marked usages" (1983, p. 90). According to Pawley and Syder, language learners need to learn a means of "knowing which of the well-formed sentences are nativelike – a way of distinguishing those usages that are normal or unmarked from those that are unnatural or highly marked" (p. 94).

In the second language pragmatics literature, the terms *conventional expression* and *pragmatic routine* have begun to be distinguished from *formula* and *routine*. *Formula* and *routine* have been used for the more general terms, and *conventional expressions* and *pragmatic routines* have been used more narrowly. Bardovi-Harlig (2009) distinguished the term *conventional expression* from *formulas* to distinguish pragmatic investigations and claims from psycholinguistic ones related to processing. The term *conventional expression* emphasizes the social aspect of use, namely a speech community's preference for a particular string, and avoids the psycholinguistic claim regarding storage and retrieval. Following Erman and Warren (2000), conventional expressions are "combinations of at least two words favoured by native speakers in preference to an alternative combination which could have been equivalent had there been no conventionalization" (p. 31). In order to establish preference, Bardovi-Harlig (2009) established a cut-off of greater than 50% of all responses of native speakers in a particular, well-defined pragmatic context for the identification of a conventional expression. *Pragmatic routines*, on the other hand, show a looser association with context, but like conventional expressions transparently convey the illocutionary force of specific speech acts (for example, *I agree*, *That's true*, and *You're right* for agreement or *Yeah but* and *I agree … but* for disagreement). How these are identified for investigation is discussed in the next section.

How are Conventional Expressions Identified for Study?

In the study of L2 pragmatics, researchers need to be conservative in the identification of target language candidates for expressions and the subsequent demonstration that they are conventionally used in predictable contexts in the target language community with which the learners interact because they will be used to evaluate learner production. This helps delimit the learnability question: Can/do learners acquire conventional expressions available in the input? Whereas other areas of second language research have tackled the poverty of stimulus argument (Cook, 1991), demonstrating that second language learners are able to acquire language features that are not instantiated in the input, L2 pragmatics deals with a very different learnability issue: the acquisition of features that can be shown to be readily available in the pragmatic input, but demonstrably not present in learner production. Thus, establishing availability in input becomes a crucial issue in L2 pragmatics research. The variables that affect the acquisition of conventional expressions in pragmatics, such as noticing, learner subjectivity, and cross-linguistic influence, are only relevant if the expressions are available to learners in input.

It is important to note that individual intuition is unreliable in identifying target language expressions for either acquisition research or instruction, and this is demonstrated by the comparison of textbook "useful expressions" to corpora, and the comparison of different corpora to each other (Bardovi-Harlig, Mossman, & Vellenga, 2015b; Bardovi-Harlig & Mossman, 2016). In keeping with the multifaceted ways in which pragmatics research defines and researches FL, I divide the activity of identifying *candidate* expressions as one stage of research and confirming that they are *conventional* as a second stage.

One way to identify expressions is by observations of speech patterns in a community. This is what we did in the spring of 2006 when my seminar students and I recorded repeated uses of conventional expressions and the events in which they occurred in and around Bloomington, Indiana. In this case, native-speaker expressions were collected from authentic conversations (Bardovi-Harlig, 2009; Bardovi-Harlig et al., 2010). Other sources include field notes (Taguchi et al., 2013), television reality shows, graffiti dialogs, and diary accounts (Culpeper, 2010), multiple expression generation in response to written discourse completion tasks (Edmonds, 2014), and identification by instructors of phrases produced in written discourse completion tasks (Wong, 2012). Other sources named in the literature include translational equivalents in languages of interest (Roever, 2005), literal and figurative pairs (Kecskes, 2000), reports by learners (Yang, 2016), textbooks (Bardovi-Harlig et al., 2015a, b; Yang, 2016), reference works including phrasebooks for travelers (Taguchi et al., 2013), and subtitles from films (Furniss, 2016, 2017).

In pragmatics, even more than in other areas, there is pushback on the concept of a native-speaker standard. However, if we look back to Coulmas's (1981) definition, we see that he states that formulas are used by "reasonable co-members" of a speech community. A person can determine the degree to which he or she wishes to be regarded as a co-member of a community.

How is Conventionality Established in Second Language Pragmatics Research?

To ask the question "how is conventionality of candidate expressions established in pragmatics research?" is to assume (or even indirectly assert) that all studies establish conventionality. It is perhaps more helpful to assert that they should, and then point out that some studies establish conventionality in different ways. In acquisition research, one cannot make the claim that learners are not doing something expected (such as using a conventional expression) unless it is specifically established that the target language speakers perform the same way. Wolfson (1986) demonstrated long ago that native speaker intuition in pragmatics is unreliable; thus empirical evidence must be cited for determining what expressions are targets.[3] It is on the question of establishing conventionality that earlier and more recent studies are most clearly divided. Scarcella (1979), House (1996), Roever (2005), and Kecskes (2000) do not report how the conventionality of the formulas that they investigated was established empirically.

As more recent studies report, once candidate expressions have been identified, the next step is often to test or confirm conventionality. In pragmatics, this often means identifying the preferred expression in a context, following Erman and Warren's definition. One way to operationalize "favored in preference to alternatives" (Erman & Warren, 2000, p. 31) and "community-wide use" (Myles,

Hooper, & Mitchell, 1998, p. 325) is to set a cut score above which there would be no competing alternative. Bardovi-Harlig and colleagues operationalized that as greater than 50% of all responses to a particular scenario (Bardovi-Harlig, 2009; Bardovi-Harlig et al., 2010).

In order to determine the preferred expression for a particular context, experimental contexts were constructed based on the field notes that accompanied the original candidate expressions. Based on the field notes, short descriptions were developed for each expression; the descriptions included the addressee, context of the activity, and often a prior speaker turn and a prompt "You say". In pragmatics this is called a *scenario*. A task consisting of such scanerios is called a discourse completion task, or more commonly, DCT. The scenarios were given to native speakers in oral form and they were asked to reply orally.

(1) You give your classmate a ride home. He lives in the building next to yours. He gets out of the car and says,

(Audio Only): "Thanks for the ride".
You say: (participant speaks)

Scenarios from the pilot were advanced to the computer-delivered oral DCT used in the final elicitation task if native-speaker responses exceeded 50% for a single expression. Native speakers who had not participated in the pilot were tested on the same task as the learners to assure comparability.

Other studies have also adopted a 50% cut-off. The same cut-off practice established in Bardovi-Harlig (2009) was used for a study in L2 French (Edmonds, 2014) and Chinese (Bardovi-Harlig & Su, submitted, using oral DCTs; Taguchi et al., 2013, and Yang, 2016, using written rather than oral DCTs). Yang (2016) raised the cut-off to 67% (or two-thirds majority). Taguchi et al. (2013) supplemented the production data with a judgement task in which native speakers provided a yes/no judgement of whether the situations occur regularly: items that were retained were evaluated as occurring regularly by at least 50% of respondents.

The 50% cut-off for native speaker production was used independently by Culpeper (2010) who compared spontaneous production of candidate impoliteness formulas to their occurrence in a corpus. For a candidate sequence to be considered an impoliteness formula, at least 50% of the uses of an expression had to be impolite as confirmed by uses in the Oxford English Corpus (OEC). (Culpeper, 2010, did not have a learning component, but provides a good model for establishing a baseline combining observation and corpus validation in L2 pragmatics research.)

Instead of establishing preference, other studies establish frequency. Bardovi-Harlig et al. (2015a) distinguished frequently used expressions from conventional expressions, calling them *pragmatic routines*. Pragmatic routines lack the association with the very specific contexts with which conventional expressions are associated, but are linked to more general contexts like speech acts. Bardovi-Harlig et al. (2015a) identified as instructional targets pragmatic routines that met or exceeded the range of 10–40 occurrences per million using the Michigan Corpus of Academic Spoken English (MICASE; Simpson, Briggs, Ovens, & Swales, 2002). The range of 10–40 occurrences per million words were set by Biber and colleagues as a means of defining "frequent" occurrence of multiword sequences (Biber, Johansson, Leech, Conrad & Finegan, 1999; Biber, Conrad, & Cortes, 2004, respectively). Working with conventional expressions in Chinese, Wong (2012) consulted the Centre for Chinese Linguistics Online Corpus (the CCL Corpus), retaining only candidate expressions with five or more tokens for analysis. Out of a corpus of 477 million characters, or about 300 million words, they were considerably less frequent than Biber and colleagues have suggested.

After identifying candidate expressions from the subtitle corpus of the Russian National Corpus, Furniss (2016, 2017) ran word frequency and an n-gram list of two to five words. Multiword sequences that could function pragmatically were identified by hand. In order to qualify as routine formulas, sequences had to be recurrent, occur in specific social contexts, and uphold the social contract (Bardovi-Harlig, 2012a). Furniss's corpus-informed approach allowed her to move from corpus to pragmatics, whereas most pragmatics researchers go from pragmatics to corpus (Bardovi-Harlig et al., 2015a) or other additional pragmatic means of verification (Bardovi-Harlig, 2009; Bardovi-Harlig & Su, submitted; Taguchi et al., 2013;Yang, 2016).

How is Learner Knowledge Evaluated?

In pragmatics, the preference for production data is well established (more on that later). However, in the investigation of conventional expressions, some tasks will be more familiar to other areas of research on FL in second language acquisition. Like recognition tasks in studies of FSs in second language acquisition (without a pragmatic focus; e.g., Alali & Schmitt, 2012), multiple-choice tasks have been used in pragmatics (Roever, 2005 for English;Yang, 2016 for Chinese) in which learners are given a scenario, similar to a DCT, but with choices for an appropriate response, one of which is the target FS. However, the DCT multiple-choice format confounds sociopragmatic knowledge with recognition of expressions that are conventional and used by the speech community and those that are not conventional.

Two decontextualized recognition tasks have been used in an attempt to separate pragmatic knowledge from recognition of conventional expressions. Decontextualized expressions, spoken in isolation, were played twice for the learners and were evaluated for frequency of encounter by learners, who circled one of three options: "I frequently/sometimes/never hear this" (Bardovi-Harlig, 2009, 2010; Bardovi-Harlig &Vellenga, 2012; Furniss, 2016). A second self-assessment of knowledge of conventional expressions (Bardovi-Harlig, 2014) allowed learners to hear two isolated aural tokens of a conventional expression, then asked them to evaluate their level of knowledge and include a definition and a mini-conversation showing how they would use it (similar to Barron's, 2003, "free DCT" where a learner writes both parts of the conversation).

In second language pragmatics, learner knowledge of conventional expressions is generally evaluated through production data, requiring an exact match to the target expression, within variation exhibited by native speakers (Bardovi-Harlig, 2009; Bardovi-Harlig & Su, submitted; Yang, 2016). The native speakers in Bardovi-Harlig (2009) used both contractions and full forms. Thus, learners were given full credit for all variations of ({*I'm/I am*}) *sorry* {*I'm/I am*} *late*. Because the contexts are narrowly defined by scenarios in DCTs (shown above in Example 1), no additional scaffolding is given to elicit FL, as is done in many studies outside pragmatics which have used C-test formats with and without meaning glosses (Schmitt, Grandage, & Adolphs, 2004; Jones & Haywood, 2004, respectively), matrices (Revier, 2009), or translations (Alali & Schmitt, 2012).[4]

In keeping with the conversation simulation, Bardovi-Harlig and colleagues use oral DCTs exclusively in the target language (Bardovi-Harlig, 2009; Bardovi-Harlig et al., 2015a, for different oral tasks in English; Bardovi-Harlig & Su, submitted, for a task in Chinese.) In contrast, Taguchi and colleagues have used oral tasks in English to elicit production in L2 Chinese (Taguchi et al., 2013; Taguchi, Xiao, & Li, 2016).

Working with oral data requires additional considerations. Responding to the role that fluency plays is one of them. For example, the analyst must determine whether pauses should be counted as part of targetlike production up to a certain length; that is, a decision would need to be made as to whether *Sorry I'm late* and *Sorry* (.5) *I'm late* would both be given full credit. Longer pauses might be seen to violate the "fluency" criteria of Myles et al. (1998, p. 325): "phonologically coherent – that is, fluently articulated, nonhesitant". Interestingly, not all felicitous deliveries are fast or nonhesitant. The use of the right formula, but with infelicitous delivery, was observed by Tateyama (2001) working with L2 Japanese. She noted that some delivery, for example in apologies, was too smooth where hesitancy is required, and thus not apologetic sounding. Production may also seem abrupt or "mechanical" in delivery (House, 1996). Using oral data adds a dimension to the analysis of conventional expressions that is not present when written DCTs are used (see Yang, 2016, for a written task).

An exception to a linguistic analysis of the conventional expressions is the use of rating scales of pragmatic acceptability which incorporate conventional expressions as an element of the rating, but do not report on the expressions themselves. Taguchi and colleagues gave judges a 4-point rating scale (Taguchi et al., 2013) and later a 6-point rating scale (Taguchi et al., 2016) that incorporate a judgement of the use of conventional expressions with other pragmatic features. At each level, judges rate the form of the expression, the appropriateness, and the meaning. In the 4-point scale, 3 is perfect, 0 is no answer, opt out, or makes no sense. The judgements are based on native speaker intuitions rather than corresponding native speaker production.

There is a fundamental difference between the two approaches to evaluating learner production. Having NS complete the same task as learners highlights exactly what NS do in that same scenario. Using judges, as Taguchi et al. do, relies on the judges' intuition of what is "appropriate" and how close the expression gets to what the judges believe is nativelike production. However, using judgements does not account for subtle differences in context. For example, in one thanking scenario used by Bardovi-Harlig (2009), native speakers and learners say "{thank you/thanks} for your {time/help}" and in another they say "{Thank you/thanks}so much". It is unlikely that a rater would intuitively arrive at the distributional knowledge independent of native-speaker production. Yet, without such information, the evaluation of learner production by a rater (in place of native speaker production) only provides information about the acceptability or felicity of a single utterance, and cannot establish whether the learner is using a conventional expression in a context where native speakers would.

Furthermore, there is a fundamental difference in scoring. In Taguchi's scoring system, targetlike production is given 3 points, whereas partial production of a conventional expression is given a lower score (a 2 or 1), depending on how far from the target raters think it is. That means that multiple partial scores (let's say for the sake of argument, three scores of "1") add up to the same total (in this case, 3) as a learner who produces one expression well. The alternative is to give one point for an exact rendition of the expression and no points for interlanguage forms. This latter alternative better addresses claims outside of pragmatics suggesting that formulas seed grammar, something that they cannot do if they are subject to grammatical development themselves. Interlanguage attempts are discussed qualitatively in such analyses or assigned to separate categories.

What Do We Know So Far?

The recent focus on FL in L2 pragmatics has yielded a number of findings that could not have been anticipated at the start of the inquiries about a decade ago. The results are divided across two main sections for economy and to avoid repetition. In this section I discuss the relation of recognition and production, implementation of nativelike selection, learning environment, transfer, instruction, and evaluation of pragmatic performance. In the following section, I discuss findings and practices that might be relevant to studies of FL more broadly, namely, advantages of pragmatic elicitation tasks, syntactic development of FL, and task effects.

In Second Language Pragmatics, Learners Recognize more Conventional Expressions than they Produce

Some learner nonproduction of conventional expressions comes in part from learners not knowing a particular expression, as evidenced by results from recognition tasks. On the other hand, results from recognition tasks coupled with production tasks also reveal that learners report knowing expressions that they do not produce in appropriate contexts. This pattern has two possible interpretations: either learners do not know how to use some expressions that they report knowing (this shows up in definition tasks coupled with learner construction of dialogs; Bardovi-Harlig, 2014) or learners do know at least some of the meaning and use of the expression, but assess the context provided in the task as requiring a different speech act, which precludes its use.

Nativelike Selection: Learners can Distinguish Conventional from Modified Expressions

Learners can increasingly distinguish conventional expressions from modified strings with higher proficiency (Bardovi-Harlig, 2009, 2010) and/or instruction (Bardovi-Harlig & Vellenga, 2012; Furniss, 2016). In addition, learners of second language French (first language English, second language French, in France) were more accurate in determining appropriateness and faster at doing so for conventional expressions than for non-conventional sentences presented in the same DCT-like contexts with scenario and language (Edmonds, 2014). Instruction that brings learners' attention to conventional expressions also results in higher rates of exclusion of non-conventional expressions (Furniss, 2016). This is a clear illustration of nativelike selection (Pawley & Syder, 1983), by which learners can distinguish conventional expressions from competing grammatical strings.

Environment

Because studies of conventional expressions in pragmatics are as much about pragmatics as FL, environment (specifically, in-country – whether second language or study abroad – or foreign language classrooms) has been investigated as a variable. Environment is thought to be important in pragmatics because in in-country environments, learners would be in contact with situations in which pragmatics would be especially salient. Both the reasons for learning pragmatics and the input would be enhanced, as would the opportunities for noticing.

There is a clear advantage of target community exposure (Barron, 2003; Roever, 2005; Taguchi, 2011) and proficiency (Bardovi-Harlig, 2009, 2010; Bardovi-Harlig & Bastos, 2011; Roever, 2005; Taguchi, 2011) to the acquisition of formulas. The environment variable (and length of residence in the host environment) often interacts with the proficiency variable and intensity of interaction. Increased length of stay led to improved formula production (Barron, 2003), and study abroad experience positively affected the comprehension of routines (Taguchi, 2011). In a study of three variables (i.e., proficiency, length of residence, and intensity of interaction), Bardovi-Harlig and Bastos (2011) found that recognition of authentic formulas showed significant influence of intensity of interaction. Production of pragmatic formulas showed significant influence of both proficiency and intensity of interaction.

Length of stay did not have a significant effect on either recognition or production. This suggests that lengthy exposures positively influence acquisition because they lead to interaction, not merely because they are long.

Roever (2012) claimed that learners with in-country exposure did so much better than foreign language learners in the identification of pragmatic routines on a 12-item multiple-choice task that there is no point in teaching pragmatic routines in foreign language classrooms. However, Roever grossly overestimates the generalizability of the multiple-choice task, which is not equivalent to the pragmatic and communicative challenges that learners encounter in-country.

Finally, there is also evidence that foreign language settings are not deterministic of low success rates. Yang (2016) seems to attribute the poor performance of the foreign language learners of Chinese (CFL) in her study to environment. Yang concluded that "the results suggest that CFL learners' ability to produce native-like pragmatic routine formulae in corresponding real-life situations in China is not promising" (p. 39). However, there is also a possible task effect. Yang's learners were tested using written DCTs with scenarios presented in English. In contrast, CFL learners who were tested by oral DCTs with scenarios presented in Chinese (Bardovi-Harlig & Su, submitted) surpassed the scores of Yang's learners. Such comparisons suggest that task effect should be investigated further.

Transfer

As in other areas of language acquisition, transfer may play a role in the acquisition of FL in pragmatics. Based on the limited number of studies so far, it appears that transfer may be both lexical and pragmatic. Intermediate-level Persian learners of English in Tehran often used translations of a Persian formula for responding to compliments even when they did not use the formulas in the same context in Persian (Sharifian, 2008). In a study of Irish learners of German, transfer from L1 to L2 decreased over time, with some variation across scenarios (Barron, 2003). L2 learners from different L1 language-culture backgrounds may also differ – not in the expressions used – but in the interpretation of what speech act is appropriate in a particular setting; this then affects production of the target expression (Bardovi-Harlig, Rose, & Nickels, 2008).

Instruction

Second language pragmatics researchers tend to also be involved with pragmatics pedagogy, so it is not surprising that some pragmatics researchers have also been involved in instructional effects studies and the development of instructional materials and activities. Teaching pragmatic routines to classroom language learners, whether in second-language classrooms (Bardovi-Harlig et al., 2015a; Bardovi-Harlig, Mossman, & Su, 2017; Bardovi-Harlig, & Vellenga, 2012) or foreign-language classrooms (Furniss, 2016; House, 1996; Tateyama, 2001), has proven successful. Instruction results in the higher production of conventional expressions in expected contexts (Bardovi-Harlig et al., 2015a; Bardovi-Harlig et al., 2017; Bardovi-Harlig & Vellenga, 2012; House, 1996; Tateyama, 2001) and in greater ability to distinguish conventional expressions from grammatical equivalents (Bardovi-Harlig & Vellenga, 2012; Furniss, 2016). Reviewing materials for instruction of formulaic expressions emphasizes the lack of authentic input in textbooks, regardless of language.

Conventional Expressions Enhance Pragmatic Production by Second Language Learners

Conventional expressions help learners sound more targetlike pragmatically. They convey the illocutionary force of the utterance and, in their transparency, should clearly convey the speakers' intentions. For example, learners more clearly convey their intentions to agree and disagree in academic conversations after instruction in pragmatic routines (Bardovi-Harlig et al., 2015a; Bardovi-Harlig et al., 2017). However, in those same studies the separate rating of speech act clarity and pragmatic routines show that improvement is not entirely due to the use of routines, as speech act scores are much higher than scores for the use of the pragmatic routines. Nevertheless, pragmatic routines contribute significantly to the identification of illocutionary force. Assuming the relation of pragmatic "goodness" and the use of conventional expressions, Taguchi et al. (2013, 2016) integrated appropriate use and accurate production of conventional expressions into a rating scale for speech act production. Future work might attempt to correlate pragmatic ratings (without a formulaic component) to learner production of conventional expressions evaluated separately to determine what each contributes to the perception of learner production.

How Second Language Pragmatics Contributes to the Study of Formulaic Language

In 1998, Granger linked growing research in pragmatics to research in FL. Although relatively few studies in L2 pragmatics have directly focused on conventional expressions, research in pragmatics can contribute significantly to the general study of FL.

The first contribution is a methodological one. Discourse completion tasks used to elicit production in pragmatics directly facilitate the study of conventional expressions by eliciting relatively dense, free production of such expressions. Discourse completion tasks present participants with scenarios that specify setting, addressee, and the communicative goal of a speech event. They may also include pictures of the addressee or the item discussed, and may even include spoken turns to which the participants reply. Oral tasks can be time-pressured to simulate the online nature of conversation, and an initiating turn followed by the learners' turn can simulate the first two turns in a conversation. Time pressure has been argued to favour the use of formulas (Edmonds, 2014; Weinert, 1995), allowing learners to demonstrate their knowledge of FL for pragmatics. Using conversation simulation allows all participants to respond to an identical prompt. Moreover, the elicitation format allows easy comparison of different populations. In L2 pragmatics, learners are often compared to native speakers or to other learners at different levels of proficiency, hence allowing for interpretations of cross-sectional development and influence of proficiency.

Having such dense production of conventional expressions leads to a number of discoveries. The one I want to emphasize here is that dense production has allowed us to track the syntactic development of conventional expressions (Bardovi-Harlig, 2009; Bardovi-Harlig & Stringer, 2017). This is the second main (and unexpected) contribution of pragmatics to a more general understanding of FL. The dense production of conventional expressions by learners at multiple levels of development showed that, in addition to producing complete, targetlike conventional expressions, learners may also produce attempts at the target expression that reveal their knowledge of what response is culturally and pragmatically appropriate in a specific context, without producing the full expression. That is, such dense production of conventional expressions by members of the speech community revealed what the target was, and this assists in interpreting learner production. In addition, it shows that the acquisition of conventional expressions is not an all-or-nothing proposition; instead, syntactic development is driven by grammar. Examples include attempts at *Sorry I'm late* in apology contexts (*sorry for lating, sorry about my late, I am sorry from late,* and *sorry to/too late*), *I'm just looking* in declining an offer (*I just look, I just looking, I'll just looking,* and *Just I'm looking*), and *I really appreciate it* in thanking scenarios (*Appreciate!, I'm appreciate, I appreciate that for you, I will appreciate it to you*; Bardovi-Harlig & Stringer, 2017). An unsolicited example was produced by a graduate student the semester I was writing this paper, when she handed in her paper saying, "sorry for the late". Similar examples were reported for L2 Chinese (Bardovi-Harlig & Su, submitted; Taguchi et al., 2013).

We can relate these examples to observations about interlanguage forms of FSs that have been reported in other studies. Osborne (2008) reports examples of pluralized adjectives in FSs produced by advanced learners. He cites as examples both loose compounds (*bathrooms fittings, diets ads, adults smokers*) and formulaic units (*in others words, the good olds times, basics rights*). Dai and Ding (2010) conducted error analyses of formulas (but offered only one example), suggesting that learners use interlanguage forms of formulas. Additional examples of interlanguage forms of conventional expressions come from L2 pragmatics. These include *I very appreciate* (Eisenstein & Bodman, 1986), *I am agree with you, Are you agree with me?* (Foster, 2001) and *Watch up* (*Watch out*), and *Time is off* (*Time's up*) (Scarcella, 1979).

There are stages of development in the acquisition of conventional expressions, much like other areas of language. It helps us understand why mastery of FSs are thought to be a sign of advanced language learners (Boers & Lindstromberg, 2012;

Yorio, 1989). Learners may know the rudiments of an expression (the lexical core) before they know the whole expression. The same patterns of acquisition can be found cross-linguistically (at least in English and Chinese). One possible acquisitional sequence is suggested by the work of Bardovi-Harlig and Su (submitted):

> Nontargetlike speech act (nonalignment of speech act required by context) →targetlike speech act (alignment with context) with nontargetlike lexical resources → target lexical core→ full conventional expression

Finally, not every pragmatic context is characterized by high rates of FL (Bardovi-Harlig, 2012b, on variation; Bardovi-Harlig, 2016). For example, Taguchi et al. (2016) experimentally contrast speech acts realized by conventional expressions with those are not realized with conventional expressions.

How the Study of Formulaic Language Contributes to Second Language Pragmatics

One contribution that the general study of FL makes to the investigation of conventional expressions in pragmatics is framing the discussion of FL. There are many areas that research in pragmatics generally does not investigate, such as processing, although there are crossover studies such as Edmonds (2014). Although pragmatics research has focused on production, in order to participate in conversations, learners must constantly process incoming language in real time.

A particularly influential tool from research on FL has been the use of corpora. General corpora cannot replace traditional means of elicited production in pragmatic research (oral DCTs, role plays, and elicited conversations), but they can be very useful in determining the frequency of pragmatic routines, given a pragmatically appropriate corpus. Frequency information over a large number of speakers can complement the higher-density data collection from purpose-built pragmatics tasks as long as mode and register are matched.

Finally, instruction of pragmatic routines has drawn on both pragmatics pedagogy and instruction of FL. Instruction in pragmatic routines has used both an academic corpus (the Michigan Corpus for Academic Spoken English) for teaching English for Academic Purposes (Bardovi-Harlig et al., 2015a; Bardovi-Harlig et al., 2017) and the Russian National Corpus (Furniss, 2016, 2017) for teaching routines for social interaction. Providing authentic input is key in pragmatics instruction. (See also, Pellicer-Sánchez & Boers, this volume, on pedagogical approaches to the teaching and learning of FL.)

Conclusions and Future Directions

Just as Granger (1998) predicted, the acquisition of L2 pragmatics has proven to be a fruitful area of investigation for conventional expressions. While the elicitation tasks used in pragmatics have yielded very interesting results for both research in L2 pragmatics and in other areas of acquisition and use of FL in second language, much remains to be done. One area for future research is the identification of additional conventional expressions (and verification of their conventionality in the relevant speech communities). The range of target languages could also be expanded, as well as the speech domains within those languages, including both daily interactions and institutional and professional interactions (such as those in medical, legal, or business settings).

One more area is to investigate how and why certain conventional expressions are acquired before others. When there is variation in the target expression such as "I'll call you back" and "I'll call you later", learners seem to prefer the transparent form, "I'll call you later". Syntactic complexity may also play a role, either at the level of internal structure of the conventional expression or at the level of complementation (Bardovi-Harlig et al., 2017). Learner variables have been explored, but how do language variables such as transparency, salience, frequency, and composition (among others) influence the initial selection of target expressions for the learner?

Another avenue of exploration is the role of multifunctionality in the L2 acquisition of lexical items, such as conventional expressions and pragmatic routines. Will learners who can use "that's right" as an agreement routine notice and incorporate functional equivalents, such as "you're right" and "that's true", whether on their own or following instruction, or will they maintain one-meaning, one-form and persist in using "that's right"? That raises the final area of investigation, the effect of integrating pragmatics instruction and instruction on conventional expressions, which is still rather new, especially in pragmatics.

While there are many exciting avenues of research to explore, it is clear that the integration of pragmatics with other areas of inquiry into the second language acquisition and use of FL will enrich the inquiry on both sides.

Notes

1 For a review of formulaic language in pragmatics more generally, see Bardovi-Harlig (2012), and for Applied Linguistics, see the 2012 ARAL volume on formulaic language.
2 For a discussion of formulaicity in pragmatics, see "How formulaic is pragmatics?" Bardovi-Harlig (2016); see also Taguchi et al. (2016) for a comparison of speech acts realized by conventional expressions and those that are not.
3 One reviewer and, over the years, various audience members have pointed out that native-speaker intuition may also be questionable in other areas as well. That may be true, but I limit my claim to pragmatics and to Wolfson's well-known demonstration.
4 For a discussion of elicitation tasks, see Bardovi-Harlig et al. (2015a).

References

Alali, F. A., & Schmitt, N. (2012). Teaching formulaic sequences: The same as or different from teaching single words? *TESOL Journal*, *3*(2), 153–180.

Bardovi-Harlig, K. (2009). Conventional expressions as a pragmalinguistic resource: Recognition and production of conventional expressions in L2 pragmatics. *Language Learning, 59*(4), 755–795.

Bardovi-Harlig, K. (2010). Recognition of conventional expressions in L2 pragmatics. In G. Kasper, H. t. Nguyen, D. R. Yoshimi, & J. K. Yoshioka (Eds.), *Pragmatics and language learning* (Vol. 12, pp. 141–162). Honolulu, HI: University of Hawai'i, National Foreign Language Resource Center.

Bardovi-Harlig, K. (2012a). Formulas, routines, and conventional expressions in pragmatics research. *ARAL, 32*, 206–227.

Bardovi-Harlig, K. (2012b). Pragmatic variation and conventional expressions. In J. C. Félix-Brasdefer & D. Koike (Eds.), *Pragmatic variation in first and second language contexts: Methodological issues* (pp. 141–173). Amsterdam: John Benjamins.

Bardovi-Harlig, K. (2014). Awareness of meaning of conventional expressions in second language pragmatics. *Language Awareness, 23*(1–2), 41–56.

Bardovi-Harlig, K. (2016). How formulaic is pragmatics? In K. Bardovi-Harlig, & J. C. Félix-Brasdefer (Eds.), *Pragmatics and Language Learning* (Vol. 14, pp. 325–340). Honolulu, HI: University of Hawai'i, National Foreign Language Resource Center.

Bardovi-Harlig, K., & Bastos, M.-T. (2011). Proficiency, length of stay, and intensity of interaction and the acquisition of conventional expressions in L2 pragmatics. *Intercultural Pragmatics, 8*(3), 347–384.

Bardovi-Harlig, K., Bastos, M.-T., Burghardt, B., Chappetto, E., Nickels, E., & Rose, M. (2010). The use of conventional expressions and utterance length in L2 pragmatics. In G. Kasper, H. t. Nguyen, D. R. Yoshimi, & J. K. Yoshioka (Eds.), *Pragmatics and language learning* (Vol. 12, pp. 163–186). Honolulu, HI: University of Hawai'i, National Foreign Language Resource Center.

Bardovi-Harlig, K., & Mossman, S. (2016). Corpus-based materials development for teaching and learning pragmatic routines. In B. Tomlinson (Ed.) *SLA research and materials development for language learning* (pp. 250–267). New York, NY: Taylor and Francis.

Bardovi-Harlig, K., Mossman, S., & Su, Y. (2017). The effect of corpus-based instruction on pragmatic routines. *Language Learning & Technology, 21*(3), 76–103.

Bardovi-Harlig, K., Mossman, S., & Vellenga, H. E. (2015a). The effect of instruction on pragmatic routines in academic discussion. *Language Teaching Research, 19*(3), 324–350.

Bardovi-Harlig, K., Mossman, S., & Vellenga, H. E. (2015b). Developing corpus-based materials to teach pragmatic routines. *TESOL Journal, 6*(3), 499–526.

Bardovi-Harlig, K., Rose, M., & Nickels, E. (2008). The influence of first language and level of development in the use of conventional expressions of thanking, apologizing, and refusing. In M. Bowles, R. Foote, S. Perpiñán, & R. Bhatt (Eds.), *Selected proceedings of the 2007 Second Language Research Forum* (pp. 113–130). Somerville, MA: Cascadilla Proceedings Project.

Bardovi-Harlig, K., & Stringer, D. (2017). Unconventional expressions: Productive syntax in the L2 acquisition of formulaic language. *Second Language Research, 33*(1), 61–90.

Bardovi-Harlig, K., & Su, Y. (submitted). Conventional expressions as a pragmalinguistic resource in L2 Chinese. Manuscript submitted for publication.

Bardovi-Harlig, K., & Vellenga, H. E. (2012). The effect of instruction on conventional expressions in L2 pragmatics. *System, 40*(1), 77–89.

Barron, A. (2003). *Acquisition in interlanguage pragmatics: Learning how to do things with words in a study abroad context*. Amsterdam: John Benjamins.

Biber, D., Conrad, S., & Cortes, V. (2004). If you look at ... Lexical bundles in university teaching and textbooks. *Applied Linguistics, 25*(3), 371–405.

Biber, D., Johansson, S., Leech, G., Conrad, S., & Finegan, E. (1999). *Longman grammar of spoken and written English*. Essex: Pearson Education.

Blum-Kulka, S. (1989). Playing it safe: The role of conventionality in indirectness. In S. Blum-Kulka, J. House, & G. Kasper (Eds.), *Cross-cultural pragmatics: Requests and apologies* (pp. 37–70). Norwood, NJ: Ablex.

Boers, F., & Lindstromberg, S. (2012). Experimental and intervention studies on formulaic sequences in a second language. *Annual Review of Applied Linguistics, 32*, 83–109.

Cook, V. J. (1991). The poverty of the stimulus argument and multi-competence. *Second Language Research, 7*(2), 103–117

Coulmas, F. (1981). *Conversational routine: Explorations in standardized communication situations and prepatterned speech*. The Hague: Mouton.

Culpeper, J. (2010). Conventional impoliteness formula. *Journal of Pragmatics, 42*(12), 3232–3245.

Dai, Z., & Ding, Y. (2010). Effectiveness of text memorization in EFL learning of Chinese students. In D. Wood (Ed.), *Perspectives on formulaic language: Acquisition and communication* (pp. 71–87). London: Continuum.

Edmonds, A. (2014). Conventional expressions: Investigating pragmatics and processing. *Studies in Second Language Acquisition, 36*(1), 69–99.

Eisenstein, M., & Bodman, J. W. (1986). "I very appreciate": Expressions of gratitude by native and non-native speakers of American English. *Applied Linguistics, 7*(2), 167–185.

Erman, B., & Warren, B. (2000). The idiom principle and the open choice principle. *Text, 20*(1), 29–62.

Félix-Brasdefer, J. C., & Hasler-Barker, M. (2015). Complimenting in Spanish in a short-term study abroad context. *System, 48*, 75–85.

Forsberg, F. (2010). Using conventional sequences in L2 French. *IRAL, 48*(1), 25–51.

Foster, P. (2001). Rules and routines: A consideration of their role in the task-based language production of native and non-native speakers. In M. Bygate, P. Skehan, & M. Swain (Eds.), *Researching pedagogical tasks: Second language learning, teaching and testing* (pp. 75–93). Harlow: Longman.

Furniss, E. A. (2016). Teaching the pragmatics of Russian conversation using a corpus-referred website. *Language Learning & Technology, 20*, 38–60.

Furniss, E. (2017). Teaching pragmatics with corpus data: The development of a corpus-referred website for the instruction of routine formulas in Russian. In J. Romero-Trillo (Ed.), *Yearbook of corpus linguistics and pragmatics* (Vol. 4, pp. 129–152). Switzerland: Springer.

Granger, S. (1998). Prefabricated patterns in advanced EFL writing: Collocations and formulae. In A. P. Cowie (Ed.), *Phraseology: Theory, analysis, and applications* (pp. 145–160). Oxford: Clarendon.

House, J. (1996). Developing pragmatic fluency in English as a foreign language: Routines and metapragmatic awareness. *Studies in Second Language Acquisition, 18*(1), 225–252.

Jones, M., & Haywood, S. (2004). Facilitating the acquisition of formulaic sequences: An exploratory study in an EAP context. In N. Schmitt (Ed.), *Formulaic sequences: Acquisition, processing and use* (pp. 269–300). Amsterdam: John Benjamins.

Kecskes, I. (2000). Conceptual fluency and the use of situation-bound utterances. *Links & Letters, 7*, 145–161.

Leech, G. (1983). *Principles of pragmatics*. New York, NY: Longman.

Myles, F., Hooper, J., & Mitchell, R. (1998). Rote or rule? Exploring the role of formulaic language in classroom foreign language learning. *Language Learning, 48*(3), 323–363.

Osborne, J. (2008). Phraseology effects as a trigger for errors in L2 English: The case of more advanced learners. In F. Meunier & S. Granger (Eds.), *Phraseology in foreign language learning and teaching* (pp. 67–83). Amsterdam: John Benjamins.

Pawley, A., & Syder, F. H. (1983). Two puzzles for linguistic theory: Nativelike selection and nativelike fluency. In J. C. Richards & R. W. Schmidt (Eds.), *Language and communication* (pp. 191–226). London: Longman.

Reiter, R. M., Rainey, I., & Fulcher, G. (2005). A comparative study of certainty and conventional indirectness: Evidence from British English and Peninsular Spanish. *Applied Linguistics, 26*(1), 1–31.

Revier, R. L. (2009). Evaluating a new test of *whole* English Collocations. In A. Barfield & H. Gyllstad (Eds.), *Researching collocations in another language: Multiple interpretations* (pp.125–138). London: Palgrave Macmillan.

Roever, C. (2005). *Testing ESL pragmatics: Development and validation of a web-based assessment battery*. Berlin: Peter Lang.

Roever, C. (2012). What learners get for free: Learning of routine formulae in ESL and EFL environments. *ELT Journal, 66*(1), 10–21.

Scarcella, R. C. (1979). Watch up! *Working Papers in Bilingualism, 19*, 79–88.

Schmitt, N., Grandage, S., & Adolphs, S. (2004). Are corpus-derived recurrent clusters psycholinguistically valid? In N. Schmitt (Ed.), *Formulaic sequences: Acquisition, processing, and use* (pp 127–151). Amsterdam: John Benjamins.

Sharifian, F. (2008). Cultural schemas in L1 and L2 compliment responses: A study of Persian-speaking learners of English. *Journal of Politeness Research: Language, Behavior, Culture, 4*(1), 55–80.

Simpson, R. C., Briggs, S. L., Ovens, J., & Swales, J. M. (2002). *The Michigan corpus of academic spoken English*. Retrieved from http://quod.lib.umich.edu/m/micase.

Taguchi, N. (2011). The effect of L2 proficiency and study-abroad experience on pragmatic comprehension. *Language Learning, 61*(3), 1–36.

Taguchi, N., Li, S., & Xiao, F. (2013). Production of formulaic expressions in L2 Chinese: A developmental investigation in a study abroad context. *Chinese as a Second Language Research, 2*(1), 23–58.

Taguchi, N., Xiao, F., & Li, S. (2016). Effects of intercultural competence and social interaction on speech act production in a Chinese study abroad context. *The Modern Language Journal, 100*(4), 775–796.

Tateyama, Y. (2001). Explicit and implicit teaching of pragmatic routines. In K. Rose & G. Kasper (Eds.), *Pragmatics in language teaching* (pp. 200–222). Cambridge: Cambridge University Press.

Terkourafi, M. (2002). Politeness and formulaicity: Evidence from Cypriot Greek. *Journal of Greek Linguistics, 3*(1), 179–201.

Thomas, J. (1983). Cross-cultural pragmatic failure. *Applied linguistics, 4*(2), 91–112.

Weinert, R. (1995). The role of formulaic language in second language acquisition: A review. *Applied Linguistics, 16*(2), 180–205.

Wolfson, N. (1986). Research methodology and the question of validity. *TESOL Quarterly, 20*(4), 689–699.

Wong, H. (2012). *Use of formulaic sequences in task-based oral production of Chinese* (Unpublished doctoral dissertation). Durham University, Durham.

Yang, J. (2016). CFL learners' recognition and production of pragmatic routine formulae. *Chinese as a Second Language, 51*(1), 29–61.

Yorio, C. (1989). Idiomaticity as an indicator of second language proficiency. In K. Hyltenstam & L. K. Obler (Eds.), *Bilingualism across the lifespan* (pp. 55–72). Cambridge: Cambridge University Press.

6
HUMOR AND FORMULAIC LANGUAGE IN SECOND LANGUAGE LEARNING

Nancy Bell and Stephen Skalicky

Introduction

What does formulaic language (FL) have to do with humor, a type of discourse that is typically thought to rely heavily on innovation and surprise? A great deal, as it turns out. In fact, both humor and irony[1] frequently exploit formulaic sequences (FSs) in their construction. Veale (2012b) argues convincingly that linguistic creativity is based on our knowledge of the formulas and conventions of language and that we "use this familiar knowledge to create familiar surprises for an audience, to concoct novel uses of language that depart from the familiar yet are understandable only in relation to the familiar" (p. x). If we consider structures to range on a continuum from more to less formulaic, we might place idioms on the most formulaic side, given that these are largely frozen constructions, whose meaning cannot be deduced by understanding the individual words. Idioms are highly formulaic at the lexical level, thus it is difficult to change a word in the phrase "at the drop of a hat" and retain the meaning of doing something without hesitation. Metaphors and similes, on the other hand, are highly formulaic in terms of their syntactic structure, yet they offer greater creativity in terms of lexical items that can be used to fill the slots: as big as a house/whale/baseball/rose bush. Many social routines also draw on conventional forms, but these can often be deployed flexibly, allowing for both greater creativity and nuance. For instance, an apology can be formulated with more or fewer hedges or boosters: "I'm rather sorry about that" vs. "I'm so incredibly sorry about that". Highly creative language can be found in artistic forms of language, such as poetry, but also in the mundane efforts of a speaker – first language (L1) or second language (L2) – using circumlocutions in trying to recall or evoke a specific term.

Humor and irony fall toward the less formulaic end of the continuum. As already noted, humor thrives on the new and unexpected, yet it is frequently constructed by drawing on knowledge of FL and subverting it. Thus, the familiar joke forms of children may still get a guffaw from adults if they offer a novel take:

Question: Why did the chicken cross the basketball court?
Answer: He heard the referee calling fowls.
(www.golberz.com/2009/12/top-10-why-did-chicken-cross-road-jokes.html)

The formulaic nature of social routines, idiomatic expressions, figurative language, and collocations can all be similarly disrupted for humor, as long as both speaker and audience are familiar with the norms on which the joke is built. As Veale (2012b) notes, "Behind every creative riff on a familiar form lies an equally familiar idea or stock mental image" (p. 67). Thus, novel forms typically rely on the audience's ability to draw on cultural, as well as linguistic, knowledge.

It is clear, then, that both the appreciation and construction of much humor relies on knowledge of conventional and FL, as well as the cultural norms these refer to. Yet the identification and acquisition of formulaic expressions is highly challenging for L2 users (Bell, 2011; Kim, 2014; Shively, Menke, & Manzón-Omundson, 2008). Bell (2012b) reviewed research on formulaic expressions and L2 language play, describing the theoretical relationship between the two, as well as examining the types and functions of L2 play with FL. That review drew largely on qualitative work, and at that time, she noted that "investigations into language play and formulaic language have largely taken place without reference to each other" (p. 198) and called for the development of "a unified model that articulates the relationship between the functions and processing of formulaic language and language play" (p. 199). In the intervening years, little has been done to advance this agenda; however, given the opportunity to revisit this important topic, we have opted for a new lens and a renewed call for research. In this review, we focus primarily on work from corpus linguistics that teases apart the relationship between formulaic expressions with humor and irony. Due to the paucity of L2 studies of this phenomenon, we begin by focusing largely on L1 research, thus much of this chapter should be read as a research agenda for the study of the detection, comprehension, and use of FSs for humor and irony by L2 users using corpus linguistic methods.

First Language Corpus Studies of Humor and Irony

In this section, we focus primarily on L1 corpus investigations of humor and irony, as these studies afford the most direct insight into the formulaic profiles of humor and irony. Many of these works draw on Sinclairian corpus perspectives, which maintain that language is largely patterned at both the local, concrete level (e.g., collocations) and at larger, abstract levels (i.e., extended units of meaning; Sinclair, 1991, 2004; Stubbs, 2001), although similar arguments have been made from construction grammar perspectives (Antonopoulou & Nikiforidou, 2009, 2011; Antonopoulou, Nikiforidou, & Tsakona, 2015). In addition, we review research which has demonstrated that some examples of humor and irony, such as negative sarcasm and humorous similes, are highly formulaic (e.g., Giora, Drucker, & Fein, 2014; Veale, 2012a). As a whole, these studies depict a complex relationship among humor, irony, and FL. The purpose of this section is to briefly review these studies before discussing how these theories present challenges for L2 learners attempting to use/learn humor and irony.

Humor and Irony as Non-Formulaic

Corpus researchers from the Sinclairian perspective have posited that creative language, such as humor and irony, is the result of deviations from typified language patterns. Hoey's (2005) theory of Lexical Priming weds Sinclarian corpus linguistics with psycholinguistics by arguing that language patterns, such as collocations, colligation, and semantic associations are psychologically reinforced in the mental lexicon (i.e., a person's mental catalog of linguistic knowledge) as language users are exposed to language input. Specifically, Hoey referred to these mental associations as *priming*s, arguing that lexical items are primed to occur with certain other lexical items, in certain grammatical roles, and in certain semantic and pragmatic categories. One of the more illustrative examples Hoey uses to advance this theory is the *Drinking Problem Hypothesis*, which posits that humor, ambiguity, and other types of linguistic creativity are the result of subversions or conflicts among primings associated with different senses of polysemous words. Specifically, different senses of polysemous words will form their own primings, and that when these primings are violated, the result is ambiguous, humorous, or novel.

The *Drinking Problem Hypothesis* is based on a scene from the 1980 movie *Airplane*. In the scene, the main character is said to have a drinking problem (i.e., is unable to control the amount of alcohol he drinks). The scene then shows the main character spilling a beverage down his face while trying to drink from a glass. The drinking *problem* is thus related to physical inability and not to alcoholism. According to Hoey (2005), because the collocation *drinking problem* and its variants are more commonly associated with discussions of alcoholism, the phrase primes that specific meaning. The other, unusual meaning that *could* be a result of the collocation *drinking problem* (i.e., that one has difficulty with drinking liquids) is not typical nor expected, and thus in the scene from *Airplane* the humor is a result of the audience being forced to reinterpret the meaning of *drinking problem* in a new, unexpected context.

Hanks (2013) put forth a similar theory, wherein he described language as operating via sets of *norms* and *exploitations*. Hanks (2013) argued that words do not have inherent meanings, but rather possess "meaning potentials" (p. 73) that are fully realized once used in discourse. A meaning potential is a collection of different semantic components that are compatible or incompatible with other words' meaning potentials. While meaning potentials between words are typically used in an expected and agreeable manner, examples of humor such as puns and other word play purposefully evoke mutually incompatible meaning potentials. In other words, according to Hanks, purposeful deviations from expectations do not occur *except* when authors are attempting to be humorous or otherwise creative with language.

Goatly (2012, see also 2017) conducted an extensive analysis of multiple jokes and other examples of humor from the perspective of Lexical Priming. His work revealed that key phrases in his examples exploited primings at the levels of collocation, colligation, or semantic preference when compared to usage in generalized corpora. Goatly also identified an additional type of priming found in an example of humorous news satire: primings of genre or register expectations. This type of priming is not covered under Hoey's theory, but operates using the same basic principles (i.e., readers are primed to expect that certain genre and register conventions will be upheld). Goatly ultimately concluded that some examples of linguistic humor are heavily reliant on the purposeful replacement of expected with unexpected primings, but that Lexical Priming could not explain every instance of humor.

Other empirical investigations have produced similar results. A study of ironic poetry by Louw (1993) predates Hoey (2005) and Hanks (2013), but follows similar logic as Lexical Priming theory. Louw (1993) examined how atypical uses of the word *utterly* could trigger ironic meaning. Louw argued that because *utterly* commonly patterns with negative collocates (e.g., *utterly against, utterly burned, utterly demolished*), the word *utterly* takes on an inherently negative connotation (or prosody, as Louw described it). Therefore, when *utterly* is paired with a positive word (e.g., *utterly dedicated, utterly good, utterly grand, utterly venerable*, p. 163), the apparent positive meaning of these phrases is coloured by the negative prosody inherent in *utterly*. Thus, the positive literal meaning is interpreted negatively, resulting in an ironic opposition of intended meaning.

In a series of corpus studies, Partington (Partington, 2007, 2009, 2011a, 2011b) demonstrated how both irony and humorous word play subvert formulaic patterns at the levels of collocation, colligation, and semantic association. In regards to irony, Partington described irony as a "reversal of evaluation" (Partington, 2007, p. 1554) that functioned by exploiting a reader's expectations for the evaluation of entities through the purposeful contrasting of unexpected collocations (Partington, 2011b). For example, the phrase "*Beckett thinks there is a great deal to be said for death*" creates an ironic interpretation by placing a lexical item with an inherently negative connotation (i.e., *death*) in a lexical context that typically casts a positive evaluation on the noun or subject it precedes (i.e., *to be said for*). In terms of humor, Partington (2009) examined word play (operationalized as puns) in a corpus of British newspaper headlines from the perspective of Lexical Priming.

Partington argued that the overriding of polysemous primings in a pun such as "*Is the tomb of Karl Marx just another communist **plot**?*" forces a reader to shift from an idiomatic mode of reading (i.e., single, automatic choice) to an open choice mode of reading (i.e., manual interpretation of novel constructions).

In a study of humorous satirical headlines, Skalicky (in press) reported that certain satirical headlines employ extremely infrequent collocations or semantic associations when compared to a generalized reference corpus. For example, the satirical headline *Russian Officials Promise Low Death Toll for Olympics* contains the phrase *low death toll*, a collocation which only occurs twice in the Corpus of Contemporary American English (COCA; Davies, 2008). Instead, *death toll* is frequently preceded by adjectives related to certainty (e.g., *official death toll*) or an ongoing process (e.g., *rising death toll*). However, other satirical headlines did not deviate from linguistic patterns at all, and instead relied on background knowledge of topics and typical discourse coverage of events (e.g., *Tsunami Death Toll Rises to 36 Americans* in reference to the deadly 2011 tsunami in the Indian Ocean).

Humor and Irony as Formulaic

Although the previous studies provide evidence supporting the claim that humor and verbal irony can result from deviations from typical language patterns, other studies have demonstrated that some instances of humor and irony are highly formulaic because they employ consistent syntactic patterns. For example, several corpus and psycholinguistic studies have demonstrated that negative constructions such as *clever she is not* (Giora et al., 2013, p. 90) are recognized as sarcastic irony by default. Specifically, phrases such as *X is not his/her forte* or *X he/she is not*, when presented in a decontextualized format, are more frequently recognized as ironic (Giora et al., 2013; Giora, Drucker, Fein, & Mendelson, 2015). Follow-up corpus studies searching for these constructions revealed that in naturalistic discourse, high percentages (> 80%) of negative constructions formed in this manner are indeed sarcastic (Giora, 2016; Giora et al., 2014; Giora et al., 2013)

The notion of "linguistic readymades" (Veale, 2013b, p. 38) used as vehicles for creative purposes further attests to the potential for humor and irony to be formulaic. Specifically, syntactic patterns that form certain similes, such as *about as X as a Y*, are evidence of a speaker's intention to be creative and humorous (Veale, 2012a), and are more commonly ironic and humorous than straight (i.e., simple comparisons; Veale, 2012b, 2013a). However, even though non-humorous or ironic similes share the same structure with humorous and ironic similes, humorous similes contain an additional negative affective dimension that invites a humorous interpretation and distinguishes them from straight comparison similes (Veale, 2013a).

As a whole, the studies reviewed thus far indicate that humor and irony have a complex relation with FL. On the one hand, humor and irony can result from deviations from FL (e.g., collocations), while on the other hand, some examples of humor and irony are extremely formulaic in structure (e.g., humorous similes). Additionally, there are examples of humor and irony that do not follow humor or irony formulas and also do not deviate from expected language patterns (e.g., some humorous satirical headlines, Skalicky, in press). This complex relationship among humor, irony, and FL provides several implications for L2 learners.

Implications for Second Language Learners

Hoey's theory of Lexical Priming is a usage-based explanation of language acquisition which argues that formulaic patterns found in texts are the result of mental representations, rather than any inherent structure of a language (Pace-Sigge, 2013). Usage-based theories of language acquisition maintain that repeated exposure to language in use builds and reinforces cognitive representations of language (Bybee, 2006, 2008; Ellis & Wulff, 2015; Wulff, this volume). Therefore, one of the primary challenges an L2 user will face when attempting to recognize or produce humor or irony is developing sufficient mental representations of frequent and expected language patterns. Specifically, a catalog of polysemous senses is important in order to fully reconcile many priming violations. Empirical investigations of English L2 vocabulary development suggests that learners initially acquire the most frequent senses of polysemous words within the first four months of learning before then cataloging additional senses (Crossley, Salsbury, & McNamara, 2010). However, even advanced L2 users encounter sense overlap from their L1, which can complicate the number of available senses and interpretations when an L2 user attempts to disambiguate the meaning of an ambiguous, polysemous word (Elston-Guttler & Williams, 2008). Advanced L2 participants also demonstrate no effects of semantic priming based on polysemous word senses, suggesting the integration of polysemous senses is incomplete when compared to a native speaker of a language (Crossley & Skalicky, in press). As a whole, these studies suggest that even at advanced proficiency levels, L2 learners may still lack the requisite knowledge of polysemous senses needed in order to fully understand common and uncommon formulaic uses of those words, and thus lack the full ability to comprehend the resultant humor or irony deviations from those patterns.

The second major challenge, then, is for L2 users to develop the ability to detect purposeful deviations from these patterns with humorous or ironic intent. There are, to our knowledge, just two empirical studies that have investigated the ability for L2 learners to detect deviations from expected linguistic patterns for humorous or ironic means. Vaid, López, and Martínez (2015) directly tested the ability of 27 monolingual English and 21 bilingual Spanish L1 English L2 users to identify humorous from non-humorous sentences. In this study, participants saw either joke or non-joke stimuli and categorized the stimuli as humorous or non-humorous. Half of the jokes presented to participants involved some sort of lexical incongruity (i.e., word play or violations of semantic or syntactic expectations), while the other half involved an incongruity based on social or cultural knowledge. Their results suggested that while both monolingual and bilingual users were slower to categorize the lexical jokes compared to the social or cultural knowledge jokes, accuracy in classification was significantly higher for the lexical jokes. The results also suggested that bilinguals took longer to classify a sentence as a non-joke, and that bilinguals demonstrated a trend towards higher accuracy in classifying jokes than monolinguals. The authors interpreted this finding as evidence suggesting the bilingual participants were more careful when processing the L2 input, resulting in slower reading times but higher accuracy. However, little information about the language proficiency of these participants was reported, aside from knowing that only participants who self-rated their language ability as a 4 or higher on a 7-point scale were included in the study, making it difficult to identify solid links between L2 English proficiency and ability to identify incongruity in the form of lexical violations.

Yet, incongruity resolution (i.e., humor appreciation) is not necessary to identify an utterance as humorous, as research in L2 humor recognition has shown (Bell, 2007). At the same time, in a study with similarities to Vaid et al. (2015), Shardakova (2016a) found that "learners were unable to disentangle humor detection from humor appreciation, so when they did not like the humor they did not register it" (p. 10). In other words, when learners did not enjoy a joke, they did not report it as humorous. Shardakova's participants were 32 native speakers of Russian and 98 Americans learning Russian. Rather than using self-reports of language proficiency, the ACTFL proficiency scale was used, and the American participants ranged from Intermediate High to Superior on that scale. Even participants at the Superior level, who might be expected to identify lexical violations, did not report these if they did not find them amusing. Shardakova (2016a) did find that both native speakers of Russian and L2 learners often relied on identification of unusual words or phrases as a cue to humor. However, the learners were less successful due to their limited ability to recognize conventional versus non-conventional usages, which resulted not only in them missing cues to humor but also in incorrectly identifying as cues language that was merely a typical use of a formulaic phrase. Knowledge of generic conventions and genre expectations also played a part in the learners' assessment of humor. Shardakova used literary and news texts in this study, and although learners were readily able to comprehend meaning in both texts, they were much more successful in identifying humor in the literary texts, where humor would be more expected.

A third challenge that exists when L2 users of English attempt to violate expected linguistic patterns for the purpose of producing humor or irony lies not in their own developing linguistic or socio-cultural competence, but in the ability and willingness of their interlocutor to recognize and accept unconventional formulations from an L2 user. The use of FL is a strong marker of nativeness (Ortaçtepe, 2013), and perhaps because of this, utterances by L2 users that are clearly – and purposefully – built on formulaic structures, but which also deviate from them in some way, seem to be particularly prone to being misconstrued as errors, rather than as humor or simply creative language play (Prodromou, 2007). Scholars of English as a lingua franca (ELF) have referred to this as the *territorial imperative*. As Seidlhofer (2009) explains, the use of FL demonstrates that one is a community member and follows the norms of the community: "If you fail to conform, you reveal that you do not belong. Any departure from the accepted wording of an idiomatic turn of phrase, no matter how slight, is likely to mark you as an outsider" (p. 198). While our discussion in the following section focuses on L2 pedagogical considerations, it is worth noting here that the remedy to the often frustrating and alienating problem of having one's attempts at L2 humor be received as errors must come from educational efforts, beginning in childhood, that seek to raise awareness among those with monolingual competence of language structure and functions, the process of language learning, and intercultural communication.

Instruction in Formulaic Language and Humor

Having access to a range of formulaic expressions is clearly important to the developing repertoire of L2 users, and, particularly given the challenge emergent bilinguals have in identifying such language, it is something that should be addressed in the classroom. Furthermore, evidence is mounting that humor, with its close relationship to FL, can facilitate L2 development. How might we fruitfully bring these two aspects of language, formulaic expressions and humor, together in the L2 classroom? In this section, we begin by briefly reviewing the evidence that humor facilitates recall of language and considering the ways that it might help raise learner awareness of conventional L2 forms and provide opportunities for practicing their use. We then consider approaches to the teaching of FL and of humor and discuss how the latter might be used to draw attention to, and thus facilitate the development of, conventional L2 forms.

A number of studies have demonstrated that humorous images and language are recalled better than serious, or even simply bizarre, images or language. This has mainly been demonstrated through experimental studies (Bates, Kintsch, Fletcher & Guiliani, 1980; Carlson, 2011; Schmidt, 1994, 2002; see also Strick, Holland, van Baaren, & Van Knippenberg, 2010 for a review) and for recall where language is encountered incidentally, rather than intentionally, as in the experimental conditions (Keenan, MacWhinney, & Mayhew, 1977). The incidental/intentional aspect of exposure to humorous material is important to take into consideration as a condition of learning. Humor thrives on surprise, so it is reasonable to ask whether the memory benefit for humorous stimuli can be expected to occur when participants are expecting to be tested on material (intentional learning) or whether spontaneous, unexpected exposure can also produce this result. Using decontextualized sentences, Schmidt and Williams (2001) found a positive result on recall for humor under both conditions. Humorous language encountered in naturally occurring conversation also seems subject to better recall than serious language, whether the learning is incidental (Keenan, MacWhinney, & Mayhew, 1977) or intentional (Bates et al., 1980). Classrooms are complex environments, however, and it should be noted that studies of the effect of humor on retention of course material have had mixed results, although one meta-analysis found a small, but consistent gain in lecture material recall (Martin, Preiss, Gayle & Allen, 2006). An additional caveat to these findings is that when items are presented or retrieved by a learner, they must be mixed – humorous items and serious items – for the facilitative effect on recall to occur (McDaniel, Dornburg, & Guynn, 2005).

Puns are one form of humor in which the serious and humorous meanings are inherently juxtaposed, and two studies have demonstrated that recall of the meanings of polysemous words are strongly subject to recall when they are presented in riddle or joke form for learners to decipher together (Lucas, 2005; Tocalli-Beller & Swain, 2007). Where these two studies examined the effect of tasks that intentionally exposed learners to humor and encouraged them to play with the L2, Bell (2012a) assessed recall in incidental encounters where new L2 forms were focused on in a playful or humorous manner. In comparison to unknown lexical items that were focused on seriously, those that were the subject of humorous attention were remembered better. The results were positive but less conclusive for form-based language play (versus the meaning-based play with vocabulary), perhaps simply because there were fewer instances of jocularity around L2 forms. Thus, with regard to the memory effect of humor for language learning specifically, evidence indicates that lexical items that are encountered in a playful context are subject to better recall than those that were encountered seriously. At present this has only been established with respect to individual lexical items, but, although it remains subject to empirical verification, it seems plausible that this would extend to FSs as well, although perhaps only with respect to meaning, but not necessarily form.

In addition to facilitating recall of L2 vocabulary, there is general agreement that humorous language play offers learners valuable opportunities for experimenting safely with new forms and functions, specifically as a way of developing new social voices and subject positions, often in a way that authentically resembles the type of talk found outside of a classroom context (Åhlund & Aronsson, 2015; Broner & Tarone, 2001; Laursen & Kolstrup, 2017; Pomerantz & Bell, 2007, 2011; Shardakova, 2016b; Waring, 2013). Much of this type of humorous interaction involves the identification of linguistic patterns. For instance, the time-tested role-play activity may introduce learners to some version of the common, conventional exchange between salespeople and shoppers:

A: Can I help you?
B: Thanks, I'm just looking.

As language teachers well know, learners usually need little encouragement to build on such language in silly and outrageous ways. This type of interaction is likely to reinforce knowledge of the conventional forms, while also potentially opening up new subject positions for L2 users knowing and playing with formulaic expressions.

Recent empirical investigations aiming to teach specific aspects of humor to L2 users have had generally positive outcomes (Kim, 2014, 2017, Kim & Lantolf, 2016 on sarcasm; Prichard & Rucynski, in press on satire; Hodson, 2014 on joke identification and comprehension). Recommendations for the design and implementation of tasks for learning about humor that are based on current research and theory have also been set forth (Bell & Pomerantz, 2015; Wulf, 2010). In addition, pedagogical interventions for FL are recognized as important for L2 users, given the difficulty of learning these, and, like tasks designed with teaching humor, have generally been found to be effective (see Pellicer-Sánchez & Boers, this volume). Given what this review has demonstrated about the relationship between FSs and a great deal of humor, might the two be joined together in activities that facilitate the acquisition of both? How might humor be used in the service of acquiring L2 FSs? And, turning the question around, how might formulaic expressions help learners recognize and produce L2 humor?

Humor may aid in the expansion of L2 users' repertoire of formulaic expressions since, as described above, it has been found to increase recall of new lexical items. This is crucial for FL, which is difficult to acquire and often requires memorization. This might be done by inserting humorous examples of FL into example dialogs or role plays. For instance, the sequence "Would you mind VERB+ing" will likely be remembered better if examples such as "Would you mind helping me?" and "Would you mind moving that?" are presented with something silly (for the context), like, "Would you mind worshipping me"? For this to be most effective, recall that serious and humorous examples should be mixed (McDaniel et al., 2005). Learners might be asked to do fill-in-the-blank exercises that require them to choose the appropriate intact phrase (Boers, Dang, & Strong, 2017), which also happens to be the humorous one.

Humorous pictures that illustrate the literal meaning of figurative formulaic phrases may aid in learning; however, Szczepaniak and Lew (2011, see also Boers, Lindstromberg, Littlemore, Stengers, & Eyckmans, 2008), who found that literal but non-humorous depictions facilitated idiom recall, caution that images that draw on the literal meaning of a phrase humorously may mislead learners about the meaning of the phrase. This remains an empirical question, however, as it also seems possible that the additional challenge of decoding the humor might lead to greater semantic elaboration and thus greater retention. Although less humorous and more likely to be broadly playful, it is also worth recalling that phonological repetition occurs in a good deal of FL. Boers (2013) estimates that nearly 20% of FL involves some type of repetition, including rhyming, alliteration, and assonance, while Eyckmans and Lindstromberg (2017), restricting their examination of sound repetition to alliteration or assonance in figurative idioms, find these occurring in up to 35% of those forms. Eyckmans and Lindstromberg

(2017) further noted learners recalled idioms more accurately following activities designed to raise awareness of phonological patterning.

As L2 users expand their repertoire of conventional L2 phrases, they can be encouraged to identify and produce purposeful deviations to create humor. Not only is this creative use of FL likely to reinforce knowledge of the conventional form and further linguistic development in general, but it is also the type of activity that can help L2 users gain a sense of ownership over their new language and expand their sociolinguistic competence (Tarone, 2000), as they subvert the typical sayings of common social actors, such as teachers and doctors, or in expressing emotions not usually unleashed in the classroom, such as anger or love. Bell and Pomerantz (2015) provide a framework for systematically integrating humor into the teaching of what are otherwise typically serious lessons in purely utilitarian uses of the L2, but we provide two examples here that are particularly relevant to the teaching of FL.

As learners begin to understand that FSs can be subverted for humorous ends, activities can be implemented that encourage the identification and even creation of humorous versions of conventional phrases. As an example, students can consider what other words they might put in place of "heart" in the phrase "Home is where the heart is", and imagine scenarios where they might jokingly use these. A recent meta-analysis found the use of corpus tools in L2 learning to be highly effective (Boulton & Cobb, 2017), and the evaluation of FSs is one productive use of linguistic corpora, allowing learners to check to see whether and how often their versions occur, as well as examine occurrences of the unusual phrase in its context to see how it is used. As noted earlier, infrequent collocations are often a cue to humor (Goatly, 2017; Skalicky, in press). A quick check on Google for "Home is where the head is" (a change that is easy to imagine a context for, and that maintains the alliteration) received 375,000 hits on Google, many as titles of magazine articles or in literary texts or song lyrics. The insertion of "leg", on the other hand, garners just a single hit and is much more difficult to imagine a context for. Students can imagine things other than body parts, as well, that might be where a "home" is, and check their usage.

Memorization, repetition, and rehearsal, reviled for some time, are again being recognized as legitimate L2 learning practices. Ding (2007) reports that memorization not only allows L2 users to learn language as FSs, rather than through rules and individual lexical items, but helps them attend in detail to the form of such chunks. In reviewing the role of repetition in L2 development, Larsen-Freeman (2012) emphasizes that no performance is ever exactly the same, as each results in some change to the system. What happens when a performance is repeated, then, is better described by the term *iteration*. Iteration, she explains, generates variation in the L2 system, which potentially opens up new language resources that the L2 user can deploy to communicate more effectively and in more nuanced ways across social situations. While FSs may need to be memorized, humorous play with such language can deliberately introduce iteration, not to mention make recitation less tedious. Many language learning tasks are relatively open, with the idea that learners will construct their own meanings, yet research has shown that activities that constrain learners' options by forcing them to be creative and construct new meanings result in richer, more complex language (Kim & Kellogg, 2007; Tin, 2011). Tin (2012, see also Tin, 2013) provides a framework and examples of three types of constraints – goal, input, and outcome – that can be placed on tasks to encourage creative L2 play, all of which could be applied to tasks involving the study of FL.

Finally, for overworked teachers, it is helpful to know that humor does not necessarily need to be formally and systematically incorporated into the L2 classroom. How teachers orient to humor – as off-task behaviour and therefore subject to sanction, or as a learning opportunity – may be just as important in providing learning opportunities. A growing number of studies have found greater experimentation, engagement, and authentic interaction in L2 classrooms where humorous play with language is accepted and even encouraged by teachers (e.g., Illés & Akcan, 2017; Lehtimaja, 2011; Reddington & Waring, 2015; van Dam & Bannink, 2017). With knowledge of the ways that FSs are constructed and how they function, language instructors may contribute a great deal to their acquisition simply by alerting students to features like phonological repetition, and by modelling and being receptive to play with these forms.

Conclusions and Future Directions

In this chapter, we have reviewed recent L1 corpus research that examines the relationship between FL and humor, and have considered how that research, in conjunction with the growing number of studies of L2 use and acquisition of humor, might inform our understanding of their development for L2 users and our pedagogical decisions. By necessity, the discussions were largely parallel, with inferences drawn about the implications of one on the other. We hope, however, that this review has demonstrated the close relationship between FSs and humor, as well as that, and how, these two might facilitate mutual development. In closing, we briefly set forth a research agenda to explore the intersection between conventional language and humor, and establish whether and how they might be used in conjunction in the L2 classroom to facilitate L2 development.

First, basic research must be conducted to understand how L2 users process, perceive, understand, and are able to produce humor with FSs. These issues must be explored with respect to different types of humor (e.g., pre-scripted jokes, sarcasm, teasing) and different types of FSs (e.g., conventional metaphors, collocations, social routines), as well as teasing apart questions of meaning versus form. Much of this work can be modelled on existing psycholinguistic and corpus-based studies of L1 users; however, additional avenues of inquiry specific to L2 users must also be addressed. For instance, how does L2 proficiency affect different learners' ability to engage with humor and FL? How do various aspects of formulaicity, requiring knowledge of linguistic, social, or generic conventions, interact with identification, appreciation, and production of L2 humor? What challenges does language versus culture pose for L2 users encountering humorous FSs?

Second, given the recognized need for L2 users to develop a repertoire of FSs, along with the potential of humor to facilitate that development, it is clear that there is a need to study a variety of pedagogical tasks that join the two aspects of language to assess whether and to what extent they are effective for learning either or both FSs and humor. Here again, replication of prior studies is possible. Specifically, those that have involved interventions that attempt to teach FL can be redesigned to incorporate an element of humor to test its effect on recall of conventional forms. Other studies might involve teaching formulaic aspects of humor, including polysemous words and any conventional structures that are used for cuing or responding to humor. The possibilities for research at the intersection of humor and FSs are wide ranging and show great promise for influencing L2 classroom practice.

Note

1 In this chapter, we review research related to both humor and irony because many examples of irony can result in humor. However, it is important to note that we do not consider irony to be a specific type of humor itself.

References

Åhlund, A., & Aronsson, K. (2015). Stylizations and alignments in a L2 classroom: Multiparty work in forming a community of practice. *Language & Communication, 43*, 11–26.

Antonopoulou, E., & Nikiforidou, K. (2009). Deconstructing verbal humour with construction grammar. In G. Brône & J. Vandaele (Eds.), *Cognitive poetics: Goals, gains and gaps* (pp. 289–317). Berlin: Mouton de Gruyter.

Antonopoulou, E., & Nikiforidou, K. (2011). Construction grammar and conventional discourse: A construction-based approach to discoursal incongruity. *Journal of Pragmatics, 43*(10), 2594–2609.

Antonopoulou, E., Nikiforidou, K., & Tsakona, V. (2015). Construction grammar and discoursal incongruity. In G. Brône, K. Feyaerts, & T. Veale (Eds.), *Cognitive linguistics and humour research* (pp. 13–47). Berlin: Mouton de Gruyter.

Bates, E., Kintsch, W., Fletcher, C., & Guiliani, V. (1980). The role of pronominalization and ellipsis in texts: Some memory experiments. *Journal of Experimental Psychology: Human Learning and Memory, 6*(6), 676–691.

Bell, N. (2007). Humour comprehension: Lessons learned from cross-cultural interaction. *Humour, 20*, 367–387.

Bell, N. (2011). Humour scholarship and TESOL: Applying findings and establishing a research agenda. *TESOL Quarterly, 45*(1), 134–159.

Bell, N. (2012a). Comparing playful and non-playful incidental attention to form. *Language Learning, 62*(1), 236–265.

Bell, N. (2012b). Formulaic language, creativity, and language play in a second language. *Annual Review of Applied Linguistics, 32*, 189–205.

Bell, N., & Pomerantz, A. (2015). *Humour in the classroom: A guide for language teachers and educational researchers*. New York, NY: Routledge.

Boers, F. (2013). Cognitive linguistic approaches to teaching vocabulary: Assessment and integration. *Language Teaching, 46*(2), 208–224.

Boers, F., Dang, T. C. T., & Strong, B. (2017). Comparing the effectiveness of phrase-focused exercises: A partial replication of Boers, Demecheleer, Coxhead, and Webb (2014). *Language Teaching Research, 21*(3), 362–380.

Boers, F., Lindstromberg, S., Littlemore, J., Stengers, H., & Eyckmans, J. (2008). Variables in the mnemonic effectiveness of pictorial elucidation. In F. Boers & S. Lindstromberg (Eds.), *Cognitive linguistic approaches to teaching vocabulary and phraseology* (pp. 189–216). Berlin: Mouton de Gruyter.

Boulton, A., & Cobb, T. (2017). Corpus use in language learning: A meta-analysis. *Language Learning, 67*(2), 348–393.

Broner, M., & Tarone, E. (2001). Is it fun? Language play in a fifth-grade Spanish immersion classroom. *The Modern Language Journal, 85*(iii), 363–379.

Bybee, J. (2006). From usage to grammar: The mind's response to repetition. *Language, 82*(4), 711–733.

Bybee, J. (2008). Usage-based grammar and second language acquisition. In P. Robinson & N. C. Ellis (Eds.), *Handbook of cognitive linguistics and second language acquisition* (pp. 216–236). New York: Routledge.

Carlson, K. (2011). The impact of humour on memory: Is the humour effect about humour? *Humour, 24*(1), 21–41.

Crossley, S., Salsbury, T., & McNamara, D. (2010). The development of polysemy and frequency use in English second language speakers: Polysemy and frequency use in English L2 speakers. *Language Learning, 60*(3), 573–605.

Crossley, S. A., & Skalicky, S. (in press). Making sense of polysemy relations in first and second language speakers of English. *International Journal of Bilingualism*.

Davies, M. (2008). *The corpus of contemporary American English*. Provost, UT: Brigham Young University.

Ding, Y. (2007). Text memorization and imitation: The practices of successful Chinese learners of English. *System, 35*(2), 271–280.

Ellis, N. C., & Wulff, S. (2015). Useage based approaches to SLA. In B. VanPatten & J. Williams (Eds.), *Theories in second language acquisition: An introduction* (pp. 75–93). New York: Routledge.

Elston-Guttler, K. E., & Williams, J. N. (2008). First language polysemy affects second language meaning interpretation: Evidence for activation of first language concepts during second language reading. *Second Language Research, 24*(2), 167–187.

Eyckmans, J., & Lindstromberg, S. (2017). The power of sound in L2 idiom learning. *Language Teaching Research, 21*(3), 341–361.

Giora, R. (2016). When negatives are easier to understand than affirmatives: The case of negative sarcasm. In P. Larrivée & C. Lee (Eds.), *Negation and polarity: Experimental perspectives* (pp. 127–143). Cham: Springer.

Giora, R., Drucker, A., & Fein, O. (2014). Resonating with default nonsalient interpretations: A corpus-based study of negative sarcasm. *Belgian Journal of Linguistics, 28*(1), 3–18.

Giora, R., Drucker, A., Fein, O., & Mendelson, I. (2015). Default sarcastic interpretations: On the priority of nonsalient interpretations. *Discourse Processes, 52*(3), 173–200.

Giora, R., Livnat, E., Fein, O., Barnea, A., Zeiman, R., & Berger, I. (2013). Negation generates nonliteral interpretations by default. *Metaphor and Symbol, 28*(2), 89–115.

Goatly, A. (2012). *Meaning and humour*. Cambridge: Cambridge University Press.

Goatly, A. (2017). Lexical priming in humorous discourse. *European Journal of Humour Research, 5*(1), 52–68.

Hanks, P. (2013). *Lexical analysis: Norms and exploitations*. Cambridge, MA: MIT Press.

Hodson, R. (2014). Teaching 'humour competence'. *Proceedings of CLaSIC, 2014,* 149–161.

Hoey, M. (2005). *Lexical priming: A new theory of words and language*. London and New York, NY: Routledge.

Illés, E., & Akcan, S. (2017). Bringing real-life language use into EFL classrooms. *ELT Journal, 71*(1), 3–12.

Keenan, J., MacWhinney, B., & Mayhew, D. (1977). Pragmatics in memory: A study of natural conversation. *Journal of Verbal Learning and Verbal Behavior, 16,* 549–560.

Kim, J. (2014). How Korean EFL learners understand sarcasm in L2 English. *Journal of Pragmatics, 60,* 193–206.

Kim, J. (2017). Teaching language learners how to understand sarcasm in L2 English. In N. Bell (Ed.), *Multiple perspectives on language play* (pp. 317–346). Boston and Berlin: Walter de Gruyter.

Kim, J., & Lantolf, J. (2016, Online First). Developing conceptual understanding of sarcasm in L2 English through explicit instruction. *Language Teaching Research,* 1–22.

Kim, Y-H., & Kellogg, D. (2007). Rules out of roles: Some differences in play language and their developmental significant. *Applied Linguistics, 28*(1), 25–45.

Larsen-Freeman, D. (2012). On the roles of repetition in language teaching and learning. *Applied Linguistics Review, 3*(2), 195–210.

Laursen, H., & Kolstrup, K. (2017, Advance Access). Multilingual children between real and imaginary worlds: Language play as resignifying practice. *Applied Linguistics,* 1–25.

Lehtimaja, I. (2011). Teacher-oriented address terms in students' reproach turns. *Linguistics and Education, 22,* 348–363.

Louw, B. (1993). Irony in the text or insincerity in the writer? The diagnostic potential of semantic prosodies. In M. Baker, F. Gill, & E. Tognini-Bonelli (Eds.), *Text and technology: In honour of John Sinclair* (pp. 157–176). Amsterdam: John Benjamins.

Lucas, T. (2005). Language awareness and comprehension through puns among ESL learners. *Language Awareness, 14*(4), 221–238.

Martin, D., Preiss, R., Gayle, B., & Allen, M. (2006). A meta-analytic assessment of the effect of humorous lectures on learning. In B. Gayle, R. Preiss, N. Burrell, & M. Allen (Eds.), *Classroom communication and instructional processes* (pp. 295–313). Mahwah, NJ: Lawrence Erlbaum.

McDaniel, M., Dornburg, C., & Guynn, M. (2005). Disentangling encoding versus retrieval explanations of the bizarreness effect: Implications for distinctiveness. *Memory & Cognition, 33*(2), 270–279.

Ortaçtepe, D. (2013). Formulaic language and conceptual socialization: The route to becoming nativelike in L2. *System, 41,* 852–865.

Pace-Sigge, M. (2013). The concept of lexical priming in the context of language use. *ICAME Journal, 37,* 149–173.

Partington, A. (2007). Irony and reversal of evaluation. *Journal of Pragmatics, 39*(9), 1547–1569.

Partington, A. (2009). A linguistic account of wordplay: The lexical grammar of punning. *Journal of Pragmatics, 41*(9), 1794–1809.

Partington, A. (2011a). "Double-speak" at the White House: A corpus-assisted study of bisociation in conversational laughter-talk. *Humour, 24*(4).

Partington, A. (2011b). Phrasal irony: Its form, function and exploitation. *Journal of Pragmatics*, *43*(6), 1786–1800.

Pomerantz, A., & Bell, N. (2007). Learning to play, playing to learn: FL learners as multicompetent language users. *Applied Linguistics*, *28*(4), 556–578.

Prichard, C., & Rucynski, J. (in press). Second language learners' ability to detect satirical news and the effect of humor competency training. *TESOL Journal*, e366.

Prodromou, L. (2007). Bumping into creative idiomaticity. *English Today*, *89*, *23*(1), 14–25.

Reddington, E., & Waring, H. (2015). Understanding the sequential resources for doing humour in the language classroom. *Humour*, *28*(1), 1–23.

Schmidt, S. (1994). Effects of humour on sentence memory. *Journal of Experimental Psychology: Learning, Memory, & Cognition*, *20*(4), 953–967.

Schmidt, S. (2002). The humour effect: Differential processing and privileged retrieval. *Memory*, *10*(2), 127–138.

Schmidt, S., & Williams, A. (2001). Memory for humorous cartoons. *Memory & Cognition*, *29*(2), 305–311.

Seidlhofer, B. (2009). Accommodation and the idiom principle in English as a Lingua Franca. *Intercultural Pragmatics*, *6*(2), 195–215.

Shardakova, M. (2016a). American learners' comprehension of Russian textual humour. *The Modern Language Journal*, *100*(2), 1–18.

Shardakova, M. (2016b). Playful performances of Russianness and L2 symbolic competence. In K. Bardovi-Harlig & J. César Félix Brasdefer (Eds.), *Pragmatics & language learning* (Vol. 14, pp. 179–206). Honolulu, HI: University of Hawai'i, National Foreign Language Resource Center.

Shively, R., Menke, M., & Manzón-Omundson, S. (2008). Perception of irony by L2 learners of Spanish. *Issues in Applied Linguistics*, *16*(2), 101–132.

Sinclair, J. (1991). *Corpus, concordance, collocation*. New York: Oxford University Press.

Sinclair, J. (2004). *Trust the text: Language, corpus, and discourse*. New York: Routledge.

Skalicky, S. (in press). Lexical priming in humorous satirical newspaper headlines. *Humour*.

Strick, M., Holland, R., van Baaren, R., & Van Knippenberg, A. (2010). Humour in the eye tracker: Attention capture and distraction from context cues. *The Journal of General Psychology*, *137*(1), 37–48.

Stubbs, M. (2001). *Words and phrases: Corpus studies of lexical semantics*. Oxford: Blackwell.

Szczepaniak, R., & Lew, R. (2011). The role of imagery in dictionaries of idioms. *Applied Linguistics*, *32*(3), 323–347.

Tarone, E. (2000). Getting serious about language play: Language play, interlanguage variation and second language acquisition. In B. Swierzbin, F. Morris, M. Anderson, C. Klee, & E. Tarone (Eds.), *Social and cognitive factors in second language acquisition: Selected proceedings of the 1999 second language research forum* (pp. 31–54). Somerville, MA: Cascadilla Press.

Tin, T. B. (2011). Language creativity and co-emergence of form and meaning in creative writing tasks. *Applied Linguistics*, *32*(2), 215–235.

Tin, T. B. (2012). Freedom, constraints and creativity in language learning tasks: New task features. *Innovation in Language Learning and Teaching*, *6*(2), 177–186.

Tin, T. B. (2013). Towards creativity in ELT: The need to say something new. *ELT Journal*, *67*(4), 385–397.

Tocalli-Beller, A., & Swain, M. (2007). Riddles and puns in the ESL classroom: Adults talk to learn. In A. Mackey (Ed.), *Conversational interaction in second language acquisition: Empirical studies* (pp. 143–167). Oxford: Oxford University Press.

Vaid, J., López, B. G., & Martínez, F. E. (2015). Linking the figurative to the creative: Bilingual's comprehension of metaphors, jokes, and remote associates. In R. R. Heredia & A. B. Cieślicka (Eds.), *Bilingual figurative language processing* (pp. 53–86). New York: Cambridge University Press.

Van Dam, J., & Bannink, A. (2017). The first English (EFL) lesson: Initial settings or the emergence of a playful classroom culture. In N. Bell (Ed.), *Multiple perspectives on language play* (pp. 245–279). Boston and Berlin: Walter de Gruyter.

Veale, T. (2012a). A computational exploration of creative similes. *Metaphor in Use: Context, Culture, and Communication, 38*, 329.

Veale, T. (2012b). *Exploding the creativity myth: The computational foundations of linguistic creativity*. New York, NY: A&C Black.

Veale, T. (2013a). Humorous similes. *Humour, 26*(1), 3–22.

Veale, T. (2013b). Linguistic readymades and creative reuse. *Journal of Integrated Design and Process Science, 17*(4), 37–51.

Waring, H. (2013). Doing being playful in the second language classroom. *Applied Linguistics, 34*(2), 191–210.

Wulf, D. (2010). A humour competence curriculum. *TESOL Quarterly, 44*(1), 155–169.

7
FORMULAIC LANGUAGE AND ITS PLACE IN INTERCULTURAL PRAGMATICS

Istvan Kecskes

Introduction

Although many studies report low rate of use of formulaic expressions in L2 (e.g., Ellis, Simpson-Vlach, & Carson, 2008; Kecskes, 2007; Prodromou, 2008; Warga, 2005), formulaic language (FL) use is as important in a second language (L2) as in a first language (L1). Several scholars called our attention to how important prefabricated units are in L1 and L2 production and comprehension. This work started in L1 research (see Hymes, 1962; Fillmore, 1976) and L2 scholars followed suit (e.g., Hakuta, 1974; Krashen & Scarcella, 1978; Weinert, 1995). Hymes (1962) pointed out that an immense portion of verbal behaviour consists of linguistic routines. Bolinger (1976) suggested that speakers do at least as much remembering as they do putting together. Fillmore (1976) also found that an enormously large amount of natural language is formulaic, automatic, and rehearsed, rather than propositional, creative, or freely generated. Sinclair (1991) argued that language production alternates between word-for-word combinations and prefabricated multiword combinations. This is so because all languages have particular ways of putting words together, which is eloquently represented in the domain of phraseology and is supposed to be a major mechanism contributing to the formation and reinforcement of a person's language use and cultural identity (Cowie, 1998). Kecskes (2007, 2013) claimed that preferred ways of saying things and preferred ways of organizing thoughts in a language are best reflected in the use of FL that has received particular attention over the last four decades, especially idioms, speech formulas, and metaphors.

As far as L1s are concerned, the development of formulaicity and idiomaticity is a natural consequence of language socialization and socialization through language. There is psycholinguistic evidence that fixed expressions and formulas have an important economizing role in speech production (cf. Miller & Weinert, 1998; Wray, 2002) (see Chapter 2 in this volume). Sinclair's (1991) idiom principle says that the use of prefabricated chunks may illustrate a natural tendency to economy of effort. This means that in communication we want to achieve more cognitive effects with less processing effort. Formulaic expressions ease the processing overload not only because they are ready-made but also because their salient meanings are easily accessible in online production and processing. There is no doubt about this in L1 (e.g., Ellis et al., 2008; Giora, 2003; Kecskes, 2002). But how about intercultural communication in which interlocutors do not share core common ground or lingua franca communication where the medium of interaction is not the L1 of any of the participants? Will formulaic expressions play the same role in L2 use as they do in L1? Is FL the essential part of language use when L2 is put to use in intercultural interactions? These are some of the important questions that intercultural pragmatics seeks answers for. In fact, the use of FL is one of the central issues of research in intercultural pragmatics (e.g., Kecskes, 2007, 2013; Minakova & Gural 2015; Osuka, 2017).

Intercultural Pragmatics is concerned with the way the language system is put to use in social encounters between human beings who have different L1s, communicate in a common language, and, usually, represent different cultures (Kecskes, 2010, 2013). What is common in interlocutors in intercultural interactions is that they use their L2 or Lx for communication. The communicative process in these encounters is synergistic in the sense that in them existing pragmatic norms and emerging, co-constructed features are present to a varying degree.

An important reason for the emergence of Intercultural Pragmatics as a new field of inquiry at the beginning of the 2000s was to distinguish research on intercultural interaction and discourse from interlanguage and cross-cultural pragmatics, as well as to emphasize the importance of developing a subfield of pragmatics with a multilingual angle. Interlanguage pragmatics focuses on the acquisition and use of pragmatic norms in L2: how L2 learners produce and comprehend speech acts, and how their pragmatic competence develops over time (e.g., Kasper & Blum-Kulka, 1993; Kasper, 1998). Cross-cultural pragmatics (e.g., Boxer, 2002; Wierzbicka, 2001) is comparative in nature. It focuses on cross-cultural similarities and differences in the linguistic realization and sociopragmatic judgement in context. By now, it has become clear that each of these three disciplines has its own legitimacy. However, it is almost unavoidable that these three fields have some overlap, which is a natural consequence of some of the issues that each addresses from its own perspective.

Intercultural Pragmatics represents a socio-cognitive perspective in which individual prior experience and actual social situational experience are equally important in meaning construction and comprehension. If we want to answer the questions raised earlier about FL use in L2, first we will need to give a brief overview of the main tenets of the socio-cognitive approach (SCA) that constitutes the theoretical basis of research in Intercultural Pragmatics. In SCA there is emphasis on the interplay of cooperation (actual situational experience) and egocentrism (prior experience) in language production and comprehension, which help us better understand the differences between L1 and L2 in the use of FL.

The Socio-Cognitive Approach (SCA)

The main goal of SCA is to bring together the two seemingly antagonistic lines of research in pragmatics: the *"individualistic"*, intention-based cognitive-philosophical line and the *"societal"*, context-based sociocultural-interactional line to better explain intercultural interactions. This looks like a necessary attempt because we human beings have a double nature: we are both individuals and social beings at the same time. This fact is reflected in our communicative behaviour and is very important if we want to understand the differences in FL use in L1 and L2. Recently, SCA has been used in several studies focusing on a variety of issues both in L1 and L2 including FL (e.g., Khatib & Shakouri, 2013; Macagno & Bigi, 2017; Schenck & Choi, 2015).

One of the main differences between the cognitive-philosophical approach and the socio-cultural interactional approach is that the former considers intention *a prior mental state* of speakers[1] that underpins communication, whereas the latter regards intention as a *post factum* construct that is achieved jointly through the dynamic emergence of meaning in conversation in which socio-cultural factors play the leading role. Since the two approaches represent two different perspectives, it would be difficult to reject either of them entirely. According to SCA, the complexity of the issue requires that we consider both the a priori and co-constructed, emergent sides of intention when analyzing communicative processes. SCA was proposed by Kecskes (2008, 2010, 2013) and Kecskes and Zhang (2009) as an attempt to unite the two perspectives and to emphasize that there is a dialectical relationship between a priori intention (based on individual prior experience) and emergent intention (based on actual social situational experience), as well as egocentrism (individual) and cooperation (social).

In this approach interlocutors are considered social beings searching for meaning with individual minds embedded in a socio-cultural collectivity. SCA argues that Grice was right when he tied cooperation to the speaker-hearer's rationality. However, egocentrism must be added to the speaker-hearer's rationality. We human beings are just as egocentric (as individuals) as cooperative (as social beings). Several studies (e.g., Barr & Keysar, 2005; Giora, 2003; Keysar, 2007) claimed that speakers and hearers commonly ignore their mutual knowledge when they produce and understand language. Their behaviour is called "egocentric" because it is rooted in the speakers-hearers' own knowledge instead of their mutual knowledge. If this claim is accepted, then a speaker's utterance cannot be just recipient design because it is also affected by individual prior experience.

"Egocentrism" in the SCA refers to attention-bias that is the result of prior experience of an individual. It means that interlocutors activate and bring up the most salient information to the needed attentional level in the construction (by the speaker) and comprehension (by the hearer) of the communication. This issue is especially important when interlocutors use their L2 or Lx. What is most salient for an L2 user is usually motivated by her/his L1 prior experience or limited L2 experience. There is nothing negative about egocentrism if the term is used in this sense. It should not be confused with "egotistic" that refers to a person who is self-centred and focuses only on his/her agenda.

Communication is a dynamic process, in which individuals are not only constrained by societal conditions but also shape them at the same time. As a consequence, the process is characterized by the interplay of two sets of traits that are inseparable, mutually supportive, and interactive:

Individual traits	*Social traits*
prior experience	actual situational experience
salience	relevance
egocentrism	cooperation
attention	intention

Individual traits (prior experience → salience → egocentrism →attention) interact with societal traits (actual situational experience → relevance → cooperation → intention). Each trait is the consequence of the other. Prior experience results in salience which leads to egocentrism that drives attention. Intention is a cooperation-directed practice that is governed by relevance which (partly) depends on actual situational experience. Integrating the pragmatic view of cooperation and the cognitive view of egocentrism, SCA emphasizes that both cooperation and egocentrism are manifested in all phases of communication, albeit in a varying degree.

Communication is the result of the interplay of intention and attention motivated by the socio-cultural background that is privatized individually by interlocutors. The socio-cultural background is composed of the environment (actual situational context in which the communication occurs), the encyclopedic knowledge of interlocutors deriving from their "prior experience", tied to the linguistic expressions they use, and their "current experience", in which those expressions create and convey meaning. So, language is considered both individual (as part of prior experience knowledge) and social (part of the actual situation). In communication, we show our two sides. We cooperate by generating and formulating intention(s) that is/are relevant to the given actual situational context.[2] At the same time, our egocentrism means that we activate the most salient information to our attention in the construction (speaker) and comprehension (hearer) of utterances.

The interplay of cooperation (social) and egocentrism (individual) has a profound effect on language processing. This is where we should look for the origin of FL use. Cooperation and common prior experience within a speech community result in the development of prefabricated linguistic units that mean the same thing for the members of that community and make interaction smooth. At the same time, individual differences in prior experience and different communicative goals are reflected in freely generated language. The two types of language processing (analytic – holistic) could be viewed as forming a continuum. Speakers of any language in their actual language use move up and down on a continuum whose hypothetical ends are "prefabricated language" and "ad hoc generated language" as follows:

<-->
Prefabricated language   Ad hoc generated language

Language users, no matter whether they use the given language as L1, L2, or Lx, are always in between the two poles. This means that they use more or less prefabricated and ad hoc generated language depending on several factors such as communicative need, intention, topic, actual situational context, speech partners, etc. If we want to understand why FL is as important in L2 as in L1, first we should review the most important issues in L1 use that have relevance in L2 as well.

Formulaic Language in L1

By FL we usually mean multiword collocations which are stored and retrieved holistically rather than being generated de novo with each use. Collocations, fixed semantic units, frozen metaphors, phrasal verbs, speech formulas, idioms, and situation-bound utterances can all be considered as examples of FL (Howarth, 1998; Kecskes, 2000; Wray, 2002, 2005). These word strings occurring together tend to convey holistic meanings that are either more than the sum of the individual parts or else diverge significantly from a literal or word-for-word meaning and operate as a single semantic unit (Gairns & Redman, 1986).

However, with the appearance of huge corpora, understanding FL has become more complicated. Working with large corpora, Altenberg (1998) went so far as to claim that almost 80% of our language production can be considered formulaic. Whatever the proportion actually is, one thing is for sure: speakers in conventional speech situations tend to do more remembering than putting together. Our everyday conversations are often restricted to short, routinized interchanges where we act as the given situational "frame" requires. So, a typical conversation between a customer and a store assistant may look like this:

(1) Conversation between store assistant (A) and Customer (C).

    A: What can I do for you?
    C: Thank you, I am just looking.
    A: Are you looking for something particular?

C: No, not really.
A: If you need help, just let me know.

The expressions that the speakers used do not look freely generated. Each of them can be considered a formula that is tied to this particular kind of situation. A great deal of linguistic performance, both speech and writing, does not involve improvising phrases and sentences ex nihilo from a vocabulary of several thousand words or lexical items and a basic stock of internalized grammatical patterns or rules, as the generative syntacticians believed (see, for instance, Chomsky, 1981).

Pawley and Syder (1983) claimed that although few people are able to encode, either in advance or while speaking, anything longer than a single clause of eight to ten words, they all regularly produce far longer fluent, pause-free, multi-clause utterances in spontaneous speech, mainly because they employ many prefabricated units and utterances. What we seem to do is to retain language in chunks, and this way much of our mental lexicon is stored in lexical expressions. This is basically what we do, no matter whether we use or L1, L2, or Lx. Kecskes (2016) argued that real linguistic creativity appears to be a discourse phenomenon rather than a sentence phenomenon as generative syntacticians have claimed. The economizing role of memorized lexical phrases allows addressees to pay attention to the larger structure of the discourse rather than to individual lexical items. What Pawley and Syder (1983) said about the size of the postulated stock of familiar usages is very interesting. Whereas "the number of single morpheme lexical items known to the average mature English speaker is relatively small; a few thousand", they suggest that "the number of sentence-length expressions familiar to the ordinary mature English speaker probably amounts, at least, to several hundreds of thousands" (p. 194). What about L2 users? It is essential that this number will be much less for them because of lack of or limited exposure and other factors that will be discussed later.

The huge stock of prefabricated units in the mind that are ready to be called upon when need occurs is mainly the result of normativization, standardization, emergence of shared expectations, and core common ground development of native speakers in a particular language or speech community. There is evidence (e.g., Eckert, 1992; Gumperz, 1968; Kecskes, 2015) that when people are together even only for a short time they create a speech community that starts to develop their language use norms from scratch. Kecskes (2015, 2016) claimed that the endeavour of creating normative use by developing formulas in a speech community is part of human rationality just like Gricean cooperation. He demonstrated through two research projects that the idiom principle is on in L2 as well, but it generates less FL than is the case in L1. However, as a compensation, L2 learners produce their own formulas in the course of interaction even if they spend only a short time together. Gumperz (1968) defined a speech community as any human aggregate characterized by regular and frequent interaction by means of a shared body of verbal signs and set off from similar aggregates by significant differences in language usage. Based on all this we may say that the more time a group or community of people spend together, the more we can expect that they start to give special meaning to certain strings of linguistic signs and units. As a result, their language use will be more and more characterized by the use of formulaic expressions that will be combined by ad hoc generated linguistic units. Kecskes (2016) argued that in SCA creativity in language use is considered a dynamic process in which formulaic units are combined with ad hoc generated elements in a syntax and discourse affecting way. Research in L2 confirms that (see Ellis, 2003; Ellis et al., 2008; Howarth, 1998).

Psychological Saliency of Formulaic Sequences

People use accessible categories to make sense of their social and linguistic context and environment. For a social or linguistic category to affect behaviour, it must be psychologically salient as the basis for perception and self-conception. From the perspective of L2 use, it is important to discuss the psychological salience of formulaic units. That will help us better understand why FL use differs in L1 and L2. Examining the role of psychological saliency in the use of formulaic units highlights that psychologically salient formulas behave like coherent, synergistic lexico-functional units and not as multiword chunks whose meaning can be calculated on the basis of its composition. The question for L2 users is as follows: can they develop this psychological saliency in L2? What factors affect that process?

Simpson-Vlach and Ellis (2010) argued that psycholinguistically salient sequences like *on the other hand, suffice it to say, welcome abroad, you are all set* cohere much more than would be expected by chance. Thus, measures of association, rather than raw frequency, keep them glued together.

If we want to understand how formulas and idiomatic units function, we will need to answer the following questions: do native language users perceive particular word sequences as formulaic-functional units, and other word sequences only as loose collocations that are often used together? What is the difference, for instance, between the "glued together" word sequences such as *suffice it to say, as a matter of fact*, and ad hoc frequent word sequences such as *if they were* . . . or *I have been* . . . ? What is needed for considering a word sequence a formulaic-functional unit? How does psychological saliency work in L2 use?

With the emergence of corpus linguistics, the interest in multiword sequences has increased to a great extent. Corpus linguists go beyond the Bolingerian "remembering and putting together" dynamism of language use and mostly side with Altenberg (1998), who claimed that 80% of our language production can be considered formulaic (see previous discussion). This appears to be so if we accept Wray's definition of formulaic sequences:

> a formulaic sequence [is] a sequence, continuous or discontinuous, of words or other elements, which is, or appears to be, prefabricated: that is, stored

and retrieved whole from memory at the time of use, rather than being subject to generation or analysis by the language grammar.

(Wray, 2002, p. 9)

Based on this definition there is hardly anything in language production that cannot be considered formulaic.

There is no doubt about the fact that an immense portion of verbal behaviour consists of linguistic routines. But what is the nature of these linguistic routines? Why do they exist in the language? Are they the results of the functioning of the linguistic system or are they the results of socio-cultural needs? The right answer to this question is both. Multiword sequences clearly demonstrate the distinction between conventions of language and conventions of usage. This division has been made by several researchers, including Searle (1979) and Morgan (1978). Searle said: "It is, by now, I hope, uncontroversial that there is a distinction to be made between meaning and use, but what is less generally recognized is that there can be conventions of usage that are not meaning conventions" (1979, p. 49). This distinction is expressed even more clearly by Morgan:

> In sum, then, I am proposing that there are at least two distinct kinds of convention involved in speech acts: conventions of language ... and conventions in a culture of usage of language in certain cases.... The former, conventions of language, are what make up the language, at least in part. The latter, conventions of usage, are a matter of culture (manners, religion, law. . .).
>
> (Morgan, 1978, p. 269)

To demonstrate the difference between the two types of conventions, let us look at the following examples:

(2) Renting a car

Clerk: Can I help you, sir.
Customer: Yes, I have a reservation.
Clerk: Your name, please.
Customer: James Cunning.
Clerk: May I see your driver's license, Mr. Cunning?

None of the expressions used by the interlocutors look freely generated. Each of them can be considered a formula. However, if we consider the following conversation, we may see something different.

(3) Bill and David are talking.

Bill: **If we want to** be on time **we will need to** take a taxi.
David: OK, **my friend.**

Can the expressions in bold be considered formulas? Are they in any way different from the ones in example (2)? There is no doubt that the expressions in bold consist of words that are frequently used together. But are they formulas here? Do they have some kind of psychological saliency as formulas for the speakers? We must be careful with the answer because frequency of occurrence of word sequences is only one of the criteria based on which we can identify formulaic expressions. The problem is that the role of frequency seems to be overemphasized in present-day linguistics, especially in corpus linguistics. Recent research analyzing written and spoken discourse has established that highly frequent, recurrent sequences of words, variously called lexical bundles, chunks, and multiword expressions, are not only salient but also functionally significant (e.g., Biber et al., 1999; Ellis et al., 2008). Cognitive research demonstrated that knowledge of these ready-made expressions is crucial for fluent processing. The recurrent nature of these units is discussed in the relevant literature (Biber et al., 1999; McEnery & Wilson, 1996). Simpson-Vlach and Ellis (2010) confirmed that large stretches of language are adequately described as collocational streams where patterns flow into each other. However, Sinclair's (1991) idiom principle is based primarily not on frequency that results in long lists of recurrent word sequences (Biber, Conrad, & Cortes, 2004; Biber et al., 1999). The problem with lists of reoccurring word sequences is that they can hardly give us any chance to distinguish where we have conventionalized formulas or where we have just frequently occurring word chunks that lack psychological saliency. We need a criterion other than frequency to distinguish between frequently occurring collocations and formulaic expressions. Corpus linguistics does not help us much with that distinction. Biber et al. (1999, p. 990), in their study of lexical bundles, defined FL as sequences of word forms that commonly go together in natural discourse, irrespective of their structural make-up or idiomaticity, and argued that conversation has a larger amount of lexical bundle types than academic prose. However, there seems to be a clear difference from the perspective of psychological saliency between sequences such as *to tell the truth, as a matter of fact, on the one hand*, and *if they could, we will need to, huge suitcase*, or *that is probably what* ... although all of these expressions are high on any frequency-based list. This is why we need to distinguish between groups of prefabricated expressions that have psychological saliency for speakers of a particular language community and loosely tied, frequently occurring word sequences such as *if they want, to do with it, tell them to*, etc.

L2 studies that are relevant for intercultural pragmatics show something different. They also emphasize the importance of frequency in processing FL. Ellis et al. (2008) argued that formula processing by non-natives, despite their many years of English as a second language (ESL) instruction, was a result of the frequency of the string rather than its coherence. For learners at that stage of development, it is the number of times the string appears in the input that determines fluency. Ellis et al. argued that tuning the system according to frequency of occurrence alone is not enough for nativelike accuracy and efficiency. According to those authors, what is additionally required is tuning the system for coherence – for co-occurrence greater than chance. Ellis et al. (2008) claimed that this is what solves the two puzzles for linguistic theory posed by Pawley and Syder (1983), native-like selection and nativelike fluency. Native speakers have extracted the underlying co-occurrence information, often implicitly from usage. Non-native speakers, even advanced ESL learners with more than 10 years of English instruction, still have a long way to go in their sampling of language. These learners are starting to recognize and become attuned to more frequent word sequences, but they need help to recognize distinctive formulas.

Based on the socio-cognitive approach, intercultural pragmatics gives a different explanation for this phenomenon. It argues that the development of psychological validity/saliency of these expressions in L2 is a matter of not only frequency and exposure to language use but also immersion in the culture, acceptance, and wish of the non-native speaker whether he/she wants to use those formulaic expressions or not (see details of Ortactepe, 2012 and Kecskes, 2015 studies discussed later). Frequent encounters with these expressions for non-native speakers help but are not enough to develop psychological saliency, as the following encounter between a Korean student and a clerk at the Registrar's office demonstrates:

(4) Korean student (Lee) and Registrar (Clerk) encounter.

    Lee: Could you sign this document for me, please?
    Clerk: Come again?
    Lee: Why should I come again? I am here now.

In spite of the distinctive intonation used by the clerk when uttering come again, the Korean student processed the expression not as a formula but as a freely generated expression with literal meaning. So, what really counts is the type of association between the lexical units in a sequence, rather than raw frequency. What creates psychological saliency is the discursive function in a particular context of that expression. As mentioned at the beginning of this section, the formula behaves like one coherent synergistic lexico-functional unit and not as a multi-word chunk whose meaning can be calculated on the basis of its composition. This functional aspect is what makes immersion in the target culture important for non-native speakers, because that is where those functions come from. But as we will see later, that may not be enough.

How does Intercultural Pragmatics Explain Formulaic Language Use?

Several studies within the confines of intercultural pragmatics have aimed to look at how formulas are used in intercultural interaction or by bilingual speakers (e.g., Cakir, 2008; Minakova & Gural, 2015; Ortactepe, 2012; Taguchi, Li, & Xiao, 2013; Zhou, 2012). They all mention that non-native speakers struggle with the use of

FL for several reasons, including lack of knowledge of conceptual load attached to formulas, no fit into synergistic communicative style, unwillingness to use certain expressions, preference for ad hoc generated expressions, etc. When we examine intercultural interactions, two more problems occur. One of them is that interlocutors in intercultural interactions cannot be sure that their partners understand the given formula the same way they do because they may lack the core common ground that native speakers share. Let us take the following example:

(5) Jianwei, Mary, Andy, and Liya are sitting at a table and eating.

Jianwei: Can I eat that last piece of sandwich?
Liya: Be my guest.
Jianwei: But it's not yours.

This example shows the problem very well. There are three non-native speakers and one native speaker at the table. The Chinese student asks for permission to eat the last piece of sandwich. The Russian student uses a formula to respond, which is a situation-bound utterance, encouraging or allowing someone else to take action like in the following encounter: A: *Do you mind if I order another glass of beer?* B: *Not at all, be my guest.*

The possessive pronoun *my* in the set phrase *be my guest* does not necessarily refer to possession. However, the Chinese student processes the utterance based on its literal meaning because he may not know the functional meaning of the situation-bound utterance *be my guest*. So, a slight misunderstanding occurs.

The socio-cognitive approach emphasizes the importance of prior experience and actual situational experience. When formulas are used in L1, native speakers almost never misunderstand each other because they have the necessary prior experience with the use of formulas, and the actual situational frame makes their use smooth and clear. In intercultural interactions, the interlocutors' prior experience with target language (L2) formulas significantly differs because of the factors mentioned previously, such as acceptance, preference, willingness to use, etc., that are not present in L1 to the same extent. Besides, the situational frame does not play the same triggering and/or clarifying role as it does in L1 because interactants may not be equally familiar with it.

The other problem that intercultural pragmatics research highlights is the contradiction that exists between the default processing principles (idiom principle and economy principle) and the low rate of target language formulas in intercultural communication. Being the default processing strategy, the formulaic option is expected to be most salient in language production in L1 (Sinclair, 1991; Miller & Weinert, 1998; Wray, 2002). The open choice principle is invoked in L1 only when the idiom principle fails or is blocked for some reason. This looks like a logical mechanism in L1 production where participants can rely on mutual understanding of formulaic expressions that are motivated by common ground, conventions, commonalities, norms, common beliefs, and mutual knowledge. This explains why we find much "remembering", i.e., FL use in L1. However, this is not the case in L2 where the idiom principle generates much less FL. But why? Does it mean that L2 users' mind is not prewired for the *idiom principle* the way L1 users' mind is? And what about the economy principle? Are these two principles blocked in L2, or do they function in a different way in L2?

Based on the socio-cognitive approach, we can argue that neither of the principles is blocked in L2 production and intercultural interactions (see Kecskes, 2015). What we have is a shift of emphasis from the communal to the individual, and that move causes changes in how the two principles operate. The key issue here is the extent to which interlocutors have access to core common ground. If societal circumstances in the speech community provide broad core common ground, speakers in that community may rely on a wide range of FL provided by presumed background information shared by participants in interactions. However, if this core common ground is not present to the extent it is in L1, then L2 users must co-construct it, which is not an easy task given the different sociocultural background the participants represent in intercultural interactions. So, it is not that the individual becomes more important than the societal. Rather, since there is limited core common ground, it should be created in the interactional context in which the interlocutors function as core common ground creators rather than just common ground seekers and activators, as is mostly the case in L1. As a consequence, there is more reliance on language created ad hoc by individuals in the course of interaction than on prefabricated language and pre-existing frames in the target language. But the idiom principle and economy principle are on: L2 users' primary choice is formulaic units if they have access to any in the target language. And the natural tendency to the economy of effort also works. L2 users want to achieve as much as possible with the least possible effort both in production and comprehension. But how can they do that? They use the open choice principle to create formulas. There is more new formula creation than use of existing formulas in L2. We can find evidence in corpora to prove this (Kecskes, 2007, 2015):

A) L2 speakers use formulas where their proficiency and preference allow that.

Ortactepe (2012) conducted a longitudinal, mixed-method study that relied on the assumption that international students, as newcomers to the American culture, experience bilingual development through conceptual socialization, which enables them to gain competency in the target language through exposure to the target language and culture. By collecting qualitative and quantitative data three times over a year, the study examined the linguistic and social development of Turkish bilingual students as a result of their conceptual socialization in the US. Ortactepe provided evidence that L2 learners' conceptual socialization relies predominantly – contrary to what previous research says – on learners' investment in language rather than only on extended social networks. Examining FL use, she found that in case of advanced language learners, the use of FL depends not on proficiency but on acceptance, preference, and willingness of use.

B) Kecskes (2015) conducted a corpus-based study to examine if the idiom principle is blocked in L2 production or not.

Data collection was based on seven conversations that lasted 30 minutes, recording spontaneous speech on topics such as health, sports, and living in Albany. The participants were as follows: C1 Japanese and Korean, C2 Korean and Turkish, C3 Korean and Chinese, C4 Japanese and Chinese, C5 Chinese and Korean, C6 Korean and Burmese, C7 African-French and Korean. Two types of production sequences were selected within each 30-minute session: (1) how do participants introduce themselves (closed social situation) and (2) how do participants introduce a new topic (open social situation)?

Introduction is a closed social situation that requires formulaicity in most languages. The subjects (six out of seven pairs) relied on well-known situation-bound utterances rather than freely generated expressions:

- Let me introduce myself first.
- So glad to meet you. Let me ask you how long you have been here?
- Can I ask your name?
- Nice to meet you.

Introducing a new topic is an open social situation. Although the frame is well-known, language use associated with this frame is much less formalized than in close social situations.

Focus of analysis was on the first attempt to change the topic of the conversation. Results showed that subjects used mainly freely generated expressions to introduce a new topic. For instance:

(6)

    C1B: Okay, it's been three or . . . three months **so far** right? **Do you like** living in Albany? Living in America?
    C4B: So **can you please tell me** the difficulties in life here.
    C6B: And **what about** . . . do you **care more about** . . . food?

These examples demonstrate that the idiom principle must be on because the ad hoc generated utterance chunks are combined with some formulaic expressions (see in bold) that are relevant to the matter the participants attempted to talk about.

C) L2 speakers generate new formulas that are the results of cooperation and co-construction.

The more time members of a speech community spend together, the more norms of conduct they develop for themselves. There is evidence (e.g., Canagarajah, 2014; Eckert, 1992; Gumperz, 1968; Kecskes, 2015) that when people are together even only for a short time, they create a speech community that starts to develop its language use norms from scratch. They create formulas that do not exist in the target language or are modifications of existing formulaic expressions, such as *it is almost skips from my thoughts, you are not very rich in communication, take a school*, etc. Kecskes (2015) demonstrated that English lingua franca (ELF) speakers frequently coin or create their own ways of expressing themselves effectively, and the mistakes they may make will carry on in their speech, even though the correct form is there for them to imitate. For instance, he reported that several participants in a spontaneous conversation adopted the phrase *native Americans* to refer to native speakers of American English. Although in the "think aloud" conversation session, the correct expression (native speaker of American English) was repeated several times by one of the researchers, the erroneous formula *native Americans* kept being used by the lingua franca speakers. They even joked about it and said that the use of target language formulas coined by them in their temporary speech community was considered like a "joint venture" and created a special feeling of camaraderie in the group.

Several studies in ELF (e.g., Firth, 2009; Mauranen, 2009; Pitzl, 2012; Seidlhofer, 2009) reported this "creative" attitude of L2 users to idiomatic expressions. However, we have to be careful with what we actually consider creative language use and what constitutes an error in ELF. Cogo and Dewey (2012) claimed that "deciding what constitutes an error is . . . not a particularly ELF-compatible way of thinking about language" (p. 78).

Pitzl et al. (2008) talked about "creative innovations". To be creative in a language first of all means drawing on experiences and knowledge in that language and then diverging in ways which may be unexpected but still processable by other language users.

Conclusions and Future Directions

The chapter emphasized that from the perspective of intercultural pragmatics only those linguistic units should be considered formulaic that have some psychological saliency for the language users. These expressions are glued together and cohere much more than would be expected by chance or in collocations where the measure of association is only raw frequency. This approach partly explains the low level of FL use in L2 or Lx. The lack of or limited psychological saliency for L2 users bring forth factors such as acceptance, preference, and willingness to use that may be present in L1 use to a lesser extent.

It was argued that the idiom principle and economy principle are the main driving forces of any language use. They are inherent and affect the use of any language production, the question only is to what extent. Human beings want to achieve as much as possible with the least possible effort. The best way to do that is to use as many prefabricated chunks of language and possible and combine them with ad hoc generated utterances in a creative way. As it was argued in this chapter, there is little use of L2 FL in intercultural interactions, but at the same time there is quite a bit of new formula creation that is the result of individual endeavours or co-construction. So, the open choice principle is used not only for generating expressions ad hoc but also as a compensation for limited access to prefabricated units in the target language.

Future research should focus on the investigation of the nature of this compensation process. Several attempts have already been made in this direction (see Kecskes, 2016; Pitzl, 2012; Taguchi et al., 2013). These studies have focused on the creative language use of ELF speakers and sought an answer to the question: where is the limit to ELF interlocutors' "creative use of language"?

There is also a need to study further the psychological factors such as preference and willingness to use that affect the selection and use of target language formulas. This should be connected with the investigation of what types of formulaic expressions L2 users create ad hoc in temporary speech communities.

Notes

1 The notion of prior intention was initially proposed by Searle (1983, pp. 165–166). Searle's (1983) work on intentionality introduced a distinction between prior intention and intention-in-action, the latter referring to "the proximal cause of the physiological chain leading to overt behaviour" (Ciaramidaro et al., 2007, p. 3106). In our understanding, "intention-in-action" also refers to some kind of prior cause.
2 Actual situational context is both a linguistic and social phenomenon, as will be explained later. It makes the utterance socially relevant.

References

Altenberg, B. (1998). On the phraseology of spoken English: The evidence of recurrent word-combinations. In A. P. Cowie (Ed.), *Phraseology: Theory, analysis, and applications* (pp. 101–122). Oxford: Clarendon Press.

Barr, D. J., & B.Keysar. (2005). Making sense of how we make sense: The paradox of egocentrism in language use. In H. L. Colston & A. N. Katz (Eds.), *Figurative language comprehension: Social and cultural influences* (pp. 21–43). Mahwah, NJ: Lawrence Erlbaum.

Biber, D., Conrad, S., & Cortes, V. (2004). If you look at. . . : Lexical bundles in university teaching and textbooks. *Applied Linguistics, 25*, 371–405.

Biber, D., Johansson, S., Leech, G., Conrad, S., & Finegan, E. (1999). *Longman grammar of spoken and written English*. London: Pearson Education.

Bolinger, D. (1976). Meaning and memory. *Forum Linguisticum, 1*, 1–14.

Boxer, D. (2002). Discourse issues in cross-cultural pragmatics. *Annual Review of Applied Linguistics, 22*, 150–167.

Çakır, C. (2008). Basic concepts and questions of intercultural communication. *Turkish Culture and Haci Bektas Veli Research Quarterly, 46*, 181–187.

Canagarajah, A. S (2014). In search of a new paradigm for teaching English as an International Language. *TESOL Journal*, 5, 767–785.

Chomsky, N. (1981). *Lectures on government and binding*. Dordrecht: Foris.

Ciaramidaro, A., Adenzato, M., Enrici, I., Erk, S., Pia, L., & Bara, B. (2007). The intentional network: How the brain reads varieties of intentions. *Neuropsychologia, 45*, 3105–3113.

Cogo, A. & Dewey, M. (2012). *Analysing English as a Lingua Franca: A corpus-driven investigation*. New York: Continuum.

Cowie, A. P. (1998). Introduction. In A. P. Cowie (Ed.), *Phraseology: Theory, analysis, and applications* (pp. 1–20). Oxford: Clarendon Press.

Eckert, P. (1992). Communities of practice: Where language, gender and power all live. In K. Hall, M. Bucholtz, & B. Moonwomon (Eds.), *Locating power, Proceedings of the 1992 Berkeley Women and Language Conference* (pp. 89–99). Berkeley: Berkeley Women and Language Group.

Ellis, N. C. (2003). Constructions, chunking, and connectionism: The emergence of second language structure. In C. J. Doughty & M. H. Long (Eds.), *The Handbook of second language acquisition* (pp. 63–103). Malden, MA: Blackwell.

Ellis, N. C., Simpson-Vlach, R., & Carson, M. (2008). Formulaic language in native and second language speakers: Psycholinguistics, corpus linguistics, and TESOL. *TESOL Quarterly, 42*, 375–396.

Fillmore, C. J. (1976). The need for a frame semantics within linguistics. *Statistical Methods in Linguistics, 12*, 5–29.

Firth, A. (2009). The lingua franca factor. *Intercultural Pragmatics, 6*(2), 147–170.

Gairns, R., & Redman, S. (1986). *Working with words: A guide to teaching and learning vocabulary*. Cambridge: Cambridge University Press.

Giora, R. (2003). *On our mind: Salience, context and figurative language*. Oxford: Oxford University Press.

Gumperz, J. (1968). The speech community. In A. Duranti (Ed.), *Linguistic anthropology: A reader* (pp. 66–73). Cambridge: Cambridge University Press.

Hakuta, K. (1974). Prefabricated patterns and the emergence of structure in second language acquisition. *Language Learning, 24*(2), 287–297.

Howarth, P. (1998). Phraseology and second language proficiency. *Applied Linguistics, 19*, 24–44.

Hymes, D. H. (1962). The ethnography of speaking. In T. Gladwin & W. C. Sturtevant (Eds.), *Anthropology and human behavior* (pp. 13–53). Washington, DC: The Anthropology Society of Washington.

Kasper, G. (1998). Interlanguage pragmatics. In H. Byrnes (ed.), *Learning and Teaching Foreign Languages: Perspectives in research and scholarship*, (pp. 183–208). New York, NY: Modern Language Association.

Kasper, G. & Blum-Kulka, S. (1993). *Interlanguage Pragmatics*. Oxford: Oxford University Press.

Kecskes, I. (2000). A cognitive-pragmatic approach to situation-bound utterances. *Journal of Pragmatics, 32*, 605–625.

Kecskes, I. (2002). *Situation-bound utterances in L1 and L2*. Berlin and New York, NY: Mouton de Gruyter.

Kecskes, I. (2007). Formulaic language in English lingua franca. In I. Kecskes & Horn, L. R (Eds.), In *Explorations in pragmatics: Linguistic, cognitive and intercultural aspects* (pp. 191–219). Berlin and New York, NY: Mouton de Gruyter.

Kecskes, I. (2008). Dueling contexts: A dynamic model of meaning. *Journal of Pragmatic, 40*(3), 385–406.

Kecskes, I. (2010). Situation-Bound utterances as pragmatic acts. *Journal of Pragmatics, 42*(11), 2889–2897.

Kecskes, I. (2013). *Intercultural pragmatics*. Oxford: Oxford University Press.

Kecskes, I. (2015). Is the Idiom Principle Blocked in Bilingual L2 Production? In R. Heredia & A. Cieslicka (Eds.), *Bilingual figurative language processing* (pp. 28–53). Cambridge: Cambridge University Press.

Kecskes, I. (2016). Deliberate creativity and formulaic language use. In K. Allan, A. Capone, & I. Kecskes (Eds.), *Pragmemes and theories of language use perspectives in pragmatics, philosophy & psychology* (Vol. 9, pp. 3–20). Cham, Switzerland: Springer.

Kecskes, I., & Zhang, F. (2009). Activating, seeking and creating common ground: A sociocognitive approach. *Pragmatics and Cognition, 17*(2), 331–355.

Keysar, B. (2007). Communication and miscommunication: The role of egocentric processes. *Intercultural Pragmatics, 4*(1), 71–84.

Khatib, M. & Shakouri, N. (2013). Literature stance in developing critical thinking: A pedagogical look. *International Journal of Research Studies in Language Learning, 2*(4), 101–108.

Krashen, S. & R. Scarcella (1978). On routines and patterns in language acquisition and performance. *Language Learning, 28*(2), 283–300

Macagno, F. & S. Bigi (2017). Understanding misunderstandings. Presuppositions and presumptions in doctor-patient chronic care consultations. *Intercultural Pragmatics, 14*(1), 49–75.

Mauranen, A. (2009). Chunking in ELF: Expressions for managing interaction. *Intercultural Pragmatics, 6*, 217–233.

McEnery, T., & Wilson, A. (1996). *Corpus linguistics.* Edinburgh: Edinburgh University Press.

Miller, J., & Weinert, R. (1998). *Spontaneous spoken language: Syntax and discourse.* Oxford: Clarendon Press.

Minakova, L., & Gural, S. (2015). The situational context effect in non-language-majoring EFL students' meaning comprehension. *Procedia – Social and Behavioral science, 200*, 62–68. doi:10.1016/j.sbspro.2015.08.014.

Morgan, J. L. (1978). Two types of convention in indirect speech acts. In P. Cole (Ed.), *Pragmatics (Syntax and Semantics 9)* (pp. 261–280). New York, NY: Academic Press.

Ortaçtepe, D. (2012). *The development of conceptual socialization in international students: A language socialization perspective on conceptual fluency and social identity (advances in pragmatics and discourse analysis).* Cambridge: Cambridge Scholars Publishing.

Osuka, N. (2017). Development of pragmatic routines by Japanese learners in a study abroad context. In I. Kecskes & S. Assimakopoulos (Eds.), *Current issues in intercultural pragmatics* (pp. 275–297). Amsterdam and Philadelphia: John Benjamins.

Pawley, A., & Syder, F.H. (1983). Two puzzles for linguistic theory: Nativelike selection and nativelike fluency. *Language and Communication, 5*, 191–226.

Pitzl, M.-L. (2012). Creativity meets convention: Idiom variation and re-metaphorization in ELF. *Journal of English as a Lingua Franca, 1*(1), 27–55.

Pitzl, M.-L., Breiteneder, A., & Klimpfinger, T. (2008). A world of words: Processes of lexical innovation in VOICE. *Vienna English Working Papers, 17*(2), 21–46.

Prodromou, L. (2008). *English as a lingua franca: A corpus based analysis.* London: Continuum.

Searle, J. R. (1979). *Expression and meaning: Studies in the theory of speech acts.* Cambridge: Cambridge University Press.

Searle, J. R. (1983), *Intentionality: An essay in the philosophy of mind.* Cambridge: Cambridge University Press.

Seidlhofer, B. (2009). Accommodation and the idiom principle in English as a lingua franca. *Intercultural Pragmatics, 6*(2), 195–215.

Schenck, A.D. & Choi, W. (2015). Improving efl writing through study of semantic concepts in formulaic language. *English Language Teaching, 8* (1), 142–154.

Simpson-Vlach, R., & Ellis, N. C. (2010). An academic formulas list: New methods in phraseology research. *Applied Linguistics, 31*, 487–512.

Sinclair, J. (1991). *Corpus, concordance, collocation.* Oxford: Oxford University Press.

Taguchi, N., Li, S., & Xiao, F. (2013). Production of formulaic expressions in L2 Chinese: A developmental investigation in a study abroad context. *CASLAR: Chinese as a Second Language Research, 2,* 23–58.

Warga, M. (2005). Je serais très merciable: Formulaic vs. creatively produced speech in learners' request closings. *Canadian Journal of Applied Linguistics, 8,* 67–94.

Weinert, R. (1995). The role of formulaic language in second language acquisition: A review. *Applied Linguistics, 16,* 180–205.

Wierzbicka, A. (2001). *Cross-cultural pragmatics: The semantics of human interaction.* Berlin and New York, NY: Mouton de Gruyter.

Wray, A. (2002). *Formulaic language and the lexicon.* Cambridge: Cambridge University Press.

Wray, A. (2005). Idiomaticity in an L2: Linguistic processing as a predictor of success. In B. Briony (Ed.), *IATEFL 2005: Cardiff conference selections* (pp. 53–60). Canterbury: IATEFL.

Zhou, H. (2012). A study of situation-bound utterances in modern Chinese. *CASLAR: Chinese as a Second Language Research, 1*(1), 55–86.

PART III
Pedagogical Perspectives on Formulaic Language

PART III

8
PEDAGOGICAL APPROACHES TO THE TEACHING AND LEARNING OF FORMULAIC LANGUAGE

Ana Pellicer-Sánchez and Frank Boers

Introduction

The surge in vocabulary studies 20 years ago led to a greater interest in examining the effectiveness of different procedures for the teaching and learning of lexical items. These investigations have often been categorized into two main approaches: examinations of *incidental learning* and interventions to engage learners in *intentional* or *deliberate learning*. Incidental learning accrues as a by-product of a communicative activity, without a particular intention to learn language items or linguistic features (Schmitt, 2010). Lexical items acquired when learners are reading a book, listening to an interview on the radio, or watching a movie are all examples of what has been considered incidental vocabulary learning, because the primary focus during these activities is on content rather than on the linguistic packaging of that content. By contrast, intentional vocabulary learning involves a deliberate effort to commit lexical items to memory or to consolidate knowledge of items, as for instance when studying word lists, testing oneself using flashcards, or completing vocabulary exercises. In actual practice, it is hard to tell whether a given learner might be focusing temporarily on new words also during an activity such as reading a story. Consequently, it is far from easy to operationalize the distinction between incidental and intentional learning. What *is* possible, however, is to distinguish between learning *conditions* that are and are not intended to engage learners in intentional learning. Following Nation and Webb (2011), we will consider a vocabulary learning condition to be intentional if learners are forewarned of a vocabulary test and/or if task instructions explicitly direct their focus to lexical items. Intentional and incidental approaches are not mutually exclusive. Instead, they complement one another. For instance, incidental learning conditions (e.g., extensive reading) may be particularly beneficial for the fine-tuning and consolidation of newly acquired knowledge. For example, repeated contextualized encounters with a word that was first studied deliberately as a discrete item may not only entrench this item more firmly in memory but also foster familiarity with facets of the word that are possibly less amenable to deliberate study, such as its phraseological behaviour.

The vast majority of studies empirically testing the efficiency of particular activities for vocabulary learning have focused on the acquisition of single-word items. However, as illustrated in this volume, a high proportion of language is formulaic, and knowledge of multiword lexis or "formulaic sequences" (FSs) (Wray, 2002) is essential for achieving high levels of proficiency in a second language (L2) (e.g., Crossley, Salsbury, & McNamara, 2015; Durrant & Schmitt, 2009; Kremmel, Brunfaut, & Alderson, 2017; Stengers, Boers, Housen, & Eyckmans, 2011). There is now a growing consensus not only among researchers but also among authors of pedagogy-oriented books that attention to formulaic language (FL) should be an integral part of language pedagogy (Lewis, 1993; Lindstromberg & Boers, 2008a). The last decade has witnessed an unprecedented increase in the number of "intervention" studies examining the teaching and learning of FL, and the findings of these studies have the potential to inform pedagogical practice. The aim of this chapter is to provide a concise (and, of necessity, non-exhaustive) review of available empirical research to date.

The chapter is organized roughly along the traditional categories of incidental and intentional learning conditions, but we will recognize an additional category – that of *semi*-incidental learning conditions. These semi-incidental conditions are characterized by steps which direct learners' attention to particular FSs in a text (and thus potentially raising their awareness of phraseology more generally), while the learners are nonetheless expected to engage with the text first and foremost for its content. A prominent example is a reading comprehension task using a text where the visual saliency of certain lexical items has been enhanced typographically. As this typographic enhancement is intended to incite learners to shift their attention from text content to the wording of that content, we consider this intervention different from "purely" incidental learning conditions. At the same time, when no instruction to study the target items is given, it is an intervention that does not fully qualify as intentional learning (as defined previously) either. We will therefore situate this and similar interventions between the realms of incidental and intentional learning conditions.

Let it be clear that this review focuses on studies intended to gauge the effectiveness of tried methods and procedures for helping learners acquire multiword lexis. Due to constraints of space, the review does not provide coverage of the several laudable efforts made in recent years to compile lists of high-utility multiword expressions that merit prioritization in teaching and learning (e.g., Martinez & Schmitt, 2012; but see Durrant, this volume). Also outside the scope of this review is the creation and validation of a growing number of print and online resources for learners' independent exploration of the phraseological dimension of language (but see Cobb, this volume, and Meunier, 2012).

Incidental Learning of Formulaic Language

Learners can increase their lexical repertoire by picking up words and expressions from reading texts, listening input, audio-visual materials, and through interaction. Among these, reading has attracted the most attention from vocabulary researchers, but the focus has long been on single words, with FSs a relatively new addition to this strand of research.

Studies on the acquisition of single words have shown that incidental vocabulary learning is influenced by features of the target items themselves, such as word class (Kweon & Kim, 2008); characteristics of the input materials in which target words are embedded, as for instance the presence of pictorial support (e.g., Bisson, Van Heuven, Conklin, & Tunney, 2015), the provision of annotations (e.g., Chun & Plass, 1996), and the helpfulness of contextual cues (Webb, 2008); the learners' familiarity with the topic (e.g., Pulido, 2007); the learners' general proficiency level (e.g., Tekmen & Daloglu, 2006); and the learners' vocabulary knowledge in particular (Horst, Cobb, & Meara, 1998). Among the many factors, however, frequency of encounters with the same words has perhaps received the most attention from vocabulary researchers. A reliable estimate of the number of encounters required for word acquisition could help to gauge the chances that words beyond the high-frequency bands will be acquired, taking into account differing amounts of exposure (Nation, 2014). Unfortunately, while several studies have shown that more encounters with the same words tend to result in better gains, such estimates of the number of encounters necessary for successful acquisition range widely, from six (Rott, 1999) and eight (e.g., Horst et al., 1998) to more than 10 (Pigada & Schmitt, 2006; Pellicer-Sánchez & Schmitt, 2010; Webb, 2007). This range is perhaps not so surprising, as the effect of frequency of exposure is almost bound to interact with other factors, such as the semantic relevance, formal salience, and distribution of the instances of the given word (e.g., Laufer & Rozovski-Roitblat, 2015; Szudarski & Carter, 2016; Webb & Chang, 2015).

Still, frequency clearly matters, and consequently this factor also figures high on the research agenda concerning the incidental acquisition of multiword lexis. An early example is an experiment by Durrant and Schmitt (2010), who examined English as a Second Language (ESL) learners' acquisition of adjective-noun collocations (e.g., *excellent drink*) presented in sentences which the participants were asked to read aloud. The learners were assigned to one of three experimental conditions: (1) target collocations embedded in a sentence once; (2) repeated exposure to the same sentences containing the target collocations (i.e., verbatim repetition); or (3) repeated exposure to the target collocations in different sentences (i.e., varied repetition). Post-test results showed that both repetition conditions outperformed the single exposure condition. Interestingly, repetition in the same contexts led to stronger memories of the target collocations than repetition in different sentence contexts.

It may be argued that a sentence-level task as used in Durrant and Schmitt (2010) is rather different from the reading of "texts". A study which did use texts and which also found an effect for frequency was conducted by Webb, Newton, and Chang (2013). English as a Foreign Language (EFL) learners read short stories for about 35 minutes while listening to the audio-recording of these stories. Eighteen target verb–noun collocations (e.g., *break the silence*; *raise questions*) were incorporated into these texts, and participants read one of four versions of the texts, which varied in the number of instances of each target collocation (just once, 5, 10, and 15 times). Post-test results showed a significant effect of repetition and that multiple encounters with an FS are necessary for substantial learning to occur. A single encounter did not bring about noticeable learning at all, and for the majority of the learners as many as 10 encounters turned out insufficient for them to accurately recall the complete FSs.

Compelling evidence for the role of frequency was *not* found in a conceptual replication by Pellicer-Sánchez (2017) and Pellicer-Sánchez and Siyanova-Chanturia (under review), however. Participants in these studies read one of two versions of a short story that differed in the number of instances of target collocations – four versus eight instances. Results showed a significant increase in collocational knowledge with both versions, but no statistically significant difference in learning gains between them. As the authors acknowledge, the nature of the target collocations used in their experiments (i.e., collocations containing a pseudoword) needs to be borne in mind when interpreting the results, because the novelty of the pseudoword is likely to catch a reader's attention. In many cases, a learner will encounter a collocation consisting entirely of familiar words (e.g., *have an accident*), and, since familiar words attract little attention (Godfroid, Boers, & Housen, 2013), it is conceivable that their combination in a wordstring will go unnoticed, too. Approximate replications with real collocations would therefore be useful.

In sum, the findings suggest that, reminiscent of what was found for uptake of single words, frequency of encounters with FSs certainly matters, but it is only one of several variables that influence the likelihood of uptake. Other variables probably include characteristics of the expression itself (e.g., degrees of formal complexity, novelty, and semantic transparency), its relevance for text comprehension, the availability of counterparts in the learners' first language (L1), and individual differences among learners (e.g., level of proficiency). The nature of the text and the distribution of the instances of target items may also matter.

From a pedagogical perspective, it is worth bearing in mind that the learning gains attested in aforementioned studies such as Webb et al. (2013) resulted from reading modified materials that were densely packed (or "seeded") with instances of the same expressions. Non-manipulated authentic texts are extremely unlikely to expose readers to, for example, as many as 15 instances of the same collocation in a short time span (as was the case in one of Webb et al.'s reading conditions). For example, Boers and Lindstromberg (2009) screened 120 pages of a popular novel (a detective story) for instances of verb-noun collocations (e.g., *tell + truth*) and found that almost none of these occurred more than once, and none occurred often enough to come close to the frequencies associated with learning in aforementioned reading experiments (also see Cobb, this volume, for discussion). It therefore would take large amounts of unmodified input to foster incidental acquisition of many FSs, and even so, certain types of FSs might just not occur the required number of times for considerable learning to occur.

Next to frequency of encounters, another recurring theme in incidental vocabulary acquisition research has been modality of input. Studies have furnished evidence that vocabulary acquisition from listening input occurs as well (e.g., Brown, Waring, & Donkaewbua, 2008; Van Zeeland & Schmitt, 2013; Vidal, 2011), but also that the gains tend to be smaller than from reading (Brown et al., 2008; Vidal, 2011). To our knowledge, the acquisition of L2 multiword lexis from audio input alone has been investigated in only one study so far. Webb and Chang (under review) compared the learning of FSs in three input conditions: reading, reading while listening, and listening. Their college EFL learners read, listened to, or read-while-listened to a graded reader containing 17 target sequences in six sessions over a three-week period. Post-test results showed that reading while listening had an advantage over both reading-only and listening-only conditions. An explanation for the added value of listening input when it comes to helping learners pick up FSs from texts may lie with prosody (Lin, 2012; this volume). Prosody can aid the parsing of text because it often signals where the boundaries of semantic units are, and this can thus be expected to help learners identify such units, including multiword expressions.

If bi-modal input is more conducive to incidental acquisition of FSs than silent reading alone, then one may wonder whether *multi*-modal input, such as captioned videos, might also be comparatively beneficial. Research has already pointed to the usefulness of multi-modal input for single-word acquisition (Montero Perez, Van Den Noortgate, & Desmet, 2013, for a meta-analysis), and so it is definitely worth investigating whether this extends to the acquisition of FSs. A classroom experiment on incidental uptake of FSs from multi-modal input was conducted by Hoang and Boers (2016). High-intermediate ESL learners twice read and listened to a story supported by pictures, and they were told in advance that they would be asked to retell the story. Announcing this output task was deemed to prompt engagement with lexis used in the story that the learners might anticipate using to retell the story. The story contained a large number of FSs, but only a minute fraction of these (less than 7%) were recycled accurately in the learners' versions. By comparison, the learners did recycle most of the content words from the text. One explanation for their comparatively elusive nature could simply be that FSs are often longer than single words and thus more challenging to hold in (phonological) short-term memory. Another is that not all FSs are easy to decipher let alone to pinpoint their pragmatic function, and so learners may develop some receptive knowledge of such expressions but stay wary of using them productively (Dagut & Laufer, 1985). Yet another explanation is the lack of attention that precise wording attracts when texts are processed "naturally", i.e., when texts are processed with a focus on content rather than the linguistic packaging of that content (Van Patten, 2002). To address this issue, some pedagogy-minded applied linguists (e.g., Sharwood-Smith, 1993) have proposed to typographically enhance selected language features in texts, so as to make these perceptually more salient. That is the type of intervention we turn to next.

Semi-Incidental Learning of Formulaic Language

Successful incidental vocabulary learning is subject to learners' noticing of the lexical items in the input. The role of attention was emphasized by Schmidt (2001) in his *Noticing Hypothesis*. As he claims, "people learn about the things they attend to and do not learn much about the things they do not attend to" (p. 30). However, learners do not always notice unknown lexical items in the input (Laufer, 2005). This need for attention, together with the often small gains reported by incidental learning studies, has led vocabulary researchers to explore techniques to direct learners' attention to words in the input. One of such methods is pre-modifying the input through input-enhancement techniques (Ellis, 2015). In vocabulary learning, this input-enhancement is usually done by means of typographic enhancement (e.g., highlighting items in text by means of underlining, bold typeface, italics, uppercase, or use of colour).

Most studies on the effect of enhancement techniques have focused on the learning of grammatical forms, though (e.g., Jahan and Kormos, 2015; Winke, 2013). Fewer studies have examined their effect on vocabulary learning, and, when the intervention did concern vocabulary, it was typically used to signal to the reader that glosses or annotations were available for the highlighted words (e.g., Hulstijn, Hollander, & Greidanus, 1996; Laufer, 2005; Peters, Hulstijn, Sercu, & Lutjeharms, 2009).

Typographic enhancement of FSs may address one of the practical issues raised earlier in the section about incidental acquisition. While it increases the likelihood that learners will attend to the relevant word strings, it does not require the same resourcefulness on the part of the materials designer as "input flooding", i.e., inserting multiple instances of the same expression in a text (e.g., Pellicer-Sánchez, 2017; Webb et al., 2013). A recent study by Boers, Demecheleer, He, Deconinck, Stengers, and Eyckmans (2017), for example, presented learners with texts that were only manipulated by underlining FSs that were already present in them. The learners were found more likely in a post-reading test to recognize FSs from the texts if these had been typographically enhanced. Another recent study, by Szudarski and Carter (2016), compared the effect of input flooding alone with the effect of input flooding combined with typographic enhancement of the target collocations, and found that the latter condition led to greater learning gains.

While these studies support the hypothesis that typographically enhanced FSs attract attention, online reading measures can provide more direct evidence. Choi (2017) investigated the effect of typographic enhancement (bold typeface) on the processing and learning of L2 collocations. Participants were asked to read a text containing a set of target collocations in either an enhanced or unenhanced version while their eye movements were tracked. Not only did post-reading tests show an advantage for the enhanced version, but the eye-movement measures also showed that collocations in the enhanced version attracted more and longer fixations than the same collocations in the unenhanced version of the text. Worth mentioning is that the learners who had read the enhanced version of the text were found *less* successful at remembering segments from the text untouched by the enhancement than their peers who had read the version without any enhancement at all. A similar "trade-off" in learners' intake of enhanced and unenhanced phrases from a text was reported in the aforementioned study by Boers et al. (2017), where the enhancement of a small number of FSs led to particularly successful post-reading recognition of precisely these sequences but also an apparent reduction of these learners' intake of other sequences which had been left untouched in the text. It is perhaps to be expected that students will interpret enhancement as an effort on the part of the teacher/materials designer to signal the most important elements of a text, and so it is not so surprising they will focus less on what is left unenhanced. Similar concerns have been expressed about such side effects of typographic enhancement in the area of grammar acquisition research (Lee & Huang, 2008).

More studies involving typographic enhancement of FSs are available, but these will be reviewed further later because they involve intentional learning as well. Before we turn to intentional learning conditions, however, it is worth mentioning that FSs can also be made more salient in aural input. "Aural enhancement" is not uncommon in interactional feedback, for example, when a teacher uses prosodic cues to make particular language elements more perceptually salient (e.g., Nassaji, 2016, for a review of the research on interactional feedback). To the best of our knowledge, the effectiveness of prosodic enhancement for the purpose of FS acquisition in particular is as yet unexplored (but see Lin, this volume, for the potential benefits of intonation units for FS acquisition).

Intentional Learning of Formulaic Language

So far, our review has mostly concerned learning conditions where texts are manipulated with a view to increasing the likelihood of FS uptake. Crucially, however, the initiative lies with the learners as to whether they actually attend to and cognitively engage with the target FSs in manipulated texts. The interventions we discuss in the present section are ones where FSs are presented to learners more explicitly as objects of language study and where the intention of the activity is clearly to learn these items. We consider roughly three ways of creating these intentional learning conditions: (1) instructions to explore texts for the presence of FSs; (2) decontextualized FS-focused activities not necessarily linked to any input text; (3) engaging learners with particular characteristics of FSs that can render these more memorable.

It is worth mentioning that several of the studies we review here include comparisons of an intentional learning condition with an incidental and/or semi-incidental condition of the kinds discussed previously. In that regard, this line of investigation is reminiscent of comparisons conducted in the domain of single-word acquisition, such as Laufer's (2005) comparison of the effectiveness for word learning of (a) exclusively meaning-focused activities (which we have called incidental learning conditions), (b) activities with a focus on words as the need arises during primarily meaning-focused activities (akin in some ways to what we have labelled semi-incidental learning conditions), and (c) activities where words are presented as objects for language study (i.e., intentional learning conditions – the focus of the present section). As Laufer points out, this parallels the distinction originally made by Long (1991) in the realm of L2 grammar learning between "meaning-focused", "form-focused", and "forms-focused" activities.

Intentional Learning of Formulaic Language from Texts

We now turn to interventions where learners are *instructed explicitly to engage with the phraseological dimension of texts*, and which therefore belong to the realm of intentional learning as we defined it. An early investigation into the merits of such interventions was conducted by Boers, Eyckmans, Kappel, Stengers, and Demecheleer (2006). Two groups of EFL learners used the same in-class reading and listening texts in the course of a school year. One group was regularly asked to identify useful phrases in these texts, an activity – "text chunking" – advocated by Lewis (1997). The other group was not explicitly alerted to the phraseological dimension of the texts. At the end of the course, the students' oral proficiency was gauged in an interview. The text-chunking group was found to use more FSs than the comparison group. However, the greater number of FSs found in the utterances produced by the chunking group did not actually reflect greater uptake of these from the texts they had explored in class. Instead, the FSs used in the interview were mostly expressions "mined" from a text given as prompt for part of the interview. So, it seems the intervention equipped the students with a *strategic* advantage, but it is far from clear to what extent the text-chunking activities alone helped the students expand their repertoire of FS for active use in real-time communication. When the study was partially replicated with a new cohort of students, but *without* the use of an L2 text prompt in the end-of-course interview, again no compelling evidence emerged that students in the chunking group had added a greater number of FS to their repertoires than those in the comparison group (Stengers, Boers, Housen, & Eyckmans, 2010). It needs to be acknowledged, though, that an interview is probably too crude an elicitation instrument to reveal the true extent to which particular items were learned from texts spread over a whole course.

Peters (2009) conducted a shorter but more tightly controlled experiment using a post-test targeting precisely those lexical items included in a reading text. A number of lexical items were typographically enhanced and glossed. One group of EFL learners was simply instructed to focus on new vocabulary, while the second group was instructed explicitly to pay attention to collocations. Both groups showed substantial learning gains, but there was no clear effect of the instruction to pay special attention to collocations. It is likely that both groups engaged with the collocations to the same extent because of the enhancement in the text. Peters (2012) conducted a conceptual replication of her earlier study, this time with two groups of learners of L2 German. A number of words and FSs were typographically enhanced in a text, and these also came with a gloss. Other items were also glossed, but they were not enhanced in the text. On the post-test, the students performed better on the target items that were enhanced in the text (which adds to the body of evidence for the effectiveness of enhancement when it comes to FSs). As in the earlier study, one group of students was explicitly briefed beforehand about the importance of FSs. Again, however, this group did not perform noticeably better on the post-test items targeting the FSs than did their peers in the comparison group.

A number of studies have investigated the added value of "output" activities that require learners to recycle the FSs they have focused on in an input text. In Szudarski (2012), for example, intermediate learners were asked to read a short story containing verb-noun collocations. Participants were assigned to one of three conditions: reading only, reading followed by exercises on collocations from the text, and a control condition. Test results showed that the addition of exercises helped learners to acquire collocational knowledge at both receptive and productive levels. By contrast, the reading-only condition did not lead to much measurable learning. It is worth mentioning, though, that the verb-noun combinations in this study contained de-lexicalized verbs, which seem to be particularly problematic for L2 learners due to their lack of semantic distinctiveness and often due also to the non-congruency with L1 counterparts (Peters, 2016). Laufer and Girsai (2008) took a special interest in such non-congruency between L1 and L2 collocations, and investigated whether translation exercises might be a particularly beneficial addition to a reading activity. Three groups of EFL students read the same text containing as-yet-unfamiliar collocations (e.g., *hit the headlines*). Explicit steps were taken to clarify the meaning of these to the students. One group was subsequently asked to discuss the contents of the text and to debate a moral dilemma it raised. The second group did multiple-choice and completion exercises concerning the target collocations (but without involving comparisons with L1). The third group was given translation exercises, which naturally involve

L1 to L2 comparisons. In both an immediate and a delayed post-test, the latter group performed best and the group which had not done any vocabulary-focused exercises performed the poorest. It is perhaps worth mentioning that the post-test format chosen in this study – a translation test – may have given an edge to the students who had practiced the target items through translation exercises over those who had been given the collocation-focused exercises that bore less resemblance to the test format.

These studies by Szudarski (2012) and Laufer and Girsai (2008) evaluated the benefits of particular procedures in "one-off" experiments. To inform pedagogic decisions at the level of course design, however, it is also important to gauge the effects of a more sustained focus on FL throughout a course, involving various activities around FSs encountered in texts. Jones and Haywood (2004) describe an EAP course in which the students were regularly engaged in activities with a focus on FSs. While the authors found clear evidence that these students' awareness of FL increased, their actual use of FSs in their end-of-course essays did not differ markedly from that of a comparison group that had not received the FS-focused treatment. In a conceptual replication, Peters and Pauwels (2015) also examined the effect of integrating various FS-focused activities in an EAP course. They found evidence of an effect, but this evidence emerged much more clearly in an FS-focused recognition test than through the learners' spontaneous use of FSs in their end-of-course writing assignments. This illustrates again that it may take a lot of productive practice with newly learned FSs for learners to spontaneously and adequately deploy this knowledge in communicative tasks. The need to provide many opportunities for learners to consolidate knowledge to the extent that it becomes readily retrievable (i.e., "procedural") is fully recognized in the field (e.g., Gatbonton & Segalowitz, 2005; Wood, 2009).

Finally, a considerable amount of studies have explored the use of corpora as the input text for learning FSs. These data-driven learning (DDL) approaches usually set a task that involves learners working with corpus data. These conditions would also be considered intentional approaches of the sort covered in this section. However, since these are discussed in depth elsewhere in this volume (see Chapter 10), we refrain from reviewing them here.

Decontextualized Exercises on Formulaic Language

Several studies have investigated conditions for the learning of FSs that bypass their introduction through textual input. This has been done, for example, to compare the outcomes of incidental, semi-incidental, and intentional learning of collocations, as in a study by Sonbul and Schmitt (2013), who compared the outcomes of learning of collocations under three conditions: (1) reading a passage with multiple instances of the target collocations embedded; (2) reading the passage with the same target collocations typographically enhanced; (3) studying the target collocations as decontextualized items. Post-test results showed that reading enhanced text and studying decontextualized items both brought about more noticeable learning gains than the "purely" incidental learning condition.

Some experiments have compared different FS-focused study procedures with a view to evaluating what knowledge is engendered by these procedures. Webb and Kagimoto (2009) asked EFL learners to either read three example sentences containing the same verb-noun collocation (e.g., *sit exams*) or to copy the same collocation three times in gapped sentences. A series of post-tests revealed no overall difference in effectiveness between the two conditions. On the test format where the learners were prompted to recall the complete collocations, the overall success rate was under 30%. This is arguably a poor learning outcome given the time invested. If so, this may be due to the absence of any retrieval effort – the collocations were available for copying throughout the study procedure (see Karpicke & Roediger, 2008, for a review about the importance of retrieval practice in learning). A study by Alali and Schmitt (2012), for example, reported slightly better outcomes when learners completed gap-fill exercises by retrieving targets from memory than when they were asked to chorally repeat target collocations 10 times. A case for using more than a single study procedure is made by Zhang (2017), who assigned EFL learners to one of three learning conditions: (1) simply studying verb-noun collocations (e.g., *bear resemblance*); (2) inventing sentences incorporating the given collocations on display; and 3) a combination of both procedures. A control group only took the pre-test and the post-tests. The overall scores on the tests clearly indicate that the combined study procedure resulted in the greater gains. This outcome needs to be put into perspective, though, because the overall success rate obtained under this procedure was still only 35% better than what was attested in the control group. Again, it may be argued that, because the collocations were available to the students, the element of retrieval was missing from the study procedure. In a study with idioms as targets for learning, Stengers, Deconinck, Boers and Eyckmans (2016) also found that a copy exercise contributed very little to learners' retention of the expressions.

Giving participants the task to study FSs presented in a decontextualized fashion (i.e., not embedded in a text) can also help determine factors about the FSs "themselves" (rather than contextual variables) that make them relatively easy versus difficult to learn. For example, in an investigation where EFL learners were asked to study a list of idioms, Steinel, Hulstijn, and Steinel (2007) found that imageability (i.e., the ease with which an expression calls up a mental image) was one of the predictors of learning success. In another example of this line of research, Peters (2016) demonstrated that non-congruency with L1 counterparts hinders learning of collocations even when they are studied deliberately. How FSs are grouped together for deliberate study matters as well. Webb and Kagimoto (2011), for example, found that learning sets of adjective-noun collocations where the adjectives bear semantic resemblance (e.g., *narrow escape* and *slim chance*; *tall order* and *high spirits*) is much harder than learning the same collocations grouped in ways that minimize the risk of inter-item confusion. This is reminiscent of what has been found repeatedly in relation to grouping semantically related words together (e.g., Erten & Tekin, 2008).

Given that most of the studies we have reviewed so far in this chapter are framed in one way or another as initiatives to help inform pedagogical practice, it is rather surprising that very few studies to date have explicitly taken as a point of departure how FSs are actually tackled in mainstream language education, as reflected, for example, in popular commercially available course books and textbooks. One exception is a study by Boers, Demecheleer, Coxhead, and Webb (2014), who first identified exercise formats for practicing verb–noun collocations that are commonly used in EFL textbooks and then put these to the test in classroom experiments. Many of the exercise formats were variants of matching operations where the collocation is broken up into its constituent parts, and the challenge for the learner is to re-assemble them (e.g., in a gap-fill exercise where the missing verb is to be supplied to match the given noun collocate). Often a number of choices are presented to the learner (e.g., *do/give/make + a suggestion*), and the task is to discriminate between the correct choice and the lures. The learning gains in the several trials reported in Boers et al. (2014) turned out discouragingly poor: delayed post-test scores were typically just 5–10% better than the pre-test scores. In many cases, the students erroneously reproduced the lures they had contemplated (and sometimes chosen) while doing the exercises, although corrective feedback was given at the end of each exercise. In an approximate replication, Boers, Dang, and Strong (2017) found that this risk of inter-item confusion was minimized by a gap-fill exercise format where the collocations (to be chosen from) are kept intact from the start.

What is striking about many textbook exercises on FSs is that they rely on learning through trial and error. Boers et al.'s (2017) analysis of 323 exercises found in a corpus of 10 EFL textbook series revealed that more than half of these do *not* present users with examples of the targeted FSs (such as collocations) prior to or alongside the exercise. Unless the learner already knows the expressions, doing these exercises inevitably amounts to a fair amount of guesswork, and it seems the textbook authors rely on teachers' corrective feedback to override memories of wrong choices. The data from the classroom experiments reported in Boers et al. (2014) and Boers et al. (2017) suggest, however, that wrong responses made in a collocation exercise do risk leaving undesirable traces in memory, and that these may compete for selection when the learner later tries to retrieve the right expression. If so, then it is probably judicious to minimize the risk of error at the exercise stage. One way of doing this is to present learners with exemplars of the target expressions alongside the exercise, as is done in some resources for independent study, such as McCarthy and O'Dell (2005). Stengers and Boers (2015) compared this exemplar-guided implementation of a gap-fill exercise on Spanish verb–noun collocations with a trial-and-error implementation and found the former to be slightly more beneficial. At the same time, the learning gains attested for that condition in a delayed post-test were far from spectacular either

(18%). This again suggests that practice without any retrieval effort should not be expected to work wonders.

Using exemplars is also a core feature of approaches known as data-driven learning (DDL), often associated with the use of corpus tools such as concordances. However, as that rapidly expanding area merits a chapter of its own (Cobb, this volume), we shall refrain from discussing it here.

Making Formulaic Language Memorable

The interventions reviewed so far involve steps to expose learners to multiple instances of selected FSs, to increase the salience of those FSs in texts, to prompt learners to imitate or reproduce FSs they have been presented with, to give learners feedback on FSs they have generated, and to engage learners in the exploration of sets of exemplars. Generally absent from such interventions are attempts on the part of the teacher or materials designer to engage learners with facets of the target FSs that may render them memorable. Two such facets have received a fair amount of attention from applied linguists.

The first applies mostly to figurative idioms and concerns steps to connect their (abstract) idiomatic meaning (e.g., *take a back seat* = allowing someone else to take control and make the important decisions) to a literal reading of the expression (e.g., one can take a back seat in a car and thus leave the driving to someone else) (e.g., Boers, Demecheleer, & Eyckmans, 2004; Boers, Eyckmans, & Stengers, 2007). Sometimes learners can presumably make these associations autonomously, but for many idioms it helps if learners are at least pointed in the right direction. Such resuscitation of a literal reading is likely to lend concreteness and imageability to the expression, and – in keeping with *Dual Coding* theory (e.g., Paivio, 1986) – this is believed to benefit memory. In a similar vein, figuratively used prepositional and phrasal verbs can be made more imageable by pointing out the metaphors that underpin them (e.g., Boers, 2000). For instance, the use of *out* in *find out* can be made sense of if one realizes that "seeing" is often equated with "knowing" (hence expressions such as "I see what you mean" and "I'm still in the dark about it") and that taking something "out" of a container will make it visible. A substantial number of studies have furnished empirical support for such steps that make idioms and prepositional/phrasal verbs more memorable by evoking their literal underpinnings (Boers, 2013, for a review).

The second facet of FSs that may be exploitable for the purpose of memorability is their sound patterning. A pattern that has attracted a fair amount of attention in recent years is alliteration (*cut corners; slippery slope; time will tell; toss and turn; good as gold; life-long learning; better safe than sorry*), whose incidence in various segments of English phraseology by far exceeds statistical chance. For example, approximately 17% of expressions listed in English idiom dictionaries display alliteration (Boers & Lindstromberg, 2009). A series of experiments with ESL and EFL learners has shown that alliterative FSs tend to enjoy a small advantage over non-alliterative matched controls in recall tests, but crucially also that this advantage is enhanced quite substantially when learners' attention is directed to the presence of alliteration (e.g., Boers, Lindstromberg, & Eyckmans, 2014a; Eyckmans, Boers, & Lindstromberg, 2016; Lindstromberg & Boers, 2008b). It is likely that similar effects of attention-directing can be obtained with FSs that exhibit rhyme (e.g., *steer clear; brain drain; left high and dry*) or assonance (e.g., *small talk; cook the books; hit and miss*) (e.g., Boers et al., 2014b; Lindstromberg & Boers, 2008c). Of particular interest here from a practical perspective is that it takes very little investment of time or effort for a teacher to point out a pattern such as alliteration in an expression so as to unlock its full mnemonic potential. Considering the conspicuous presence of alliteration in English phraseology, it is rather surprising to find no attempts in EFL textbooks to exploit it in some way.

Conclusions and Future Directions

In this chapter, we have reviewed diverse studies examining interventions intended to accelerate acquisition of L2 FSs. The interventions range from manipulating input texts to the use of "mnemonics". We have characterized the conditions for FS learning created in the interventions as incidental, semi-incidental, and intentional, while recognizing that these distinctions are not always easy to make. We have sometimes made evaluative comments concerning the amount of learning observed in the studies. There is an ongoing debate in the realm of L2 vocabulary research about the relative contributions of incidental and intentional learning conditions. It is generally accepted that intentional approaches bring about noticeable gains at a faster rate (e.g., Laufer, 2003; Lin & Hirsh, 2012). However, Nation and Webb (2011) argue that this needs to be put into perspective because incidental learning conditions, such as extensive reading, provide additional opportunities for skills development (such as reading comprehension and reading fluency) beyond the acquisition of a pre-selected set of new words. The effectiveness of treatment conditions is typically evaluated by comparing outcomes specifically concerning a narrow set of pre-selected targets (such as a pre-selected set of FSs), but this may overlook the possibility that learners in a comparison condition who did not fare so well on that specific front benefited from their treatment in other ways that fell outside the scope of the test measures (Boers, 2015).

In any case, comparisons of the relative effectiveness of incidental and intentional approaches to FS learning across studies will inevitably lack validity due to the many differences involved (type and number of target FSs, participant profiles, type and timing of tests, amount of time on the activity, etc.). The closest to a valid comparison are studies where incidental and intentional learning conditions were assessed within a single research endeavour, such as Sonbul and Schmitt (2013). What is nonetheless safe to say after inspecting the body of evidence on incidental FS uptake from exposure is that it tends to require multiple encounters with new FSs in a relatively short time span for measurable learning to happen. It is important to reiterate that evidence of incidental learning of new FSs emerged in these studies *only* when texts were "seeded" with sufficient numbers of instances of the target FSs – and what number is sufficient is likely to depend on circumstances (including the nature of the FSs, their dispersion in the text, the learners' proficiency level, and the modality of the text input). As pointed out, it is quite unlikely for the same FSs to occur multiple times in an authentic (i.e., non-manipulated) text, and so it would seem that the chances of "purely" incidental uptake by L2 students will ultimately depend on whether practitioners or material writers are prepared to embark on the laborious process of creating the kind of textual input that was used in some of the studies on incidental learning of collocations that we have reviewed here. If this is not realistic, it does by no means follow that authentic texts make no contribution to FS learning. As hinted in the introduction to this review, any incidental encounter with an FS that was intentionally focused on some time previously has the potential to further entrench it in memory and to help the learners fine-tune their appreciation of its usage patterns. Incidental learning is likely to be incremental, and the gradual deepening and refinement of knowledge over time is something that the offline test measures used in most studies almost inevitably fail to capture. In future research it may therefore be worth investigating (e.g., by means of eye-tracking) how brief prior intentional study of lexical items such as FSs influences learners' reading behaviour as they re-encounter the items during content-focused reading, and to compare learning outcomes from this to a reading condition with input flooding.

If intentional learning of FSs is expected to yield noticeable gains faster than incidental learning, this needs to be qualified, too. As our review shows, intentional learning procedures can vary widely in their degrees of effectiveness. For example, mere copying of FSs, without any requirement for learners to try and retrieve the items from memory, did not appear to be a particularly powerful learning practice. Neither did matching-type exercises commonly used in contemporary course books seem effective. The effectiveness of any pedagogical procedure – be it incidental, intentional, or both – will inevitably depend on the quality of its design and how it is implemented.

A part of this review concerned studies on the benefits of attention-drawing techniques such as typographic enhancement. These "semi-incidental" learning conditions seem to hold good promise – they were generally found to lead to better uptake of FSs than "purely" incidental conditions, and they may even be a match for FS-focused exercises (Sonbul & Schmitt, 2013), although it is clear that much more research is needed to confirm this theory. The benefits of typographic enhancement have been interpreted as being a direct consequence of increased attention to the target lexical items. Eye-tracking data, providing an online record of learners' attention to enhanced input, have confirmed this assumption (Choi, 2017). The practical advantage of typographic enhancement is that it is very easy to implement – easier than input flooding – although selecting items for enhancement is not straightforward. Teachers who wish to enhance FSs in a text may need familiarity with resources such as online corpus tools to be able to ascertain that the targets they are selecting actually are FSs and ones deserving of their students' attention. It may also be worth recalling that the increased attention usurped by enhanced text elements can be in detriment of text comprehension and of intake of other potentially useful language from the text. Future research should take advantage of the benefits of eye-tracking as a direct measure of learners' attention to vocabulary items and use it in combination with explicit vocabulary tests, to gain a richer and more accurate picture of the effect of different attention-grabbing techniques on learners' noticing of FL and the subsequent learning. So far, research on enhancement of FSs has focused exclusively on written text. The effect of other types of enhancement techniques, such as auditory input manipulation, remains to be explored.

We have for convenience's sake used "formulaic sequence" (Wray, 2002) as an umbrella term in this review. A downside of using an umbrella term is that it risks concealing the diversity of the phenomenon at hand. Different FSs pose different challenges for learners and may therefore require different pedagogical intervention to help learners meet these challenges. In several of the studies reviewed here, "collocation" serves a similar umbrella function and has been used to characterize word partnerships regardless of semantics. For pedagogical purposes, however, in particular with a view toward putting oneself in the learner's shoes, recognizing a difference between what have "traditionally" been called collocations and idioms may be useful (Boers & Webb, 2015), with collocations being comparatively easy to comprehend (if one knows the meaning of the constituent words) and idioms being harder to figure out due to their "non-compositionality" (in the sense that the meaning of the expression does not follow straightforwardly from adding up the meanings of the constituent words). For example, while there have been interesting attempts at exploring the role of frequency in incidental learning conditions, it stands to reason that the effect of frequency is modulated by other factors, and the semantic nature of the target items is likely to be one of them. Yet, it must be possible to take this factor into consideration (see Boers, Lindstromberg & Webb, 2014, for an example of a very modest attempt at an exploration of this kind). After all, many of the studies reviewed here used a variety of test measures, including ones that gauge uptake of form and ones that gauge uptake of meaning. It may be worth (re-)examining such test data more closely at the item level, because this may help determine what sort of learning condition benefits the learning of what sort of FS and what aspects of knowledge about certain FSs are privileged by a certain learning condition. Given the complexity and the multifaceted nature of the phenomenon at hand, a one-size-fits-all approach to the learning and teaching of FL is very unlikely to be tenable.

A final comment concerns the pedagogical orientation of the strand of research we have reviewed here. If, ultimately, the aim is to inform pedagogical practice, then one must wonder if it might not be useful to find out more systematically how teachers and course designers around the world are already addressing the challenge of FL learning. Unfortunately, little is known (apart from what is reflected in commercially available manuals and textbooks) about the materials and procedures intended for FS learning that are used in "real" classrooms (and L2 learning environments more generally). If applied research wishes to inform pedagogical practice, a legitimate question to ask is whether that research should not also be informed *by* the current realities of pedagogical practice, at least so as to prioritize those questions on the research agenda that matter the most to educational practitioners and to their learners.

References

Alali, F., & Schmitt, N. (2012). Teaching formulaic sequences: The same or different from teaching single words? *TESOL Journal, 3*(2), 153–180.

Bisson, M.-J., Van Heuven, W., Conklin, K., & Tunney, R. (2015). The role of verbal and pictorial information in multi-modal incidental acquisition of foreign language vocabulary. *Quarterly Journal of Experimental Psychology, 68*(7), 1306–1326.

Boers, F. (2000). Metaphor awareness and vocabulary retention. *Applied Linguistics, 21*(4), 553–571.

Boers, F. (2013). Cognitive Linguistic approaches to second language vocabulary: Assessment and integration. *Language Teaching, 46*(2), 208–224.

Boers, F. (2015). Weighing the merits of form-focused intervention. *Language Teaching Research, 19*(3), 251–253.

Boers, F., Dang, C. T., & Strong, B. (2017). Comparing the effectiveness of phrase-focused exercises. A partial replication of Boers, Demecheleer, Coxhead, and Webb (2014). *Language Teaching Research, 21*(3), 362–280.

Boers, F., Demecheleer, M., Coxhead, A., & Webb, S. (2014). Gauging the effects of exercises on verb – noun collocations. *Language Teaching Research, 18*(1), 54–74.

Boers, F., Demecheleer, M., & Eyckmans, J. (2004). Etymological elaboration as a strategy for learning figurative idioms. In P. Bogaards & B. Laufer (Eds.), *Vocabulary in a second language: Selection, acquisition and testing* (pp. 53–78). Amsterdam and Philadelphia: John Benjamins.

Boers, F., Demecheleer, M., He, L., Deconinck, J., Stengers, H., & Eyckmans, J. (2017). Typographic enhancement of multiword units in second language text. *International Journal of Applied Linguistics, 27*(2), 448–469.

Boers, F., Eyckmans, J., Kappel, J., Stengers, H., & Demecheleer, M. (2006). Formulaic sequences and perceived oral proficiency: Putting a lexical approach to the test. *Language Teaching Research, 10*(3), 245–261.

Boers, F., Eyckmans, J., & Stengers, H. (2007). Presenting figurative idioms with a touch of etymology: More than mere mnemonics? *Language Teaching Research, 11*(1), 43–62.

Boers, F., & Lindstromberg, S. (2009). *Optimizing a lexical approach to instructed second language acquisition*. Basingstoke: Palgrave Macmillan.

Boers, F., Lindstromberg, S., & Eyckmans, J. (2014a). Is alliteration mnemonic without awareness-raising? *Language Awareness, 23*(4), 291–303.

Boers, F., Lindstromberg, S., & Eyckmans, J. (2014b). When does assonance make L2 lexical phrases memorable? *The European Journal of Applied Linguistics and TEFL, 3*(1), 93–107.

Boers, F., Lindstromberg, S., & Webb, S. (2014). Further evidence of the comparative memorability of alliterative expressions in second language learning. *RELC Journal, 45*(1), 85–99.

Boers, F., & Webb, S. (2015). Gauging the semantic transparency of idioms: Do natives and learners see eye to eye? In R. Heredia & A. Cieslicka (Eds.), *Bilingual figurative language processing* (pp. 368–392). Cambridge: Cambridge University Press.

Brown, R., Waring, R., & Donkaewbua, S. (2008). Incidental vocabulary acquisition from reading, reading-while-listening, and listening. *Reading in a Foreign Language, 20*(2), 136–163.

Choi, S. (2017). Processing and learning of enhanced English collocations: An eye-movement study. *Language Teaching Research, 21*(3), 403–426.

Crossley, A. S., Salsbury, T., & McNamara, D. S. (2015). Assessing lexical proficiency using analytic ratings: A case for collocation accuracy. *Applied Linguistics, 36*(5), 570–590.

Chun, D. M., & Plass, J. L. (1996). Effects of multimedia annotations on vocabulary acquisition. *The Modern Language Journal, 80*(2), 183–198.

Dagut, M., & Laufer, B. (1985). Avoidance of phrasal verbs – A case for contrastive analysis. *Studies in Second Language Acquisition, 7*(1), 73–79.

Durrant, P. & Schmitt, N. (2009). To what extent do native and nonnative writers make use of collocations? *International Review of Applied Linguistics, 47*, 157–177.

Durrant, P., & Schmitt, N. (2010). Adult learners' retention of collocations from exposure. *Second Language Research, 26*(2), 163–188.

Ellis, R. (2015). *Understanding second language acquisition*. Oxford: Oxford University Press.

Erten, I. H., & Tekin, M. (2008). Effects on vocabulary acquisition of presenting new words in semantic sets versus semantically unrelated sets. *System, 36*(3), 407–422.

Eyckmans, J., Boers, F., & Lindstromberg, S. (2016). The impact of imposing processing strategies on L2 learners' deliberate study of lexical phrases. *System, 56*, 127–139.

Gatbonton, E., & Segalowitz, N. (2005). Rethinking communicative language teaching: A focus on accuracy and fluency. *Canadian Modern Language Journal, 61*(3), 325–353.

Godfroid, A., Boers, F., & Housen, A. (2013). An eye for words: Gauging the role of attention in L2 vocabulary acquisition by means of eye-tracking. *Studies in Second Language Acquisition, 35*(3), 483–517.

Granger, S. (1998). Prefabricated patterns in advanced EFL writing: Collocations and formulae. In A. P. Cowie (Ed.), *Phraseology: Theory, analysis, and applications* (pp. 145–160). Oxford: Oxford University Press.

Hoang, H., & Boers, F. (2016). Re-telling a story in a second language: How well do adult learners mine an input text for multiword expressions? *Studies in Second Language Learning and Teaching, 6*(3), 513–535.

Horst, M., Cobb, T., & Meara, P. (1998). Beyond a clockwork orange: Acquiring second language vocabulary through reading. *Reading in a Foreign Language, 11*(2), 207–223.

Hulstijn, J. H., Hollander, M., & Greidanus, T. (1996). Incidental vocabulary learning by advanced foreign language students: The influence of marginal glosses, dictionary use, and reoccurrence of unknown words. *Modern Language Journal, 80*(3), 327–339.

Jahan, A., & Kormos, J. (2015). The impact of textual enhancement on EFL learners' grammatical awareness of future plans and intentions. *International Journal of Applied Linguistics, 25*(1), 46–66.

Jones, M., & Haywood, S. (2004). Facilitating the acquisition of formulaic sequences: An exploratory study. In N. Schmitt (Ed.), *Formulaic sequences* (pp. 269–300). Amsterdam: John Benjamins.

Karpicke, J. D., & Roediger, H. L. III (2008). The critical importance of retrieval for learning. *Science, 319*, 966–968.

Kremmel, B., Brunfaut, T., & Alderson, J. C. (2017). Exploring the role of phraseological knowledge in foreign language reading. *Applied Linguistics, 38*(6), 848–870. doi: 10.1093/applin/amv070.

Kweon, S., & Kim, H. (2008). Beyond raw frequency: Incidental vocabulary acquisition in extensive reading. *Reading in a Foreign Language, 20*(2), 191–215.

Laufer, B. (2003). Vocabulary acquisition in a second language. Do learners really acquire most vocabulary by reading? *Canadian Modern Language Review, 59*(4), 565–585.

Laufer, B. (2005). Focus on form in second language vocabulary acquisition. In S. H. Foster-Cohen, M. P. Garcia-Mayo, & J. Cenoz (Eds.), *EUROSLA Yearbook 5* (pp. 223–250). Amsterdam: John Benjamins.

Laufer, B., & Girsai, N. (2008). Form-focused instruction in second language vocabulary learning: A case for contrastive analysis and translation. *Applied Linguistics, 29*(4), 1–23.

Laufer, B., & Rozovski-Roitblat, B. (2015). Retention of new words: Quantity of encounters, quality of task, and degree of knowledge. *Language Teaching Research, 19*(6), 687–711.

Lee, S-K., & Huang, H-T. (2008). Visual input enhancement and grammar learning: A meta-analytic review. *Studies in Second Language Acquisition, 30*(3), 307–331.

Lewis, M. (1993). *The lexical approach*. Hove: LTP.

Lewis, M. (1997). *Implementing the lexical approach*. Hove: LTP.

Lin, C., & Hirsh, D. (2012). Manipulating instructional method: The effect on productive vocabulary use. In D. Hirsh (Ed.), *Current perspectives in second language vocabulary research* (pp. 117–148). Bern, Switzerland: Peter Lang.

Lin, P. M. (2012). Sound evidence: The missing piece of the jigsaw in formulaic language research. *Applied Linguistics, 33*(3), 342–347.

Lindstromberg, S., & Boers, F. (2008a). *Teaching chunks of language*. Rum, Austria: Helbling Languages.

Lindstromberg, S., & Boers, F. (2008b). The mnemonic effect of noticing alliteration in lexical chunks. *Applied Linguistics, 29*(2), 200–222.

Lindstromberg, S., & Boers, F. (2008c). Phonemic repetition and the learning of lexical chunks: The mnemonic power of assonance. *System, 36*(3), 423–436.

Long, M. (1991). Focus on form: A design feature in language teaching methodology. In K. de Bot, R. Ginsberg, & C. Kramsch (Eds.), *Foreign language research in a cross-cultural perspective* (pp. 39–52). Amsterdam: John Benjamins.

Martinez, R., & N. Schmitt (2012). A phrasal expressions list. *Applied Linguistics, 33*(3), 299–320.

McCarthy, M., & O'Dell, F. (2005). *English collocations in use*. Cambridge: Cambridge University Press.

Meunier, F. (2012). Formulaic language and language teaching. *Annual Review of Applied Linguistics, 32*(2), 111–129.

Montero Perez, M., Van Den Noortgate, W., & Desmet, P. (2013). Captioned video for L2 listening and vocabulary learning: A meta-analysis. *System, 41*(3), 720–739.

Nassaji, H. (2016). *The interactional feedback dimension in instructed second language acquisition*. London: Bloomsbury.

Nation, I. S. P. (2014). How much input do you need to learn the most frequent 9,000 words? *Reading in a Foreign Language, 26*(2), 1–16.

Nation, I. S. P., & Webb, S. (2011). *Researching and analyzing vocabulary*. Boston: Heinle, Cengage Learning.

Paivio, A. (1986). *Mental representations: A dual coding approach*. New York: Oxford University Press.

Pellicer-Sánchez, A. (2017). Learning L2 collocations incidentally from reading. *Language Teaching Research*, *21*(3), 381–402.

Pellicer-Sánchez, A., & Schmitt, N. (2010). Incidental vocabulary acquisition from an authentic novel: Do things fall apart? *Reading in a Foreign Language*, *22*(1), 31–55.

Pellicer-Sánchez, A., & Siyanova-Chanturia, A. (under review). *Learning collocations incidentally from reading: A comparison of eye movements in a first and second language.*

Peters, E. (2009). Learning collocations through attention-drawing techniques: A qualitative and quantitative analysis. In A. Barfield & H. Gyllstad (Eds.), *Researching collocations in another language: Multiple interpretations* (pp. 194–207). Basingstoke: Palgrave Macmillan.

Peters, E. (2012). Learning German formulaic sequences: The effect of two attention-drawing techniques. *Language Learning Journal*, *40*(1), 65–79.

Peters, E. (2016). The learning burden of collocations: The role of interlexical and intralexical factors. *Language Teaching Research*, *20*(1), 113–138.

Peters, E., Hulstijn, J. H., Sercu, L., & Lutjeharms, M. (2009). Learning L2 German vocabulary through reading: The effect of three enhancement techniques compared. *Language Learning*, *59*(1), 113–151.

Peters, E., & Pauwels, P. (2015). Learning academic formulaic sequences. *Journal of English for academic purposes*, *20*, 28–39.

Pigada, M., & Schmitt, N. (2006). Vocabulary acquisition from extensive reading: A case study. *Reading in a Foreign Language*, *18*(1), 1–28.

Pulido, D. (2007). The relationship between text comprehension and second language incidental vocabulary acquisition: A matter of topic familiarity? *Language Learning*, *57*(1), 155–199.

Rott, S. (1999). The effect of exposure frequency on intermediate language learners' incidental vocabulary acquisition through reading. *Studies in Second Language Acquisition*, *21*(4), 589–619.

Schmidt, R. (2001). Attention. In P. Robinson (Ed.), *Cognition and second language instruction* (pp. 3–32). Cambridge: Cambridge University Press.

Schmitt, N. (2010). *Researching vocabulary*. London: Palgrave Macmillan.

Sharwood-Smith, M. (1993). Input enhancement and instructed SLA: Theoretical bases. *Studies in Second Language Acquisition*, *15*(2), 165–179.

Sonbul, S., & Schmitt, N. (2013). Explicit and Implicit lexical knowledge: Acquisition of collocations under different input conditions. *Language Learning*, *63*(1), 121–159.

Steinel, M. P., Hulstijn, J. H., & Steinel, W. (2007). Second language idiom learning in a paired-associate paradigm: Effects of direction of learning, direction of testing, idiom imageability, and idiom transparency. *Studies in Second Language Acquisition*, *29*(3), 449–484.

Stengers, H., & Boers, F. (2015). Exercises on collocations: A comparison of trial-and-error and exemplar-guided procedures. *Journal of Spanish Language Teaching*, *2*(2), 152–164.

Stengers, H., Boers, F., Housen, A., & Eyckmans, J. (2010). Does chunking foster chunk uptake? In S. De Knop, F. Boers, & A. De Rycker (Eds.), *Fostering language teaching efficiency through cognitive linguistics* (pp. 99–117). Berlin and New York, NY: Mouton de Gruyter.

Stengers, H., Boers, F., Housen, A., & Eyckmans, J. (2011). Formulaic sequences and L2 oral proficiency: Does the type of target language influence the association? *International Review of Applied Linguistics in Language Teaching*, *49*(4), 321–343.

Stengers, H., Deconinck, J., Boers, F., & Eyckmans, J. (2016). Does copying idioms promote their retention? *Computer Assisted Language Learning*, *29*(2), 289–301.

Szudarski, P. (2012). Effects of meaning- and formed-focused instruction on the acquisition of verb – noun collocations in L2 English. *Journal of Second Language Teaching and Research, 1*(2), 3–37.

Szudarski, P., & Carter, R. (2016). The role of input flood and input enhancement in EFL learners' acquisition of collocations. *International Journal of Applied Linguistics, 26*(2), 245–265

Tekmen, E. A., & Daloglu, A. (2006). An investigation of incidental vocabulary acquisition in relation to learner proficiency level and word frequency. *Foreign Language Annals, 39*(2), 220–243.

VanPatten, B. (2002). Processing instruction: An update. *Language Learning, 52*(2), 755–803.

Van Zeeland, H., & Schmitt, N. (2013). Incidental vocabulary acquisition through L2 listening: A dimensions approach. *System, 41*(3), 609–624.

Vidal, K. (2011). A comparison of the effects of reading and listening on incidental vocabulary acquisition. *Language Learning, 61*(1), 219–258.

Webb, S. (2007). The effects of repetition on vocabulary knowledge. *Applied Linguistics, 28*(1), 46–65.

Webb, S. (2008). The effects of context on incidental vocabulary learning. *Reading in a Foreign Language, 20*(2), 232–245.

Webb, S., & Chang, A. (2015). Second language vocabulary learning through extensive reading with audio support: How do frequency and distribution of occurrence affect learning? *Language Teaching Research, 19*(6), 667–686.

Webb, S., & Chang, A. (under review). *How does mode of input affect the incidental learning of multiword combinations?*

Webb, S., & Kagimoto, E. (2009). The effects of vocabulary learning on collocation and meaning. *TESOL Quarterly, 43*(1), 55–77.

Webb, S., & Kagimoto, E. (2011). Learning collocations: Do the number of collocates, position of the node word, and synonymy affect learning? *Applied Linguistics, 32*(3), 259–276.

Webb, S., Newton, J., & Chang, A. (2013). Incidental learning of collocation. *Language Learning, 63*(1), 91–120.

Winke, P. M. (2013). The effects of input enhancement on grammar learning and comprehension: A modified replication of Lee (2007) with eye-movement data. *Studies in Second Language Acquisition, 35*(2), 323–352.

Wood, D. (2009). Effects of focused instruction of formulaic sequences on fluent expression in second language narratives: A case study. *Canadian Journal of Applied Linguistics, 12*(1), 39–57.

Wray, A. (2002). *Formulaic language and the lexicon*. Cambridge: Cambridge University Press.

Zhang, X. (2017). Effects of receptive-productive integration tasks and prior knowledge of component words on L2 collocation development. *System, 66*, 156–167.

9
TESTING FORMULAIC LANGUAGE

Henrik Gyllstad and Norbert Schmitt

Introduction

As has been shown in this volume, formulaic language (FL) has been found to be a pervasive phenomenon in English, and is essential for using it effectively and appropriately. For example, it has been found that FL realizes key functions, e.g., requesting (*Would you please X?*) (Nattinger & DeCarrico, 1992) and meanings (*I'm not sure if X* = expressing uncertainty) (Biber, Johansson, Leech, Conrad, & Finegan, 1999). As the importance of FL has become increasingly apparent, moves have been made to identify Formulaic Sequences (FSs), compile lists of these items, and design tests. In comparison to single-word vocabulary, however, the identification and testing of FL is still in an embryonic stage. Single-word vocabulary testing has benefitted from the development of word lists, which have allowed the testing of the wider vocabulary of a language. For example, the *General Service List* (West, 1953) was influential in materials writing, and thus also the testing of the words appearing in those materials. Towards the end of the century, standardized tests of English single-word vocabulary began appearing, notably the *Vocabulary Levels Test* (VLT) (Nation, 1990), the *Eurocentres Vocabulary Test* (Meara & Jones, 1988), and the *EFL Vocabulary Tests* (Meara, 1992). But around the same time, as there was a growing awareness of the fact that that vocabulary consisted of much more than just individual words, attempts were made to measure knowledge of FSs with newly designed tests (e.g., the *Word Associates Test*, Read, 1998; *DISCO*, Eyckmans, 2009). However, the testing of FL has proved more difficult than that of individual words. Consequently, there is still no consensus on the best ways to measure FL and no test which has been recognized as a standard measurement. This chapter will review tests of FL to date, identify key issues, and suggest ways in which the field can move forward in developing the next generation of formulaic measurement.

Tests of Formulaic Language

Despite a growing interest in FL generally over the last couple of decades, the field is far from having developed anything close to a standardized test. This is very different from single-word vocabulary where several tests are accepted and widely used (e.g., those previously mentioned). Several factors make the testing of FL a particularly challenging endeavour. First, FL is made up of numerous disparate categories, which all have their own particular characteristics: e.g., idioms (focus on non-compositionality), collocations (focus on word partnerships), lexical bundles (focus on recurring exact word strings), and phrasal verbs (focus on verb-based multiword units which typically are non-compositional). Therefore, creating a test format which can adequately measure every different category equally well is practically impossible. Second, there are a very large number of FSs, with Pawley and Syder (1983) suggesting that they amount at least to "several hundreds of thousands" (p. 213), while Jackendoff (1995) concludes that the phrasal lexicon may be the same or larger than the lexicon of single words. These two factors work against both the identification of the target population and the representative sampling of items from that population. This leaves researchers in a very challenging position, and it is probably next to impossible to develop a definite list of all the existing FSs in a language, and then to develop a test for these sequences.

Another factor involves the definition of FL (also connected with Point 1), obviously a prerequisite for testing. Definitions containing statistical criteria can be precise and measurable, e.g., MI scores in the frequency approach to collocations. But many criteria are much more subjective, e.g., the degree of compositionality for idioms (Grant & Nation, 2006), as they tend to rely on researcher intuition to some extent. An even fuzzier criterion is that of "holistic storage", which is mentioned in some definitions of FL (such as Wray, 2002), but is virtually impossible to operationalize. Also, as has been argued by Read and Nation (2004), what is "holistic" varies from person to person, and even varies from time to time within a person:

> the means of storage and retrieval of the same sequence can differ from one individual to another, and can differ from one time to another for the same individual depending on a range of factors such as changes in proficiency, changes in processing demands, and changes in communicative purpose.
>
> (p. 25)

Clearly, the rather complex and heterogeneous nature of FL presents challenges when it comes to testing and assessment, and there is a shortage of research to date on how it can and should be measured. A telling sign of this is the absence of assessment and testing as one of the identified main strands of activity in a thematic issue on FL in the *Annual Review of Applied Linguistics* in 2012 (Wray, 2012). The present situation is, thus, that there is no established best practice for how to test FL, let alone a standardized test of FL ability.

Research Including Assessment of Formulaic Language

Despite the absence of tests of overall FL, a number of tests target knowledge of particular categories (e.g., collocations, idioms, word associations and phrasal verbs). Whereas idioms have received much attention in research on processing, from a testing point of view, the most frequent type of FS targeted is seemingly collocation. A number of studies have involved analyses of corpora of L2 essays written in English (e.g., Howarth, 1996; Laufer & Waldman, 2011; Nesselhauf, 2005; Siyanova-Chanturia, 2015) (see Chapter 12 in this volume for a discussion of these studies).[1] Furthermore, there are a number of studies in which some sort of elicitation technique has been used (e.g., Bahns & Eldaw, 1993; Farghal & Obiedat, 1995; Garnier & Schmitt, 2016). Finally, there are a handful of published studies in which the overarching aim has been to develop tests of collocation knowledge: Eyckmans (2009), Gyllstad (2009), and Revier (2009). There are also tests of word associations that are relevant in this regard: Read (1993), Vives Boix (1995), and Wolter (2005). Due to length restrictions, we will focus here on seven tests which exemplify a range of formats and that illustrate key issues for the development of FL tests.

The Word Associates Test (Read, 1993, 1998)

The *Word Associates Test* (WAT) is one of the oldest tests, which measures collocation knowledge as one type of FL as part of the test format (it also measures meaning knowledge based on synonyms[2]). It is probably also the best-known of the tests reviewed here. It was originally developed by Read (1993), and in its initial conception it was intended to measure knowledge of academic English vocabulary, as represented by the words in the University Word List (UWL) (Xue & Nation, 1984), an 800-word compilation based on various frequency counts of academic texts. In its revised version, it is aimed at measuring "the extent to which learners were familiar with the meanings and uses of a target word" (Read, 1998, p. 43), with the "uses" part measured by a matching collocation format. The test presents 40 adjectives like the example shown in Figure 9.1. The task is to circle the four words which associate with the target item, for example, in the figure, *quick* and *surprising* (synonyms) and *change* and *noise* (collocations).

The test features relatively few words selected for having strong and recognizable collocates. (This is one reason for using only adjectives for target words.)

Sudden

Beautiful	quick	surprising	thirsty

change	doctor	noise	school

FIGURE 9.1 An example task item from the Word Associates Test (new version). (from Read, 2000, p. 184)

Notably, the WAT was never designed to generalize to inferences about wider collocation knowledge, but rather a test which uses collocation knowledge as a proxy for "depth of knowledge". This concept is extremely vague (see Read, 2004), and it is interesting that Read used a type of FL to represent this more advanced quality of lexical knowledge. Perhaps this should not be surprising, as most research spanning from Bahns and Eldaw (1993) to Siyanova-Chanturia (2015) points to mastery of FL being one of the later aspects of lexical knowledge to be acquired.

The WAT uses a recognition format, partly due to practical constraints. Research shows that productive mastery of collocation is much more difficult than receptive knowledge, with Laufer and Waldman (2011) finding only about half the number of collocations in non-native essays compared to native ones. Read used a receptive format to ensure he would elicit collocation responses, even though they would be at the relatively easier receptive level of mastery. However, use of what is essentially a multiple-choice format leads almost inevitably to problems with examinees using test-taking strategies to answer the items (Gyllstad, Vilkaitė, & Schmitt, 2015). Schmitt, Ng, and Garras (2011) found that the method of scoring was crucial, and they suggested giving credit for items only if all correct options were selected, in order to compensate for guessing. The fact that the test is still in development 23 years after its inception (i.e., Read, 2016) illustrates the difficulty of measuring depth of knowledge, and for our current purposes, collocation knowledge in particular, as one type of FS.

COLLEX and COLLMATCH (Gyllstad, 2009) /DISCO (Eyckmans, 2009)

In an edited volume on researching L2 collocations (Barfield & Gyllstad, 2009), no fewer than four tests of collocation knowledge are presented: COLLEX and COLLMATCH (Gyllstad, 2009), DISCO (Eyckmans, 2009), and CONTRIX (Revier, 2009). The first three tests use versions of a recognition format and will be discussed in this section.

The COLLEX and COLLMATCH tests were designed to measure advanced Swedish learners' (upper secondary school and university) receptive recognition knowledge of English verb+noun word combinations. The tests were developed and evaluated through a series of test administrations, aimed at creating test versions yielding reliable and valid scores (see Gyllstad, 2007 for details). The COLLEX test is a 50-item test with a decontextualized format, as shown in Figure 9.2. The test taker must choose the alternative that is a frequent and natural word combination in English (b).

The most recent iteration of the COLLMATCH test format is essentially a yes/no test which targets collocations. It presents decontextualized items, which the examinees judge as being frequent and natural word combinations in English or not (Figure 9.3).

1. a. drive a business   b. run a business   c. lead a business

a	b	c

FIGURE 9.2 An example item from COLLEX.
(from Gyllstad, 2009, p. 157)

1 have a say   2 lose sleep   3 do justice   4 draw a breath   5 turn a reason

□ yes   □ yes   □ yes   □ Yes   □ yes
□ no   □ no   □ no   □ No   □ no

FIGURE 9.3 Five example items from COLLMATCH.
(from Gyllstad, 2007, p. 309)

Gyllstad administered both the COLLEX and COLLMATCH, along with the VLT (Schmitt, Schmitt, & Clapham, 2001), to 307 participants (mainly Swedish university students), and found that both collocation tests produced very similar scores in terms of percentage correct. They also correlated strongly with vocabulary size (VLT) (.83–.88) and with each other (.86). Thus, we find that the COLLEX (using a three-option multiple-choice format) and the COLLMATCH (using a yes/no format) provide very similar information, despite the differing formats.

This makes the yes/no format of the COLLMATCH interesting because of its advantage of speed; yes/no tests are typically quicker to take, and so more items can be tested than for other formats, e.g., COLLMATCH – 100 items; COLLEX – 50 items. Given the large number of FSs in language, this format allows a far larger sampling. A possible downside of the format is that there is no demonstration of knowledge, and cynical test takers could in theory simply guess and have a 50–50 chance of answering correctly. Yes/no tests of single words typically have non-words added (which the test takers obviously cannot know), and if these words are checked as known, then learners' scores can be adjusted downwards accordingly. (However, there is no consensus on the best adjustment formula, e.g., Pellicer-Sánchez & Schmitt, 2012.) In COLLMATCH, 70 of the 100 items are target collocations and 30 are pseudo-collocations. For all items, irrespective of category, z-scores were retrieved from the British National Corpus (BNC) to ensure significance for the target collocations and conversely lack of significance for the pseudo-collocations. Thus, it might be possible to adjust scores for guessing if a suitable adjustment formula can be found.

Another example which illustrates how the receptive format can be adapted is the Discriminating Collocations Test (DISCO) (Eyckmans, 2009). As illustrated

☐ seek advice   ☐ pay attention   ☐ express charges

FIGURE 9.4 An example item from DISCO.
(from Eyckmans, 2009, p. 146).

in Figure 9.4, the test taker is asked to tick the *two-word* combinations that are idiomatic in English (*seek advice, pay attention*).

Eyckmans found that the DISCO was sensitive enough to indicate improvement in collocation knowledge after a 60-hour period of instruction, although it had limited power in indicating production of FSs in oral output.

It is interesting that all of these tests are intended to measure collocation knowledge, and although the authors provide a number of different kinds of validity and reliability evidence (see the respective studies for details), none have sufficient validation evidence which would indicate how their scores are to be interpreted in terms of overall knowledge of collocations. This is because the item selection approach used was largely a word-centred approach, whereby collocates are identified for high-frequency node words. A more holistic approach would entail selecting whole collocations from a frequency list. This criticism, essentially pointing to a lack of a good model of collocation knowledge and use, is not specific to these tests, but could be made of virtually every collocation measure, and is a weakness we think test developers need to address in the future.

CONTRIX (Revier, 2009)

The CONTRIX format is different from the previous formats in that, although employing a receptive format, it is claimed to assess L2 learners' productive knowledge of verb-object/noun collocations (e.g., *make a complaint*) (Revier, 2009). CONTRIX items consist of a sentence prompt containing a gap to be filled by selecting words from each of the three columns to the right. Test takers are asked to select (circle) the combination of verb, article, and noun that best completes the sentence. In the example in Figure 9.5, that would be *keep + a + secret*.

Using Schmitt's matrix for what type of knowledge is tested (2010, p. 86) (see Table 9.1), the format targets "meaning recognition" (by providing the components of forms to choose from). However, Revier (2009) argues somewhat unconventionally that it could also be said to tap into "productive knowledge for test takers must not only create (i.e., produce) meaning by combining lexical constituents, but they must also grammatically encode the noun constituent for determination" (p. 129). This is an interesting claim, but unfortunately, the initial pilot only investigated differences in scores between learners of different proficiency levels, and differences in scores between transparent, semi-transparent, and non-transparent collocations. Thus, there was no evidence that the test provides an indication of productive collocation mastery as an independent construct.

The quickest way to win a friend's trust is to show that you are able to _____ .	tell	a/an	joke
	take	the	secret
	keep	--	truth

FIGURE 9.5 An example item from CONTRIX.
(Revier, 2009, p. 129)

A Productive Collocation Test (Schmitt, Dörnyei, Adolphs & Durow, 2004)

In the literature, a large number of studies have made use of tests of FL as part of traditional experimental and quasi-experimental learning designs (e.g., Henriksen, 2013; Schmitt, 2004). One example that illustrates a more conventional way of measuring productive knowledge of FSs (compared to the CONTRIX) comes from a study by Schmitt et al. (2004). The researchers created a productive test that was a type of cloze test. A range of academically based FSs were embedded in multi-paragraph contexts, with all or most of the content words in the target FS deleted, but leaving the initial letter(s) of each word. The meaning of the targeted sequence was provided next to the item in parentheses to ensure that the ability to produce the "form" of the formulaic sequence was measured, not comprehension of its meaning. One paragraph is extracted, which contains two items (*first of all, it is clear that*) (Figure 9.6).

This format is reminiscent of Laufer and Nation's (1999) format used for a single-word productive VLT. It has the advantage of being difficult to guess if one does not know the target item, while seemingly relatively easy to complete if the target sequence is known. The format would be classified as "form recall" according to Schmitt's (2010, p. 86) terminology, and the test would seem to provide evidence that a learner can spell the sequences in question. However, this is far from demonstrating that learners can think of the sequences unprompted on their own and independently use them in their writing and speaking. This highlights another problem common to almost all tests of FL: the uncertainty of how to interpret the scores in terms of how much FL learners can employ in their everyday use of the four skills.

The PHRASE Test (Martinez, 2011)

One of the few tests where the scores can be related to a fixed set of FSs is the PHRASE test (Martinez, 2011), which is directly linked to the 505 phrasal

Learning English as a second language is a difficult challenge, but we do know several ways to make learning more efficient.

Fi_____ of a_____, almost every research study   (the initial one)
shows that you need to use English as much as possible.

I_____ is cl_____ that the more you use English,   (this is obvious)
the better you will learn it. There is not disagreement about this.

FIGURE 9.6 Example items for testing production of FS.
(Schmitt et al. (2004, pp. 58–59)

> At once: I did it **at once**.
> a. one time
> b. many times
> c. early
> d. immediately

FIGURE 9.7 An item for the PHRASE Test.
(Martinez, 2011, Slide 54)

expressions on the *PHRASE List* (Martinez & Schmitt, 2012). It uses a fairly standard four-option multiple-choice format, with the target item and a short, non-defining sentence as context (d) (Figure 9.7).

The key thing to note about this experimental test is that it was sampled from a finite list of phrasal expressions, and so the percentage correct on the test can be interpreted as the percentage known on the whole PHRASE List. This is in stark contrast to the other tests discussed, where there is no way to know how to interpret the scores in terms of overall size. This suggests that future tests of FL may need to focus on much more constrained, and thus identifiable, subsets of FL, in order to make the resulting scores more meaningful.

Principles for Developing New Tests of Formulaic Language

The previous review shows that, although measurement of FL subtypes has progressed in its short lifetime, each of the existing tests has limitations, and test writers will need to enhance their development procedures to write tests that provide valid and reliable scores that are useful for teachers and students. Length constraints prohibit us from outlining every issue that needs to be considered when developing valid tests of FL, but we feel the following key issues need to be addressed.

Defining Constructs

In any language testing endeavour, there is a need to link an individual's test performance to a specific ability in reference to a construct. In terms of procedures for this, Bachman (1990, p. 40) suggests a sequence of three steps: (1) defining the construct theoretically, (2) defining the construct operationally, and (3) establishing procedures for quantifying observations. Once such definitions are in place, we can start working with the population of items that supposedly belong to the construct. Over the last couple of decades, a number of influential definitions of FL have been presented in the literature, most notably Wray's oft-cited 2002 version:

> a sequence, continuous or discontinuous, of words or other elements, which is, or appears to be, prefabricated: that is, stored and retrieved whole from memory at the time of use, rather than being subject to generation or analysis by the language grammar.
>
> *(p. 9)*

Wray's definition was designed to capture as wide a range of FL as possible for discussion in her seminal book, but this open-ended definition is simply too broad to operationalize in the development of tests (e.g., if something *is* or *appears to be* prefabricated, then it does not have to be prefabricated, thus making this criterion unworkable). In her 2008 book-length follow-up, Wray provides an excellent discussion on the way in which different definitions lead to wider or narrower scope when it comes to identification of formulaic exemplars, and how different research purposes require different approaches (Wray, 2008: Chapter 8). This applies to testing too, and the last point creates a natural link to the next issue, that of having a particular purpose in mind when designing a test.

Tests Need to be Developed for Particular Purposes

Tests of individual words have tended to be generic, with no indication given about which particular purposes, contexts, or learners the tests were suitable for. For example, developers of the well-known VLT only indicated that it provided an estimate of the vocabulary size at different frequency levels, but never specified what kind of learners it would be appropriately used with. This is true for both the original version (Nation, 1990) and the enhanced, revised version (Schmitt et al., 2001). Likewise, users of the *Vocabulary Size Test* (VST) (Nation & Beglar, 2007) were initially given no guidance of whom to use it with or how. Nevertheless, Nation and Coxhead (2014) later found that some New Zealand participants performed quite differently on the test when a personal test administrator talked them through it and kept them engaged, compared to doing it themselves. Furthermore, this difference was the greatest for people in the lowest quartile of test takers. This discrepancy is not surprising, because no test works for every person in every situation. This means that the current situation where "one-size-fits-all" tests dominate is no longer tenable. Testing of FL must follow the lead of mainstream testing where tests are developed and validated for specific contexts and learners (Bachman & Palmer, 2010; Read & Chapelle, 2001) (see Voss (2012) for an example of this), and where appropriate statistical methods are used (see Bachman, 2004). Developers of formulaic measurement need to be clear about what their tests are trying to achieve, what the resulting scores mean, and whom to use the test with and in which situations. The reason for this is straightforward: if no context is specified for a test, then how can validation evidence be collected that it works? This calls for the creation of some type of manual accompanying the test which outlines (in plain speak) the essential requirements for choosing, administrating, and marking the test, and then for interpreting the resulting scores.

Selecting the Formulaic Sequences to Test

FL is ubiquitous in language. With so many FSs in language, it becomes essential to narrow them down in some way to have a reasonable chance of obtaining a viable measurement.

As explained in this volume, FL is not a homogeneous phenomenon, but is on the contrary, quite varied, made up of a range of different categories (e.g., idioms, phrasal verbs, lexical phrases, collocations, phrasal expressions, and discourse organizers). Each category has its own particular characteristics. Idioms and some phrasal verbs have idiomatic meanings. Other categories, like lexical bundles and discourse markers, have meanings that are typically transparent from the individual words in the sequence but bound in conventionalized strings expected by the speech community. Some categories, like collocations, can have both idiomatic and literal meanings (*top drawer* = highest drawer in a cabinet, and best example of something). The various categories are used for different functions, e.g., discourse markers are used to signpost discourse organization, while idioms usually express meaning (*silver lining* = there is hopefully some good in a bad situation).

With such a range and variety of FL, it is not surprising that no single, comprehensive compendium exists. Even if it did, it would almost certainly not be measurable. This makes it important to understand the reason for testing, in order to define which category or categories of FL to measure. For example, if the purpose is to measure knowledge of the most common FS, then testing phrasal expressions (Martinez & Schmitt, 2012) makes sense, as their defining characteristic is high frequency (among the most frequent 5,000 lexical items in English). Another purpose might be to measure writing ability, and testing discourse organizers might be a sensible part of this approach.

Once the category (or categories) of FL has been determined, the test developer needs to identify the population of FSs in that category, from which to sample in order to build the test. Most developers will rely on existing descriptions of the category, in the form of either a dictionary or list. There are numerous dictionaries focusing on various categories of FL. Idioms, phrasal verbs, and collocations are well supported with dictionaries from most of the major publishers. However, it should be noted that these resources vary greatly in how they were compiled, but because they are written for learners and not researchers, the rationale/procedure for inclusion (or omission) of items is either vague or left completely unstated.

The existing dictionaries have large numbers of items: e.g., the *Cambridge Idioms Dictionary* (2006, 2nd ed.) has approximately 7,000 items, *Collins COBUILD Phrasal Verbs Dictionary* (2012) has more than 4,000 items, and the *Oxford Collocations Dictionary for Students of English* (2009, 2nd ed.) has approximately 250,000 items. These large numbers of items can leave the test developer overwhelmed, as any sample small enough to be testable will only include a tiny fraction of the total items in the dictionaries (see sample rate identified later). To address this issue, a number of lists have been developed to identify a smaller number of the most useful items to teach and test, usually as indicated by high frequency. For example, Liu (2011) narrowed the nearly 9,000 phrasal verbs he analyzed down to 150, which made up nearly two-thirds of the phrasal verb occurrences in the BNC corpus. Likewise, Liu (2003) used frequency and range criteria to identify 302 idioms which occurred in the spoken discourse of professional, academic, and media language. Other lists which provide frequent and pedagogically relevant items include the Pearson *Academic Collocation List* (2,469 items; Ackerman & Chen, 2013) and the *PHRASE List* (505 items; Martinez & Schmitt, 2012).

But lists are not limited to indicating the most useful items in an FS category; they can also provide beneficial information about the items. For example, many lexical items are polysemous, and lists can potentially give information about the frequency of various meaning senses. For single-word vocabulary, this was most notably done by the *General Service List* (West, 1953), which gave percentages of the various meaning senses of the key 2,000 words in English. The same format was provided by the *PHaVE List* (Garnier & Schmitt, 2015), which provides percentage information about the meaning senses of the most frequent 150 English phrasal verbs. Another type of information is how FSs are used. The *Academic Formulas List* (Simpson-Vlach & Ellis, 2010) categorizes the identified formulas according to their function (e.g., Quantity specification – *both of these*, Contrast and comparison – *as opposed to*).

As useful as dictionaries and lists may be, it is important for test developers to understand how they were compiled, so that accurate judgements can be made about their appropriacy for the specified test purpose.

If word lists are not used, then the test developer must rely on other means to select the FSs to include on the test. Particularly for collocations and lexical bundles, statistical frequency-based criteria are often used (e.g., t-score, Mutual Information (MI), DeltaP, a certain number of occurrences in a corpus). Some researchers favour semantically based criteria based on the "phraseological school" approach (e.g., degree of compositionality, amount of variation allowed). It is beyond the remit of this chapter to go into these in detail (see Barfield & Gyllstad, 2009 and Schmitt, 2010, for overviews), but a logical requirement is that test developers need to carefully consider their purposes and which criteria are best suited to achieving those purposes.

Sampling

Once a source of appropriate FS has been selected, the next step is to sample a suitable number of items from it to fix on the test. This brings up the issue of sampling rate. With some language constructs, a limited number of items can give a good indication of the knowledge of the construct. For example, if a learner can answer several test items correctly demonstrating the past form of regular English verbs (*-ed*), this probably gives a good indication they can use this grammatical "rule" across the range of regular verbs. But FL is not a rule-based, but rather an item-based construct. Just because a learner knows one collocation or idiom, for example, does not imply they know a different one. Therefore, each lexical item, whether individual word or FS, needs to be tested separately. Given the large number of lexical items in any language, this causes problems for the test developer, as it is simply impossible to test every item.

The standard solution is to draw a representative sample from the overall population of items, and then use these to extrapolate to the complete population. For example, at the 3,000 level of the revised VLT (Schmitt et al., 2001), 30 items represented the 1,000 words in the level. If learners answered 50% of the items correctly (15), then the interpretation was that they also knew 50% of all the words in that level (500). Sampling always involves a tension between validity (more items give better test information) and practicality (fewer items lead to shorter and more practical tests). This leads to the obvious question of what is the lowest sampling rate which can produce valid test scores.

The answer to this question partly stems from the purpose of the test. If the intention is to obtain a very rough idea of the number of words/sequences a person knows, then a lower sampling rate might suffice. But if the test is supposed to produce a relatively accurate estimate, then a higher sampling rate is required. Unfortunately, there has been little research into how sampling rate affects the validity of vocabulary tests. Use of sophisticated statistics from *Item Response Theory* like Rasch analysis can allow the measurement of homogenous constructs with relatively few items (see McNamara, 1996), but it is very debatable whether this approach can work with item-based language aspects like vocabulary and FSs. Most tests of vocabulary size have used 10–30 items to represent 1,000-word frequency bands (e.g., *VST* – 10 items; *X-Lex Test* (Meara & Milton, 2003) – 20; *VLT* – 30), with the unverified assumption that this was enough. Unfortunately, there has been little research into minimum sample rates for vocabulary tests, and none to our knowledge for tests of FL.

One study which does shed light on sampling is Gyllstad, Vilkaitė, and Schmitt (2015). They compared test scores from the 10 items on a four-option multiple-choice test (*VST*) with scores from a much more comprehensive 100-item test (which was assumed to be a better estimate of the 1,000-word frequency level). The 10-item test correlated at .50–.86 (r^2 = .25–.74). Unsurprisingly, more items led to increasingly higher correlations, with 30 items producing correlations of .85–.95 (r^2 = .73–.90). The researchers concluded that 10 items per 1,000 were sufficient to give a ballpark indication of vocabulary size, but that more items led to more accurate estimates, while any more than 30 items may well lead to practicality issues due to excessive test length. However, while this study is informative, the *VST* measures individual words, and it is unclear whether tests of FL would behave in a similar manner. Given the lack of research in this area, test developers will need to run their own validation studies to determine what sampling rate is appropriate for their particular purposes and needs. However, unless the set of FSs is quite constrained (e.g., the 207 core formulas on the *Academic Formulas List*, Simpson-Vlach & Ellis, 2010), the number of items on any FL test will likely need to be substantial.

However, the tests reviewed so far have not attempted to map onto a defined set of FS, but rather have attempted to measure more general collocation knowledge. The WAT has 40 items, the CONTRIX 45 items, the DISCO and COLLEX 50, and the COLLMATCH 100, but the number of items necessary to indicate general collocation knowledge as a construct is still undetermined. Future research will need to look at all of these formats in order to determine the number of items needed to provide useful information.

Choosing Appropriate Item Formats

We have looked at a number of different formats, but there is no way of saying that any format is better than the others. It all comes down to the test purposes and the type of learner taking the test. In this sense, tests of FL are no different from any kind of vocabulary test. As a way to avoid using terms like *receptive* and *productive*, Schmitt (2010), based on work by Laufer and Goldstein (2004), proposed the use of a two-by-two matrix for what particular type of form-meaning knowledge is targeted in a test. The matrix is aimed at single-word knowledge but can also be useful in guiding thought about tests of FL (Table 9.1).

Once a test developer is clear what degree of mastery should be tested for the specified purpose of the test, then Table 9.1 can help the developer think about what kind of item format is required to tap into that level.

TABLE 9.1 *Matrix for deciding what aspect and level of mastery an item is tapping into*

		\multicolumn{2}{c}{Formulaic sequence knowledge tested}	
		RECALL	RECOGNITION
Formulaic sequence knowledge given	MEANING	Form recall (supply all or part of the L2 sequence)	Form recognition (select the L2 sequence)
	FORM	Meaning recall (supply definition/ L1 translation etc.)	Meaning recognition (select definition/ L1 translation etc.)

Source: (adapted from Schmitt, 2010, p. 86)

Taking Advantage of Technology

Most tests of single-word vocabulary and FL to date have traditionally been of the paper-and-pencil variety. Some of these tests have been moved to computerized or Internet-based platforms, but for the most part, they are simply electronic versions of the paper-and-pencil formats. For example, the *Lextutor* website (www.lextutor.ca/tests/) provides web-based versions of a number of existing tests (e.g., the *VLT*, the *VST*, the *EFL Vocabulary Tests*, the *Phrasal Vocabulary Size Test*, BNC Version, Martinez, 2011). But the electronic age offers more possibilities than just reworking existing tests. One opportunity is to use adaptive tests to achieve a better and more focused sampling. With paper-and-pencil tests, the number of items at each level is fixed on the page, and learners must go through all of the items, regardless of whether they are too easy (e.g., high-frequency items which are very well-known) or too difficult (e.g., low-frequency items which may not be known at all). Computer-adaptive tests can use a few items at each frequency level to gauge the particular learner's general level, and then give many items at the frequency point where some, but not all, of the words/sequences are known. This allows many more items to be given in the "window", which is most informative of the learner's vocabulary size. However, the most sensible adaptive formula has not yet been established from the many options available, and research has only begun on the advantages and disadvantages of various algorithms (Kremmel, in preparation).

Adaptive tests also have the potential to give information on the quality (depth) of lexical knowledge. This has been demonstrated by the *Computer Adaptive Test of Size and Strength (CATTS)* test (Laufer & Goldstein, 2004), which gives examinees tests of form recall, meaning recall, form recognition, or meaning recognition, depending on the learner's responses. The result is an indication of the strength of knowledge of the form-meaning link, and the idea of using a computer-adaptive format should also work with FL.

Conclusions and Future Directions

In this chapter, we have concluded that there is a lack of standardized tests of FL, and instead that a number of tests exist that target subtypes of FS, such as idioms, collocations, phrasal verbs, and lexical bundles. Many are still experimental, and most of them lack the type and scope of validation research necessary to truly know how they work, and what their scores mean. For the majority, it is still difficult to determine what their scores say about knowledge of wider-ranging formulaic knowledge. Our suggestions for future tests largely revolve around a call for a much more rigorous specification of test purpose, and with it, a tighter description of the category(s) and scope of FL being measured. Ideally, this should be done through the issuing of a "user manual" accompanying the test. With this, desirable formats and the selection of target items will be much more obvious to achieve the stated purpose(s).

Beyond our suggestions, what might the future bring for the testing and researching of FL? In a conference colloquium dedicated to FL, Vilkaitė and Gyllstad (2014) discussed several possibilities. For example, in terms of identification of FS, they foresaw that intuition will continue to play a role, but with an increased use of several raters/judges to improve judgements (inter-rater reliability). Also, whereas offline/paper-and-pencil tests will continue to have appeal in traditional classroom settings, more sophisticated psycholinguistic and neurolinguistic approaches (e.g., eye-tracking, EEG, ERP, and fMRI) will be used in researching FL, especially when it comes to the question of holistic storage and researching differences (cross-sectionally) between groups of native speakers and learners, and within individuals over time (longitudinally).

It stands to reason that no one can truly foresee the future, but if future test developers follow up on our suggestions, and take on-board the other wealth of information available in this volume, the next generation of FL tests cannot help but be much improved.

Notes

1 Text analysis studies that have examined the use of FL in learner production could be seen as measurements/tests of productive FL ability, as are rating criteria and scoring rubrics.
2 This makes it difficult to interpret the scores as FL knowledge, as half the test measures a non-FL construct (i.e., single-word meaning).

References

Ackermann, K., & Chen, Y.-H. (2013). Developing the academic collocation list (ACL) – A corpus-driven and expert-judged approach. *Journal of English for Academic Purposes, 12*, 235–247.

Bachman, L. F. (1990). *Fundamental considerations in language testing.* Oxford: Oxford University Press.

Bachman, L. (2004). *Statistical analyses for language assessment*. Cambridge: Cambridge University Press.
Bachman, L. F., & Palmer, A. S. (2010). *Language assessment in practice: Developing language assessments and justifying their use in the real world*. Oxford: Oxford University Press.
Bahns, J., & Eldaw, M. (1993). Should we teach EFL students collocations? *System, 21*, 101–114.
Barfield, A., & Gyllstad, H. (Eds.). (2009). *Researching collocations in another language: Multiple interpretations*. Basingstoke: Palgrave Macmillan.
Biber, D., Johansson, S., Leech, G., Conrad, S., & Finegan, E. (1999). *Longman grammar of spoken and written English*. Harlow: Longman.
Cambridge Idioms Dictionary (2006). Cambridge: Cambridge University Press.
Collins COBUILD Phrasal Verbs Dictionary (2012). Glasgow: HarperCollins.
Eyckmans, J. (2009). Toward an assessment of learners' receptive and productive syntagmatic knowledge. In A. Barfield & H. Gyllstad (Eds.), *Researching collocations in another language* (pp. 139–152). New York, NY: Palgrave Macmillan.
Farghal, M., & Obiedat, H. (1995). Collocations: A neglected variable in EFL. *International Journal of Applied Linguistics, 28*(4), 313–331.
Garnier, M., & Schmitt, N. (2015). The PHaVE List: A pedagogical list of phrasal verbs and their most frequent meaning senses. *Language Teaching Research, 19*(6), 645–666.
Garnier, M., & Schmitt, N. (2016). Picking up polysemous phrasal verbs: How many do learners know and what facilitates this knowledge? *System, 59*, 29–44.
Grant, L., & Nation, P. (2006). How many idioms are there in English? *ITL International Journal of Applied Linguistics, 15*(1), 1–14.
Gyllstad, H. (2007). *Testing English collocations* (Unpublished PhD thesis). Lund: Lund University.
Gyllstad, H. (2009). Designing and evaluating tests of receptive collocation knowledge: COLLEX and COLLMATCH. In A. Barfield & H. Gyllstad (Eds.), *Researching collocations in another language* (pp. 153–170). New York, NY: Palgrave Macmillan.
Gyllstad, H., Vilkaitė, L., & Schmitt, N. (2015). Assessing vocabulary size through multiple-choice formats: Issues with guessing and sampling rates. *ITL International Journal of Applied Linguistics, 166*, 276–303.
Henriksen, B. (2013). Research on L2 learners' collocational competence and development – A progress report. In C. Bardel, C. Lindqvist, & B. Laufer (Eds.), *L2 vocabulary acquisition, knowledge and use: New perspectives on assessment and corpus analysis* (pp. 29–56). Eurosla Monograph Series 2.
Howarth, P. (1996). *Phraseology in English academic writing: Some implications for language learning and dictionary making*. Lexicographica Series Maior 75. Tübingen: Max Niemeyer.
Jackendoff, R. (1995). The boundaries of the lexicon. In M. Everaert, E. van der Linden, A. Schenk, & R. Schreuder (Eds.), *Idioms: Structural and psychological perspectives* (pp. 133–166). Hillsdale, NJ: Lawrence Erlbaum.
Kremmel, B. (in preparation). Algorithms for vocabulary size tests.
Laufer, B., & Goldstein, Z. (2004). Testing vocabulary knowledge: Size, strength, and computer adaptiveness. *Language Learning, 54*(3). 399–436.
Laufer, B., & Nation, P. (1999). A vocabulary-size test of controlled productive ability. *Language Testing, 16*(1), 33–51.
Laufer, B., & Waldman, T. (2011). Verb-noun collocations in second language writing: A corpus analysis of learners' English. *Language Learning, 61*(2), 647–672.

Liu, D. (2003). The most frequently used spoken American English idioms: A corpus analysis and its implications. *TESOL Quarterly, 37*(4), 671–700.
Liu, D. (2011). The most frequently used English phrasal verbs in American and British English: A multicorpus examination. *TESOL Quarterly, 45*, 661–688.
Martinez, R. (2011). *Putting a test of multiword expressions to a test*. Paper presented at the IATEFL Testing, Evaluation and Assessment SIG. University of Innsbruck: September 16, 2011. Retrieved from https://ufpr.academia.edu/RonMartinez/Talks.
Martinez, R., & Schmitt, N. (2012). A Phrasal Expressions List. *Applied Linguistics, 33*(3), 299–320.
McNamara, T. (1996). *Measuring second language performance*. Harlow: Longman.
Meara, P. (1992). *EFL Vocabulary Tests*. University College, Swansea: Centre for Applied Language Studies.
Meara, P., & Jones, G. (1988). Vocabulary size as a placement indicator. Retrieved from www.lognostics.co.uk/vlibrary/meara&jones1988.pdf.
Meara, P., & Milton, J. (2003). *X_Lex, the Swansea levels test*. Newbury: Express.
Nation, I. S. P. (1990). *Teaching and learning vocabulary*. New York, NY: Newbury House.
Nation, I. S. P., & Beglar, D. (2007). A vocabulary size test. *The Language Teacher, 31*(7), 9–13.
Nation, P., & Coxhead, A. (2014). Vocabulary size research at Victoria University of Wellington, New Zealand. *Language Teaching, 47*(3), 398–403.
Nattinger, J. R., & DeCarrico, J. S. (1992). *Lexical phrases and language teaching*. Oxford: Oxford University Press.
Nesselhauf, N. (2005). *Collocations in a learner corpus*. Amsterdam: John Benjamins.
Oxford Collocations Dictionary for Students of English (2009). Oxford: Oxford University Press.
Pawley, A., & Syder, F. H. (1983). Two puzzles for linguistic theory: Nativelike selection and nativelike fluency. In J. C. Richards & R. W. Schmidt (Eds.), *Language and communication* (pp. 191–225). London: Longman.
Pellicer-Sánchez, A., & Schmitt, N. (2012). Scoring Yes – No vocabulary tests: Reaction time vs. nonword approaches. *Language Testing, 29*(4), 489–509.
Read, J. (1993). The development of a new measure of L2 vocabulary knowledge. *Language Testing, 10*, 355–371.
Read, J. (1998). Validating a test to measure depth of vocabulary knowledge. In A. Kunnan (Ed.), *Validation in language assessment* (pp. 41–60). Mahwah, NJ: Lawrence Erlbaum.
Read, J. (2000). *Assessing vocabulary*. Cambridge: Cambridge University Press.
Read, J. (2004). Plumbing the depths: How should the construct of vocabulary knowledge be defined? In P. Bogaards & B. Laufer (Eds.), *Vocabulary in a second language* (pp. 209–227). Amsterdam: John Benjamins.
Read, J. (2016). *A fresh look at measuring depth of vocabulary knowledge*. Paper presented at the Vocab@Tokyo conference. September 12–14, 2016, Tokyo.
Read, J., & Chapelle, C. (2001). A framework for second language vocabulary assessment. *Language Testing, 18*(1), 3–32.
Read, J., & Nation, P. (2004). Measurement of formulaic sequences. In N. Schmitt (Ed.), *Formulaic sequences: Acquisition, processing and use* (pp. 23–35). Amsterdam: John Benjamins.
Revier, R. L. (2009). Evaluating a new test of whole English collocations. In A. Barfield & H. Gyllstad (Eds.), *Researching collocations in another language: Multiple interpretations* (pp. 125–138). New York, NY: Palgrave Macmillan.
Schmitt, N. (Ed.). (2004). *Formulaic sequences: Acquisition, processing and use*. Amsterdam: John Benjamins.
Schmitt, N. (2010). *Researching vocabulary: A vocabulary research manual*. Basingstoke: Palgrave Macmillan.

Schmitt, N., Dörnyei, Z., Adolphs, S., & Durow, V. (2004). Knowledge and acquisition of formulaic sequences: A longitudinal study. In N. Schmitt (Ed.), *Formulaic sequences: Acquisition, processing, and use* (pp. 55–86). Amsterdam: John Benjamins.

Schmitt, N., Ng, J. W. C., & Garras, J. (2011). The word associates format: Validation evidence. *Language Testing, 28*(1), 105–126.

Schmitt, N., Schmitt, D., & Clapham, C. (2001). Developing and exploring the behaviour of two new versions of the vocabulary levels test. *Language Testing, 18*(1), 55–88.

Simpson-Vlach, R., & Ellis, N. C. (2010). An academic formulas list: New methods in phraseology research. *Applied Linguistics, 31*(4), 487–512.

Siyanova-Chanturia, A. (2015). Collocation in beginner learner writing: A longitudinal study. *System, 53*, 148–160.

Vilkaitė, L., & Gyllstad, H. (2014). *Formulaic language: How can it be assessed?* Paper presented at the AAAL conference. March 23, 2014, Portland, Oregon.

Vives Boix, G. (1995). *The development of a measure of lexical organisation: The association vocabulary test* (Unpublished PhD thesis). University of Wales, Swansea.

Voss, E. (2012). *A validity argument for score meaning of a computer-based ESL academic collocational ability test based on a corpus-driven approach to test design* (Unpublished PhD thesis). Iowa State University.

West, M. (1953). *A general service list of English words*. London: Longman.

Wolter, B. (2005). *V_Links: A new approach to assessing depth of word knowledge* (Unpublished PhD thesis). University of Wales, Swansea.

Wray, A. (2002). *Formulaic language and the lexicon*. Cambridge: Cambridge University Press.

Wray, A. (2008). *Formulaic language: Pushing the boundaries*. Oxford: Oxford University Press.

Wray, A. (2012). What do we (think we) know about formulaic language? An evaluation of the current state of play. *Annual Review of Applied Linguistics, 32*, 231–254.

Xue, G., & Nation, I. S. P. (1984). A university word list. *Language Learning and Communication, 3*(2), 215–229.–

10

FROM CORPUS TO CALL

The Use of Technology in Teaching and Learning Formulaic Language

Tom Cobb

Introduction

Linguists discovered formulaic language (FL) through computer analysis of large texts, and this chapter makes the case that second language (L2) learners should follow in their footsteps, though probably with more learner-oriented or CALL (computer-assisted language learning) types of software. Non-computational approaches to FL do not deal adequately with what is known about FL (the extent, distribution, or true nature of it) nor its acquisition (that it requires both awareness and massive exposure). While a CALL approach in this area is yet to be extensively developed or conclusively tested, this chapter will furnish concrete ideas for why and how this can be achieved and will report on progress and prospects.

Linguists and Learners

It is reasonable there should be a role for computer technology in the teaching and learning of FL, because linguists themselves learned of the existence and extent of FL by looking at large texts, or corpora, with computer technologies. Prior to corpus analysis, it could be assumed that, apart from a relatively small number of idioms and set expressions ("How are you?" or "Good morning"), languages consisted mainly of words and rules – individual words assembled into phrases and sentences through the application of grammatical rules. What corpus analysis revealed, however, was that of the infinite number of phrases that can be assembled by the application of rules to words, only a few of these are actually used by speakers of any language. Furthermore, this usage is shared by all users of a language and is an important part of what we know when we know a language. In other words, there is another principle in addition to grammar that is operating in the construction of any utterance. It is what Sinclair (1991) called "the idiom principle", though it applies equally to literal and metaphorical or idiomatic expressions. Of all the many grammatically permissible ways of proposing marriage to someone ("Would you consider marriage? Does your marrying me seem plausible?" etc.), the precise formula "Will you marry me?" claims the vast majority of instances – whether in linguistics, literature, or life – and learners should know this.

The idiom principle was suspected to exist by many in the pre-computational era of linguistics (Pawley & Syder, 1983), but what was new with corpus analysis was its extent. Starting in the mid-1980s, computer software was written that could analyze texts of several million words, tallying among other things the amount of word-group recurrence, and this turned out to be unexpectedly large. A classic finding from Erman and Warren (2000) is that 52% of word tokens in typical spoken text and 40% in written text are involved in some sort of word-group recurrence. A further twist is that if one or two intervening words are allowed to count as part of the group ("big *shiny* car" as well as "big car") and members of word families are counted as repeated words ("big shiny cars") then these figures can rise by another 15%. (Explore this claim at N-Gram on the author's *Lextutor* Website, http://lextutor.ca/n_gram/, by manipulating any text with the "Intervenors" and "Families" settings.)

Admittedly, there is a question about the true formulaicity of computer-generated phrase repetitions or "bundles". Is the recurrent string "of the many" a meaningful unit? Such items must form a large part of Erman and Warren's figure. This question has led to a reaction against pure computational approaches by the phraseologists (e.g., Cowie, 1998), who propose either intuition, hand work, or hand checking of computer work as the most reliable source of insight about FL. The fact remains, however, that the extent of formulaicity in language was first learned of through computational analysis, and this remains an awareness-raising insight that is important for language learners to experience, so in principle such analysis can also be a source of insight for them, too. But does the argument for computation in learning about formulaic language extend beyond "in principle"?

One reason for believing so is that while computer analysis of a text or corpus may occasionally focus a learner's attention on a non-formulaic string like "of the many", this at least is a true recurring word group which will cause no harm if attended to, as cannot be said for those proposed in some other approaches to teaching and learning formula. Boers, Dang, and Strong (2017) found that most formula exercises across 10 current EFL textbooks invited learners to fill in blanks with suitable items from memory or imagination, or else make matches on a table between, e.g., *drive/ride* and *bike/car*, either of which left many with a strong memory for precisely the non-standard association, possibly because of the processing effort committed to raking memory and/or guessing. Non-standard associations simply could not be produced from the consideration of concordance lines, or any pedagogical exercise derived from these, for the simple reason that they are not present in that output. Figure 10.1 shows a selected concordance from a graded reader corpus for the keyword *ride* with typical collocates italicized by a teacher (and hence a hand-checked computer output, in terms of the prior discussion). The concordance lines bear nothing resembling "ride a car" but rather bear numerous words that typically do harmonize with *ride*, like *horse*, *bicycle*, and *bus*. In other words, the pedagogical case for using corpus technology to learn formulaic sequences (FSs) at least extends as far as providing little or no unsuitable learning stimuli, or "doing no harm" (in the words of a well-known formula).

The ways a concordance interface can explore the FL of a text or corpus are basically two. First is a search with hypothesis in hand, which consists of entering an intact phrase ("bus ride") with the options of intervening items, either item first, or alternative morphologies. Second is an exploratory search, which consists of entering a keyword ("ride") in one or all morphologies, with the option to sort adjacent words by first, second, or third word to the right, or left – one of these sortings should expose any repeated associations. The output in Figure 10.1 is an all-forms search sorted by keyword from which a teacher has extracted promising formulaic pieces. Most concordance programs can perform these basic functions, with the difference between programs lying mainly in cost, ease of use, size of corpus treatable, whether exploiting a grammatically tagged or only "flat" corpus, and the level of sophistication in formatting the output (with Lextutor.ca at one extreme being free of cost and easy to use with smallish, flat corpora and the minor highlighting shown in Figure 10.1, and SketchEngine.co.uk, Kilgarriff, 2004, at the other providing colour-coded comparison insights from enormous corpora, either flat or tagged – but requiring some training to use and a user fee).

With whatever degree of sophistication, however, does the argument for corpus technology as a learning resource for FSs not extend beyond just "doing no harm"? In fact, the empirical case for substantial learning from corpus work is quite strong. In a meta-analysis of data-driven learning (DDL) approaches to language learning (involving the use of a corpus as a learning resource), Boulton and Cobb (2016) found that lexicogrammar (the category that FSs fall under)

Concordance extract for family RIDE
User selected output: 10 selected from 54 available in Corpus=corpus_graded_2k.txt on lextutor.ca/conc/

```
014.    was happy to agree that Brat would ride one of her horses, Chevron. Be
019.    er. After the boat there was a bus ride which took us past brightly pa
020.    rses. She hires her own jockeys to ride these horses in the Grand Nati
025.    I am a very keen swimmer and horse-rider. My hobby is collecting the p
026.    the 36-year-old Philadelphia woman rides a bike. She has become a fost
045.    Murdoch felt cross and tired as he rode home on his bicycle from schoo
046.    he bag into his bicycle basket and rode off towards Jericho. Yes you h
047.    r on his black horse, and with him rode a beautiful lady, her black cu
052.    riage, on a beautiful black horse, rode Quintus, the new Commander of
053.    free. He jumped onto the horse and rode fast toward one chariot. The d
```

FIGURE 10.1 Doing no harm with corpus data.

comprised 49 of the total 64 studies in their cull, with an average effect size of 1.54 standard deviations for within-groups studies (pre-post designs) and .75 standard deviations for between-groups studies (experimental and control groups designs). These effect sizes are "very large" and "large" by the field-specific standards of applied linguistics (Plonsky & Oswald, 2014, p. 889). Examples from this collection of FS studies with strong results include Chan and Liou (2005), Chen (2011), Daskalovska (2014), Huang (2014), Liou et al. (2006), and Sun and Wang (2003).

These DDL studies are quite diverse in the tasks they set for learners and the type of corpus presentation they adopt, but Chan and Liou (2005) provides a good example of the approach. The researchers had Chinese EFL learners use a bilingual Chinese-English parallel sentence concordance (sentences in English on one side and in Chinese on the other for a given search pattern) to fill gaps in a sentence which typically involved a pair of strongly associating verb-noun pairs ("The man tried to ____ fire to his neighbor's house with gas", with *set* the missing item). Learners were given strategies for discovering the missing word in the concordances (search for instances of *fire* sorted by the word on the left, which should pull out several instances of *set* in a corpus of any size) but pretty much left to work independently and develop personal search strategies. The overall effect size for this study was 2.41 standard deviations, compared to traditional ways of doing this same learning. This pedagogical sequence resembles many in the DDL tradition, namely a worksheet of some kind to be completed, usually collaboratively, through consulting and generalizing from corpus data.

Rationale for Using Corpus Data to Learn Formulae

Even if corpus data was the source of linguists' discovery of the extent of formulaicity in language in the 1980s, and has similarly shown itself to help learners in the DDL studies to become aware of this generally and learn some patterns specifically, we still do not have any reason to believe that concordance work is uniquely positioned to help learners with FL. The unique value of corpus data in learning about formulae arises from the fact that formulae are "difficult" in the first place.

The difficulty of FL is notorious and well documented. (Since the learning of formulae is the topic of Chapter 8 in this volume, only aspects relevant to computation are discussed here.) As early as Bahns and Eldaw (1993), formulaicity in general, and collocation in particular, has consistently been described as the final aspect of language to be even partially mastered by language learners. The problem seems to be that formulae, whether for receptive or productive language use, are learned at a glacial pace through massive exposure that is relatively unmediated by intention or cognition, compared to comparatively straightforward word meanings or grammar patterns (Ellis, 1994). In language reception, Martinez and Murphy (2011) found that even when learners knew all the words in a reading passage *qua* single words, they still had poor comprehension for its overall meaning when the passage contained idiomatic formulae (where individual words do not add up to a predictable meaning, like *beat around the bush*). In language production, the result of this glacial learning rate for FL is that learners with a strong grip on grammar and extensive single-word lexicons are often able to produce utterances that strike native speakers as "odd" or "foreign", which Kjellmer (1991) attributed to the fact that "in these learners' production, the building material is individual bricks [words] rather than prefabricated sections [lexicalised phrases]" (p. 124).

But is it really worth learners' trouble to get FL right? Apart from the avoidance of linguistic *faux-pas*, there is the larger matter that it is probable the smooth, automatic handling of FL is basic to the memory processing requirements of using a second or any language. Pawley and Syder (1983), at the beginning of the formulaic era and arguably its instigators, speculated that language processing would be an impossibly complex task if every word of an utterance had to be handled separately (as learners show they are doing when they ask, "Do you want to marry me?"). These researchers proposed instead that "native-like fluency" depends on large parts of language processing consisting of low-cost handling of formulaic patterns *qua* chunked, single items, with working memory thereby left free to handle a relatively small number of truly novel, unpredictable constructions.

The fact that recurring formulae were also problematic for professional linguists prior to the corpus era should give learners some cheer, in that the source of the problem was the same in both cases, and the linguists have solved it – or at least solved it on the level of awareness if not on the level of detail. What linguists discovered is that while formulaicity is pervasive in language, particular formulae sadly are not. Apart from a small number of extremely frequent formulae (as identified by Shin & Nation, 2008, or Martinez & Schmitt, 2012), the vast majority, though known to native speakers, are rare. A common joke at learners' expense is the misuse of the expression "to pull somebody's leg" (meaning to tease, which ends up as "pull somebody's legs", etc.). Why should this be so hard to learn? It is simple lack of exposure. Even in the TenTen corpus ("enTenTen13", comprising 22,728,686,012 word tokens, as analyzed by SketchEngine set to count all lemma variants and one intervening word), there are just 5,654 instances involving "pull" + my/your/his/etc. + "leg", or one instance per 5 million words, and about 15% of these are literals which do not involve the teasing idea.

The TenTen corpus probably represents something in the order of all the words a native speaker would hear or read in a lifetime. One humorous estimate of the words we speak in a lifetime is 860,341,500 (Brandreth, 1980), or about 1/26th of the TenTen, so if we hear or read 26 times as many as we produce, this estimate is not implausible for native speakers. For learners, a more realistic sample of the language they might encounter can be found in the purpose-built pedagogical corpus of 14 million words of basic English, including graded stories and informal speech in UK and US variants, compiled by Nation (2012) for use in the higher frequency levels of his *Range* software. In this corpus, there are 16 instances of

Concordance extract for family **PULL** With leg on EITHER side sorted 1 wds left of key

```
003.    forty nine oh oh w 0 laughs 0 yeah just PULLING your leg um that s drawls er dra
004.    um i just wondered if he pulled your le PULLED your leg so how he used to take t
005.    ell no that s alright I m having my leg PULLED here Probably hadn t been in the
006.    ow she got quite annoyed No He was only PULLING your leg Oh He can take a joke a
007.    old Ireland She thought he was probably PULLING her leg but wouldn t actually ha
008.    o Feargal she burst out laughing You re PULLING my leg Indeed he is not Feargal
010.    diff City And so of course they started PULLING his leg then see And he said he
015.    had passed It s all right Robbie I was PULLING your leg You so obviously expect
016.    r No I think well I said I think he was PULLING your leg slightly you could have
```

User selected output: 9 selected from 16 available in Corpus=bncoca_1-2.txt on lextutor.ca/conc/ set to 999 max on 2017/11/6

FIGURE 10.2 Years' worth of exposure assembled in a moment.

leg-pulling, including all legal family variants and sequences ("having my leg pulled" etc.), of which only nine involve the "teasing" metaphor, or one instance per nearly 2 million words. In other words, a learner who reads a million words a year might never encounter it. The individual items are of course far more numerous (2,372 for "pull', 1,503 for "leg"). So how would "pull somebody's leg" ever be observed, let alone learned, except by luck? It will happen only if a teacher knows it is a reasonably important thing to know at a certain stage of learning and uses some means like a concordance to bring it together (as shown in Figure 10.2).

And further, leg-pulling is a colourful idiomatic formula which is presumably easier to become aware of and learn than the huge number of far less striking literal formulae (e.g., riding bikes, not driving them), where computer search is if anything more needed to replace or supplement natural observation.

It is the thesis of this chapter that massive exposure to formula information is required for complete language learning, and that only computationally assembled data can provide this exposure. Concordance output can assemble more formula information, more effectively, than any other pedagogy is capable of. Making it pedagogically interesting is, of course, another story, to be dealt with in the following sections. But first, is a concordancing approach a truly necessary component of any pedagogy of FL?

Low-Technology Alternatives

It has been argued that the reading of texts in general, and graded readers in particular, can also be a source of formula acquisition, which takes place in a more contextually meaningful way than is provided by dissociated concordance lines (which in addition are not always simple to interpret, Figure 10.2). In an incidental acquisition study, Webb, Newton, and Chang (2013) found that if learners read while listening for roughly one hour to a graded story, of between 4,000 and 7,000 words within their existing vocabulary knowledge, seeded with different frequencies of the same formulaic expressions (verb-object collocations like *face facts* and *blow nose*), then with 15 occurrences they learned to recognize appropriate matches from a multiple-choice selection in 75% of the 18 available test items, with productive knowledge only slightly less. In other words, formula acquisition can occur incidentally through reading and is sensitive to frequency (see discussion in Chapter 8).

But while this is an interesting result in principle, it is also highly limited as a pedagogy for formula acquisition. Learners will typically not be reading and listening at the same time (a particularly propitious arrangement for many types of vocabulary growth; Horst, Cobb, & Meara, 1998). They will not be reading texts with all vocabulary known other than the FSs. They will not meet the same FSs as many as 15 times in one hour of reading, though they will meet far more than 18 distinct FSs, of which many will also be unknown. They will not be given the base form of formulae to identify in a test (test items required only recognition of *face facts* or *blow nose*) but instead left to work these out for themselves over time from items with morphological variation and intervening items (*facing hard facts* and *blowing big noses*).

Would anything like this study's learning conditions be replicated in unseeded graded readers? The original text used in Webb et al. (2013), Oxford Bookworms' version of *New Yorkers* (from Henry, Hedge, & Bassett, 2000), when run through the "Clusters/N-Gram" feature of Anthony's (2014) *AntConc* Concordancer, yields surprisingly few formula learning opportunities. The story contains only 11 two to five word sequences that are repeated 15 times, and none of these are verb-object units, or any sort of independently meaningful unit. In other words, extensive reading might be a source in principle of learning FSs, if the learning opportunities were present, except that they will probably not be, and Webb et al. do not discuss the number of hours of unmodified graded readers that would be required for a comparable rate of acquisition.

For the demonstration of a frequency effect, and an attempt to find formula acquisition within a pleasurable context of story-reading, and an implementation of Boers et al.'s (2017) counsel that learners be exposed only to intact formula, Webb et al.'s (2013) study is commendable. Yet it still leaves us rather far from a practical solution to the FSs acquisition problem. The proposition of this chapter is that some form of corpus searching is at present the only complete and even provisionally proven pedagogy for making language learners aware of and proficient in the handling of FSs. The question is what form this corpus searching will take.

Contextualized Corpus Work

The worksheet and concordancer approach typical of DDL as described previously in the discussion of Chan and Liou (2005; namely worksheet for completion with corpus information leading to measurably raised awareness) is just one possible type of corpus work. The limits of this type of pedagogy are not hard to imagine. The learning takes place in a very narrow semantic context, as may be reflected in the less impressive results at delayed post-test in Chan and Liou (as was also found across DDL studies generally by Boulton & Cobb's, 2017, meta-analysis). This possibly reflects the general truth of cognitive psychology (e.g., Anderson, 2015) that memories are not strong for low-meaning inputs such as might characterize disjointed worksheet questions or concordance lines. This explains the motivation to search for formula learning in more meaningful contexts such as reading graded stories, as Webb et al. (2013) do in their study. But concordancing work can be imagined, which is less decontextualized, with concordancing embedded within a more CALL-like environment, which typically keeps records, includes game elements, incorporates considerations of motivation, context of learning, etc.

The benefits of this idea are largely speculative to this point, however, since CALL developers and enterprises have not focused significantly on formula learning. In a review paper on CALL and the teaching of FL, Nesselhauf and Tschichold (2002) found this topic "largely neglected", and since none of the 68 Google Scholar citations to this paper up to November 2017 is a comparable treatment of the topic, their verdict appears to remain correct. One reason may be the ongoing migration of CALL vocabulary work to the small screen (*DuoLingo*, *Free Rice*, or the many other flashcard apps enumerated at https://en.wikipedia.org/wiki/List_of_flashcard_software), which for space constraints do not emphasize lexical information beyond the single word. Indeed, the present writer, as consultant to a gaming software project (reported in Cobb & Horst, 2012), witnessed first-hand the difficulty of evolving the single-word version of the Nintendo game *My Word Coach* to a v.2 incorporating formulaic information (the project was abandoned). For these reasons, much of the interesting work being done on CALL and modified concordancing approaches to integrating formulae within lexis takes place on the periphery of the CALL universe, on teacher-developer websites like Lextutor (www.lextutor.ca).

Two elements of the basic concordancing experience are modifiable within a CALL context: the nature of the corpus and the learning context.

Modifying the Corpus

Concordance searches in applied linguistics are normally performed on full corpora which claim to represent a language as a whole, such as the British National Corpus (BNC; Oxford University Computing Services, 2001) or Corpus of Contemporary American English (COCA; Davies, 2008). Using such corpora, an applied linguist or teacher can determine something about a language that is relevant to learning it, such as that a particular formulaic expression like "pull someone's leg" is probably not frequent enough to be learned incidentally. But for pedagogical purposes, the corpus involved in a formula learning activity need not represent the language as a whole, but might instead reflect the purposes of a learner or a teacher more than a linguist or applied linguist. Cobb (1999) had learners search for lexical information in a 50,000-word corpus assembled from the same learners' own study materials (e.g., course books, language lab assignments, classroom tests, and worksheets) such that some or most of the concordance lines in any given activity were probably familiar, especially when expanded to paragraph size. Interestingly, vocabulary acquired through the use of this corpus had not begun to dwindle by delayed post-test, as compared to some of the DDL studies mentioned earlier.

Modifying the Learning Context

Even if the language of a corpus is familiar, asking learners to use it to answer questions they do not currently have is nonetheless a decontextualized exercise. This is not the case however if the question comes from learners themselves. For example, learners are seeking corpus information in a meaningful context when they click on a word or expression in a text to see a concordance output for it, as shown in Figure 10.3, where concordance lines serve as a type of gloss. This technology has been provisionally validated for single-word learning by Lee, Warschauer, and Lee (2017). Users of such a tool are almost certainly seeking mainly single-word information in the concordance lines, but what they seek is not necessarily the only thing they get. Notice that in Figure 10.3 the concordances are set up by the developer to provide a secondary focus on any repeated sequences there may be in the output by left-of-keyword sorting. Thus, the most likely

HYPERTEXT FILE: in_progress_59
Click twice for concordance (50 lines) & dictionary, with AltKey (Option) to pronounce word and put into Word Box

This article shows how language processing is intimately tuned to input frequency. Examples are given of frequency effects in the processing of phonology and phonotactics, reading, spelling, lexis, morphosyntax, formulaic language, language comprehension, grammaticality, sentence production, and syntax. The implications of these effects for the representations and developmental sequence of SLA are discussed.

Usage-based theories hold that the acquisition of language is exemplar based. It is the piecemeal learning of many thousands of constructions and the frequency-biased abstraction of regularities within them. Determinants of pattern productivity include the power law of practice, cue competition and constraint satisfaction, connectionist learning, and effects of type and token frequency. The regularities of language emerge from experience as categories and prototypical patterns.

The typical route of emergence of constructions is from formula, through low-scope pattern, to

Concordance for *family* frequency in brown_strip.txt sorted 1 wd left of key   Dictionary Eng_Eng

```
009.   he dream was a reality on the infinite progressions of universal, gradient frequencies, across which the m
010.   ifier, no ballast resistor was required for stability of operation. A high frequency starter was used to s
011.   s, apparently obtained at least in part by emphasizing the middle and high frequencies. The penalty for th
012.   ion of a barbiturate into the posterior hypothalamus causes a lessening in frequency and amplitude of cort
013.   arations indicative of such an intention is being reported with increasing frequency from a variety of sou
014.   creative. What does it mean to be creative, a term we hear with increasing frequency these days? When we t
015.   th of the receiver; therefore, only with precise foreknowledge of the line frequencies is an astronomical
016.   py has been started. Since conventional methods are insensitive at the low frequencies of these molecular
017.   tion of a strong magnetic field to the radical vapor, which shifts the low- frequency spectra to a conveni
```

FIGURE 10.3   Sneaking formula insights into lexical search.

Text is from Ellis (2002); corpus is Brown (Kucera & Francis, 1971); routine is http://lextutor.ca/hyp/1/.

formulae are delivered along with the lexical information. Formula information is "sneaked in" to the single-word search for "frequency" ("high frequency", "increasing frequency", and "low frequency"). Whether learners notice this extra information has not been formally investigated.

Other examples of sneaked-in formula information on the Lextutor website are *List_Learn* (http://lextutor.ca/list_learn/), where learners build their own comprehensive flashcard glossaries by generating concordances from a word list to engage in a choose-the-definition quiz (shown in Figure 10.4, where "cease to" and particularly "cease to be" and "cease to exist" have been serendipitously generated); and *Concord_Writer* (www.lextutor.ca/cgi-bin/conc/write/), in which a writer's own emerging text is fully linked to a concordancer, such that "possible next words" can be generated from any of several corpora.

The learning context can also include what teachers do. Still in the context of a reading activity, a teacher can use a corpus tool to determine which repeated strings in a text they should draw learners' attention to. A teacher who runs a text through AntConc's or Lextutor's *N-Gram* routines can learn which strings are recurring, a feature which normally lies below the radar of even native-speaker awareness. Then, once such strings have been identified, these can form the content of concordance-based worksheets or quizzes tied to the text under study, on paper or online. The paper exercise shown in Figure 10.5 is made using Lextutor's concordance "gap" routine, where the keyword is replaced by a gap. The text in this case is about driving, and the search word is *car* with any of *drive*, *driver*, *truck*, or *ride* in the context. The main learning affordance here would be in a

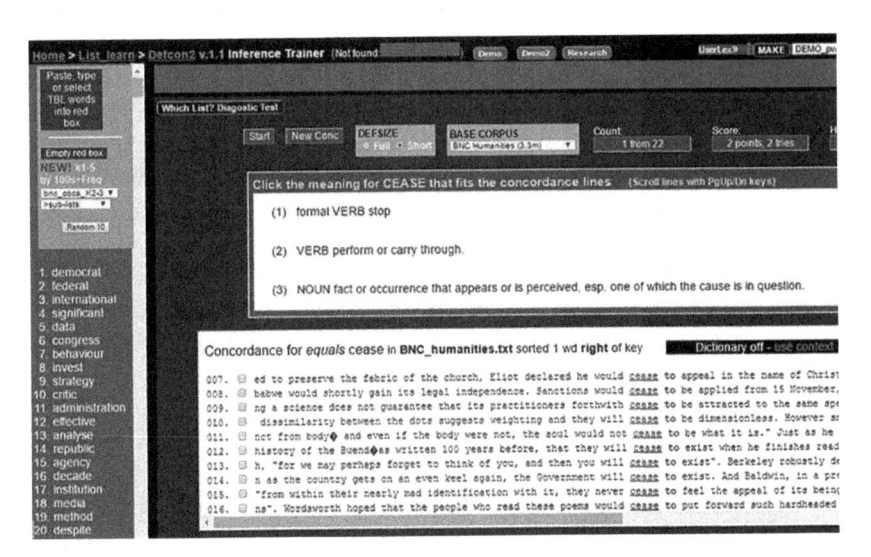

FIGURE 10.4 Combined word and formula trainer.

Defcon2 is from www.lextutor.ca/cgi-bin/list_learn/defcon2.pl; word lists are from Nation's (2012) BNC-COCA lists; dictionary is drawn from the *Concise Oxford Dictionary*; Corpus is BNCs' humanities subcorpus.

Instructions: Write in the word that fits all the gaps

```
001.   it is a matter of fact that Smith cannot drive a ____. There is nothing to suggest that the brain ca
002.   status when I am driven up in front of work in a ____ driven by my wife, who is only a woman. Even t
004.   , North Providence, with injuries suffered when a ____ he was driving struck a utility pole on Woonas
007.   nside of the door-frame on the driver's side of a ____. She called softly, 'Barney'. He looked in her
008.   of appealing to them for help. Perhaps they had a ____ or truck and would drive him into town. Then h
013.   For those who need or want and can afford another ____, buying one and driving it on the grand tour,
017.   you insure five or more rigs. This means either a ____ or a truck. Discounts run up to 2% of cost. Us
020.   avaughn Huntley is accused of driving the getaway ____ used in a robbery of the Woodyard Bros.' Groce
022.   transported, may think of the engine driving his ____ as 'a mystical beast under the hood'. The Ital
```

FIGURE 10.5 CALL-concordance worksheet contextualized for post-reading.

From Brown corpus; made by routine at http://lextutor.ca/conc/eng.

teacher-led discussion of the roll of the words associated with *car* (*drive, driver, driving*, etc.) in determining the correct answer. A point to address here is that asking learners to supply a missing piece of a formula may look like an instance of the bad pedagogy discovered by Boers et al. (2017) and discussed prior, except that it targets and reviews an expression recently encountered.

A similar activity could also be put into the hands of learners through an online CALL-Concordancing activity. The activity shown in Figure 10.6 comes from a text with a strong presence of non-overlapping *make* and *do* verbs. Learners are asked to choose the word that will fill all the gaps in each concordance, and then repeat the exercise with a new randomization of concordance lines from the same or a different corpus. A paper task (like the one shown in Figure 10.5) can be simply created by the teacher to follow the online work, employing a new randomization, thus affording an opportunity for re-use of inputs and for transfer. Again, teacher involvement in discussion and feedback would help highlight the formulaic and collocational information that determines the correct answers.

Another learner-meaningful context for a CALL-Concordance activity is when the concordance is offered as a response to learners' writing errors. In the event of a writing error in an online submission, a teacher can use Lextutor's concordance input form (at http://lextutor.ca/conc/eng) to click together the pieces of a URL that generates a concordance bearing a more correct version of what the learner was trying to say, then copy-paste the URL into the learner's document to return for correction (the procedure is described with examples in Gaskell & Cobb, 2004). Here is an example of such a URL showing a CALL-concordance error feedback (Corpus is graded readers collection from OUP's Bookworm series; routine is Corpus Concordance English at http://lextutor.ca/conc/eng/):

www.lextutor.ca/cgi-bin/conc/wwwassocwords.pl?SearchStr=marry%20me&SearchType=equals&Corpus=corpus_graded_2k.txt&SortType=left&LineWidth=120&AssocWord=will&Fam_or_Word=word

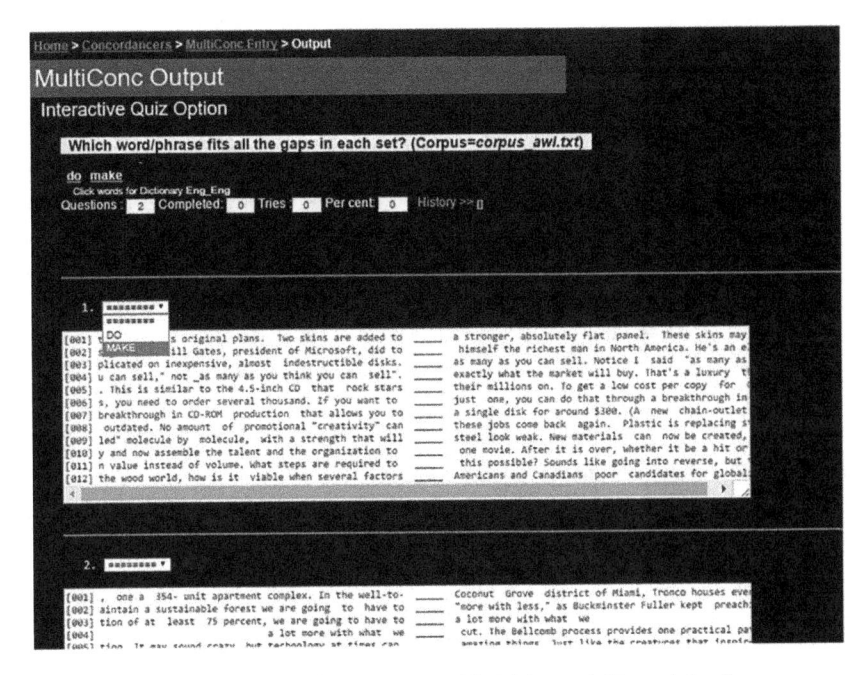

FIGURE 10.6 CALL-Concordancing repeatable Make-and-Do activity from a text. Corpus is graded readers collection from OUP's Bookworm series; routine is MultiConcordance at http://lextutor.ca/conc/multi.

CALL-concordance feedback can be used with any type of productive error, but it is particularly apt for errors in FL. Figure 10.7 is taken from a tutorial routine employing typical formula errors that was developed to prepare learners in the Gaskell et al. study for corpus-based correction. Here the concordance for "marry me", from a corpus of graded readers, makes it reasonably clear that "Will you marry me?" is the standard formulation for this idea while "Do you want to marry me?" while not impossible is marked or non-standard. The learner considers the concordance information and then makes a correction in the corresponding space on the right. Not obvious in the screen-print is that the learner can easily reformulate the search, for example using "marry me" as the keyword and "want" as an associated word to the left. From this it will be obvious that while "want to marry me?" is used in certain contexts, "Do you want to marry me?" rarely appears as a direct question.

In summary, there are several ways of presenting concordancing information to learners in contexts they are normally motivated to attend to, with formulaic information as either the direct or indirect focus of the exercise.

204 Tom Cobb

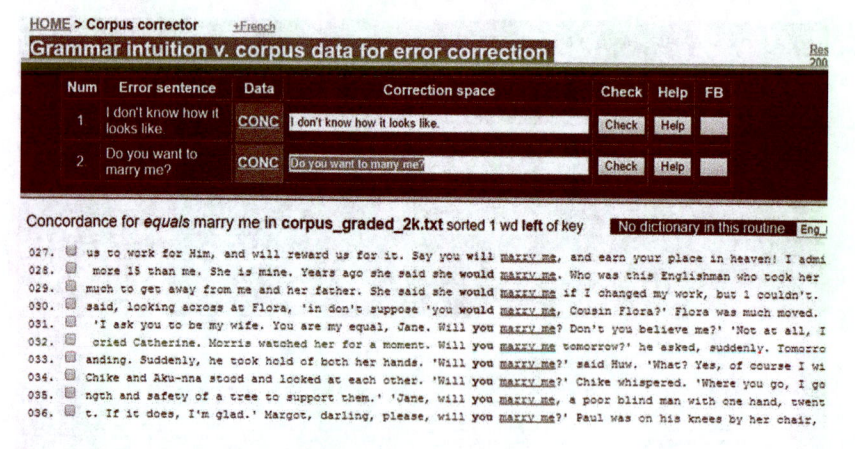

FIGURE 10.7   Corpus-based formula adjustment.

"Will you marry me?" is the archetypal formulaic sequence from Pawley and Syder (1983); Corpus corrector quiz is from www.lextutor.ca/conc/gram/.

CALL Formula Work other than Concordancing

So far in this discussion it may have seemed that concordancing is the only possible way to have learners work with FL in CALL. But there are two other responses worth talking about: formulaic cloze passages and single-word work with formulaic spin-off.

Formulaic Cloze Passages

While CALL approaches to lexical development have traditionally focused on single words (Cobb & Horst, 2011), and indeed were often versions of the word-to-meaning or L1-to-L2 word flashcard concept (Nakata, 2011), various kinds of FSs are gradually being accommodated within the genre. Some of these involve drag-and-drop versions of the textbook activities found ineffective by Boers et al. (2017). The other major tendency in CALL vocabulary work that does not employ matching or word cards is the cloze passage, which presents words in a context but also has tended to work on the level of single words. There is no reason, however, that computer cloze passages cannot find and remove entire formulaic expressions for learners to return to their places in a text. Boers et al.'s counsel to have workers attend only to intact formulae is not thereby violated. In Figure 10.8, Lextutor's "Cloze Builder" displays the lyrics with accompanying sound file for David Bowie's song *Space Oddity* (1969). The teacher has chosen some intact (without intervenors) multiword units for removal, with varying degrees of success as to what constitutes a true formula, and the learner's task is to put them back in their original places. Resources to aid the learner in this task include the sung rendition

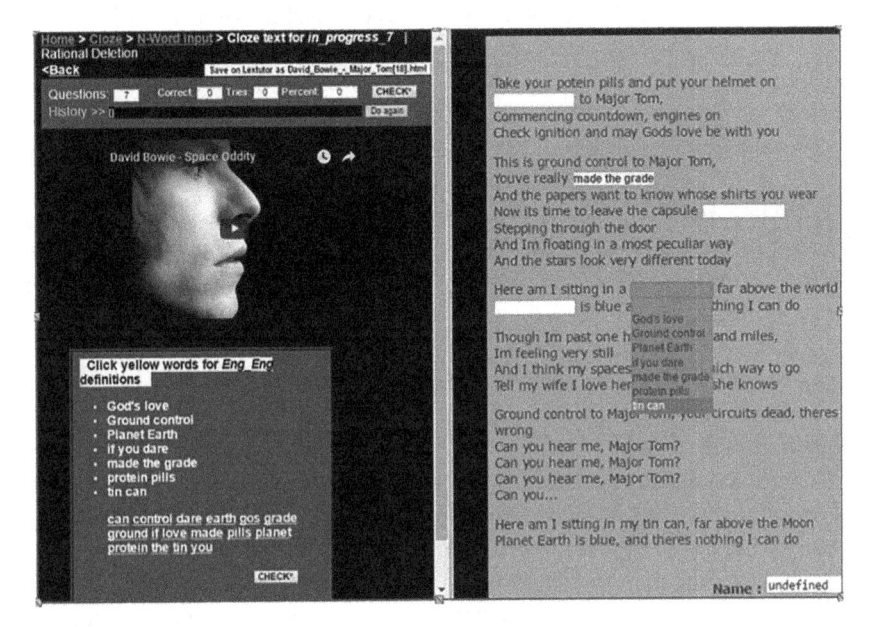

FIGURE 10.8 CALL cloze for sequences, not words.

From David Bowie's *Major Tom* (1969); cloze passage from http://lextutor.ca/cgi-bin/cloze/n/ ; video from www.youtube.com/watch?v=VrERLeFseDA; WordReference from http://mini.wordreference.com.

of the text, a listing of the items that have been removed, and a glossary for looking up their individual words in a mono- or bilingual dictionary (English to nine other languages). Apparently, no research has been done to determine the value of this type of activity for formula learning; the value will presumably be whatever it is for single-word cloze passages, possibly with additional awareness raising for the "togetherness" of some words and its accompanying prosody in the sound rendition.

Single-Word CALL and Formulaic Sequences

On the single-word level, both the computer and its update, the mobile smart phone, have proven to be highly effective vocabulary teachers (Cobb, 1997; Cobb & Horst, 2011). However, CALL vocabulary approaches have focused almost entirely on single words, despite researchers' growing awareness of the existence and importance of recurring FSs. A single-word focus is probably inevitable and indeed acceptable in this context for two reasons. First is the relatively small number of single words that must be learned to get a basic grip on a language, namely 3,000 high-frequency families for 95% coverage in average texts (Schmitt, Cobb, Horst & Schmitt, 2017), compared to the truly stupendous number of FSs involving just those same few items (probably tens of thousands that, though low in frequency, are nonetheless known to all native speakers). In other words, the practicality of direct teaching of all those FSs is of doubtful value. Who could remember them? Second is the fact that learning single words in any case appears to facilitate the subsequent learning of formulae in which they feature.

Some researchers have argued that given the prevalence of FSs, particularly within particular domains, single-word work is a waste of time (Hyland & Tse, 2007). This argument has been leveled particularly against the teaching of the 580 items of the corpus-based Academic Word List (Coxhead, 2000), whose items are shown to function differently within different formulaic expressions in different domains, leading to the possibility that this is how they should be presented and learned. Hyland et al's may be an extreme position, yet it is supported by a general lack of clarity within vocabulary research and instruction as to whether words or formulaic sequences should be taught, or when, in what proportions, and with what handover points.

There is some evidence, however, to suggest that assuming a dichotomy between single-word teaching and FS teaching is probably not useful. It now appears likely that single-word learning can be a precursor of multiword learning; that is to say, once a single-word form and basic meaning have been fixed in memory, then further learning of formulae involving that word is facilitated. And yet that the converse is not true: learning a formula does not necessarily facilitate learning the items that compose it. Wray's (2002) famous example is that few people can state what Rice Krispies are made of. There has been for some reason little investigation of this interesting question, apart from Bogaards (2001). He asked Dutch learners of French to learn idiomatic FSs (in which the meanings of the individual words did not add up to the intended overall meaning), half of whom had previously learned the individual words of the sequences and half had not. Those who had previously learned the words were significantly better able to both comprehend and retain the sequences.

This insight from French gradually made its way into English as a second language research. Nguyen and Webb (2017) looked for the predictors of L2 learners' learning of FSs, and found the strongest predictor to be the frequency of the node word of a sequence, this presumably reflecting roughly the number of times a learner would have seen this word *qua* single word. These researchers also found significant positive correlations between learners' knowledge of single words and their knowledge of FSs. In other words, learning words and learning sequences tends to go hand in hand, and there is little evidence of a word-formula dichotomy. Indeed, it is known to any language teacher that there are few learners with large single-word lexicons who do not also know large numbers of FSs, and vice versa.

This is not to say that the whole process from single-word to multiword learning needs only be left to nature to happen by itself, or that it happens most efficiently left to itself. Martinez and Murphy's (2011) subjects knew all the single words in a story passage rich in idiomatic formulae but nonetheless did not comprehend the main idea of the passage. In other words, single-word learning had not (yet) transferred to formulaic knowledge, at least in the case of idiomatic formulae. This suggests that specific training in the interpretation of word groups is required, though it is not at present clear whether this should amount to awareness raising for formulae generally or focused work with particular formulae.

What does all this mean for CALL and the acquisition of formulaic sequences? Basically, that the single-word successes of CALL probably did not come at the expense of formulaic skill but rather facilitated it, long term, for the many learners who have used this software in the past 20 years – but also that more could probably be done to raise awareness of formula at the same time as working on single words. The CALL program that is needed is hence one that is legitimately focused mainly on single-word acquisition, but with some simultaneous attention to the groupings and formulae that these words are likely to enter ("sneaked in" in the idiom adopted above, but perhaps more explicitly).

Conclusions and Future Directions

This chapter has argued that corpus technology is key to exposing the extent and nature of formulaic language to second and foreign language learners. Without seeing "pull someone's leg" in a corpus, learners will never notice it, or if they do, have any way to evaluate its importance as a learning object. A carefully built and properly analyzed corpus can show both the extent of the formulaic phenomenon (raise awareness of it) as well as the usage characteristics of particular formula. Such a corpus can do this in an engaging manner without either breaking formulae apart (and running the risks elaborated by Boers et al., 2017) or misrepresenting their distribution characteristics (as Webb et al., 2013, have implicitly done). However, the chapter also argues, concordance work can probably be accomplished best in a pedagogical context where motivation, curriculum integration, and learner purpose are taken into account – that is, in a CALL context.

But as mentioned, however, Nesselhauf and Tshichold's (2002) conclusion was that formula instruction was "largely neglected in CALL", and this would appear to still be the case with two exceptions, concordance work in the DDL approach and a handful of CALL experiments that integrate concordancing within a tutorial context. In other words, despite the historical connection between text computing and FL, the connection has not been extensively exploited instructionally. A number of operational ideas for integrating formula work within ongoing CALL vocabulary work have been shown in this chapter, and some of it has received preliminary empirical validation (Boulton & Cobb, 2017, for lexicogrammar by DDL generally; Gaskell & Cobb, 2004, for concordance error feedback; Lee et al., 2017, for concordance glossing). The strong result for DDL in lexicogrammar will presumably transfer positively to effectively designed CALL-concordancing, with its greater attention to learner variables and pedagogy.

An issue humming in the background of this chapter is the unresolved question whether formulae can be tackled in detail in L2 instruction (particular formulae highlighted and practiced), or only generally in the form of awareness raising (learners made aware they should pay attention to how words go together). Both sides of this question have their proponents. Simpson-Vlatch and Ellis (2010) built and then crunched a corpus of academic lectures for specific to-be-learned formulae for that setting; Thornbury (2002) argues that for general English, the number of formulae and quasi-formulae is so vast that only an awareness-raising approach can be effective. In the opinion of the preseent writer, corpus work appears to be effective whichever answer turns out to be correct.

The progress of this work will to some extent await resolution of some other issues in learning research and technology development. Questions that will have a bearing on this and which to some extent fall out of concerns raised in this chapter are the following:

- Should formula work involve mainly awareness raising or mainly teaching of particular formulae, or does this depend on the learning purpose?
- Should FSs be taught before, after, or along with the single words they are composed of?
- Can formulae knowledge and skill be incorporated within the small screen and short learning time that have typified recent CALL success in vocabulary acquisition, or is a different technology or paradigm needed?
- If the vocabulary money is now riding on the small screen, and the small screen is inherently unsuited to formulaic information, where will this new paradigm come from?
- Is there any need for learners to perform corpus analysis themselves, or can they simply be shown the insights of experts who have done so?

The ideal way forward in this area can be indicated by the behaviours and strategies of learners themselves, the best of whom already use the Web as their prime resource for information about formulae and which words go together. But it should be possible for applied linguistics as a profession to do better than just let learners roam the Web for their language insights. We should be able to offer them learning technologies for formula work that incorporate specialized corpora, feedback, motivation to persist, opportunities to review – in short, pedagogy.

References

Anderson, J. (2015). *Cognitive psychology & its implications* (8th Ed.). New York, NY: Worth Publishers.

Anthony, L. (2014). *Antconc 3.4.4w*. Computer program. Retrieved October 20, 2017 from www.laurenceanthony.net/software/antconc/.

Bahns, J., & Eldaw, M. (1993). Should we teach EFL students collocations? *System, 21*(1), 101–114.

Brandreth, G. (1980). *The joy of lex: How to have fun with 860,341,500 words*. New York, NY: Morrow.

Boers, F., Dang, T., & Strong, B. (2017). Comparing the effectiveness of phrase-focused exercises: A partial replication of Boers, Demecheleer, Coxhead, and Webb (2014). *Language Teaching Research, 21*(3), 362–380.

Bogaards, P. (2001). Lexical units and the learning of foreign language vocabulary. *Studies in Second Language Acquisition, 23*(3), 321–343.

Boulton, A., & Cobb, T. (2016). Corpus use in language learning: A meta-analysis. *Language Learning, 65*(2), 1–46.

Chan, T. P., & Liou, H. C. (2005). Effects of web-based concordancing instruction on EFL students' learning of verb – Noun collocations. *Computer Assisted Language Learning, 18*(3), 231–251.

Chen, H.-J. (2011). Developing and evaluating a web-based collocation retrieval tool for EFL students and teachers. *Computer Assisted Language Learning, 24*(1), 59–76.

Cobb, T. (1997). Is there any measurable learning from hands-on concordancing? *System, 25*(3), 301–315.

Cobb, T. (1999). Applying constructivism: A test for the learner-as-scientist. *Educational Technology Research & Development, 47*(3), 15–31.

Cobb, T., & Horst, M. (2011). Does word coach coach words? *CALICO Journal, 28*(3), 639–661.

Cowie, A. P. (1998). *Phraseology: Theory, analysis, & applications*. Oxford: Oxford University Press.

Coxhead, A. (2000). A new academic word list. *TESOL Quarterly, 34*(2), 213–238.

Daskalovska, N. (2014). Corpus-based versus traditional learning of collocations. *Computer Assisted Language Learning, 28*(2), 130–144.

Davies, M. (2008). *The corpus of contemporary American English*. Provost, UT: Brigham Young University.

Ellis, N. (1994). Vocabulary acquisition: The implicit ins & outs of explicit cognitive mediation In N. Ellis (Ed.), *Implicit & explicit learning of languages* (pp. 211–282). London: Academic Press.

Ellis, N. (2002). Frequency effects in language processing. *Studies in Second Language Acquisition, 24*, 143–188.

Erman, B., & Warren, B. (2000). The idiom principle and the open choice principle. *Text, 20*(1), 29–62.

Gaskell, D., & Cobb, T. (2004). Can learners use concordance feedback for writing errors? *System, 32*(3), 301–319.

Henry, O., Hedge, T., & Bassett, J. (2000). *New Yorkers: Short stories* [Oxford Bookworms Library Stage 2]. Oxford: Oxford University Press.

Horst, M., Cobb, T., & Meara, P. (1998). Beyond a clockwork orange: Acquiring second language vocabulary through reading. *Reading in a Foreign Language, 11*(2), 207–233.

Huang, Z. (2014). The effects of paper-based DDL on the acquisition of lexico-grammatical patterns in L2 writing. *ReCALL, 26*(2), 163–183.

Hyland, K., & Tse, P. (2007). Is there an 'Academic Vocabulary'? *TESOL Quarterly, 41*(2), 235–253.

Kilgarriff, A. (2004). *The sketch engine*. Computer program. Retrieved October 20, 2017 from www.sketchengine.co.uk/.

Kjellmer, G. (1991). A mint of phrases. In Aijmer, K., & Altenberg, B. (Eds.), *English corpus linguistics* (pp. 111–127). London: Longman.

Kucera, W., & Francis, H. (1971). *The brown corpus of present-day edited American English*. Princeton: University Press.
Lee, H., Warschauer, M., & Lee, J. (2017). The effects of concordance-based electronic glosses on L2 vocabulary learning. *Language Learning & Technology, 21*(2), 32–51.
Liou, H.-C., Chang, J. S., Chen, H. J., Lin, C.-C., Liaw, M.-L., Gao, Z. M., Jang, J.-S. R., Yeh, Y., Chuang, T. C., & You, G.-N. (2006). Corpora processing and computational scaffolding for an innovative web-based English learning environment. *CALICO Journal, 24*(1), 77–95.
Martinez, R., & Murphy, V. (2011). Effect of frequency and idiomaticity on second language reading comprehension. *TESOL Quarterly, 45*(2), 267–290.
Martinez, R., & Schmitt, N. (2012). A phrasal expressions list. *Applied Linguistics, 33*(3), 299–320.
Nakata, T. (2011). Computer-assisted second language vocabulary learning in a paired-associate paradigm: A critical examination of flashcard software. *Computer Assisted Language Learning, 24*, 17–38.
Nation, P. (2012). *The BNC/COCA words family lists*. Retrieved November 8, 2017 from www.victoria.ac.nz/lals/about/staff/publications/paul-nation/Information-on-the-BNC_COCA-word-family-lists.pdf.
Nesselhauf, N., & Tshichold, C. (2002). Collocations in CALL: An investigation of vocabulary-building software for EFL. *Computer Assisted Language Learning, 15*(3), 251–279.
Nguyen, T., & Webb, S. (2017). Examining second language receptive knowledge of collocation and factors that affect learning. *Language Teaching Research, 21*(3), 298–320.
Oxford University Computing Services. (2001). *The British National Corpus*, version 2 (BNC World). Distributed on behalf of the BNC Consortium. URL: http://www.natcorp.ox.ac.uk/.
Pawley, A., & Syder, F. (1983). Two puzzles for linguistic theory: Nativelike selection and nativelike fluency. In J. Richards & R. Schmidt (Eds.), *Language and communication* (pp. 191–225). London: Longman.
Plonsky, L., & Oswald, F. L. (2014). How big is "big"? Interpreting effect sizes in L2 research. *Language Learning, 64*(4), 878–912.
Shin, D., & Nation, P. (2008). Beyond single words: The most frequent collocations in spoken English. *ELT Journal, 62*, 339–348.
Simpson-Vlach, R., & Ellis, N. (2010). An academic formulas list: New methods in phraseology research. *Applied Linguistics, 31*, 487–512.
Sinclair, J. (1991). *Corpus, concordance, collocation*. London: Oxford University Press.
Schmitt, N., Cobb, T., Horst, M., & Schmitt, D. (2017). How much vocabulary is needed to use English? Replication of Van Zeeland & Schmitt (2012), Nation (2006), and Cobb (2007). *Language Teaching, 50*(2), 212–226.
Sun, Y.-C., & Wang, L.-Y. (2003). Concordancers in the EFL classroom: Cognitive approaches and collocation difficulty. *Computer Assisted Language Learning, 16*(1), 83–94.
Thornbury, S. (2002). *How to teach vocabulary*. Harlow: Longman.
Webb, S., Newton, J., & Chang, A. (2013). Incidental learning of collocation. *Language Learning, 63*(1), 91–120.
Wray, A. (2002), *Formulaic language and the lexicon*. Cambridge: Cambridge University Press.

11
FORMULAIC LANGUAGE IN ENGLISH FOR ACADEMIC PURPOSES

Phil Durrant

Introduction

English for Academic Purposes (EAP) is concerned with understanding and teaching the use of English in university settings. Its primary motivation is the practical one of helping students who do not speak English as their first language succeed in English-medium university study. A number of reasons have been put forward for a focus on formulaic language (FL) in EAP. Some of these echo reasons given for a focus on FL in general; others are more specific to the EAP context.

The most fundamental reason for focusing on FL comes from the theoretical position that formulas are basic linguistic units. This view is influenced by Sinclair's (1991) *idiom principle* and by *pattern grammar* (Hunston & Francis, 2000) and *construction grammar* (Goldberg, 2006). It is captured well by O'Donnell et al.'s observation that "the phrase is the basic level of language representation where form and meaning meet with greatest reliability" (O'Donnell, Roemer, & Ellis, 2013, pp. 83–84). From the learner's perspective, this translates to the point that formulas are often irreducible syntactic/semantic units, which cannot be properly understood if they have not been specifically learned. It is this motivation which drives, for example, Hsu's (2014) list of semantically opaque formulas commonly found in academic readings and DeCarrico and Nattinger's (1988) similar list of items found in lectures.

A second motivation is found in the ideas that formulas have a special psycholinguistic status and that they play an important role in language acquisition. The former point suggests that phrases support fluent processing, making the learner's job correspondingly easier and freeing up resources for focusing on the content of the language which they are producing or trying to understand (e.g., Cortes,

2006; Simpson-Vlach & Ellis, 2010). The latter, based on models of first language learning suggested by, amongst others, Tomasello (2003) and Lieven (2008), and adapted for second language learning most prominently by Ellis (2008), sees the learning of formulas as a crucial stage in language learning, with command of the creative language system (grammar) being constructed through the gradual analysis of formulas (e.g., Lewis, 2000; Nattinger & DeCarrico, 1992).

A further rationale for incorporating formulas in EAP is the claim that there is a link between learners' use of FL and their perceived proficiency in the language (Chen & Baker, 2016; Cortes, 2004; Staples, Egbert, Biber, & McClair, 2013). Accordingly, it has been suggested that appropriate use of formulas enables learners to achieve higher grades in assessments (AlHassan & Wood, 2015; Jones & Haywood, 2004). At its most simple, this has sometimes been equated to the claim that learners who use more formulas will be perceived as more proficient (Haswell, 1991), but recent work has shown that the relationship is considerably more complex than this (see following discussion).

The link between FL and proficiency is closely related to Pawley and Syder's (1983) widely cited suggestion that appropriate use of formulas is important to achieving "nativelike" production. The term "nativelike" is probably misleading here as it suggests the issue is about sounding like someone born into a community, which is not quite right. The key point is rather that particular discourse communities (including those, like the various EAP communities, which people enter into later in life, and hence into which no one is really born) develop conventional ways of expressing frequently occurring meanings, which often take the form of formulaic utterances. Because such formulas are familiar to members of the community, they are considered "natural" (Hoey, 2005), and because formulas can be specific to particular communities, they can act as powerful signals of group membership (Wray, 2002). Since EAP is centrally concerned with helping learners meet the expectations of particular academic communities, these aspects of FL become central: by far the most commonly cited reasons for exploiting FL in EAP are couched in terms of their importance in *meeting expectations* (e.g., Li & Schmitt, 2009; McKenny, 2006), achieving *appropriateness* (e.g., Byrd & Coxhead, 2010; Chon & Shin, 2013), *naturalness* (e.g., Ackermann & Chen, 2013; AlHassan & Wood, 2015), or *idiomaticity* (e.g., Ädel & Erman, 2012), and in signalling *membership* of a group (e.g., Ädel & Erman, 2012; Davis & Morley, 2015; Hyland, 2012). It has been argued, further, that meeting expectations and signalling membership is a mark of "competent participation" (Hyland, 2008b, p. 5) in the community, implying that evaluations of the quality of learners' academic work are likely to be influenced by their effective use of formulas (AlHassan & Wood, 2015).

The association between formulas and discourse communities is related to the more general point that formulas tend to be highly context-dependent. Formulas are associated not only with particular communities, but with particular topics, particular registers, and particular genres. This feature has made FL an important analytical tool for researchers interested in language variation. EAP researchers have used formulas to study, for example, variation across academic disciplines (e.g., Durrant, 2017; Groom, 2005; Hyland, 2008b) and genres (e.g., Biber & Barbieri, 2007; Biber, Conrad, & Cortes, 2004; Groom, 2005), and across writers at different stages of their academic careers (e.g., Ädel & Römer, 2012; Cortes, 2004; Hyland, 2008a) or from different linguistic and cultural backgrounds (e.g., Chen & Baker, 2010; McKenny & Bennett, 2011; Pérez-Llantada, 2014).

One reason that analysis of this sort can be enlightening is that formulas are strongly associated, not only with particular contexts, but with particular meanings. Thus, as well as showing *where* texts vary, they also give clues as to *how* they vary in terms of the types of meanings that are created. In Hyland's (2012, p. 153) words, they "reveal lexico-grammatical community-authorized ways of making-meanings", so offering insights into the ways those communities, and the texts they produce, work. From the language learners' perspective, formulas offer ready-made ways of expressing the most common meanings which are required of them, and may even serve as "triggers to help thinking" (Davis & Morley, 2015, p. 28). Formulas may, in other words, act as a kind of scaffolding which supports learners in constructing academic texts, offering a set of ready-made meanings and ways of expressing those meanings. Like all forms of scaffolding, they provide support by restricting movement and biasing their users towards particular positions. While they serve an important pragmatic function, therefore, we also need to ask to what extent formulas constrain and limit originality in academic work and student learning.

Of the points just outlined, those related to the status of formulas in linguistic theory, in psycholinguistics, and in language acquisition are discussed in greater detail elsewhere in this volume (see Chapters 1, 2, 5, and 7). This chapter will rather focus on four issues which are more distinctive of EAP and which capture much of the important research done in this area. Specifically, it will address the following questions:

- What can corpus analysis of FL, and the ways in which it varies across texts, tell us about the language which EAP students need to learn?
- How does FL relate to originality and critical thought in academic work?
- Does using FL improve students' grades?
- How can we identify appropriate formulas to teach for academic purposes?

What can Analysis of Formulaic Language in Academic Texts Tell us about the Language Which EAP Students Need to Learn?

Corpus analysis has shown that academic texts make extensive use of recurrent expressions. The majority of these are used to "frame" novel stretches of language, showing the reader how a particular piece of information is to be interpreted, how it fits into the surrounding text, or what aspect of a phenomenon the writer or speaker wants to focus on (Biber et al., 2004). Biber et al. (2004) describe such sequences as *anchors* for new information. They note that recurrent four-grams usually function as the openings of clauses or phrases, providing "structural 'frames', followed by a 'slot'" (2004, p. 399). This is seen in cases such as:

1. *It is important to* note that Derrida does not assert. . .[1]
2. I want to talk *a little bit about* process control from that point of view.

(Biber et al., 2004, pp. 391, 395)

Similarly, Durrant and Mathews-Aydınlı (2011) show how the common rhetorical function of signalling the organization of an upcoming text comprises a subject+verb combination which is highly formulaic, followed by a much more creative object/complement, for example:

3. *Section 3 evaluates* the consequences of strategic assortment reductions. . .
4. *Part III outlines* the significance of intimate discrimination at a structural level

Cortes (2013) adds to this picture the important distinction between formulas acting as *triggers*, which signal the start of a rhetorical move (as in 5), and those acting as *complements*, which appear later within a move (as in 6). In both cases, however, the formula provides a routine frame for the content which follows:

5. However, *little is known about the* narrative skills of. . .
6. The objectives here are to determine if hedge funds exhibit persistence *in the sense that* some funds consistently have higher returns than others. . .

In examples 1–6, the balance between formulaic frame and novel content shows in microcosm the balance between the formulaic and novel which academic texts need to achieve. On the one hand, to be of value, a text needs to present new information or a new perspective. On the other hand, to count as a valid contribution to an academic discipline, it needs to locate this information or perspective in an accepted framework of understanding. These shared frameworks distinguish academic disciplines from pre-theoretical ways of understanding the world, and learning these frameworks is at the heart of learning how to do academic work. Much of the interest of FL in EAP rests on the fact that formulas reflect these frameworks.

This insight has been put to good effect in helping analysts understand the nature of academic texts and how they vary both from non-academic texts and from each other. This can be seen most clearly, perhaps, in comparisons of FL across academic disciplines. Durrant (2017), for example, shows how a quantitative analysis of overlaps in the use of four-grams between texts can map similarities and differences in language use across students working in different subject areas. Analysis of the recurring word sequences (*lexical bundles*) distinctive of texts in humanities/social sciences on the one hand and science/technology on the other hand reflects the distinct approaches to knowledge of each, with the former focusing on, for example:

- abstract constructs (*the idea of a; the nature of the*)
- autonomous agents (*the role of the; the power of the*)
- evaluations (*at the heart of; one of the main*)
- multiple contingent viewpoints (*it can be argued that; can be seen as*)
- setting things in interpretive viewpoints (*in relation to the; in the context of*)

And the latter focusing on, for example:

- the physical world (*the presence of a; the shape of the*)
- passive instruments (*it can be used; will be used to*)
- quantification (*a large number of; the difference between the*)
- received knowledge (*it is thought that; was found to be*)
- cause and effect (*is due to the; the reason for this*)

Analysis of repeated forms has also revealed characteristic differences between different genres of academic discourse. Biber et al. (2004), for example, show how most recurrent sequences found in university textbooks are based around noun and prepositional phrases and have referential functions. Characteristic formulas of this type include *the size of the; the nature of the; in the case of; in the absence of*. This contrasts with non-academic conversation, where most recurrent forms are based around verb phrases or dependent clauses and have a more interpersonal function (which Biber et al. call *stance*). Characteristic examples include *I don't want to; you don't have to; I was going to*. Interestingly, classroom teaching turns out to combine these styles, drawing on both the NP/PP-based referential formulas of academic writing and the VP/dependent clause-based stance formulas of conversation, resulting in a hybrid, and highly formulaic, form of discourse.

How does Formulaic Language Relate to Originality and Critical Thought?

While contemporary writers have focused mostly on the benefits of FL, George Orwell's classic essay *Politics and the English Language* (1946) took a more critical view. The cognitive processing efficiencies which researchers have seen as so important to attaining fluency are cast by Orwell in a very different light:

> The attraction of this way of writing is that it is easy. . . . By using stale metaphors, similes, and idioms, you save mental effort, at the cost of leaving your meaning vague, not only for yourself but for your reader.
>
> (p. 259)

Where applied linguists have seen formulas as providing a useful way of indicating "in-group membership", Orwell sees numbing conformity:

> Orthodoxy, of whatever colour, seems to demand a lifeless, imitative style. . . . When one watches some tired hack on the platform mechanically repeating the familiar phrases – *bestial atrocities, iron heel, bloodstained tyranny, free peoples of the world, stand shoulder to shoulder* – one often has a curious feeling that one is not watching a live human being but some kind of dummy. . . . A speaker who uses that kind of phraseology has gone some distance towards turning himself into a machine. The appropriate noises are coming out of his larynx, but his brain is not involved as it would be if he were choosing his words for himself. If the speech he is making is one that he is accustomed to make over and over again, he may be almost unconscious of what he is saying, as one is when he utters the responses in church. And this reduced state of consciousness, if not indispensable, is at any rate favourable to political conformity.
>
> (Orwell, 1946, p. 261)

Orwell's argument is an important reminder that both the cognitive and the social aspects of FL are not unambiguously beneficial. They provide a cognitive crutch by automating some aspects of language production, allowing us to focus more attention on other aspects of our message. However, the fact that the automated parts of our message go uninspected may lead to a lack of clarity or a failure to fully grasp our own assumptions. They provide a way of identifying with a group and access to ways of constructing knowledge which have evolved within our chosen disciplines, but identification with a group may also imply unthinking conformity and self-alienation.

This issue finds an echo in the concern sometimes expressed by teachers that students use formulaic phrases without properly understanding the ideas they express (Davis & Morley, 2015). It is also reflected more broadly in the debates between pragmatic approaches to EAP, which aim to teach students the conventions of their disciplines, more critical approaches which argue that EAP should help students actively challenge the practices of academic discourse, and academic literacies approaches, which address the issues of alienation that students may feel if forced to adopt a voice they feel is not their own (Hyland, 2006).

A very concrete example of the relationship between formulaicity and originality in student writing is seen in discussions about plagiarism. Plagiarism has been described as a form of *transgressive intertextuality* (Borg, 2009) – an illicit re-use of prior texts. One reason for students' problems with plagiarism is that most academic work actively requires the use of licit forms of intertextuality, and distinguishing the licit from the illicit is not always an easy task. Indeed, judgements about which individual cases constitute plagiarism can differ dramatically among professional academics (Borg, 2009; Davis & Morley, 2015; Pecorari &

Shaw, 2012). Pecorari and Shaw (2012), for example, find disagreement as to what constitutes "common knowledge" and thus is not in need of citation. Importantly for our topic, they also disagreed as to what language is "common property", and so not requiring a reference.

This raises the point that FL is itself a licit form of intertextuality. A key challenge for students is to learn to re-use prior language in ways that are expected of them while avoiding the types of re-use which will be seen by their teachers as transgressive. Moreover, they need to do this in a context where, as with plagiarism in general, what is considered legitimate re-use can vary widely from discipline to discipline, from genre to genre, and even from section to section of a single paper (Flowerdew & Li, 2007; Pecorari & Shaw, 2012).

Flowerdew and Li (2007) and Davis and Morley (2015) report surveys of faculty attitudes towards language re-use which offer some guidance on what distinguishes re-usable formulas from plagiarism. From both studies, the central message is that faculty perceive a sharp distinction between the *form* and the *content* of texts, which drive their perceptions of plagiarism. Davis and Morley report that re-use was seen as most unacceptable where language expresses a particular opinion or judgement (e.g., *deliberately and decisively debunks this myth*) or is stylistically distinctive (e.g., *Dawkins is deaf to theology*).

This view of legitimate FL tallies well with the descriptive work of Biber et al. (2004), described in the second section in this chapter, which portrayed formulas as structural frames which opened up slots for novel content. To describe these as entirely lacking in content is perhaps inaccurate. As I have argued earlier, formulaic frames encode the ways of thinking and writing which construct academic ways of making sense of the world. The academics surveyed by Flowerdew and Li and Davis and Morley, however, clearly perceive a difference between this type of underlying disciplinary thought (what one of Davis and Morley's respondents called the disciplinary *lingua franca* (2015, p. 27)) and more specific content.

Does Using Formulaic Language Improve Students' Grades?

A number of researchers have looked into the relationship between use of FL and perceptions of proficiency.[2] Studies have been of two main types: those which look at learners' use of sequences which are thought to be formulaic in native-speaker English, and those which look at sequences which are frequent within a learner corpus. Within the first type, a number of different methods have been used. AlHassan and Wood (2015) focus on 65 formulas which were taught to students as part of an intervention. In students' responses to an IELTS-style writing prompt at the end of the intervention, they found strong correlations ($r = .71$ and .60) between the number of target formulas used and the grades awarded to texts for two of the three raters who independently marked each text. Paquot (2017) takes a more wide-ranging approach, looking at the extent to which texts use adjective-noun, adverb-adjective, and verb-direct object combinations from Ackermann and Chen's (2013) *Academic Collocations List* (see following section). In a corpus of research papers written by French EFL students for a university linguistics course, and which had been rated at one of three CEFR levels (B2, C1, and C2), she found no systematic differences across levels.

Whereas these studies looked at lists of selected sequences which had been identified in advance as formulaic, others have been more comprehensive, quantifying the formulaicity of a text by checking the frequency of all of its constituent word sequences against a reference corpus. Granger and Bestgen (2014), for example, automatically extracted all bigrams (two-word sequences) in a corpus of L2 English essays which had been graded against the Common European Framework of Reference (CEFR). The status of the extracted bigrams as formulaic was checked based on their frequencies in the British National Corpus (BNC). Formulaicity was quantified using two statistical measures of association:

- *T-score*: a measure of the degree of certainty with which we can claim that a word pair occurs more frequently than chance would predict. This measure emphasizes high-frequency collocations, e.g.: *other hand; long time; little bit*
- *Mutual information (MI)*: a measure of the strength of the association between two-word pairs. This measure emphasizes the exclusivity of the two words to each other. Words which are not often found without each other tend to have high mutual information scores, e.g.: *pop music; juvenile delinquency; vicious circle*

Essays scoring in the "advanced" C1/C2 range of the CEFR were found to have higher proportions of bigrams with high mutual information scores and lower proportions of bigrams with high T-scores than essays scoring in the "intermediate" B1/B2 range. In a separate study which used a similar methodology with a different corpus of L2 timed writing, and quantifying frequencies using the Corpus of Contemporary American, the same authors (Bestgen & Granger, 2014) found that the mean mutual information score of bigrams in a text positively correlated with quality ratings, while the mean T-score showed no correlation. Similarly, Paquot (2017) looked at the mean mutual information score of adjective-noun, adverb-adjective, and verb-direct object combinations in the corpus of CEFR-rated EFL research papers mentioned before, with mutual information scores for each item being based on their frequencies in a reference corpus of published L2 research. She also found significant increases in mean scores across proficiency levels.

A rather different approach to understanding the relationship between formulaicity and perceptions of text quality is taken by studies which have looked at word sequences which are repeated within the learner corpus itself (Appel & Wood, 2016; Biber & Gray, 2013; Chen & Baker, 2016; Staples et al., 2013; Vidakovic & Barker, 2010). The key conceptual difference between these and the studies reviewed earlier is that they focus on sequences which are common in student writing, rather than those which are common in the target academic language community. Though I have not been able to locate any studies of this sort looking directly at authentic academic language (i.e., language written for university-based teaching or research), three have looked at writing from academic language proficiency exams.

Staples et al. (2013) studied lexical bundles in low, medium, and high-rated TOEFL writing scripts. They found that the median frequency of bundles decreased as proficiency increased, implying that there was greater repetition of bundles in the lower-level texts. They also found that lower-rated texts tended to use more bundles lifted directly from the task prompts. Similarly, Appel and Wood (2016), comparing high- versus low-scoring texts written for the Canadian Academic English Language (CAEL) assessment, found that the low-scoring texts used a greater number of bundles and made greater use of longer bundles and bundles taken from the task prompts. While Staples et al. did not find any functional differences between the bundles used in texts at different levels, Appel and Wood found that low-scoring texts made greater use of stance bundles (especially opinion statements) and discourse-organizing bundles (used to reference materials from the readings which formed part of the text prompt), while high-scoring texts made greater use of referential bundles.

Biber and Gray (2013) looked at the use of both lexical bundles and collocations in written and spoken responses to the TOEFL iBT. As with the studies reviewed earlier, they found that many bundles were recycled from task prompts. Whereas the other studies found a decrease in quantity of bundles as grades increased, Biber and Gray found a slightly more complex pattern, with texts achieving mid-level grades having more bundles than both those achieving the lowest and those achieving the highest grades. They argue that this implies a developmental pattern whereby learners at the lowest levels have not yet acquired fixed expressions; intermediate levels overuse the expressions they have learned; and learners at the highest levels move back towards greater creativity. A similar pattern is also suggested by their analysis of the collocations associated with five high-frequency verbs (*get*, *give*, *have*, *make*, and *take*), identifying which collocates are used within a three-word window of these nodes at least five times per 100,000 words. As with the analysis of lexical bundles, the mid-level texts were found to have more collocations than either the lowest- or the highest-scoring texts. For lexical bundles, this regular pattern is slightly modulated by the discourse function of bundles, with discourse-organizing bundles in speech and epistemic bundles in writing being most common at the highest levels. These final points stand in contrast to Appel and Wood (2016), who found extensive stance and discourse bundles to be associated with lower-level texts.

These complex results suggest that there is much still to be understood about the relationship between use of formulas and the grades students are likely to receive. Moreover, it is noteworthy that, with the exception of Paquot (2017), none of the studies reviewed analyzed authentic academic texts. The tasks from academic language proficiency tests studied by various researchers are clearly of some relevance to understanding academic writing but given what we know about the contextual specificity of FL use, it is also plausible that the way such language is evaluated in genuine academic contexts will differ from these. Given its importance to understanding the roles of FL use in student writing (and, accordingly, their potential roles in teaching and testing), the relationship between use of formulas and the perceived quality of academic texts is one which requires substantial further research.

How can We Identify Appropriate Formulas to Teach?

Originating in the broader *English for Specific Purposes* (Hutchinson & Waters, 1987) movement, a founding principle of EAP is that language teaching can be made more effective if we first identify what learners will be using the language for. This, the thinking goes, allows us to narrow the scope of teaching from the unattainable target of "English" as a whole, to a more manageable sub-section of the language. By identifying the language which is most important for the learner's target areas of use, we can make their learning both more efficient and more motivating.

In line with this philosophy, several studies have asked how we can select academic formulas for teachers and learners to focus on. The most common approach has been to produce a list, modelled on the lists of academic words (especially Coxhead's (2000) influential *Academic Word List*) which are already widely used in EAP programs (Burkett, 2015). As with word lists, the rationale for formula lists is that, given the huge number of formulas in English, teachers need to prioritize particular items for their learners to focus on. Again as with word lists, the primary criterion for prioritizing items is that of frequency, which, it is assumed, gives a good indication of the importance of particular formulas for learners.

Beyond simple counts of items, three more sophisticated types of frequency information are also commonly included:

- *Dispersion*: the extent to which items are used across a wide range of texts, rather than being concentrated in a few sources. In some studies (Ackermann & Chen, 2013; Eriksson, 2012), items are required to appear in more than a set number of distinct texts. In others, they are required to reach a particular frequency threshold across a range of distinct disciplinary areas (Ackermann & Chen, 2013; Durrant, 2009; Liu, 2012; Simpson-Vlach & Ellis, 2010). The latter is an attempt to ensure that formulas are relevant to a wide range of students.
- *Keyness*: the extent to which items are distinctive of the target text type. It is likely that many formulaic items which are frequent in academic texts are also frequent in the language as a whole. To identify items which are

distinctively academic, some studies (Durrant, 2009; Simpson-Vlach & Ellis, 2010) incorporate information on the relative frequencies of items in an academic corpus versus a corpus of general English and focus on those items where the gap between these is largest. A different use of keyness is made by Eriksson (2012), who focuses on items which are more common in published academic texts than in texts written by students. The logic here is that these are likely to be the items which students need but do not yet use.

- *Association*: measures of association usually focus either on how confident we can be that a combination of words occurs more frequently than chance would predict (see the description of *T-score* in the previous section) or on how strongly words in a formula are associated with each other (see the description of *mutual information* in the previous section). Many researchers have claimed that these provide a more valid way of identifying important collocations than frequency alone (e.g., Simpson-Vlach & Ellis, 2010)

While frequency data are key to formula list construction, they are not by themselves sufficient to generate a pedagogically useful list. One issue is that items which are identified on frequency grounds alone are frequently not meaningful units (e.g., *as well but*). Relatedly, frequency-based lists return a number of items which are clearly overlapping variants of a central formula (e.g., *were statistically significant*; *statistically significant differences between*; *no statistically significant*). Furthermore, some teachers and researchers wish to focus on particular subsets of items (e.g., items which are semantically opaque or items which do not translate directly in the L1) which cannot be identified on frequency grounds alone. For these reasons, studies often supplement their frequency data with manual filtering of items. Ackermann and Chen (2013), for example, manually exclude from their list linguistically incomplete items, fixed combinations, adverbs of time/frequency, common transparent adjectives, concrete geographical references, and combinations which are often hyphenated. Hsu (2014) uses a checklist to identify formulaic sequences (FSs) which are both meaningful and require holistic learning.

With extensive lists, such manual analysis is obviously arduous. Simpson-Vlach and Ellis (2010) take the ambitious step of estimating qualitative judgements about the teach-worthiness of items using frequency data alone. After asking a panel of teachers to rate a subset of 108 candidate formulas for teaching value, they use a regression analysis to determine a "formula teaching worth" formula, which they use to estimate how teachers would have rated the remainder of their items. While this is an intriguing approach, it is striking that Simpson-Vlach and Ellis do not report the goodness of fit between their model and teacher ratings. They also do not report how well the model generalized beyond the initial set of 108 items. The real effectiveness of their approach, and whether a frequency-based formula can effectively substitute for manual judgement, therefore remain unclear.

I noted previoulsy that the motivation for academic phrase lists is parallel to that for academic word lists. However, one important difference needs to be acknowledged. A key part of the justification for academic word lists is that the majority of the language we meet is made up of a relatively small number of distinct words (Durrant (2016) provides a discussion of the principles behind word lists). Coxhead (2000), for example, reports that the 570 words in her *Academic Word* List achieves 10% coverage of an academic corpus, while Durrant (2016) shows that the most frequent 587 lemmas in the Academic Vocabulary List (Gardner & Davies, 2014) account for 25% of lexical words in a corpus of student writing. There is little research into whether similar patterns exist for FL, however. Intuitively, it seems likely that the pay-off will be substantially less: FSs are, by definition, more specific, and hence rarer, than words. As we saw above, they also vary strikingly between even closely related contexts. We therefore cannot expect the same high levels of coverage as have been achieved by word lists.

The existing work on phrase lists shows that coverage can vary based on the type of formula studied and the type of academic writing studied. Durrant's (2009) list of 1,000 collocations appeared with a total frequency of between 17,677 (in Arts and Humanities disciplines) and 35,306 (in Social Science disciplines) occurrences per million words. Since each item comprises two words, and assuming each token in the corpus appears in only one collocation (a mostly plausible assumption for two-word combinations), this translates into a coverage of between 3.5% and 7.1% of words. Hsu (2014) also reports a reasonable coverage of 2.08% for a list of 475 two- to five-word sequences. It is important to note, however, that Durrant's list comprises largely combinations of lexical + function words (e.g., *associated with; as shown*), while Hsu's list includes combinations of function words (e.g., *along with; as to*) and a small number of colligations (e.g., *[auxiliary verb] + hardly*). In contrast, Ackerman and Chen's (2013) list, which includes only combinations of lexical words and which (as described earlier) excluded a number of particular types of combinations, achieves a coverage of only 1.4% with 2,468 lemmatized collocations. While there is great variation in these figures, none comes close to the high levels of coverage achieved by word lists, suggesting that listing may not be a particularly effective pedagogical approach for formulas.

A further issue with formula lists is that, as discussed before, formulas tend to be highly contextually specific. For researchers, this has been a boon as it has made formulas an excellent tool for identifying and characterizing differences between text types. It is also the chief reason why a learner's use of the most apposite formula can be so impressive. The flip side, however, is that a generic list for EAP students in general can be of only limited use. The formulas which would help a physicist write a research report will vary sharply from those which would help an historian write an essay.

Given these limitations of formula lists, it is worth asking whether there are other ways of helping learners decide what to focus on, preferably more closely tailored to their individual needs. Vincent (2013) offers one way forward here, setting out a methodology through which teachers can use corpus resources to identify FSs within specific texts that their learners are working with. His method involves identifying in a text candidate phrases which include particular high-frequency, closed-class words and then checking a reference corpus to determine their formulaic status. While Vincent's method is rather labor intensive, it is not hard to imagine systems which could make the process much easier and help learners to highlight formulas (of various types) in the texts they are reading/writing.

Conclusions and Future Directions

This chapter has explored a number of issues around the role of FL in EAP. I have suggested that formulas act as conventional frames in which academics set the novel content of their texts, that these frames carry important characteristic meanings which academics use to create knowledge in approved ways, and that they vary in interesting ways across academic communities and contexts. These features of formulas make them important both for researchers interested in how academic texts work and for students who are learning to create their own texts. We have seen that the conventions inherent in formulas are useful in helping to construct meanings but also potentially dangerous in that they embody conformity to a norm. It may also be difficult for students to distinguish legitimate from illegitimate re-use of forms (otherwise known as *plagiarism*). While many researchers have claimed that use of appropriate formulas can make learners sound more proficient, we have seen that evidence regarding the precise relationship between formulaicity and perceptions of proficiency is currently ambiguous. I have also reviewed a number of attempts to create pedagogically oriented lists of FL. While these offer an important resource, I have pointed out that they may not prove as useful as academic word lists have, and that alternative approaches to identifying language on which learners can focus may be needed.

On the basis of this review, a number of issues suggest themselves as important focuses for future work:

- The relationship between use of FL and perceptions of linguistic proficiency remains unclear. This is a crucial issue as it is this putative link which provides the ultimate rationale for students' learning FL. If formulas don't improve perceptions of learners' language, there seems little reason to study them. Moreover, a better understanding of the formula-proficiency link would help us enrich our understanding of the construct of academic language proficiency. This is crucial both for theoretically oriented tasks such as understanding academic language development and for practically oriented tasks such as establishing the validity of high-stakes tests of academic language proficiency.
- Orwell's claim that using FL prevents us from thinking critically and originally is a striking one. Traditionally, applied linguists have stayed away from

research on the language-thought interface, and I am not aware of any systematic research on the implications of formulaicity for critical or original thought, though formulaic thinking is an issue touched on by Wray (2008), and some work has looked at the role of formulas in linguistic creativity more broadly (see Bell, 2012 for an interesting review). The recent resurgence in research perspectives on the relationship between thought and language (e.g., Pavlenko, 2014) may open up possibilities for work in this area.
- We do not yet have a satisfying means of identifying formulas for teaching. A "list" approach has significant shortcomings, as discussed above. More "responsive" methods which help students to identify formulas they encounter may offer a useful way forward.

It can be hoped that future research will expand our understandings in these directions.

Notes

1 In this chapter, I will use bold italics to identify stretches of text which are assumed to be formulaic. This will not always reflect emphases made in the original texts from which I am quoting.
2 Since most assessment in universities involves written, rather than spoken work, the former has been the main focus of attention, and the current review will not deal with studies of spoken language.

References

Ackermann, K., & Chen, Y.-H. (2013). Developing the academic collocation list (ACL) – A corpus-driven and expert-judged approach. *Journal of English for Academic Purposes, 12*(4), 235–247.

Ädel, A., & Ermann, B. (2012). Recurrent word combinations in academic writing by native and non-native speakers of English: A lexical bundles approach. *English for Specific Purposes, 31*(2), 81–92.

Ädel, A., & Römer, U. (2012). Research on advanced student writing across disciplines and levels: Introducing the *Michigan Corpus of Upper-level Student Papers. International Journal of Corpus Linguistics, 17*(1), 3–34.

AlHassan, L., & Wood, D. (2015). The effectiveness of focused instruction of formulaic sequences in augmenting L2 learners' academic writing skills: A quantitative research study. *Journal of English for Academic Purposes, 17*, 51–62.

Appel, R., & Wood, D. (2016). Recurrent word combinations in EAP test-taker writing: Differences between high- and low-proficiency levels. *Language Assessment Quarterly, 13*(1), 55–71.

Bell, N. (2012). Formulaic language, creativity, and language play in a second language. *Annual Review of Applied Linguistics, 32*, 189–205.

Bestgen, Y., & Granger, S. (2014). Quantifying the development of phraseological competence in L2 English writing: An automated approach. *Journal of Second Language Writing, 26*, 28–41.

Biber, D., & Barbieri, F. (2007). Lexical bundles in university spoken and written registers. *English for Specific Purposes, 26*(3), 263–286.

Biber, D., Conrad, S., & Cortes, V. (2004). If you look at. . . : Lexical Bundles in University teaching and textbooks. *Applied Linguistics, 25*(3), 371–405. doi:10.1093/applin/25.3.371.

Biber, D., & Gray, B. (2013). Discourse characteristics of writing and speaking task types on the TOEFL iBT test: A lexico-grammatical analysis. *TOEFL iBT Research Report, 19*.

Borg, E. (2009). Local plagiarisms. *Assessment and Evaluation in Higher Education, 34*(4), 415–426.

Burkett, T. (2015). An investigation into the use of frequency vocabulary lists in university intensive English programs. *International Journal of Bilingual and Multilingual Teachers of English, 3*(2), 71–83.

Byrd, P., & Coxhead, A. (2010). On the other hand: Lexical bundles in academic writing and in the teaching of EAP. *University of Sydney Papers in TESOL, 5*, 31–64.

Chen, Y.-H., & Baker, P. (2010). Lexical bundles in L1 and L2 academic writing. *Language Learning and Technology, 14*(2), 30–49.

Chen, Y.-H., & Baker, P. (2016). Investigating criterial discourse features across second language development: Lexical bundles in rated learner essays, CEFR B1, B2 and C1. *Applied Linguistics, 37*(6), 849–880.

Chon, Y. V., & Shin, D. (2013). A corpus-driven analysis of spoken and written academic collocations. *Multimedia-Assisted Language Learning, 16*(3), 11–38.

Cortes, V. (2004). Lexical bundles in published and student disciplinary writing: Examples from history and biology. *English for Specific Purposes, 23*, 397–423.

Cortes, V. (2006). Teaching lexical bundles in the disciplines: An example from a writing intensive history class. *Linguistics and Education, 17*, 391–406.

Cortes, V. (2013). *The purpose of this study is to:* Connecting lexical bundles and moves in research article introductions. *Journal of English for Academic Purposes, 12*(1), 33–43.

Coxhead, A. (2000). A new academic wordlist. *TESOL Quarterly, 34*(2), 213–238.

Davis, M., & Morley, J. (2015). Phrasal intertextuality: The reponses of academics from different disciplines to students' re-use of phrases. *Journal of Second Language Writing, 28*, 20–35.

DeCarrico, J. S., & Nattinger, J. R. (1988). Lexical phrases for the comprehension of academic lectures. *English for Specific Purposes, 7*(2), 91–102.

Durrant, P. (2009). Investigating the viability of a collocation list for students of English for academic purposes. *Journal of English for Specific Purposes, 28*(3), 157–179.

Durrant, P. (2016). To what extent is the academic vocabulary List relevant to university student writing? *English for Specific Purposes, 43*(1), 49–61.

Durrant, P. (2017). Lexical bundles and disciplinary variation in university students' writing: Mapping the territories. *Applied Linguistics, 38*(2), 165–193.

Durrant, P., & Mathews-Aydınlı, J. (2011). A function-first approach to identifying formulaic language in academic writing. *Journal of English for Specific Purposes, 30*(1), 58–72.

Ellis, N. C. (2008). Usage-based and form-focused language acquisition. In P. Robinson & N. C. Ellis (Eds.), *Handbook of cognitive linguistics and second language acquisition* (pp. 372–405). London: Routledge.

Eriksson, A. (2012). Pedagogical perspectives on bundles: Teaching bundles to doctoral students in biochemistry. In J. Thomas & A. Boulton (Eds.), *Input, process and product: Developments in teaching and language corpora* (pp. 195–211). Brno: Masaryk University Press.

Flowerdew, J., & Li, Y. (2007). Language re-use among Chinese apprentice scientists writing for publication. *Applied Linguistics, 28*(3), 440–465.

Gardner, D., & Davies, M. (2014). A new academic vocabulary list. *Applied Linguistics, 35*(3), 305–327.

Goldberg, A. E. (2006). *Constructions at work: The nature of generalization in language.* Oxford: Oxford University Press.

Granger, S., & Bestgen, Y. (2014). The use of collocations by intermediate vs. advanced non-native writers: A bigram-based study. *International Review of Applied Linguistics, 52*(3), 229–252.

Groom, N. (2005). Pattern and meaning across genres and disciplines: An exploratory study. *English for Academic Purposes, 4*(3), 257–277.

Haswell, R. (1991). *Gaining ground in college writing: Tales of development and interpretation.* Dallas: Southern Methodist University Press.

Hoey, M. (2005). *Lexical priming: A new theory of words and language.* London: Routledge.

Hsu, W. (2014). The most frequent opaque formulaic sequences in English-medium college textbooks. *System, 47*, 146–161.

Hunston, S., & Francis, G. (2000). *Pattern grammar: A corpus-driven approach to the lexical grammar of English.* Amsterdam: John Benjamins.

Hutchinson, T., & Waters, A. (1987). *English for specific purposes.* Cambridge: Cambridge University Press.

Hyland, K. (2006). *English for academic purposes: An advanced resource book.* London: Routledge.

Hyland, K. (2008a). Academic clusters: Text patterning in published and postgraduate writing. *International Journal of Applied Linguistics, 18*(1), 41–62.

Hyland, K. (2008b). As can be seen: Lexical bundles and disciplinary variation. *English for Specific Purposes, 27*(1), 4–21.

Hyland, K. (2012). Bundles in academic discourse. *Annual Review of Applied Linguistics, 32*, 150–169.

Jones, M., & Haywood, S. (2004). Facilitating the acquisition of formulaic sequences. In N. Schmitt (Ed.), *Formulaic sequences: Acquisition, processing and use* (pp. 269–300). Amsterdam: John Benjamins.

Lewis, M. (Ed.) (2000). *Teaching collocations: Further developments in the lexical approach.* Boston: Thomson.

Li, J., & Schmitt, N. (2009). The acquisition of lexical phrases in academic writing: A longitudinal case study. *Journal of Second Language Writing, 18*, 85–102.

Lieven, E., V. M., & Tomasello, M. (2008). Children's first language acquisition from a usage-based perspective. In P. Robinson & N. C. Ellis (Eds.), *Handbook of cognitive linguistics and second language acquisition* (pp. 168–196). London: Routledge.

Liu, D. (2012). The most frequently-used multi-word constructions in academic written English: A multi-corpus study. *English for Specific Purposes, 31*(1), 25–35.

McKenny, J. A. (2006). A corpus-based investigation of the phraseology in various genres of written English with applications to the teaching of English for academic purposes (PhD thesis). University of Leeds.

McKenny, J. A., & Bennett, K. (2011). Polishing papers for publication: Palimpsests or procrustean beds? In A. Frankenberg-Garcia, L. Flowerdew, & G. Aston (Eds.), *New trends in corpora and language learning* (pp. 247–262). London: Continuum.

Nattinger, J. R., & DeCarrico, J. S. (1992). *Lexical phrases and language teaching.* Oxford: Oxford University Press.

O'Donnell, M. B., Roemer, U., & Ellis, N. C. (2013). The development of formulaic sequences in first and second language writing: Investigating effects of frequency, association, and native norm. *International Journal of Corpus Linguistics, 18*(1), 83–108.

Orwell, G. (1946). Politics and the English language. *Horizon, 13*(76), 252–265.

Paquot, M. (2017). The phraseological dimension in interlanguage complexity research. *Second Language Research*, 1–25.

Pavlenko, A. (2014). *The bilingual mind and what it tells us about language and thought*. Cambridge: Cambridge University Press.

Pawley, A., & Syder, F. H. (1983). Two puzzles for linguistic theory: Nativelike selection and nativelike fluency. In J. C. Richards & R. W. Schmidt (Eds.), *Language and communication* (pp. 191–226). New York, NY: Longman.

Pecorari, D., & Shaw, P. (2012). Types of student intertextuality and faculty attitudes. *Journal of Second Language Writing, 21*, 149–164.

Pérez-Llantada. (2014). Formulaic language in L1 and L2 expert academic writing: Convergent and divergent use. *Journal of English for Academic Purposes, 14*, 84–94.

Simpson-Vlach, R., & Ellis, N. C. (2010). An academic formulas list: New methods in phraseology research. *Applied Linguistics, 31*(4), 487–512. doi:10.1093/applin/amp058.

Sinclair, J. M. (1991). *Corpus, concordance, collocation*. Oxford: Oxford University Press.

Staples, S., Egbert, J., Biber, D., & McClair, A. (2013). Formulaic sequences and EAP writing development: Lexical bundles in the TOEFL iBT writing section. *Journal of English for Academic Purposes, 12*, 214–225.

Tomasello, M. (2003). *Constructing a language: A usage-based theory of language acquisition*. Cambridge, MA: Harvard University Press.

Vidakovic, I., & Barker, F. (2010). Use of words and multi-word units in skills for life writing examinations. *University of Cambridge ESOL Examinations Research Notes, 7–14*(41).

Vincent, B. (2013). Investigating academic phraseology through combinations of very frequent words: A methodological exploration. *Journal of English for Academic Purposes, 12*(1), 44–57.

Wray, A. (2002). *Formulaic language and the lexicon*. Cambridge: Cambridge University Press.

Wray, A. (2008). *Formulaic language: Pushing the boundaries*. Oxford: Oxford University Press.

12

FORMULAIC SEQUENCES[1] IN LEARNER CORPORA

Collocations and Lexical Bundles

Sylviane Granger

Introduction

The significant role played by corpus linguistics in establishing pre-patterned word combinations as a key dimension of language is widely acknowledged. The combined use of large electronic corpora and powerful automated methods and tools has considerably extended the scope of the traditional field of phraseology and highlighted multifarious manifestations of Sinclair's (1991) "idiom principle" in a wide range of native varieties of language. In view of these developments, it seemed reasonable to expect similar benefits from the analysis of corpora sampling non-native (L2) varieties, commonly referred to as "learner corpora". As will be apparent from this overview, the benefits have been quite remarkable, the most significant of them being a gradual move away from the single-word focus that until recently characterized the majority of L2 lexical studies towards an increasing recognition of the critical part played by multiword lexis.

The contribution of learner corpora to the study of L2 formulaic language (FL) is a reflection of two general characteristics of learner corpora. First, learner corpora tend to be quite large, in terms of numbers of both words and learners, and are therefore less prone to the representativeness problem that besets many second language acquisition (SLA) studies. This is especially important in the case of lexical studies, and even more so studies of multiword lexis, as they require a large volume of data, unlike grammatical studies, for which a smaller data set often suffices. Second, learner corpora impose as few constraints as possible on L2 learners' language choices, which makes them an excellent resource for investigating FL. They form a useful complement to more experimental data types, which can give a distorted view of reality, as "[w]hat we think we would say in a given situation is not necessarily the same as what we would actually say"

(Gass & Selinker, 2008, p. 68). However, two main factors limit the contribution of learner corpus data. First, learner corpora can only be used to investigate the production of formulaic lexis; they cannot give any information on perception. Second, they constitute performance data and as such provide only an imperfect mirror of learners' competence. They should therefore be seen as a complement to experimental studies, not a substitute for them (Gilquin & Gries, 2009).

There are many types of formulaic sequences (FSs), and only some lend themselves well to the automated methods afforded by learner corpora (LC). The two types of unit that have been studied most in LC-based studies are collocations, i.e., arbitrarily restricted pairs of lexical words (e.g., *heavy smoker*), and lexical bundles, i.e., highly recurrent sequences of contiguous *n* words (e.g., *on the other hand*). Owing to space limitations, this survey will deal exclusively with these two categories. Idioms – semantically non-compositional, often figurative, units (e.g., *beat about the bush*) – have been much less studied in learner corpus research, not only because they are more difficult to extract automatically, but also because they have been shown to be relatively infrequent and hence arguably a less useful subject for investigation in a production perspective.

A close analysis of approximately 50 recent LC-based studies allowed me to identify some general trends that apply equally to studies of collocations and of lexical bundles. These trends concern the static versus developmental perspective adopted in the studies, the targeted language and medium, and the proficiency level of the learners.

In most studies the perspective is static, i.e., the use of FL by one or more learner populations is investigated at a particular point in time. Typical examples are Nesselhauf's (2005) study of the use of collocations by learners of English with a German mother tongue (L1) background and Chen and Baker's (2016) study of lexical bundles by L1 Chinese learners of English. In the majority of cases the learner data is compared to a native speaker (NS) reference corpus of novice or expert writing.

Although static studies are still dominant today, recent years have witnessed a surge of interest in the development of L2 formulaic use. The ideal resource for this kind of study is a longitudinal learner corpus which samples the same learners over a given period of time. Given the scarcity of this type of corpus, longitudinal studies of L2 FL are still quite rare, and an increasing number of researchers approach L2 development via a pseudo-longitudinal design, i.e., they make use of learner data that samples learners at different proficiency levels (Gass, 2013, p. 36).

In the overwhelming majority of studies, the targeted language is English. However, the dominance of English is gradually being eroded by the emergence of studies of L2 FL in a range of other L2s – French (Forsberg, 2010), German (Krummes & Ensslin, 2015), Italian (Siyanova-Chanturia, 2015), Japanese (Suzuki & Umino, 2012), and Spanish (Vincze, García-Salido, Orol & Alonso-Ramos, 2016), to cite but a few. Within L2 English studies, learners of English as a foreign language (EFL) dramatically outnumber learners of English as a second language (ESL). This is partly due to the availability of the International Corpus of Learner English (ICLE; Granger, Dagneaux, Meunier & Paquot, 2009), a large collection of argumentative essays that samples EFL learners from 16 different mother tongue backgrounds, which has been used in many studies. One of the key desiderata for future research is to produce more studies (such as Yoon, 2016) focused on ESL learners in order to assess the impact of native language exposure on the acquisition of FL.

Another common feature relates to the medium. Most LC-based studies target the use of FL in writing rather than speech. The relatively small number of spoken learner corpora makes studies such as Crossley and Salsbury (2011) the exception rather than the rule. Comparisons of spoken and written data (De Cock, 2000) are particularly valuable as they highlight differences in the quantity and quality of FL in the two mediums. In each medium the corpus data tend to represent the same text types – argumentative essays in the case of writing and informal interviews in the case of speech. This can be seen as an advantage as it facilitates cross-study comparisons, but greater diversification is desirable for a better understanding of the impact of text type on the use of FL.

One final characteristic that LC-based studies of collocations and lexical bundles have in common is that they centre on the upper end of the proficiency continuum, i.e., the intermediate (often higher intermediate) and advanced levels. Apart from some rare exceptions (e.g., Siyanova-Chanturia, 2015), the early stages of acquisition are not covered. This limitation stems partly from the fact that formulaic competence is viewed as a hallmark of nativelike fluency.

It is important to bear these general trends in mind as they help put in perspective the results achieved to date by learner corpus studies. The main findings on collocations and lexical bundles are presented in the following sections. In each of the sections, the following five issues are addressed: definition and operationalization, frequency, accuracy and appropriacy, L1 transfer, and development. Concluding remarks and avenues for future research are offered in the last section.

Collocations

Definition and Operationalization

Studies of collocations are generally difficult to compare as they involve different definitions and operationalizations, and LC-based studies are no exception. Two main definitions are used, in keeping with the two main trends in phraseology studies: the traditional approach, which relies on linguistic criteria to define FSs, and the frequency-based approach, which relies on quantitative criteria (Granger & Paquot, 2008; Nesselhauf, 2005).

In the traditional sense, collocations are pairs of words that are in a syntactic relation, and display restricted commutability and some degree of semantic opacity or specialization. The last two criteria are particularly fuzzy and difficult to apply and give rise to different configurations and interpretations. Nesselhauf (2005), for example, uses only the first two criteria on the grounds that commutability and semantic opacity "although correlating to some degree, do not regularly coincide" (p. 25). In the frequency-based sense, collocations are pairs of words that co-occur in close proximity to each other with a frequency greater than chance. To measure the strength of the association, researchers use statistical tests, the most common being Mutual Information (MI), sometimes combined with other tests such as T-score (Biber, Conrad, & Reppen, 1998). Opting for the linguistic or the quantitative definition is far from being a trivial matter, as the resulting data sets of collocations only partly overlap. Statistical collocations may contain combinations of words that would be excluded by proponents of the phraseological approach. This is true, for example, of *prime minister*, which is included in Durrant and Schmitt's (2009) study but would be excluded from studies focused on collocations in the traditional sense on the grounds that it does not qualify as a collocation but as a compound. For the sake of clarity, I will henceforth refer to the traditionally defined units as "restricted collocations" (Cowie, 1998, p. 6) and the frequency-based ones as "statistical collocations".

It would be wrong to assume, however, that the frequency-based approach entirely avoids the fuzziness of the phraseological approach. In the case of statistical collocations, decisions have to be made concerning the size of the span to the left and/or right of the node word, the inclusion of a dispersion criterion and, most importantly, the frequency and statistical thresholds used to establish collocation status. Depending on the options chosen, the sets of collocations can differ quite dramatically.

In fact, both approaches have their strengths and weaknesses. The main advantage of the frequency-based approach in an L2 perspective is that it casts its net wide and does not make prima facie judgements as to which categories are worthy of investigation. In addition, statistical collocations can be presented on a continuum of collocational strength, while the phraseological approach forces researchers to make binary choices between restricted collocations and non-collocations, thereby failing to reflect the gradual nature of collocation. The downside of the frequency-based approach, however, is that it lumps together units that are linguistically quite different and may pose different challenges for learning and teaching. There are therefore strong arguments for combining the two approaches.

Frequency

To ensure valid interpretation of the results, a distinction needs to be made between the number of collocation tokens and the number of collocation types, respectively referred to by Tsai (2015) as "collocation density" and "collocation diversity" (p. 728). Studies focused on collocation density show major discrepancies. For example, Wang (2016) reports clear signs of overuse, while Laufer and Waldman (2011) establish that "learners at all three proficiency levels produced far fewer collocations than native speakers" (p. 647). Still others observe no difference in the total number of collocations between the non-native (NNS) and NS groups (Vincze et al., 2016). In addition to differences in the criteria used to identify collocations and learner populations, as well as in the control corpus used, these discrepancies are most probably related to differences in the scope of the analysis: all collocations (Vincze et al., 2016), only one specific structural category (verb + noun collocations in Laufer & Waldman) or subcategory (six high-frequency delexical verbs in Wang, 2016). In this connection, it is interesting to note that Vincze et al., using the same definitional criteria and learner population, observe overuse of verb + noun (v-n) collocations but underuse of adjective + noun collocations, which suggests that not all syntactic categories fare equally.

When it comes to collocation diversity, however, a broad consensus is reached. Whether based on restricted or statistical collocations, the majority of studies point to a lack of diversity in L2 collocation use. In his study of statistical verb–noun collocations by Taiwanese learners of English, Tsai (2015) found that, compared with the NS reference corpus, learner writing exhibited very high collocational density but limited collocational diversity, resulting in a considerable difference in type/token ratio between the two groups (NNS: 13.63% vs. NS: 56.23%). Tsai's explanation is that learners "tend to 'cling to' a limited range of low stakes collocations with which they are familiar" (pp. 735–6). Wang (2016, p. 123) also noted a lack of diversity in the learner populations he investigated. He looked up the frequency of learners' delexical v-n collocations in the British National Corpus (BNC) and established that the collocations used by learners tended to be fairly frequent combinations, such as *make + decision*, or rather fixed combinations, such as *give + rise to*, *take + part in*, or *make + use of*. The tendency to over-rely on high-frequency collocations was also established by Durrant and Schmitt (2009) on the basis of statistical collocations (see following section).

Accuracy and Appropriacy

One convergent result emerges from LC-based studies of collocation misuse: the proportion of deviant collocations is rather high. In Nesselhauf's (2005, p. 222) study, some 50% were found to lead to deviation. Laufer and Waldman (2011) report a somewhat lower but still quite significant proportion: "About a third of all collocations produced by learners are erroneous regardless of their level" (p. 662). The difference may be due to the fact that Nesselhauf (2005) included both lexical errors (i.e., the accuracy of the verb and the noun in the case of v-n collocations) and grammatical errors, such as erroneous article or preposition use, while Laufer and Waldman (2011) appear to have focused exclusively on lexical errors.

One factor that seems to have an impact on error rates is the distance between the learners' mother tongue and the L2. Wang and Shaw (2008) show that L1 Swedish learners, whose mother tongue is close to English, tend to take more risks and therefore produce more errors. Chinese learners, on the other hand, assume a larger L1-L2 distance and therefore tend to be more conservative and to produce fewer errors. As shown by Wang (2016), typological differences also play a role: the fact that there are no articles in Chinese induces many more grammatical errors involving articles (e.g., *take stand, have a close contact with*) among Chinese learners than among Swedish learners, who mainly produce lexical errors (e.g., *make an opinion, take damage*).

All these studies, while undeniably instructive, suffer from one major weakness, namely the fuzziness of the criteria used to establish the error status of a collocation. The procedure usually includes dictionary lookup and, in some cases, corpus or web searches, followed by consultation with NS informants in case of doubt. Aware that collocation is a graded phenomenon, Nesselhauf (2005) uses a scale of acceptability consisting of five degrees, but recognizes that, in view of the small number of NS judges, the acceptability judgements "remain an approximation" (p. 54). The frequency-based approach offers a much more objective basis for assessing the adequacy of collocations. On the basis of a large reference corpus such as the BNC (www.natcorp.ox.ac.uk/corpus/), it is possible to assign to each collocation in a learner corpus one or more statistical association scores, thereby providing a fine-grained picture of their degree of naturalness or typicality. As convincingly shown by Durrant and Schmitt (2009), by using these scores it is possible to classify word combinations "across a scale of collocational strength" (p. 168), rather than dividing them into correct versus incorrect collocations. This method is particularly effective in tracing the development of L2 collocation use (see section on development of collocations).

One important limitation of LC-based studies of collocation errors is that learners generally tend to play it safe, using collocations of which they are sure. As a result, absence of error is not necessarily a reflection of learners' competence. This is convincingly demonstrated by Gilquin's (2007) study of v-n delexical combinations with the verb *make* based on the L1 French subcorpus of the ICLE. While the learner corpus study revealed a mere 7% of erroneous uses, two elicitation tests submitted to similar-type learners brought out much higher error rates of 51% (fill-in exercise) and 43% (judgement test). This highlights the benefit to be gained from combining corpus and experimental data.

L1 Transfer

As rightly pointed out by Ellis (2006), the L2 mind is not a *tabula rasa*; learners perceive the L2 "through the L1-tuned *tabula repleta*" (p. 186). This means that L2 learners already have a store of FSs deeply entrenched in their L1 mental lexicons, which can be expected to have a significant impact on their L2 productions. LC-based collocation studies show that this is indeed the case.

One factor that plays a key role in the amount of transfer – whether positive or negative – is the existence or not of a congruent collocation, i.e., a word-for-word equivalent combination, in the learners' L1. In an interesting collostructional analysis[2] of *make*-collocations by French-speaking learners of English and native English speakers, Gilquin (2007) established that all the learner-specific combinations were congruent (e.g., *make an effort* = *faire un effort*), while only one of the collocates that was distinctive for NS had a direct equivalent in French.

Studies report consistently high rates of L1 influence on collocation errors: 48% in Nesselhauf (2005, p. 181) and as much as 67% in Wanner et al.'s (2013, p. 498) study of miscollocations in L2 Spanish. Although incongruent collocations result in a much higher error rate than congruent ones, it would be wrong to assume that congruent collocations are unproblematic. There is compelling evidence of learners shying away from congruent equivalents. To illustrate this phenomenon, which they refer to as "L1 avoidance", Alonso Ramos et al. (2010, p. 3211) give the example of English learners of Spanish producing the verb *cambiar* (lit. "to change") in *cambiar al cristianismo* instead of *convertirse* in spite of the existence of the congruent verb *to convert* in English. Wang (2016, p. 68) notes a similar trend in Chinese learners of English.

One important caveat needs to be added. In all the aforementioned studies, the only criterion used to establish transfer is the presence of a congruent unit in the learner's L1. This is undoubtedly a necessary criterion to establish transfer but certainly not a sufficient one. To achieve a more rigorous interpretation along the lines advocated by Jarvis (2000), it is necessary to compare learner corpora representing different mother tongue backgrounds. This makes it possible to establish whether the collocations used are specific to one particular L1 background, which would confirm a transfer interpretation, or shared by several L1 populations, which might point to a developmental feature of interlanguage (for further discussion of this issue, see section on L1 transfer of lexical bundles).

Development

As most studies of L2 collocation use are non-developmental, there are as yet few findings in this area, but some interesting trends emerge, among which are the following two.

First, collocation use is a feature of interlanguage that tends to develop late. Using a pseudo-longitudinal approach, Laufer and Waldman (2011) found that the number of restricted collocations only increased at the advanced level: "there was a statistically significant relationship between the number of verb–noun collocations and learner proficiency only in the comparison of the advanced learners with basic learners" (p. 661). However, studies based on statistical collocations provide a more fine-grained picture of learners' development. This research strand originated in a study by Durrant and Schmitt (2009), which compared modifier (adjective or noun) + noun combinations in learner and native writing, and found that learners tend to overuse high-frequency collocations such as *hard work*, characterized by high T-score, and underuse lower frequency, but strongly associated, combinations such as *immortal souls*, characterized by high MI. Granger and Bestgen (2014) used Durrant and Schmitt's approach to compare intermediate and advanced learners and obtained similar results, i.e., intermediate learners used a larger proportion of high-frequency collocations and a smaller proportion of lower frequency, but strongly associated, collocations. In the same vein, Paquot (2017) found that the mean MI scores increased systematically from CEFR[3] B2 (higher intermediate) to C1 (advanced) and C2 (very advanced), while none of the traditional single-word-based measures yielded any significant result. A particularly important result of the study is that there are differences depending on the structural composition of the collocation. For example, adj-n collocations proved to be the least powerful in distinguishing between different proficiency levels, while v-object dependencies were the best discriminators of the most advanced level (C2).

A second finding is that the acquisition or learning of collocations takes time. Significant improvement is therefore unlikely to take place in longitudinal studies that cover a short period of time. This is demonstrated by Yoon's (2016) longitudinal study of v-n statistical collocations in argumentative and narrative essays written by ESL learners over one semester. The results showed no significant development of MI scores in either genre over time. Interestingly, in a study covering the same time span, Bestgen and Granger (2014) obtained similar results for MI scores but observed a significant decrease in the number of collocations identified by T-score, a finding which can be related to the frequency of the units in learners' input and, more generally, to Ellis's (2002) formula-based approach to language acquisition. Li and Schmitt's study (2010), although covering a one-year period, failed likewise to observe any significant development. A divergent result is found in Siyanova-Chanturia (2015), one of the rare studies to focus on beginner language, which showed a significant increase in statistical adj + noun collocations produced by Chinese learners of Italian over the course of a five-month intensive Italian course. This type of discrepancy is only to be expected, as many variables can have an impact on the rate of acquisition, including the time span, the proficiency level and the quantity and quality of the input. There is a clear need for further tightly controlled studies involving larger data sets.

Lexical Bundles

Definition and Operationalization

While in the case of collocations learner corpora have added new perspectives to an existing L2 research strand, with the study of lexical bundles they have brought a completely new dimension to the field of L2 phraseology studies. Lexical bundles (Biber, Johansson, Leech, Conrad & Finegan, 1999) refer to fully corpus-driven sequences of *n* contiguous words such as *you know what I mean* or *as a result of*, which recur frequently in speech or writing. The definition underlines one major feature that clearly distinguishes collocations from lexical bundles: the contiguity of the word combination, which is a possibility in collocations but a defining feature of lexical bundles. In addition, unlike collocations, lexical bundles are extracted "disregarding any pre-defined linguistic categories" (Ädel & Erman, 2012, p. 82) and therefore often fail to display syntactic integrity (e.g. *one of the*). They are the building blocks that characterize fluent spoken and written discourse and are therefore an essential addition to the types of FSs commonly studied in L2 studies.

The three main criteria that underlie the operationalization of lexical bundles are bundle size, frequency threshold and dispersion. While many L2 researchers opt for the standard bundle size of three (Paquot, 2013) or four words (Chen & Baker, 2016), some focus on bigrams[4] (two-word sequences) (Crossley & Salsbury, 2011). Still others adopt a range of sizes, such as two to six words (De Cock, 2000, 2004), three to four words (Krummes & Ensslin, 2015) or three to five words (O'Donnell, Römer & Ellis, 2013). The frequency thresholds vary in accordance with the size of the corpus. They usually rely on a minimum number of occurrences of the bundle in the corpus or a minimum number of occurrences per million words. The third criterion – the degree of dispersion of the bundle – is intended to ensure that the findings are representative of the corpus as a whole. This criterion, which unlike the other two is absent from some LC-based studies, is usually established on the basis of a minimum number of texts in which the bundles occur or a minimum number of learners using them. Needless to say, all these differences affect the comparability of the studies, but fortunately, as will be shown in the following sections, they do not prevent some general tendencies from emerging.

Frequency

The majority of the studies compare the frequency of the bundles in a learner corpus and a comparable native corpus of novice or expert writing. Analyses in terms of overall frequencies are difficult to generalize beyond the confines of each study, owing partly to the adoption of different criteria in terms of size, frequency, and dispersion, but perhaps more importantly to the varying degrees of processing performed after the bundles have been extracted. Three factors in particular have a major impact on the overall number of bundles. The first concerns overlapping bundles such as *due to the fact* and *to the fact that*. While some researchers count them as two separate bundles, others, like Ädel and Erman (2012, p. 84), merge them into one bundle, *due to the fact + that*. The second issue relates to the bundles that have been copied from the prompt or are clearly topic- or task-dependent. While in many L2 studies these bundles are kept, some researchers exclude them. As shown by Staples, Egber, Biber, and McClair (2013), this feature has a major impact on the results. The third issue has to do with the decision to include or exclude learner-specific bundles. Results will naturally be quite different if only targetlike bundles are included in the analysis or if all the bundles used by the learners are investigated, whether targetlike or not.

This said, the general trend that emerges is one of learner overuse in bundle tokens coupled with underuse in bundle types, a trend that has also been established for collocations. L2 learners make use of a large number of recurrent sequences, but they have their "phraseological teddy bears" (Hasselgård, in press), i.e., overused phrases that learners use in contexts where NS would opt for other phrases or abstain from using a phrase altogether. This trend emerges clearly from a comparison of the most frequent bundles in learner and native data. In Hasselgård's study, for example, the top bundle in learner writing (*on the other hand*) has a frequency of 38.1 per 100,000 words, while the top native bundle (*it is important to*) only has a frequency of 19.1.

Although this general trend is instructive, it is arguably more interesting to find out which types of bundle tend to be over- or underused. De Cock (2000), for example, notes a highly marked underuse of "vagueness tags" (e.g., *or something, and things like that*) in the speech of French-speaking learners of English (p. 61). Ädel and Erman (2012), on the other hand, note an underuse of typical features of academic writing in Swedish learner writing, such as unattended "this" bundles (e.g., *this may be because, this shows that the*). In parallel with this, learner productions are also characterized by register mismatch, i.e., overuse of bundles typical of writing in speech, and vice versa (see following section).

Most studies compare the frequency of (categories of) bundles in learner and native corpora without considering the degrees of association strength holding between the words in the bundles. Here, too, as in the case of collocations, the use of association-defined bundles, i.e., bundles measured according to their statistical association score, constitutes a promising new direction. O'Donnell et al. (2013) show that three- to five-word sequences that have a significant MI score, which they call "MI-grams" (p. 95), are used significantly less by L2 learners than by expert native writers. Interestingly, they observe the same underuse in novice native writers. This may be due to the fact that the reference corpus they used to compute the association scores was an academic corpus (BNC Baby Academic corpus, www.natcorp.ox.ac.uk/corpus/babyinfo.html), and the acquisition of academic phraseology constitutes a challenge for all novice writers, including native ones. Using a general English corpus, such as the whole BNC, might well have generated different results.

Accuracy and Appropriacy

The learner corpus literature contains numerous examples of what De Cock (2000) calls "learner idiosyncratic combinations", i.e., "sequences that are used by learners only" (p. 58). These learner-specific uses are not taken into consideration in studies that explore L2 FL through the lens of native language, such as the study by Leńko-Szymańska (2014), which restricts the analysis to bundles extracted from a large native corpus.

Some of the misused lexical bundles are simply not found in native language. Granger (2015, p. 493), for instance, gives the example of *on the other side* used as a connector in lieu of *on the other hand*, which is well attested in the ICLE. Another example is *according to me* used instead of *in my view* or *in my opinion*, a bundle favoured by French-speaking learners. More frequently, the learner corpora contain sequences that qualify as bundles in the learner corpus, but not in the control native corpus, either because they are absent from that corpus or because they do not have enough occurrences in that corpus to reach the required frequency threshold. As will be shown in the following section, L1 transfer accounts for a large number of these cases, but other factors, in particular stylistic and semantic or pragmatic ones, are also in play.

One of the most frequent causes of inappropriacy is register mismatch. Learners often use spoken-like bundles in academic writing. In a study of metadiscursive bundles in six subcorpora of the ICLE and corpora of novice and expert writing, Granger (2017) found an overuse of verb-based bundles (e.g., *I would like to, we can say that*), which are typical of speech, coupled with an underuse of noun-based bundles (e.g., *in the case of, on the issue of*), which are frequent in academic writing (Biber et al., 1999, p. 991). The bundles used by learners also display a higher degree of involvement, manifested by the use of first-person pronouns, while writers, both novice and expert, favour impersonal structures (*it is clear that, it has been suggested*). Although this is less well documented, there is also evidence in learner speech of bundles that are more typical of writing, such as *for example* (De Cock, 2000, pp. 61–62). These mismatches explain why the difference between speech and writing is less marked in learner corpora than in NS corpora (De Cock, 2000, p. 58).

Misuse may also be semantic or pragmatic. For example, Chen and Baker (2016) point to learners' semantic misuse of *on the other hand* "as a multi-functional discourse marker to link whatever ideas they have, no matter whether these ideas contrast or not" (p. 13). In speech, De Cock (2004) notes the pragmatically inappropriate use of *(yes/yeah) of course*, which "may well make learners sound overemphatic and even impolite" (p. 242).

L1 Transfer

The overwhelming majority of LC-based studies highlight a significant influence of the learner's mother tongue on the use of lexical bundles. De Cock (2000, p. 65) identifies four manifestations of L1 transfer: misuse of a target language sequence, overuse, underuse, and use of learner idiosyncratic combinations. An example is the connector *on the contrary*, which is both overused and misused by French learners under the influence of the French congruent connector *au contraire*.

It is important to note, however, that L1 transfer is rarely the main focus of the studies. Most of the time, it is simply mentioned as a likely factor accounting for the presence and/or frequency of one or other bundle. In addition, in the majority of cases the presence of L1 influence is exclusively based on the existence of a similar bundle in the learner's L1, a criterion which may lead to an over-estimation of L1 transfer. Hasselgård (in press) uses a more fine-grained approach. She has recourse to a Norwegian-English translation corpus to identify the frequency of the presumed cross-linguistic equivalents of bundles overused by Norwegian learners of English. On this basis, she is able to establish that in the case of a bundle like *on the other hand* transfer is unlikely, as the Norwegian equivalent is much less frequent, while in the case of *when it comes to* it is very likely, as the Norwegian equivalent has approximately the same frequency and function of use. Paquot (2013) adopts an even more rigorous method. Like Hasselgård, she looks up frequencies in a corpus representing the learners' L1 (in her case, a corpus of French), but in addition she compares the verb-based bundles used by L1 French writers with those found in learner corpora from a range of L1s. Using a fully corpus-driven method, based on Jarvis's (2000) framework and appropriate statistical tests, she is able to identify the bundles that clearly set French learners apart from the other learner groups and concludes that "over a half of French learners' idiosyncratic use of lexical bundles with verbs can be attributed to L1 influence" (p. 401). These two studies show that the existence of a congruent form in the learners' L1 is not enough: L1 frequency also has a major impact on transferability.

Development

The study of the development of lexical bundle use by learners has mostly relied on a pseudo-longitudinal approach, i.e., a comparison of the quantity and quality of the bundles at well-defined proficiency levels. A representative study is that of Staples et al. (2013), who investigated the use of lexical bundles across three proficiency levels (low, intermediate, and high) in the TOEFL iBT (www.ets.org/toefl/ibt/about). The results show that the number of lexical bundle tokens tends to decrease with proficiency: "The participants with the highest proficiency level ... used significantly fewer bundle tokens than both the lowest scoring group and intermediate level group" (p. 219).

The quality of the bundles also varies across levels. On the basis of Biber et al.'s (1999, 2004) structural categorization, Chen and Baker (2016, p. 14) establish that the lowest-level learners have the highest proportion of verb-based bundles (*there are a lot of, I think it is*) and the lowest proportions of NP- and PP-based bundles (*a great deal of, in the case of*). The opposite tendency is found at the highest level. As verb-based bundles are especially frequent in speech, and noun-based bundles are typical of academic texts, this finding provides evidence of a "transition from a more colloquial tone to a more literate style" (p. 23). As regards functions, there appears to be no difference in the overall proportion of Biber et al.'s three main categories (referential, discourse, and stance), but Chen and Baker (ibid.) identify differences in the subcategories and in the actual bundles used. For example, they observe more overt writer visibility (*I hope I can, I think this is*) at the least proficient level (B1) and more impersonal stance bundles (*it is obvious that, it is believed that*) at the advanced (C1) level.

In one of the few longitudinal studies of lexical bundles to date, Crossley and Salsbury (2011) focused on the accuracy of bigrams (i.e., two-word bundles) measured as learners' use of "native-like lexical bundles at native-like frequencies" (p. 10) and found that the accuracy of bigram use improved significantly over the course of a year. In addition, bigram accuracy growth was found to correlate with TOEFL score growth, which suggests that "L2 learners develop lexical bundle accuracy as a function of increasing English proficiency" (p. 15).

Conclusions and Future Directions

Learner corpora have a lot to offer studies of L2 formulaic expressions. This is thanks to the wide and highly diversified empirical basis they rely on and the powerful automated methods they offer. The most innovative perspectives result from the use of corpus-driven approaches which have allowed the extraction and exploration of statistical collocations and lexical bundles. Lexical bundles, in particular, open new ground and move the study of L2 phraseology into the domain of discourse and register analysis. As regards collocations, the use of quantitative methods has made it possible to go beyond traditional dichotomies, such as the sharp division between collocations and free combinations, or between correct and incorrect collocations. These dichotomies often rely on fuzzy intuition-based criteria, which are both complex to implement and difficult to replicate. This is not to belittle the value of corpus-based studies of restricted collocations, which often offer more in-depth qualitative insights into the types of restrictedness – semantic, lexical, syntactic – displayed by FSs. In fact, each type of approach has its advantages, and nothing prevents them from being combined in one and the same study (see, for example, García Salido & Garci, 2017).

The fact that both collocations and lexical bundles are defined and operationalized in many different ways makes comparisons among studies difficult. However, it is possible to identify some converging results, of which the following three seem to me particularly important. First, L2 learners use a large number of collocations and lexical bundles, and many of them are correct, but they tend to cling to a small number of high-frequency combinations with which they feel comfortable. These pet phrases are easy to identify on the basis of learner corpora and may serve as a basis for targeted pedagogical intervention aimed at enlarging learners' repertoire. Second, learners do not constitute virgin territory when it comes to FSs: L1 transfer proves to play a major role in the L2 phrasicon. As collocations and lexical bundles tend to be semantically compositional, they are not particularly salient, and learners, unaware of their formulaic status, often translate them literally into the L2. This results in positive transfer when the units happen to be the same in L1 and L2 but, as this is often not the case, negative transfer regularly occurs. Third, the quantity and quality of collocations and lexical bundles develop with proficiency. One of the most solid signs of development is the gradual increase in association strength holding between the words within the units. This finding opens up exciting avenues for language testing and automatic assessment, which have so far restricted themselves to single-word measures.

Although I have made every effort to produce a comprehensive survey, restrictions of space have led me to exclude a number of interesting studies. First, as the focus of the paper was on FL in learner corpora, I have exclusively covered studies that make explicit use of learner corpus data and corpus-analytic methods. This leaves out many interesting studies that analyze natural language use data with more traditional methods. Second, the survey focuses only on collocations and lexical bundles and therefore leaves out findings related to the use of other types of FSs, such as phrasal verbs.

As research into L2 FL on the basis of learner corpora is still rather young, the scope for future research is very wide. The following three avenues seem to me to be particularly worth pursuing.

The first has to do with the group versus individual perspective. LC-based studies of the L2 phrasicon and, in fact, learner corpus research in general have tended to use aggregate data. While admittedly a limitation, this should be seen in the light of one of the main objectives of learner corpus research, namely the wish to contribute to the design of teaching materials tailored to the needs of particular learner populations. It is important to bear in mind, however, that "there can be no logical expectation that the pattern found in generalisations at the group level is the same as the actual development of the individual learner" (Lowie & Verspoor, 2015, p. 84). As shown by Li and Schmitt's studies, nothing prevents learner corpora from being used as a basis for the study of individual trajectories, as sole research focus or as a complement to a group perspective, and it would be good to see more studies of this type in the future.

The second is a call for more mixed-methods studies. Corpus data and experimental data each have their limitations. Both have been used to study L2 FL, but rarely have the two types of data been used conjointly, and even more rarely from the same students. And yet the potential of this two-pronged approach is great. As shown by Gilquin's (2007) study, the concurrent use of learner corpus data and experimental data provides a much more precise view of learners' collocation errors. Similarly, as shown by Li and Schmitt (2009), combining learner corpus data and interview data gives valuable information on the way phrases are learned and the degree of confidence with which they are used.

The third is an appeal for more replication studies. In a field that involves so many variables, replication studies are essential. However, replication is only possible if all the criteria used to operationalize the units have been clearly described.

This is unfortunately not always the case. Even when the information is present, it tends to be scattered over the study, making it hard for researchers to identify the criteria used. While writing this survey, I had to read a good many articles several times in order to know exactly what units had been analyzed and how they had been operationalized. It would be ideal if, in the future, all studies involving collocations and lexical bundles were to provide in a separate appendix, as well as precise information on the learner and reference corpus data, a fact sheet containing some of the key variables used to define and operationalize collocations and lexical bundles. A preliminary attempt at designing this fact sheet is provided in Appendix 12.1. If researchers were to adopt this fact sheet or an improved version of it, it would help them to compare their results with those obtained in other studies as well as to replicate previous studies, two desirable objectives likely to strengthen the contribution of LC-based studies to the highly topical and exciting field of L2 FL acquisition.

Notes

1 With a view to ensuring consistency with the terminology used in the volume, the terms "formulaic language" and "formulaic sequence" are used as umbrella terms to refer to the use of multiword sequences. It is important to note that they do not necessarily imply holistic processing and storage.
2 Collostructional analysis investigates the interaction of lexemes and the grammatical constructions associated with them (Stefanowitsch & Gries, 2003).
3 Common European Franmework of Reference for Languages (Council of Europe, 2001).
4 Biber restricts the term "lexical bundle" to sequences longer than two words on the grounds that "many of them are word associations that do not have a distinct discourse-level function" (Conrad & Biber, 2004, p. 58). However, many two-word sequences do have a discourse function (e.g., *of course, for example, if so*).

References

Ädel, A., & Erman, B. (2012). Recurrent word combinations in academic writing by native and non-native speakers of English: A lexical bundles approach. *English for Specific Purposes, 31*, 81–92.

Alonso Ramos, M., Wanner, L., Vincze, O., Casamayor del Bosque, G., Vázquez Veiga, N., Mosqueira Suárez, E., & Prieto González, S. (2010). Towards a motivated annotation schema of collocation errors in learner corpora. In *Proceedings of the international conference on language resources and evaluation* (pp. 3209–3214), May 17–23, 2010, Valletta, Malta.

Bestgen, Y., & Granger, S. (2014). Quantifying the development of phraseological competence in L2 English writing: An automated approach. *Journal of Second Language Writing, 26*, 28–41.

Biber, D., Conrad, S., & Reppen, R. (1998). *Corpus linguistics: Investigating language structure and use*. Cambridge: Cambridge University Press.

Biber, D., Johansson, S., Leech, G., Conrad, S., & Finegan, E. (1999). *Longman grammar of spoken and written English*. Harlow: Pearson Education.

Biber, D., Conrad, S., & Cortes, V. (2004). If you look at...: Lexical bundles in university teaching and textbooks. *Applied Linguistics, 25*(3), 371–405.
Chen, Y. H., & Baker, P. (2016). Investigating criterial discourse features across second language development: Lexical bundles in rated learner essays, CEFR B1, B2 and C1. *Applied Linguistics, 37*(6), 849–880.
Council of Europe (2001). *Common European framework of reference for languages: learning, teaching, assessment.* Cambridge: Cambridge University Press.
Cowie, A. P. (1998). Introduction. In A. P. Cowie (Ed.), *Phraseology: Theory, analysis and applications* (pp. 1–20). Oxford: Oxford University Press.
Crossley, S., & Salsbury, T. L. (2011). The development of lexical bundle accuracy and production in English second language speakers. *IRAL, 49*, 1–26.
De Cock, S. (2000). Repetitive phrasal chunkiness and advanced EFL speech and writing. In C. Mair, & M. Hundt (Eds.), *Corpus linguistics and linguistic theory* (pp. 51–68). Amsterdam: Rodopi.
De Cock, S. (2004). Preferred sequences of words in NS and NNS speech. *Belgian Journal of English Language and Literature*, New series, *2*, 225–246.
Durrant, P., & Schmitt, N. (2009). To what extent do native and non-native writers make use of collocations? *IRAL, 47*, 157–177.
Ellis, N. (2002). Frequency effects in language acquisition: A review with implications for theories of implicit and explicit language acquisition. *Studies in Second Language Acquisition, 24*(2), 143–188.
Ellis, N. (2006). Selective attention and transfer phenomena in L2 acquisition: Contingency, cue competition, salience, interference, overshadowing, blocking, and perceptual learning. *Applied Linguistics, 27*(2), 164–194.
Forsberg, F. (2010). Using conventional sequences in L2 French. *IRAL, 48*, 25–51.
García Salido, M., & Garcia, M. (2017). Comparing learners' and native speakers' use of collocations in written Spanish. *IRAL*. Online view. doi:https://doi.org/10.1515/iral-2016-0103.
Gass, S. (with J. Behney, & L. Plonsky). (2013). *Second language acquisition: An introductory course* (4th Ed.). New York: Routledge.
Gass, S. M., & Selinker, L. (2008). *Second language acquisition: An introductory course* (3rd Ed.). New York and London: Routledge.
Granger, S., & Bestgen, Y. (2014). The use of collocations by intermediate vs. advanced non-native writers: A bigram-based study. *IRAL, 52*(3), 229–252.
Gilquin, G. (2007). To err is not all. What corpus and elicitation can reveal about the use of collocations by learners. *Zeitschrift für Anglistik und Amerikanistik, 55*(3), 273–291.
Gilquin, G., & Gries, S. Th. (2009). Corpora and experimental methods: A state-of-the-art review. *Corpus Linguistics and Linguistic Theory, 5*(1), 1–26.
Granger, S. (2015). The contribution of learner corpora to reference and instructional materials design. In S. Granger, G. Gilquin & F. Meunier, F. (Eds.), *The Cambridge handbook of learner corpus research* (pp. 485–510). Cambridge: Cambridge University Press.
Granger, S. (2017). Academic phraseology: A key ingredient in successful L2 academic literacy. In R. Vatvedt Fjeld, K. Hagen, B. Henriksen, S. Johansson, S. Olsen, & J. Prentice (Eds.), *Academic language in a Nordic setting: Linguistic and educational perspectives* (Vol. 9(3), pp. 9–27). Oslo, Norway: Studies in Language.
Granger, S., Dagneaux, E., Meunier, F., & Paquot, M. (2009). *The international corpus of learner English.* Handbook and CD-ROM. Version 2. Louvain-la-Neuve, Belgium: Presses Universitaires de Louvain.

Granger, S., & Paquot, M. (2008). Disentangling the phraseological web. In S. Granger & F. Meunier (Eds.), *Phraseology: An Interdisciplinary Perspective* (pp. 27–49). Amsterdam and Philadelphia: John Benjamins.

Hasselgård, H. (in press). Phraseological teddy bears: Frequent lexical bundles in academic writing by Norwegian learners and native speakers of English. In M. Mahlberg & V. Wiegand (Eds.), *Corpus linguistics, context and culture*. Berlin: De Gruyter Mouton.

Jarvis, S. (2000). Methodological rigor in the study of transfer: Identifying L1 influence in the interlanguage lexicon. *Language Learning, 50*(2), 245–309.

Krummes, C., & Ensslin, A. (2015). Formulaic language and collocations in German essays: From corpus-driven data to corpus-based materials. *The Language Learning Journal, 43*(1), 110–127.

Laufer, B., & Waldman, T. (2011). Verb-noun collocations in second language writing: A corpus analysis of learners' English. *Language Learning, 61*, 647–672.

Leńko-Szymańska, A. (2014). The acquisition of formulaic language by EFL learners: A cross-sectional and cross-linguistic perspective. *International Journal of Corpus Linguistics, 19*(2), 225–251.

Li, J., & Schmitt, N. (2009). The acquisition of lexical phrases in academic writing: A longitudinal case study. *Journal of Second Language Writing, 18*, 85–102.

Li, J., & Schmitt, N. (2010). The development of collocation use in academic texts by advanced L2 learners: A multiple case study perspective. In D. Wood (Ed.), *Perspectives on formulaic language: Acquisition and communication* (pp. 23–45). London: Continuum.

Lowie, W., & Verspoor, M. (2015). Variability and variation in second language acquisition orders: A dynamic reevaluation. *Language Learning, 65*(1), 63–88.

Nesselhauf, N. (2005). *Collocations in a Learner Corpus*. Amsterdam: John Benjamins.

O'Donnell, M. B., Römer, U., & Ellis, N. C. (2013). The development of formulaic sequences in first and second language writing. *International Journal of Corpus Linguistics, 18*(1), 83–108.

Paquot, M. (2013). Lexical bundles and L1 transfer effects. *International Journal of Corpus Linguistics, 18*(3), 391–417.

Paquot, M. (2017). The phraseological dimension in interlanguage complexity research. Special Issue on Linguistic Complexity. *Second Language Research*. Online view. doi: 10.1177/0267658317694221.

Sinclair, J. (1991). *Corpus, concordance, collocation*. Oxford: Oxford University Press.

Siyanova-Chanturia, A. (2015). Collocation in beginner learner writing: A longitudinal study. *System, 53*, 148–160.

Staples, S., Egber, J., Biber, D., & McClair, A. (2013). Formulaic sequences and EAP development: Lexical bundles in the TOEFL iBT writing section. *English for Specific Purposes, 12*, 214–225.

Stefanowitsch, A., & Gries, S. Th. (2003). Collostructions: Investigating the interaction between words and constructions. *International Journal of Corpus Linguistics, 8*(2), 209–243.

Suzuki, A., & Umino, T. (2012). Corpus-based analysis of lexical collocations by intermediate Japanese language learners – With a focus on the verb suru. In Y. Tono, Y. Kawaguchi, & M. Minegishi (Eds.), *Developmental and crosslinguistic perspectives in learner corpus research* (pp. 333–353). Amsterdam and Philadelphia: John Benjamins.

Tsai, K.-J. (2015). Profiling the collocation use in ELT textbooks and learner writing. *Language Teaching Research, 19*(6), 723–740.

Vincze, O., García-Salido, M., Orol, A., & Alsonso-Ramos, M. (2016). A corpus study of Spanish as a foreign language learners' collocation production. In M. Alonso-Ramos (Ed.) *Spanish learner corpus research: Current trends and future perspectives* (pp. 299–331). Amsterdam and Philadelphia: John Benjamins.

Wang, Y. (2016). *The idiom principle and L1 influence. A contrastive learner-corpus study of delexical verb + noun collocations.* Amsterdam and Philadelphia: John Benjamins.

Wang, Y., & Shaw, P. (2008). Transfer and universality: Collocation use in advanced Chinese and Swedish learner English. *ICAME Journal, 32*, 201–232.

Wanner, L., Alonso Ramos, M., Vincze, O., Nazar, R., Ferraro, G., Mosqueira, E., & Prieto, S. (2013). Annotation of collocations in a learner corpus for building a learning environment. In S. Granger, G. Gilquin, & F. Meunier (Eds.), *Twenty years of learner corpus research: Looking back, moving ahead* (pp. 493–503). Louvain-la-Neuve, Belgium: Presses universitaires de Louvain.

Yoon, H-J. (2016). Association strength of verb-noun combinations in experienced NS and less experienced NNS writing: Longitudinal and cross-sectional findings. *Journal of Second Language Writing, 34*, 42–57.

APPENDIX 12.1

Fact Sheet for Collocations and Lexical Bundles

Collocations

Restricted collocations	• Linguistic criteria 　○ Syntactic relation 　○ Restricted substitutability 　○ Semantic opacity or specialization 　○ Other criteria • Structural categories (v-n, adj-n, etc.)
Statistical collocations	• Quantitative criteria 　○ Span size 　○ Frequency threshold 　○ Dispersion 　○ Statistical association measure(s) 　　○ Measure(s) used (MI, T-score, etc.) 　　○ Statistical association threshold(s) 　○ Other criteria • Structural categories (v-n, adj-n, etc.)

Lexical bundles

Frequency-defined bundles	• Quantitative criteria 　○ Bundle size 　○ Frequency threshold 　○ Dispersion 　○ Other criteria • Structural categories (e.g., verb-based bundles only) • Discourse functions (e.g., hedges)

Lexical bundles	

Association-defined bundles	• Quantitative criteria
	  ○ Bundle size
	  ○ Frequency threshold
	  ○ Dispersion
	  ○ Statistical association measure(s)
	    ○ Measure(s) used (MI, T-score, etc.)
	    ○ Statistical association thresholds
	  ○ Other criteria
	• Structural categories (e.g., verb-based bundles only)
	• Discourse functions (e.g., hedges)

13

CONCLUDING QUESTION

Why don't Second Language Learners More Proactively Target Formulaic Sequences?

Alison Wray

Introduction

The chapters in this volume have each explored in detail the state-of-the-art knowledge about an aspect of formulaic language (FL) research in the second language (L2) context and drawn conclusions from it. But jointly, they offer more than a simple assembly of and reflection on existing knowledge. They create the opportunity for new enquiry. A volume of this sort constitutes a significant research resource that deserves to be harvested in a systematic way. Consequently, this concluding chapter takes an innovative approach. Rather than simply summarizing and commenting on what has already been said, the preceding chapters are drawn upon more creatively, to address a new topic that spans their combined domains of reference, and that can contextualize their findings through comparison and contrast. By means of this exercise, new insights are offered about the nature of FL and the ways we tend to think of it. It is suggested that alternative ways of conceptualizing FL learning may cast new light on perplexing aspects of its nature.

The question to be addressed here is one that, as far as I am aware, has not been directly asked before: *Why do post-childhood L2 learners appear not to proactively seek out formulaic sequences (FSs) that will map onto the ones they find so useful in their first language (L1)?* Answering this question has potential significance for our more general understanding of what formulaicity in language is and how we should interpret our research evidence thus far. As the discussion will reveal, many different aspects of data and theory, relating to FSs[1] specifically, and to language more generally, need to be taken into account. Every chapter in this book has something to offer in either shaping the question, rationalizing it, or casting light on the answer, while reference will also be made to other important research in field.

The first major task is to establish the legitimacy of this loaded question. Thus, the next two sections of this chapter ask why we should *expect* that post-childhood L2 learners would target FSs, and then why we might believe that they don't. After that, we explore a series of possible explanations for why learners might not target FSs in the L2 more. The penultimate section asks whether we need to rethink the question and unpack some underlying assumptions around formulaicity and what is learned. Finally, conclusions and thoughts about future research are offered.

In the remainder of this section, the scope and core intention behind the question are outlined. Firstly, it is clearly not true that learners don't seek out *any* FSs equivalent to those in the L1. Like any tourist, they will probably expect expressions in the L2 for greeting, thanking, leave-taking, apologizing, congratulating, and so on. The question is why that awareness doesn't seem to extend to a much broader range of expressions and collocations. Why does an L1 English speaker appear not to target finding an L2 expression for *by and large* or *what on earth . . . ?* or *get ahead of oneself* or *rancid butter?*

Secondly, it will be useful to clarify the relationship between the question posed here and a paradox identified by Kecskes (this volume). He points out that the idiom principle and the economy principle are assumed to be the default in processing; that is, language users prefer to work with multiword items over single words where available, provided they are semantically coherent. Yet in intercultural (including interlinguistic) communication, relatively few FSs are observed (Kecskes, this volume). He asks whether we should infer that the idiom and economy principles are blocked in L2 use, or whether they still apply, but differences in the context and priorities of the L2 learner mean that they are realized differently. He concludes, on the basis of his own work and that of Ortactepe, that the idiom principle is not blocked in L2, but that the demands of communication tend to be different, and this determines when it can be invoked (compare *needs only analysis*, Wray, 2002, 2008b).

For this chapter, however, we need to go beyond Kecskes' observations, to ask why the massive potential benefits of having a large repertoire of multiword units do not prevail over the locally imposed expectations or perceived imperatives that create the need to break input down, or, in Kecskes' terms, over any local demands of communication. There are many habits arising from deep-seated natural preferences that learners struggle to break despite teachers' best efforts. Why is this not one of them?

Why Might Second Language Learners be Expected to Seek Out Formulaic Sequences?

The dominant claim in the research literature is that FSs are beneficial to, and prioritized by, L1 speakers (e.g., Pawley & Syder, 1983; Sinclair, 1991; Wray, 2002). It is therefore not unreasonable to assume that these benefits would also be recognized and valued when someone is learning an L2. L1 speakers will have experienced the ubiquity and processing advantages of FSs, as well as their usefulness in shaping discourse and communicating social information (Bardovi-Harlig, this volume; Coulmas, 1991; Gleason & Weintraub, 1976; Kecskes, this volume; Wray, 2002). So long as FSs are detectable, and thus potentially learnable, existing theories would seem to predict that learners would prioritize learning them, as a fast road to both proficiency and communicative competence.

The same theories, along with the more general belief that all languages are shaped by the opportunities and limitations of the human brain, predict that learners should find a roughly equivalent quantity of FSs in an L2 as in their L1. That is, it is reasonable to assume that all languages will accumulate easy-to-process expressions (Kecskes, this volume). Having said that, until recently, this assumption has been accepted rather than demonstrated.

Buerki (in press), however, takes a major step towards showing that it is in fact the case. He compares the levels of formulaicity in English, German, and Korean, using a method that addresses the challenges arising from typological differences, which affect how many words are needed to express an idea. In English, an isolating language, a complex meaning is likely to be composed of more than one word. Korean, a highly synthetic language, may well capture the same meaning within one word, which therefore won't count as formulaic.[2] German falls between the two on this continuum. Buerki shows that these typological differences can be neutralized using two procedures that are legitimate within linguistic theory and current analytic practice: (a) combining morphological variants of the same word, by removing case and gender markers; (b) detaching common bound morphemes (Korean) and compounds (German) to make separate "words". He shows that, after applying these procedures, the number of items identified as formulaic in English, German, and Korean is very similar, offering support for the idea that all humans have an equal need for fast-track processing. These three languages are typologically different enough to suggest generalizability of the finding across many others. Notwithstanding this, even if FSs are present in equal measure across languages, there is, of course, no guarantee of a direct equivalent for a given expression.

Another reason why L2 learners might target FSs is the social function that some have. Bardovi-Harlig (this volume) notes that "specific FSs characterize language use within speech communities, and may mark speakers' membership within those communities" (p. 97), as well as "often indicat[ing] the illocutionary force of an utterance when it occurs" (p. 97). She quotes Coulmas's (1981) proposal that they are sociopragmatic "tacit agreements, which the members of a community presume to be shared by every reasonable co-member" (p. 99). The community-wide shared pragmatic value of FSs adds weight to the supposition that learners would seek out expressions that they expect to perform the same vital social functions as ones in their L1, even if this has some unintended consequences (see later discussion).

Further support comes from research suggesting that learners can fairly easily identify FSs in the L2 (e.g., Hernández, Costa, & Arnon, 2016; Jiang & Nekrasova, 2007), for "even when speakers have a relatively limited exposure to a language, they are still remarkably attuned to phrase frequency distributions, at least in language comprehension" (Siyanova-Chanturia & Van Lancker Sidtis, this volume, pp. 42–43). Siyanova-Chanturia and Van Lancker Sidtis also note that FSs often have phonological features marking them out, such as assimilated consonants, reduced vowels, and a single tone unit structure (p. 49), something that Lin (this volume) explores in more depth.

Finally, research from at least two quarters predicts that FSs would be on the L2 learner's radar. Conklin and Carrol (this volume) conclude, on the basis of their review, that "when L1 formulaic expressions exist, information about them is activated and influences processing in the L2" (p. 75). Meanwhile, Wulff (this volume) explores formulaicity from the perspective of Construction Grammar (CxG), which does away with the lexicon-grammar distinction and considers "a speaker's knowledge of their language(s) . . . a huge warehouse of constructions that vary in complexity and abstraction" (p. 21). CxG thus recognizes direct cognitive links between semantics and both single words and multiword strings (Fillmore, Kay, & O'Connor, 1988; Goldberg, 2013). Indeed, usage-based CxG is likely to rather *overpredict* the learner's expectation of an L2 equivalent. This is because compositionality is viewed as scalar rather than a binary pairing (Wulff, 2013, p. 280). As such, seeking equivalent multiword constructions across languages arguably becomes rather indistinct from seeking other linguistic units (morphemes words and grammatical patterns). If so, then as Ellis (1996, 2012) proposes, looking for multiword-to-multiword mappings is just a natural subpart of general L2 learning.

How do We know Learners *don't* Look for Formulaic Equivalents?

As noted earlier, it is not that learners don't show awareness of the usefulness of *any* L2 FSs, only that they seem not to take full advantage of the potential for seeking them out to support their speed and accuracy of learning. Were learners to be more attuned to how L2 expressions might map exactly or even partly onto ones they already know in their L1, surely their inventory would quickly grow. However, research consistently finds that learners know fewer L2 FSs than they ideally need (Hendriksen, 2013; Laufer & Waldman, 2011), and they "tend to cling to a small number of high-frequency combinations with which they feel comfortable" (Granger, this volume, p. 240). As a result, research and teaching activity has typically focussed on how to improve levels of FS knowledge (e.g., Cobb, this volume; Pellicer-Sanchez & Boers, this volume).

One source of evidence that FSs are under-exploited by L2 learners is the occurrence of errors. It has been proposed (see Wray, 2002 for discussion) that grammatically regular multiword strings, if internalized, can act as a travelling repository of linguistic patterns for the learner, in addition to, themselves, delivering accuracy and idiomaticity. Yet Granger (this volume) cites evidence that about one-third of L2 collocations have errors in them. Errors in output could occur because the configuration is not recognized as a useful holistic unit, with the result that its formal features are not sufficiently trusted. Why does L1 experience not alert learners to the need to attend to form, if the meaning or function is to be sustained? For example, *under the table* means "drunk", but *beneath the table*, *under a table*, and *under the tables* can only have a literal meaning.

With respect to functionally oriented wordstrings, Bardovi-Harlig (this volume, p. 110) cites a possible acquisitional sequence proposed in another of her papers:

> Nontargetlike speech act (nonalignment of speech act required by context) → targetlike speech act (alignment with context) with nontargetlike lexical resources → target lexical core → full conventional expression → conventional expression with targetlike expansion.

This sequence sees the L2 formula learned rather late, which is incompatible with the learner specifically seeking out an L2 form equivalent to the L1 one. As such, it is consistent with the impression that post-childhood L2 learners do not approach FS learning in that way.

Why don't Second Language Learners Target Formulaic Sequences more than they (Apparently) do?

We turn now to potential reasons why post-childhood L2 learners appear not to make a beeline for FSs, despite finding them useful in the L1.[3] Five possibilities will be reviewed. Three, mirroring but extending a suggestion from Wulff (this volume), accept that they do not: they can't; they don't want to; they don't need to. One entails their looking for FSs but not in the anticipated way. The fifth steps outside the frame to consider whether external factors incorrectly implicate their learning as the cause.

Post-Childhood Learners are Unable to Successfully Target Formulaic Sequences in the Second Language

Suppose learners do try to target FSs, but it doesn't work, or it leads to unhelpful outcomes. To learn vocabulary, whether single or multiple words, one needs to encounter the item at least once, and depending on how much attention is paid to it, probably many times (Bell & Skalicky, Pellicer-Sanchez & Boers, and Siyanova-Chanturia & Van Lancker Sidtis, all in this volume; Taylor, 2012). Learners' textbooks typically fail to provide sufficient formulaic material (Bardovi-Harlig, this volume). Perhaps, then, learners try to identify examples but don't encounter enough of them. According to Wulff (this volume), rare FSs are harder to acquire than common ones, even if they are distinctive and idiomatic and, hence, potentially easy to detect. Furthermore, since learners may identify formulas before there is sufficient evidence of how they can appear and can be used, there is a risk that the parameters of inherent variability will be misjudged, resulting in "learner idiosyncratic combinations" (Granger, this volume, p. 238). If they "know the rudiments of an expression (the lexical core) before they know the whole expression" (Bardovi-Harlig, this volume, p. 110), errors are likely, and feedback might discourage seeking out FSs in the future.

Another possibility is that learners don't encounter items often enough even to detect that they are formulaic. As Cobb (this volume, p. 196) says, "while formulaicity is pervasive in language, particular formulae sadly are not". Whereas L2 learners do show evidence of favouring, indeed over-favouring, word pairs with a high absolute frequency, they differ from L1 speakers in not using less-frequent pairs with high mutual information (MI) scores, that is, where the words are statistically likely to occur together (Ellis & Simpson-Vlach, 2009; Ellis, Simpson-Vlach, & Maynard, 2008). According to Bardovi-Harlig (this volume, pp. 105–106), "learners report knowing expressions that they do not produce in appropriate contexts". Perhaps this indicates a part-learning that has stalled pending further evidence that the form is recurrent for that meaning or function. There could, indeed, be a major stumbling block for learners in stacking up evidence for FSs. If, not knowing they are formulaic, they break them down, and thus do not retain a trace of the sequence as a whole, they can't track the sequence's frequency. Meanwhile, breaking down wordstrings and interpreting them literally may impair comprehension, making the formulation less salient (Bell & Skalicky, this volume).

A third possibility is that the mode of input makes it difficult to identify FSs. Classroom learners are often quite reliant for learning on written rather than spoken input (Gyllstad & Schmitt, this volume). In writing, the gaps between words obscure the larger structure (Wray, 2015), whereas in speech, phonological patterns tend to signal a single unit (Lin, this volume; Siyanova-Chanturia & Van Lancker Sidtis, this volume). However, detecting formulaicity is not always straightforward in speech either (Lin, this volume). Unless speakers use certain phonological features, formulaic and literal meanings of the same wordstring may not be distinguishable (Van Lancker, Canter, & Terbeek, 1981). Van Lancker Sidtis (2003) also found that L2 learners lack sensitivity to some auditory cues. Meanwhile, the general assumption that FSs are fluently spoken runs into some problems. Pausing within formulaic material can be effective in holding the turn while planning, since the hearer knows the speaker hasn't finished. Furthermore, as Bardovi-Harlig (this volume) notes, for sociopragmatic reasons, some formulas should be delivered with hesitation. Gruber (2009) found that in law courts, fluently delivered formulas came across as insincere.

Fourth, difficulties could arise in matching the L1 model with the L2 target, if they are very different in form. Although the L1 often plays a part in lexical inferencing in an L2 (Paribakht & Wesche, 2015), and the transfer of information from the L1 to assist in L2 learning is not necessarily a bad thing (Singleton, 2015), it has its limits. As Conklin and Carrol (this volume) point out, "an English speaker learning French cannot simply assume that *throw money out of the window* is the same in French" (p. 63). Nor will a multiword string in one language (e.g., French *s'il vous plait*) necessarily be one in another (e.g., English *please*). Failing always to find a one-to-one mapping could leave learners under-confident about looking them (cf. Bardovi-Harlig, this volume; Chamizo-Domínguez, 2008; Conklin & Carrol, this volume; Granger, this volume; Hulstijn & Marchena, 1989).

Another possibility is that where all the individual words in an expression are already known in their own right, the formulaicity of the phrase is overlooked (cf. Pellicer-Sanchez & Boers, this volume; Wray, 2002; Wulff, this volume), something that Granger (this volume) certainly considers likely for collocations that have low saliency.

Finally, there is a difference between knowing the form of an expression (pragmalinguistic competence) and knowing how to use it (sociopragmatic competence) (Leech, 1983; Thomas, 1983), as explored by Bardovi-Harlig (this volume; compare also Granger, this volume, on misaligned register). When learners target L2 expressions for important functions, they may only look for a *form* and not realize that they are in danger of inappropriately transferring the L1 sociopragmatics to the L2 situation (Bardovi-Harlig, this volume). Successfully seeking out expressions would have to involve focussing on context and function in a broader sense (i.e., what does one say in this situation?) rather than a narrower mapping (i.e., what is the expression for an apology, given that that is what I [mistakenly] believe I need?). Repeated failure on the part of an L2 learner to deploy an expression in a culturally accurate way could be discouraging. Although learners don't always, in a natural setting, get clear feedback that something was not the right thing to say, deviations from the social norm may distance learners from the in-groups that might have helped them forge a new identity and enhance further learning (Bell & Skalicky, this volume). Indeed, having such experiences, along with being corrected in their use of what they thought were equivalent words and referential expressions, may lead them to the insight that there are, perhaps, few if any direct mappings across languages at all.

Learners Have Reasons Not to Want to Target Formulaic Sequences in the Second Language

The sociolinguistic implications of using L2 expressions could also make targeting FSs undesirable. Bardovi-Harlig (this volume, p. 101) notes that "A person can determine the degree to which he or she wishes to be regarded as a co-member of a community". In Fitzpatrick and Wray's (2006) study, a Chinese L2 learner of English was supposed to memorize (i.e., make formulaic) nativelike ways of expressing specific ideas that he wanted to convey in upcoming conversations. He found this unpalatable, and commented that he felt he had to edit the expressions away from nativelikeness, because he could not abandon his Chinese (and hence L2 speaker) identity (pp. 50–51). Bardovi-Harlig's observation, cited earlier, that L2 learners recognize more expressions with pragmatic functions than they use, could be explained in the same way: the expressions' formulaicity is a mark of an in-group status they don't consider appropriate for them (compare Kecskes, this volume). Such difficulty fully identifying with a new speech community seems to develop after childhood, which could partly explain why children typically have better outcomes in L2 learning than adults do (Wray, 2008b).

A related possibility is that certain FSs are avoided because using them entails projecting linguistic and cultural familiarity that the learners don't feel they have yet. Bell and Skalicky (this volume) point out that the familiar form of certain expressions makes them a candidate for word play. Misjudging how to use humor in FL is not only about missing accuracy in form and nuance, but also about how the learner's efforts are received. Indeed, a deviation interpreted as humorous if produced by a native speaker may be viewed as defective from a learner, and result in the learner feeling socially exposed and embarrassed (Vandergriff, 2016, p. 161). As Bell and Skalicky point out, it is difficult to unpack formula-based humor because you need to know the formula *and* the other meanings of the constituent words, as well as seeing why the outcome is funny. It may be, therefore, that humorous uses of FL create a challenging barrier for L2 learners.

The way learners encounter FSs might also discourage them from seeking them out. The learning environment of a classroom learner presents very different pragmatic affordances from those in naturalistic learning (Cook, 2013, p. 155). Classroom learning typically puts more emphasis on single words than on multiword strings, and where multiword strings are directly taught, they may be in lists rather than a textual and/or functional context (Gyllstad & Schmitt, this volume), so they are not associated with any communicative event or need. Also, a significant proportion of the input of a classroom learner is from other learners and thus not a good model, which is counter-productive if an expression's frequency of encounter is vital (Pellicer-Sanchez & Boers, this volume).

Finally, there can be a tendency for teachers to conflate teaching with pseudo-testing, whereby, for example, learners are asked to complete cloze tasks for word-strings they have not yet fully mastered (Cobb, this volume). This, again, will increase their experience of non-optimal forms, something that Cobb recommends avoiding by exposing learners to examples from corpora.

Learners Have Less Need of Second Language Formulaic Sequences

FSs have, variously, referential, discourse, and social/pragmatic functions (Wray, 2002). Perhaps L2 learners do not need a full range of expressions performing one or more of those functions, because of the limited uses to which they put the

L2. For example, expressions used for managing academic essays will not be of interest to learners until they are engaged in that activity (Durrant, this volume). Learners experiencing little genuine practical interaction in the L2 will not need many communicative FSs. And those whose communication is predominantly in a lingua franca context may adopt compensatory mechanisms for avoiding formulaicity (Kecskes, this volume) or create their own inventory (Seidlhofer, 2009). If so, then changes in the learner's environment and context should result in an increase in the targeting of L2 FSs. Bardovi-Harlig (this volume) confirms that when a learner starts to live in an L2 environment, formulaic production increases, with greatest gains associated with greatest intensity of interaction, rather than purely the length of stay. However, this does not necessarily mean that there is any change in the learner's propensity to actually seek out FSs, as opposed to encounter and adopt them.

Another possibility relates to learners' tendency to pick up one suitable expression for a given meaning or function and then stop (Granger, this volume), even though others could also be acquired. Bardovi-Harlig (this volume) asks, "Will learners who can use *that's right* as an agreement routine notice and incorporate functional equivalents such as *you're right* and *that's true* . . . ?" (p. 111). Do learners perhaps not need any more granularity than one expression provides? Or are the subtle differences in usage between broadly equivalent expressions difficult for learners to distinguish? Do these differences, associated with fine-grained meanings such as irony or identity, exclude learners at the very point where they are encountered? Or could it simply be that the post-childhood learner has an unhelpful basic belief that one only need look for "the" expression that maps perfectly onto an L1 one, to the effective exclusion of all other possibilities (c.f. Granger, this volume)?

Learners Target Formulaic Sequences, but with a Different Outcome

Or perhaps learners only *appear* not to be targeting many FSs, because when they do, the outcome does not resemble the knowledge that L1 users display. The optimum deployment balance between formulaic and non-formulaic material might be different in one's L1 and L2. If so, knowing that one has a formula in the L1 associated with a given meaning might not trigger a need for a formula in the L2, because a non-formulaic alternative is preferable. That could be because the formulaic version is unfamiliar (Dagut & Laufer, 1985) or because, as we already saw, using an L2 formula signals social identity features that the learner does not align with. Alternatively, and more subtly, perhaps L2 speakers cannot identify common social ground with others and then mark it formulaically, but rather must first create that common ground: that is, establish *how* they are a legitimate in-group member rather than just asserting that they are. If so, they might find themselves not so much picking up on existing turns of phrase as creating new ones (Seidlhofer, 2009). This, certainly, is Kecskes' view with regard to the fluidity of internationalized codes, where "there is more reliance on language created ad hoc by individuals in the course of interaction than on prefabricated language and pre-existing frames in the target language" (Kecskes, this volume, p. 143).

Learners' Low Level of Formulaic Language is Due To Something Else

Our final consideration is whether the challenges that L2 learners have with mastering FSs are in fact better explained in some way that is external to the learner and/or not primarily a function of their being a learner.

First, perhaps FSs in the L1 don't constitute the kind of knowledge that can trigger targeting it in the L2. If expressions are acquired holistically in the L1 (Wray, 2002), with a direct link between form and meaning/function, we may rarely, in the L1, encounter situations in which we first know the complex idea, and then wonder what word or wordstring can be used to express it. That is, the language creates the access to the idea, and not the reverse. If so, working from idea to expression, while clearly not impossible, might not be instinctive.

Furthermore, the formulaic learning that L2 learners engage in might not (as has been supposed thus far) be driven by a specific search for wordstrings to perform particular semantic jobs. That is, it might not be primarily indexical. In line with Sinclair's (1991) "idiom principle", picking up formulas might be a broader, more functional means of managing input for immediate interactional and learning goals. Indexing the whole, or sub-parts, to meanings might be an incidental longer-term benefit: a kind of bootstrapping into linguistic detail. This is in essence what emergent learning entails, as outlined by Ellis (2012), Goldberg (2013) and Wulff (2013; this volume).

Finally, perhaps learners' attempts to pin down FSs are hampered not only by some or all of the constraints outlined previously, but also by the sheer complexity of what they are juggling, as they simultaneously learn a language and use it. Of course, they have done this before, in first language acquisition, but the parameters are far from the same. In the next section, this complexity is unpacked, with respect to the nature of FSs.

Rethinking the Question

So far, we have considered why L2 learners appear not to exploit the potential of FL more than they do. Explanations have included a range of potential impediments to successful targeting, reasons why learners might not need, or want, to target FSs, and ways in which their "failure" might be a function of how we look at L2 achievement. We turn now to how we look at what is "formulaic" and, thus, what we are expecting L2 learners to do.

Is the Single-Word Versus Multiword Distinction a Useful One?

The discussion so far raises the old question of whether there is really any difference between single words and multiword strings (cf. Wray, 2002, 2008a). To what extent are puzzles about how FSs are learned just an extension of those about how vocabulary and grammar more generally are learned, as Construction Grammar maintains (Buerki, 2016)? In what sense is there really any difference between a learner seeking the L2 term for *tea towel*, *microwave oven*, or *deckchair cover* and seeking the term for *dustbin* or *bookshelf*? Is this not more about the conventions around word space locations? As we saw, Buerki's recent work is a stark reminder that word boundaries are a local issue for the language in hand. However, while terms for entities, like the given examples, suggest there really is little difference (Wray, 2015), not all FSs are like that.

At the level of form, a simple way to divide up FSs is into those that can be replaced by a single word or proform and those that cannot. The examples in the previous paragraph all fall into the former category, and this is why the distinction between single and multiword items seems so minimal. But many FSs have a grammatical role that encompasses more than one grammatical constituent, such as a verb and object (e.g., *run a business*, *boil eggs*, *book a holiday*, *fell a tree*). Here, it is typically not possible to make a paradigmatic replacement with a single word. A proform replacement would need to be something like *do it* rather than just *do* or *it*. Other FSs span part of a higher-level grammatical constituent, such as *in the middle of the*, and *I'd like you to*, though it can be argued that gaps for open-class items should be considered part of the formula, making the constituent grammatically complete.

While the cognitive view of FL supposes all FSs to be single items in memory, irrespective of their internal composition or grammatical role in use, it can certainly be argued that grammatically complex and incomplete items demand a registered valency, by which it is known how many, and what kind, of additional items are required for the formula to be usable. Notwithstanding the way Construction Grammar can handle all formulations as single constructions, this incompleteness does render such FSs substantially different from those playing a simple noun or verb role, in terms of form, nature, onward processing implications, and, importantly, learnability. Granger (this volume) reports research showing that adjective-noun collocation knowledge is not a reliable gauge of proficiency, whereas verb-object collocation knowledge is. This may be because of the additional linguistic requirements entailed in deploying FSs that occupy a higher grammatical constituent level.

What Qualifies as Not Formulaic in the First and Second Language?

The premise of the question posed in this paper has been that an L2 learner has some basic awareness of formulaicity in the L1, which would underpin a recognition of its usefulness in the L2. However, particularly if we allow for the boundary between single and multiword items to be a weak one, and for FSs to contain gaps for open-class items, what exactly would count as *not* formulaic in one's L1? Unless something is expressly un-idiomatic, is it not likely to be, at one level or another, formulaic? Again, that is how Construction Grammar construes language: entirely made up of constructions, just of different sizes, fixedness, and internal complexity.

If we do take this position, then when we identify errors and/or a lack of idiomaticity in L2 learners' output, it is close to saying that, in those locations, it lacks formulaicity. In turn, we are at risk, when examining learner output, of more or less ignoring all the language that is formulaic, and homing in only on the small proportion that is not, because that is where the errors are. Teachers and testers may become blind to the majority of the learner's success in acquiring idiomatic patterns in the L2. One study demonstrates that this can happen and why it is a problem. Wray and Pegg (2009) addressed an issue identified by some IELTS markers, whereby prefabricated wordstrings appeared to be inflating scores on the writing task. It is not uncommon for essays to contain prefabricated material taken from the essay prompt or from source materials, and Appel and Wood (2016), having found that lower-proficiency learners increased their accuracy in writing by copying multiword strings from source texts, warn that "an increased use of recurrent word sequences in the writing of non-native English users should not automatically be taken as a sign of increased proficiency" (p. 66).

In IELTS marking, material copied from the question is discounted, so there is no problem there. However, the use of pre-*memorized* material is harder to deal with, because, firstly, it is actual knowledge, and, secondly, even native speakers use formulaic material to manage the structure of an argument in an essay, so on what basis can it be considered wrong? Insofar as we view memorized multiword strings as a lexical resource equivalent to single words, why shouldn't learners know and use some? The problem was that, in some cases, correct and idiomatic chunks of generic material (e.g., *This interesting question can be viewed from several different angles. Firstly . . . Secondly . . . Lastly*; *A further consideration, before concluding this discussion, is . . .*) were interspersed with rather chaotic English such as *email can helps to child fast to give them friends* (p. 203). Since the chunks, in terms of word count, outnumbered the chaotic text, rewarding the former would give a higher score than the latter suggested was appropriate. Yet ignoring the former would fail to give credit for appropriate use of English, while concentrating the assessment on only a small part of the whole. As a principle this is dangerous, for learners of high proficiency are more likely than less able ones to amend what they have memorized, and add additional material, better to match the demands of the task, and as such are more liable to introduce errors. As a result, higher-proficiency learners might be penalized more than lower ones. In response to this conundrum, Wray and Pegg (2009) offer a procedure for establishing whether the idiomatic material in an essay is likely to signal an over-reliance on memorization, by subcategorizing it according to the effort entailed in making it available for use, and by mapping the different subtypes across the essay and noting characteristics of the intervening errors.

The Bricks and Mortar of Text

Following from this last discussion, we might ask, "why are certain elements idiomatic/formulaic in an L2 learner's output, when other elements are not?" What has prevented the learner from seeking out the L2 formulaic material for the rest? Are L2 learners more successful in targeting and learning some types of FSs than others? To address this, perhaps we should separate FSs into two types that often, in the research literature, sit rather uneasily together (Cobb, this volume). One is lexical bundles, which are the wordstrings of highest frequency in a corpus, typically things like *such as*; *and a lot of*; *the extent to which* (Biber, Conrad, & Cortes., 2004). The other is the broad range of more semantically intact wordstrings, from two-word nouns like *pool table* and *deep sea*, through idiomatic collocations like *allay fears*, *luke warm*, and *positive advantage*, to the phrasal and clausal expressions that, for many, represent the core of FL, like *one more time*, *mind how you go*, and *a stitch in time saves nine*. These two types sit on a continuum, for, as Cobb (this volume) demonstrates, if you have a generous enough frequency threshold for what counts as a lexical bundle, content items of the latter type will start to turn up both on their own and as frequent completions of the former type.

Nevertheless, we may usefully conceptualize language as being composed of frequently recurring configurations of "mortar" holding together a wide selection of freely selected "bricks", some a single word long, some collocating word pairs, others longer strings. For example, in *The deep ocean is one of our most precious resources*, the "bricks" are *deep ocean* and *precious resources*. They can be attributed meaning on their own: there could be a dictionary entry for each phrase as well as for the individual words. The "mortar", *is one of our most*, is not devoid of meaning, but it would be difficult to list in a dictionary by itself. Yet we can consider it a formulaic constituent because it is likely to turn up as a lexical bundle in any appropriately calibrated search of a large corpus.

L2 learners need command of both types, if they are to produce fluent, coherent output. But would both be learned in the same way? If learners were able to target FSs, which type would they be looking for? And which type is likely to be the focus of teaching? Research, including that reviewed in this volume, suggests that most attention is paid to content items, the "bricks", while the "mortar", despite its greater frequency in the language learners are exposed to, is either not noticed, not prioritized, or sidelined as too difficult to teach. Yet, were lexical bundles to be taught, or were learners encouraged to spot useful ones in resource texts, they would surely surmount a significant hurdle with regard to idiomaticity and accuracy. Indeed, even the verbatim copying of material that Appel and Wood (2016) found in lower-ability learners (e.g., *synthetic compounds containing carbon fluorine and*; *killing of certain forms of aquatic life*) would have been effective original language if the writers had been able to substitute new noun phrases for those in the original, so that only the joining material (verb and function words) was actually verbatim from the reference text (e.g., *important materials containing chemicals and*; *killing of types of animals*). A frequency search would not pick these up as copied, even though the structures were intact: and indeed, a learner could adopt complete sentence structures from the source without it showing, if they replaced the key lexical material.

Thus, lexical bundles do begin to seem like useful items to learn, even if, being relatively invisible (even in the L1) compared to substantive content material, they would be unlikely to register in the learner as potential targets without assistance from a teacher. Although challenging in its own ways, the technique of changing the substantive items (which could of course be ones occurring elsewhere in the text) would be more likely to render accurate, original output than only having a command of words, collocation pairs, and short phrases that the writer is unable to put together using the "mortar" of common lexical bundles.

Seeing Versus Doing

Another generally recognized, broad distinction that can be put to new uses as we explore whether, and how, L2 learners target and/or learn FSs, is that of reference versus function: that is, items that talk about the world, versus those that intervene in it. This distinction might seem at first unnecessary in the context of asking what formulaic material learners can target, because it is equally easy to imagine them seeking out an L2 equivalent for *tennis racquet* and *see you later*. However, whereas for referential items a need for learning can be relatively easily stimulated in the somewhat sterile environments of the classroom and home study, functional expressions only really come alive when the speaker wants to perform the function. A small number of the latter, it's true, might well be pursued on the basis of wanting to know what to say one day, rather than the need to say it right now, but these will probably only be the most common. Others may not be salient for the learner until the need to say them arises, and that is highly dependent on the learning context.

As the proponents of communicative approach and task-based learning suppose, even if a keen learner does have sufficient awareness to make decisions about which useful functional expressions to target, it may be cognitively difficult to anchor them in memory without practicing them in genuine communication. For example, Wray (2002) proposes that lexical items with social functions are indexed in the brain areas associated with facial recognition, social awareness, etc., a proposal since evidenced neurologically (e.g., Bonner & Grossman, 2014). If the keen learner wants to find out how these interactional functions are achieved in the L2, he or she will be dependent on access to a large enough range of functionally induced language. As various of the chapters in this book suggest, reference to a corpus would be desirable. However, we still lack the facility comprehensively to search corpora by function rather than form (c.f. Durrant & Mathews-Ayadinli, 2011), and there is no full dictionary of FSs organized by function and meaning yet.

In the absence of many function-first options for searching out function-heavy FSs, we return to the matter of adequate exposure. We can hypothesize that in order successfully to identify and internalize from general exposure a targeted FS with a primarily sociopragmatic functional role (see discussion in "How do we know learners *don't* look for formulaic equivalents?"), the following would have to apply:

(1) A relevant interaction regularly takes place, that the learner observes.
(2) The learner knows there will soon be a need to engage in that interaction.
(3) The learner is sufficiently semantically engaged each time the formula is observed, for the functional associations to be internalized.
(4) The learner is able to pick out and accurately delineate the target form from surrounding material, including identifying constraints on filling any open-class slots.
(5) The learner can transfer this passive knowledge into active knowledge in advance of its use.
(6) The learner has sufficient general confidence to take the step of using an FS, the internal make-up and exact sociopragmatic features of which may not be fully understood. Not all learners will have this confidence and may feel that the use of non-transparent phrases is a bit like buying and selling something in a sealed box.
(7) The learner is willing to cope with the responses that using the item may trigger in others, such as those associated with signalling more advanced L2 proficiency than previously.

As with the "bricks" and "mortar" distinction earlier, both referential and functional FSs are needed if one is to avoid social stumbles and refer widely. It is the referential items of such low frequency that they are not a central part of the teaching canon that mark out high-end proficiency. Appel and Wood (2016) found that less-proficient learners relied more than proficient ones on discourse-organizing expressions and suggest that proficient learners had more scope to express interesting, novel ideas, because they had the (single and multiword) vocabulary to do so.

The Dynamics of Learning

Finally, in our quest for why L2 learners seem not to target FSs as much as they might, we need to consider the ways in which L1 and L2 FL knowledge accumulates, and how this might be a hindrance as much as a potential stimulus for onward learning. There are several aspects to this, as befits the complexity of FL. One is the outright order of acquisition. Arnon, McCauley, and Christiansen (2017) report that earlier acquired words and phrases are quicker to process; and we have already seen how earlier L2 learning may affect later learning. For instance, the overuse of a small set of formulas (Granger, this volume) may indicate that learners are satisfied with one L2 form for each (broad) meaning. Thus, the breadth of designated meaning/function for one item will determine the lexical gaps still to fill.

But could an L2 learner have a different level of sensitivity towards, or different level of urgency about knowing, L2 items, according to when the L1 equivalent was learned? It seems unlikely that the repertoire of a 2-year-old is the most salient material for an adult L2 learner, but it could be, conversely, that the way this early-learned material is anchored cognitively leaves the learner relatively blind to it, making it harder to annex in the L2. The "sociointeractional bubble" within which infants acquire their first language (Wray, 2002), along with their cognitive immaturity, naturally filters and orders the FSs that they pick up in the early years. Children are protected from many types of functional interaction (e.g., the responsibilities of financial transactions; expression of condolences), whereas others are given a higher priority than in later life (e.g., asking permission). Young children have fewer of the social identity pressures that later draw them into linguistic coding choices. Indeed, they may, early on, be unaware of how their direct imitation of models places them in a strange pragmatic space: Namba's (2012) sons used the female forms in Japanese politeness expressions, having learned them from their female teacher.

Figure 13.1 offers a representation of the potential events at the interface of L1 knowledge and L2 learning, and how they might impact on the capacity to match FSs across languages. Along the top is a roughly time-ordered (but iterative) series of learning events for the L1, from short referential items, through expressions with a social function, to the broadening of referential vocabulary to include full and partial synonyms, and then the accumulation of group-specific options signalling identity. Collocations are acquired as an annex of word learning. The acquisition of the "mortar", i.e., the configurations that turn lexical material into coherent grammatical language, is not included in Figure 13.1: it is not likely to be part of what an L2 learner targets on the basis of L1 awareness.

The bottom row similarly lays out a time-ordered series of learning events for the post-childhood learned L2. There is scope for arguing that the order could be more different from that of the L1, but for present purposes it is easier not to add that complication. It will be noted that the L2 learner does not have a separate stage for formulas associated with socialization. This is to acknowledge that only the young child is introduced to a major set of ritual formulas for appropriate behaviour. Of course, classroom learners might have FSs to greet the teacher and ask a question, but other than that, it is envisaged that in post-childhood contexts, functional social discourse simply absorbs, as adult-style expressions, any formulas that for the child have a socializing (as opposed to a social) role.

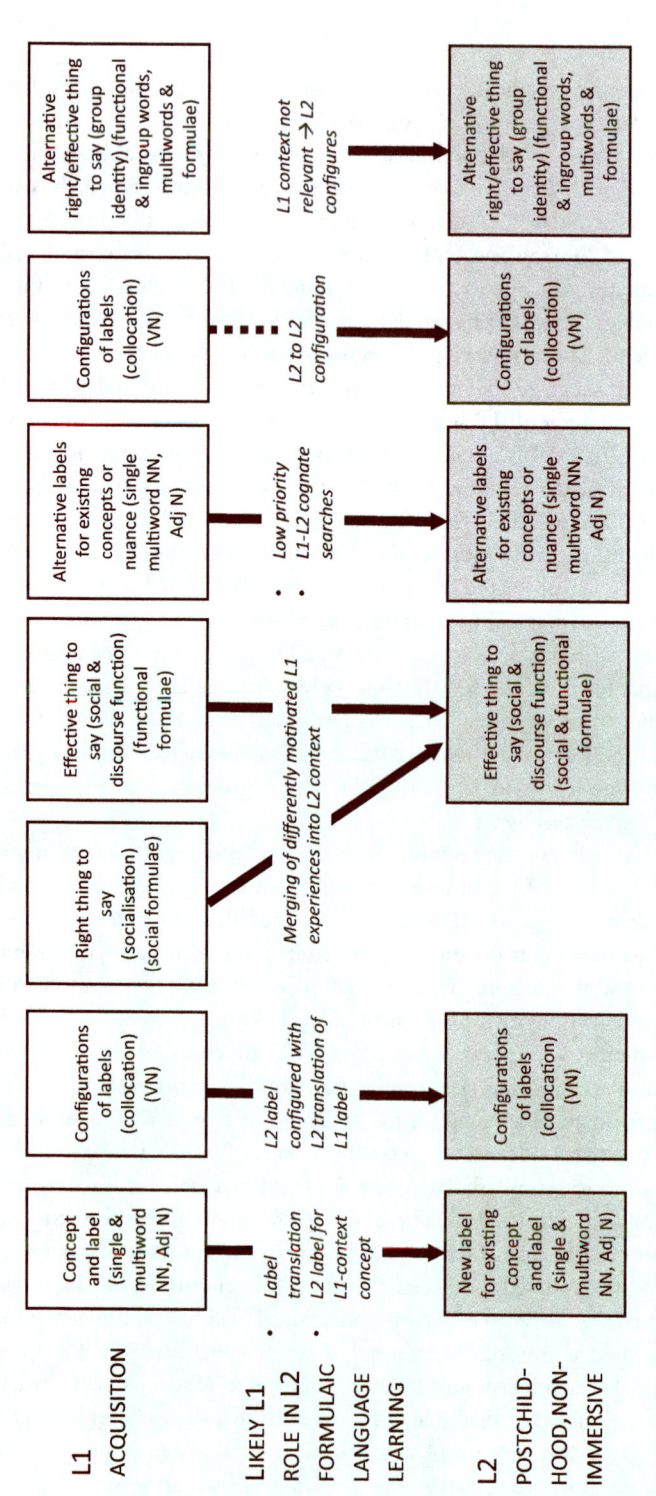

FIGURE 13.1 A simplified representation of the L1-L2 interface for learning L2 formulaic sequences.

Between the two sets of learning events is a depiction of potential interface events: how knowledge of the L1 might impact on learning the L2. First, we see the potential for the learner to target an item in the L2 that is a direct translation of a known L1 item, or to label with an L2 item the conceptual space that they annexed when learning the L1 word. This, for single words, has been discussed in research over many years. In the present case, the potential for this process extends beyond single words to multiword strings. At the second stage, we see how, transcending the nominal (NN, AdjN, etc.) collocations, to now work at the higher constituent level (e.g., VN), one L2 word, already learned, might become configured as collocating with another L2 word that is, however, a translation of an L1 item, rather than a legitimate, attested L2 collocate. This is the way in which classic non-nativelike collocates would arise (e.g., *make a photograph*).

Thirdly, as outlined by Bardovi-Harlig (this volume), the L1 experiences of social interaction influence the learning of L2 social formulas, so an L2 expression is used in its correct form but in a situation that is not culturally appropriate. Fourthly, the learner begins to accumulate alternative ways of saying the same thing. Where in the L1 this micro-filling of the semantic space is a continuation of the natural exposure-into-acquisition process, in the L2 there may, as discussed earlier, be constraints on the drive to seek out words and phrases that, while offering variation and nuance, are not strictly needed for the learner to make him/herself understood, since there is already something that can be used. Some learning will no doubt take place on the basis of exposure. But where the learner specifically looks for an alternative option for expressing an idea, there may be a strong influence from the L1, regarding what sort of alternative is targeted and how it is conceived to be different from what is already known.

Next comes the second round of non-nominal collocation configurations. By this stage, the learner is more likely to make legitimate L2 pairings, in part because the items contributing to them have themselves been learned rather later in the process. Finally, the L2 learner becomes able to make selections that favour one social identity over another, whether that be to signal non-native status, or to align with one L2 group over another (e.g., adopting dialect words; street speak, etc.). By now, L1 social contexts are barely relevant, and so the linguistic encoding is likely to be L2-centric and thus more authentic, though, as Kecskes (this volume) points out, one strong source of social identity can be that of "international speaker of a lingua franca", which has its own codes potentially different from those of native speakers.

Figure 13.1, although a gross simplification, offers some insights into why L2 learners might progressively target and not target different types of FS, according to stage and context of learning and the particular influences of the L1 on FL with different functions.

Conclusion and Further Observations

It seems that the reasons why L2 learning appears not to target FSs to the extent that it might, given their ubiquity and usefulness in the L1, are complex. Of the various explanations explored, perhaps many simultaneously contribute to a reduction in the capacity, or willingness, of a learner to seek out formulaic configurations, with the result that they can only accrue gradually through the processes of teaching and natural exposure, while being potentially compromised by influences from the L1. The different factors explored may help future researchers and teachers tease apart the dynamics of the learner's multifaceted experience.

At a theoretical level, it has been suggested that while there is general explanatory value in viewing both single words and multiword strings as types of lexical unit, doing so under-plays the more grammatically complex nature of some multiword strings. Evidence suggests that the challenges for L2 learners may reside disproportionately with those FSs that, while capable of being holistically learned, do not map onto a single grammatical constituent. Similarly, it has been proposed that the trajectories, in terms of learning, may be different for the collocation pairs and more canonical formulaic phrases that are the "bricks", versus the "mortar" of classic lexical bundles; and for referentially versus functionally oriented expressions. We have asked whether researchers and teachers are judging learners' knowledge of FSs unfairly, and whether shortfalls in FL and use might be caused by patterns of previous learning. There remain, of course, many questions to answer and opportunities for new empirical projects.

One example is whether a given post-childhood learner would be expected to develop similar formulaic knowledge across several different L2s. If learners have a natural reflex, albeit somewhat compromised by their learning context, to target FSs in the L2, then we would predict that, proportionate to their proficiency level, their knowledge would be broadly equivalent across different languages learned, in terms of quantity and/or actual instances. A quantity match would arise if the impulse to seek out FSs is driven by the learning experience (i.e., what you look for depends on what you need to do). A match of actual instances (i.e., knowing the equivalent formula across all languages) would arise if the impulse is more programmatic at a cognitive level. For example, perhaps the learner would seek new L2 nodes to link with an L1 network, or to consolidate a new, independent L2 network of similar shape to the L1 network. In line with the discussion earlier, the same predictions would be made for multiword strings and single words.

Conversely, if L2 learners are not able, or willing, to focus on looking for FS matches, we would predict that the formulaic knowledge they have is a direct result of what they have been taught and asked to learn, or have encountered in conditions conducive to inductive learning. As such, the differences in the teaching input across languages would be the main factor in determining what the learner knew, making research into teaching techniques particularly relevant. Furthermore, insofar as learners are directed towards single-word learning, we would predict the learning trajectory for words and multiword strings to be markedly different. There is little research into how similar people's knowledge of different languages is, and so we simply don't know whether a learner might transcend a substantial proportion of any differences in input type and quantity, to end up with a rather similar level of formulaic knowledge.

In terms of form and approach, this chapter has been an experiment in drawing together the contents of a significant collection of state-of-the-art reviews, supplemented by other sources, to contribute answers to a new question – one that it would have been impossible to answer through a single empirical study or, probably, even a series of them, for, as we have seen, there are a great many variables to consider. Rather, addressing the question has benefitted from the breadth and weight of combined findings about FL in the L2, across the domains of cognition, social interaction, pragmatics, and pedagogy, as expertly reviewed and discussed in the preceding chapters of this book.

Given the inherent complexity of FL as a phenomenon, there are no doubt other new questions that could be similarly addressed by drawing down insights from the most up-to-date research reports available, and engaging in comparison, reasoning, and argument. As we have seen, there is no guarantee of a single, simple answer to such questions. But finding *the* answer is far from the only purpose of the exercise. The process of enquiry involves surfacing assumptions and teasing apart small but important differences, and in that way increasing the intimacy of our knowledge and understanding of the phenomena at the heart of our interest.

Notes

1 *Formulaic sequence* (FS) (count noun) refers here to any multiword string that is perceived by the agent (i.e., learner, researcher, etc.) to have an identity or usefulness as a single lexical unit (see Wray, 2002, p. 9). *Formulaic language* (FL) (mass noun) is used for the collective of such instances.
2 Although some definitions allow for a single word to count as formulaic (e.g., Wray, 2002, 2008a), most researchers and teachers confine their interest to multiword strings.
3 Some might argue that learners are not aware of formulaicity in their L1 in the first place (see the later discussion on bricks and mortar). My view is that they are, at least in part, and that the discussion here is valid for the subset of wordstrings that they do recognize as having a special status.

References

Appel, R., & Wood, D. (2016). Recurrent word combinations in EAP test-taker writing: Differences between high- and low-proficiency levels. *Language Assessment Quarterly*, *13*(1), 55–71.
Arnon, I., McCauley, S. M., & Christiansen, M. H. (2017). Digging up the building blocks of language: Age-of-acquisition effects for multiword phrases. *Journal of Memory and Language*, *92*, 265–280.
Biber, D., Conrad, S., & Cortes, V. (2004). *If you look at* . . . Lexical bundles in university teaching and textbooks. *Applied Linguistics*, *25*, 371–405.
Bonner, M. F., & Grossman, M. (2014). The neural basis of semantic memory. In L. G. Nilsson & N. Ohta (Eds.), *Dementia and memory* (pp. 207–224). London: Psychology Press.

Buerki, A. (2016). Formulaic sequences: A drop in the ocean of constructions or something more significant? *European Journal of English Studies, 20*(1), 15–34.

Buerki, A. (in press). (How) is formulaic language universal? Insights from Korean, German and English. In E. Piirainen, N. Filatkina, S. Stumpf, & C. Pfeiffer (Eds.), *Formulaic language and new data: Theoretical and methodological implications*. Berlin and Boston: DeGruyter Mouton.

Chamizo-Domínguez, P. J. (2008). *Semantics and pragmatics of false friends*. New York, NY: Routledge.

Cook, V. (2013). *Second language learning and language teaching* (4th ed.). London: Routledge.

Coulmas, F. (1981). *Conversational routine: Explorations in standardized communication situations and prepatterned speech*. The Hague: Mouton.

Dagut, M., & Laufer, B. (1985). Avoidance of phrasal verbs: A case for contrastive analysis. *Studies in Second Language Acquisition, 7*(1), 73–80.

Durrant, P., & Mathews-Ayadinli, J. (2011). A function-first approach to identifying formulaic language in academic writing. *English for Specific Purposes, 30*, 58–72.

Ellis, N. C. (1996). Sequencing in SLA: Phonological memory, chunking, and points of order. *Studies in Second Language Acquisition, 18*, 91–126.

Ellis, N. C. (2012). Formulaic language and second language acquisition: Zipf and the phrasal teddy bear. *Annual Review of Applied Linguistics, 32*, 17–44.

Ellis, N. C., & Simpson-Vlach, R. (2009). Formulaic language in native speakers: Triangulating psycholinguistics, corpus linguistics, and education. *Corpus Linguistics and Linguistic Theory, 5*, 61–78.

Ellis, N. C., Simpson-Vlach, R., & Maynard, C. (2008). Formulaic language in native and second-language speakers: Psycholinguistics, corpus linguistics, and TESOL. *TESOL Quarterly, 42*, 375–396.

Fillmore, C., Kay, P., & O'Connor, M. C. (1988). Regularity and idiomaticity in grammatical constructions: The case of *let alone*. *Language, 64*(3), 501–538.

Fitzpatrick, T., & Wray, A. (2006). Breaking up is not so hard to do: Individual differences in L2 memorisation. *Canadian Modern Language Review, 63*(1), 35–57.

Gleason, J. B., & Weintraub, S. (1976). The acquisition of routines in child language. *Language in Society, 5*, 129–136.

Goldberg, A. (2013). Constructionist approaches. In D. Hoffman & G. Trousdale (Eds.), *The Oxford Handbook of Construction Grammar* (pp. 15–31). New York, NY: Oxford University Press.

Gruber, M. C. (2009). Accepting responsibility at defendants' sentence hearings: No formulas for success. In R. Corrigan, E. A. Moravcsik, H. Ouali, & K. M. Wheatley (Eds.), *Formulaic language. Vol 2: Acquisition, loss, psychological reality, and functional explanations* (pp. 545–566). Amsterdam: John Benjamins.

Hendriksen, B. (2013). Research on L2 learners' collocational competence and development: A progress report. In C. Bardel, C. Lindqvist, & B. Laufer (Eds.), *L2 vocabulary acquisition, knowledge and use: New perspectives on assessment and corpus analysis* (pp. 29–56). Eurosla Monographs Series 2. Retrieved from www.eurosla.org/monographs/EM02/EM02home.php.

Hernández, M., Costa, A., & Arnon, I. (2016). More than words: Multiword frequency effects in non-native speakers. *Language, Cognition and Neuroscience, 31*(6), 785–800.

Hulstijn, J., & Marchena, E. (1989). Avoidance: Grammatical or semantic causes? *Studies in Second Language Acquisition, 11*(3), 242–255.

Jiang, N., & Nekrasova, T. M. (2007). The processing of formulaic sequences by second language speakers. *Modern Language Journal, 91*(3), 433–445.

Laufer, B., & Waldman, T. (2011). Verb-noun collocations in second-language writing: A corpus analysis of learners' English. *Language Learning*, *61(2)*, 647–672.
Leech, G. (1983). *Principles of pragmatics*. New York, NY: Longman.
Lin, P. (2018). *The prosody of formulaic language*. London: Bloomsbury
Namba, K. (2012). *English-Japanese code-switching and formulaic language: A structural approach to bilingual interactions*. Saarbrücken: Lambert Academic Publishing.
Paribakht, T. S., & Wesche, M. B. (2015). L1 influences in L2 lexical inferencing. In L. Yu & T. Odlin (Eds.), *New perspectives on transfer in second language learning* (pp. 76–106). Bristol: Multilingual Matters.
Pawley, A., & Syder. F. H. (1983). Two puzzles for linguistic theory: Nativelike selection and nativelike fluency. In J. C. Richards & R. W. Schmidt (Eds.), *Language and communication* (pp. 191–227). London and New York, NY: Longman.
Seidlhofer, B. (2009). Accommodation and the idiom principle in English as a Lingua Franca. *Intercultural Pragmatics*, *6(2)*, 195–215.
Sinclair, J. McH. (1991). *Corpus, concordance, collocation*. Oxford: Oxford University Press.
Singleton, D. (2015). Cross-lexical interaction and the structure of the mental lexicon. In L. Yu & T. Odlin (Eds.). *New perspectives on transfer in second language learning* (pp. 51–62). Bristol: Multilingual Matters.
Taylor, J. R. (2012). *The mental corpus*. Oxford: Oxford University Press.
Thomas, J. (1983). Cross-cultural pragmatic failure. *Applied Linguistics*, *4*, 91–112.
Vandergriff, I. (2016). *Second-language discourse in the digital world*. Amsterdam: John Benjamins.
Van Lancker-Sidtis, D. (2003). Auditory recognition of idioms by first and second speakers of English. *Applied Psycholinguistics*, *24*, 45–57.
Van Lancker, D., Canter, G., & Terbeek, D. (1981). Disambiguation of ditropic sentences: Acoustic and phonetic cues. *Journal of Speech and Hearing Research*, *24*, 330–335.
Wray, A. (2002). *Formulaic language and the lexicon*. Cambridge: Cambridge University Press.
Wray, A. (2008a). *Formulaic language: Pushing the boundaries*. Oxford: Oxford University Press.
Wray, A. (2008b). The puzzle of language learning: From child's play to "linguaphobia". *Language Teaching*, *41(2)*, 255–273.
Wray, A. (2015). Why are we so sure we know what a word is? In J. Taylor (Ed.), *The Oxford handbook of the word* (pp. 725–750). Oxford: Oxford University Press.
Wray, A., & Pegg, C. (2009). The effect of memorized learning on the writing scores of Chinese IELTS test takers. *IELTS Research Reports*, *9*, 191–216.
Wulff, S. (2013). Words and idioms. In T. Hoffman & G. Trousdale (Eds.), *The Oxford handbook of construction grammar* (pp. 274–289). New York, NY: Oxford University Press.

INDEX

Note: Page numbers in *italic* indicate a figure on the corresponding page.

abstract syntactic frames, as constructions 21
Academic Collocations List 218
Academic Formulas List 184, 186
academic language 12, 211–224
academic language proficiency tests 219–220
academic texts, analysis of formulaic language in 213–215
Academic Vocabulary Lists 222
Academic Word List 206, 220, 222
accentuation patterns, prosody and 78–80
acquisition of language: formulaic language 7–9; order of 263; from a usage-based perspective 19–31; *see also* child first language acquisition; first language acquisition; second language acquisition
adaptive tests 187
adjective-noun collocation 163, 258
adverbs, salience of 24
age-of-acquisition (AoA) effects 43
alliteration 165–166
ambiguous idioms 44–45, 51–53, 55
AntConc Concordancer 198, 201
apology 115
articulation latency 49–50
association, measures of 221
associative learning 24
attention: role in learning 158; typographic enhancement and 158–159, 161, 167–168
aural enhancement 159

Bardovi-Harlig, Kathleen 9
Bell, Nancy 10
binomial expressions: articulation and phrase frequency 50; ERP study of 47; frequency and 55; processing of 42
BNC Baby Academic corpus 237
Boers, Frank 11
bootstrapping 19, 84, 257
British National Corpus (BNC) 178, 187, 199, 218, 232–233, 237
bundles *see* lexical bundles

CALL (computer-assisted language learning) 12, 192, 199, 202–207; cloze passages and 204–205, *205*; single-word CALL and formulaic sequences 205–207
CALL-Concordancing activity 202–203, *203–204*
Cambridge Idioms Dictionary 184
Canadian Academic English Language (CAEL) assessment 219
Carroll, Gareth 8
categories of formulaic language 183–184
CATTS (Computer Adaptive Test of Size and Strength) test 187
CEFR (Common European Framework of Reference) 218, 235
child first language acquisition: comprehension and age-of-acquisition of phrases 43; foetal response to

linguistic prosody 82–83; holistically learned chunks 82, 84–85; prosody and 81–83
children: prefabricated language, use of 27–28; sociointeractional bubble 263
chunking, of constructions 22
circumlocutions 115
clauses, as correlates of intonation units 83–84
Cloze Builder, Lextutor 204
cloze passages 204–205, *205*
Cobb, Tom 11–12
code-switching, idiom processing and 66
cognitive-philosophical approach 134
cohesion 39
COLLEX 177–178, 186
Collins COBUILD Phrasal Verbs Dictionary 184
COLLMATCH 177–178, 186
collocational streams 140
collocations 8, 12, 38; in academic language proficiency exams 219; accuracy and appropriacy of use 232–233; acquisition of 263, *264*, 265; adjective-noun 163, 258; as constructions 21; definitions 230–231; density 231; development of use 234–235; dictionaries 184; dispersion 231; distinction from lexical bundles 236; diversity 231–232; ease of comprehension 168; errors in use 232–234, 252; first language influence on second language 64–66, 70, 75; first language transfer 233–234; frequency and 68, 140, 155–156, 222, 231–232; holistic storage and retrieval 136; humor 125; idiomatic 64–66, 70, 183, 260; incidental learning 155–157; input flooding 158–159; intentional learning 161–164; irony and 118–119; Japanese 64–65, 70; knowledge as a gauge of proficiency 258; operationalizations 230–231; processing of 43–44; restricted 231–232, 234, 240, 246; statistical 231–232, 234, 246; Swedish learners 65; testing and 175–180, *176, 178–179*, 185; transparency of 75, 179; typographic enhancement for 158–159, 161; verb-noun 156–157, 161, 163–164; verb-object 258
Common European Framework of Reference (CEFR) 218, 235
communication: cooperation in 134–136; interplay of individual traits and social traits 135; socio-cultural interactional approach 134
compositional formulaic language: comprehension of 40–44; production of 49–51
comprehension of formulaic language 39–48, 54–55; compositional 40–44; figurative 44–48; of non-adjacent sequences 43
Computer Adaptive Test of Size and Strength (CATTS) test 187
computer-assisted language learning *see* CALL (computer-assisted language learning)
conceptual socialization 143
concordance 194, *194*, 197, *197*, 199–203, *200–204*
Concord_Writer 201
Conklin, Kathy 8
constraint-based model, of idiom processing 75
Construction Grammar 211, 251, 258–259
constructions: chunking of 22; combining of 21; complexity level of 21–22; defined 20–21; dispersion of 23; distribution of 23; examples of 20–21; frequency of 22, 25; passive 21; prototypicality of 24–25; recency of 23–24; redundancy of 24; salience of 22, 24; second language acquisition and 22–31; storage of 21
CONTRIX 179, *180*, 186
conventional expressions 9; dense production of 109; enhancement of pragmatic production by second language learners 108; establishment of conventionality in second language pragmatics research 101–103; evaluation of learner knowledge 103–105; future areas of research 111; identification for study 100–101; instruction in 108; meaning of term 99–100; nativelike selection of 99, 106; pragmatic routines distinguished from 100, 102–103; recognition *versus* production by learners 105–106
conventions, in language 139
cooperation, in communication 134–136, 144
corpus analysis 192–195
corpus data: concordance 194, *194*, 197, *197*, 199–203, *200–204*; contextualized corpus work 198–204; rationale for using to learn formulae 195–197

Index

Corpus of Contemporary American 199, 218
creative language use 145
critical thought, relationship of formulaic language to 215–217
cross-cultural pragmatics 133
cross-language overlap influence on processing 64–75
cue-outcome association 24

data-driven learning (DDL) approaches to language learning 162, 165, 194–195, 198–199, 207
decomposability of idioms 75
decontextualized exercises on formulaic language 162–165
decontextualized recognition tasks, in pragmatics research 103–104, 106–107
dependent clauses, interpersonal function of 215
dictionaries 184
discourse communities 212–213
discourse markers, use of 183
Discriminating Collocations Test (DISCO) 174, 178–179, *179*, 186
dispersion 23, 220
distribution, of constructions 23
ditropic sentences 79
Dual Coding theory 165
DuoLingo (app) 199
Durrant, Phil 12

economy principle 142–143, 145, 249
EFL Vocabulary Test 174, 187
egocentrism, in communication 134–135
electroencephalography (EEG) 46–48
English for Academic Purposes (EAP), formulaic language in 12, 211–224; analysis of language in academic texts 213–215; future directions of 223–224; grade improvement and 217–220; identification of appropriate formulae to teach 220–223; motivations for focus on 211–213; originality and creative thought, relationship to 215–217
English for Specific Purposes (Hutchinson and Waters) 220
Eurocentres Vocabulary Test 174
event-related brain potentials (ERPs) 46–48
expletives *39*
eye-tracking 42, 44, 45, 69, 72, 168

familiarity 4, 8, 39
figurative formulaic language: comprehension of 44–48; non-compositional 39; production of 51–54; prosodic characteristics of 51–54, 56
first language: influence on a second language 62–76, *74*; representation of the L1-L2 interface for learning L2 formulaic sequences 263, *264*, 265; what qualifies as not formulaic in 258–260
first language acquisition: emergence of formulaic sequences in child 81–83; prosody and 81–85; *see also* child first language acquisition
first language speakers: comprehension of formulaic language 40–45, 47–48, 54–55; production of formulaic language 50, 52, 54–56
fixedness of formulaic language 4–5
flashcard apps 199
form-meaning pairs 20
formulaic cloze passages 204–205, *205*
formulaic constructions 7–8; *see also* constructions
formulaicity: definition 3, 5–6; detecting 253; lack of 258–260
formulaic language: categories of 183–184; definitions 5, 38, 175, 182; features of 3–5; online processing of 38–56; production of 39, 48–56; terminology, characteristics, and definition 2–6; ubiquity of 1
formulaic sequence acquisition: prosody and 83–91; spoken input 89–90; spoken *versus* written input and 86–87
formulaic sequences: categories/types of 258; definitions 3–6, 81, 138–139; features of 3–5; prosody and 78–91; psychological salience of 138–141, 145; second language acquisition and 22–31; as strings of sounds, rather than strings of words 80; visualization of and possible variations between *39*; *see also specific sequence types*
formulas: lists of 184; in pragmatics 98–99
Free Rice (app) 199
frequency 3–4, 6, 7, 8, 63; association 221; collocations 140, 155–156, 222, 231–232; comprehension of compositional formulaic language and 40–43, 54–55; of construction 22, 25; dispersion 220; formulaic sequence

acquisition and 198; of formulaic sequences 38–43; importance in processing 140; incidental learning and 155–157, 168; judgments about the teach-worthiness of items using frequency data 221; keyness 220–221; lexical bundles 140, 236–237, 260; production of formulaic language and 49–51, 54–55; psychological saliency and 141; token 22, 25; type 22; Zipf's Law 23
functional expressions 261–262, 266
function of formulaic sequences 5–6, 262

General Service List 174, 184
grammar: acquisition, prosody and 83–84; construction 211, 251, 258–259; pattern 211
Granger, Sylviane 12
group membership 212, 216, 256
Gyllstad, Henrik 11

holistic storage 3, 6, 46, 51, 175, 188
holophrase 27
humor 10, 115–127; appreciation 121; first language corpus studies of 116–120; as formulaic 119; implications for second language learners 120–122; instruction in formulaic language and humor 122–126; misjudging how to use 255; recall and 122–125

ICLE (International Corpus of Learner English) 230
identification of formulaic sequences by second language learners 253
idiomatic noun phrases, as constructions 21
idiom priming 46
idiom principle 133, 137, 140, 142–145, 193, 211, 228, 249, 257
idioms 4–5, 8, 38, *39*, 115; ambiguous 44–45, 51–53, 55; Chinese 68–70; comprehension of 196; constraint-based model of processing 75; creative attitude of second language users to 145; decomposability of 75; dictionaries 184; ditropic sentences 79; economizing role in speech production 133; ERP studies 46–48; French 62–63, 66, 73, *74*, 206; frequency 62; German 67; intentional learning of 163; low-frequency 46;

making them memorable 165; non-compositionality of 168; overlap between first and second languages 63, 66–75; processing of 44–48, 55; production of 51–53; prosody and 79–80, 88; recall 124–125; Spanish 72; Swedish 71–72; testing and 175; transparency of 75; use to express meaning 183
IELTS 217, 259
illocutionary force of an utterance 97, 100, 108, 250
incidental learning 155–158, 198; conditions for 11, 153–154; effectiveness of 166–167; frequency and 155–157, 168; modality of input and 157–158; semi-incidental 154, 158–159
incongruence 8, 64–66, 68, 72, 120–121, 234
in-group membership 216, 256
input, modality of 157–158
input-enhancement 158–159, 167–168
input flooding 158–159, 167
intentional learning: conditions for 11, 153–154; effectiveness 166–167
intercultural communication 249
intercultural pragmatics 10, 132–146; formulaic language in first language 136–138; formulaic language explained by 141–145; future directions 145–146; overview of 133–134; psychological saliency of formulaic sequences 138–141, 145; socio-cognitive approach (SCA) 133–136, 142–143
interlanguage pragmatics 133
interlinguistic communication 249
International Corpus of Learner English (ICLE) 230
intertextuality 216–217
intonation units (IUs): boundaries 78–79; sentence fragments as 84; syntactic units and 83–84
irony 10, 115–120; first language corpus studies of 116–120; as formulaic 119; implications for second language learners 120–122; as a "reversal of evaluation" 118
irreversible binomials 38, *39*
isolating language 250
Item Response Theory 185
iteration, learning humor and 125

Kecskes, Istvan 10
keyness 220–221

language processing, sensitivity to sequence information 26
latency, articulation 49–50
learner corpora 12–13, 228–242; future avenues for study 241–242; spoken *versus* written data on 230
learner-external formulaic sequences 31
learner-internal formulaic sequences 31
learning, dynamics of 262–265
learning of formulaic language: conditions for 153–154; data-driven learning (DDL) approaches 162, 165; incidental 153–154, 155–158, 166–168, 198; input-enhancement 158–159; intentional 153–154, 159–166; modality of input and 157; representation of the L1-L2 interface for learning L2 formulaic sequences 263, *264*, 265; semi-incidental 154, 158–159; from texts 160–162
learning rate for formulaic language 193–196
lemma mediation model 74
lexical bundles 5, 12, 38, *39*; in academic language proficiency exams 219; in academic texts 215; accuracy and appropriacy of use 237–238; association-defined 237, 247; bundle size 236; cross-linguistic overlap 68; definition 235–236; development of use 239–240; dispersion 236; distinction from collocations 236; first language transfer 238–239; frequency 40–41, 43, 55, 68, 140, 236–237, 260; meanings 183; as "mortar" of text 260–261, 266; operationalization 235–236; processing of 40–41, 43; storage of 51; testing and 185; usefulness of learning 261
Lextutor Website 187, 193, 199, 201, 204
Lin, Phoebe 9
linguistic cluster 31
linguistic proficiency, perceptions of 12
linguistic readymades 119
List_Learn 201
literal compositional formulaic language 39
literal meanings, *versus* idiomatic 79

mapping: form-function 7, 19, 22, 25; multiword-to-multiword 251; one-to-one 254

meaning potential 117–118
memorability, enhancing 165–166
metaphors 115, 165
morphemes 20
multiword expressions 2
multiword verbs 38
mutual information (MI) 218, 221, 253
My Word Coach (game) 199

nativelike fluency 85–86, 141, 230
nativelike selection 99, 105–106, 141
Natural Language Processing, prosodic patterns of formulaic sequences and 79–80
N-Gram, Lextutor's 193, 201
n-grams 38, 49
non-adjacent sequences, comprehension of 43
non-literal meaning 39, *39*
Noticing Hypothesis 158
nuanced semantics 39, *39*

one-to-one mapping 254
online language processing 38–56; comprehension 39–48, 54–55; first and second language correspondence 64; production 39, 48–56
opaqueness 5
open choice principle 142
order of acquisition 263
originality, relationship of formulaic language to 215–217
Orwell, George 215–216, 223
overuse of familiar formulaic sequences 86
Oxford Collocations Dictionary for Students of English 184

particle, detection in two-word phrases 40
pattern grammar 211
pauses: length as reflection on phrase organization 83; perception of 81; prosody and 78–79, 83, 85
Pearson Academic Collocation List 184
pedagogical approach to the study of formulaic language 10–12
pedagogy 153–169; conditions for learning 153–154; decontextualized exercises 162–165; incidental learning 153–154, 155–158, 166–168; input-enhancement 158–159; intentional 153–154, 159–166; learning from texts 160–162; making formulaic language memorable 165–166; semi-incidental learning 154, 158–159; single-word teaching

205–207; technology use in teaching and learning formulaic language 192–208
Pellicer-Sánchez, Ana 11
PHaVE List 184
phonetic duration of literal, compositional formulaic language 51–53
phrasal expressions, testing 183–184
phrasal verbs: dictionaries 184; idiomatic 183; making them memorable 165
Phrasal Vocabulary Size Test 187
PHRASE 11, 180–181, *181*
PHRASE List 184
phrase lists 222
pitch 81, 85; decline at syntactic boundaries 83; idioms and 52–53
plagiarism 216–217, 223
poetry, ironic 118
Politics and the English Language (Orwell) 215–216
pragmalinguistics 99, 254
pragmatic routines: distinguished from conventional expressions 100, 102–103; future areas of research 111; identification of illocutionary force and 108; teaching of 107, 110; terminology 99, 100
pragmatics 9, 250; cross-cultural 133; English for Academic Purposes (EAP) and 216; interlanguage 133; social function of formulaic sequences and 5–6, 97–100; sociopragmatics 10, 99, 103, 250, 253–254, 262; terminology 98–100; *see also* intercultural pragmatics; second language pragmatics
prefabricated language 27–28
prepositional verbs 165
prepositions, collocational complex 43
priming 24, 120
processing 8–9; default principles 142–143, 249; effort decrease by formulaic expression use 133; frequency and 40–43; importance of frequency in 140; influence of cross-language overlap on formulaic 64–75; lexical bundles 40–41, 43; native-like fluency and 196; sensitivity to sequence information 26
processing unit 31
production of familiar phrases 39
production of formulaic language 39, 48–56; compositional 49–51; figurative 51–53
prosodic breaks: classification of 83; strength of 83

prosodic processing ability 88–91
prosody 9, 39, 78–91, 157; as a bootstrapping function in language acquisition 84; child first language acquisition and 81–83; enhancement for learning 159; figurative formulaic language 51–54, 56; first language acquisition and 81–85; importance to the contextual meaning of spoken formulaic sequences 80; learners' weakness in noticing and processing prosodic cues in second language input 87–88; native *versus* non-native speakers' processing competence 88–89; of proverbs 53; second language acquisition and 85–87
prototypes 24–25
Prototype Theory 24
proverbs 4, 38, *39*, 53
psycholinguistics 132, 211
psychological saliency of formulaic sequences 10, 138–141, 145
puns 118–119, 123

Range software 196
Rasch analysis 185
recency, of constructions 23–24
redundancy, of constructions 24
reference *versus* function 261
referential expressions 261–262, 266
referential formulaic sequences 261–262
replication studies 241–242
rhyme 166
rhythm, perception of 81
role-play activity 123
routine formula, definition of 99
routines, in pragmatics 98–99

salience: aural input and 159; of constructions 22, 24; egocentrism and 135; of pragmatics 106; psychological of formulaic sequences 138–141
sampling, in test development 185–186
sarcasm 117, 119
scaffolding, formulas acting as 213
schematization 21
Schmitt, Norbert 11
second language: conceptual socialization and 143; first language influence on 62–76, 74; representation of the L1-L2 interface for learning L2 formulaic sequences 263, *264*, 265; what qualifies as not formulaic in 258–260
second language acquisition: challenges of formulaic sequence acquisition

85–87; formulaic constructions and 22–31; learners' weakness in noticing and processing prosodic cues in second language input 87–88; spoken *versus* written input and 86–87; from a usage-based perspective 19–31

second language learners: comprehension of formulaic language 40–45, 48, 54–55; constructions, presence of mental representations of 26–27; failure to proactively target formulaic sequences 248–267; humor 115–127; identification of formulaic sequences 251; production of formulaic language 50, 52, 54–56; technology use in teaching and learning formulaic language 192–208

second language pragmatics 97–111; contributions to the study of formulaic language 108–110; distinguishing of conventional from modified expressions by learners 106; enhancement of production by convention expressions 108; environment and 106–107; establishment of conventionality in pragmatics research 101–102; evaluation of learner knowledge 103–105; future areas of research 110–111; how formulaic sequences are defined in 98–100; identification of convention expressions for study 100–101; instructional effects and 107–108; recognition *versus* production of conventional expressions by learners 105–106; study of formulaic language contributions to 110; terminology 98–100; transfer and 107

semantic violations, ERP study of 47

semi-incidental learning of formulaic language 11, 154, 158–159

sentence fragments, intonation units and 84

similes 115, 119–120

single-word teaching 205–207

single-word *versus* multiword distinction 258

Siyanova-Chanturia, Anna 8

Skalicky, Stephen 10

social function of formulaic sequences 97–100, 250

socialization, conceptual 143

socio-cognitive approach 133–136, 142–143

sociopragmatic competence 254

sociopragmatics 10, 99, 103, 250, 253–254, 262

sound patterning 165–166

speech: detecting formulaicity in 253; fluency, formulaic sequences as a "shortcut" to 85–86; illocutionary force of an utterance 97, 100, 108, 250; nativelike fluency 85–86, 141, 230; prosody 78–91

spoken language: effect on formulaic sequence acquisition in a second language 89–90; percentage of formulaic language in 22

storage, holistic 3, 6, 46, 51, 175, 188

stress, perception of 81

symbolic units, in usage-based linguistics 20

synthetic language 250

targeting of formulaic sequences by second language learners 13, 248–267; decrease need of formulaic sequences 255–256; evidence of under-exploitation of formulaic sequences 251–252; inability to successfully target 252–254; outcomes of 256–257; reasons for failure to target 252–257; reasons for not wanting to target 254–255; reasons to expect 249–251

technology: for teaching and learning formulaic language 11–12, 192–208; testing use of 187

TenTen corpus 196

terminology 2–3

territorial imperative 122

test development 182–187; defining constructs 182; formats, choosing appropriate 186, **187**; for particular purposes 182–183; sampling 185–186; selection of formulaic sequences to test 183–185; technology use 187

testing of formulaic language 11, 174–188; adaptive 187; COLLEX and COLLMATCH 177–178, *178*, 186; CONTRIX 179, *180*, 186; developing new tests, principles for 181–187; Discriminating Collocations Test (DISCO) 174, 178–179, *179*, 186; future directions 188; PHRASE test 180–181, *181*; productive collocation test 180, *181*; research and 176–181; Word Associates Test 174, *176*, 176–177

textbooks: exercises on formulaic sequences 164; failure to provide sufficient formulaic material 252
text chunking 160
texts: analysis of formulaic language in academic 213–215; bricks and mortar of 260–261, 266; intentional learning of formulaic language from 160–162; typographic enhancement of 158–159, 161, 167–168
timing 81
token frequency 22, 25
tones, perception of 81
transgressive intertextuality 216–217
transparency 5; collocations 75, 179; idiom processing 75; pragmatic routines 100
truncated forms 4–5
t-score 218, 221
type frequency 22
typographic enhancement 158–159, 161, 167–168

University Word List (UWL) 176
usage-based linguistics: formulaic language acquisition and 19–31; formulaic sequences as constructions in 20–31
usage-based theories of language acquisition 120

Van Lancker Sidtis, Diana 8
verb-argument constructions 23, 25, 27
verb islands 23
verb-noun collocations: intentional learning of 161, 163–164; in texts 156–157
verb-object collocation 258
verb phrases, interpersonal function of 215
verbs, path-breaking 23
vocabulary: intentional learning 153; tests of 174, 182–183
Vocabulary Levels Test (VLT) 174, 180, 182, 185–187
vocabulary size, tests of 185–186
Vocabulary Size Test (VST) 183, 186–187
voice quality 81

Word Associates Test 174, *176*, 176–177, 186
word lists 153, 184–185, 201, 220, 222
word play 118–119
word space locations 258
Wray, Alison 13
Wulff, Stefanie 7

X-Lex Test 186

Zipf's Law 23